This I Remember

❀

By Eleanor Roosevelt

THIS IS MY STORY

❀

ELEANOR ROOSEVELT

THIS
I REMEMBER

BY

ELEANOR ROOSEVELT

ILLUSTRATED

PUBLISHERS NEW YORK
HARPER & BROTHERS

TO MY HUSBAND

FRANKLIN DELANO ROOSEVELT

AND MY CHILDREN

ANNA, JAMES, ELLIOTT

FRANKLIN, Junior, & JOHN

WHO HAVE MADE

THIS BOOK POSSIBLE

I want to record here my deep gratitude to my devoted friend and co-worker, Malvina C. Thompson. Without her aid and constant stimulus this book would never have been finished.

I must record, too, that the decision made by my son Elliott to live at Hyde Park was also a factor in the completion of the book. Had I not stayed here it would have been far more difficult to write it and I might never have done so.

If THIS I REMEMBER is any contribution to history as it will some day be written, much of the credit is theirs. To them I am deeply grateful.

CONTENTS

ILLUSTRATIONS

Eleanor Roosevelt   *Frontispiece*

*These illustrations, printed as a separate
section, will be found following page 260*

This I Remember

CHAPTER ONE

"AS I BEGIN . . ."

As I BEGIN this book, it seems to me an infinitely more difficult task than the previous volume of my autobiography. In the first place, it can no longer be only my autobiography. Naturally most people will be interested primarily in what I may have to tell about my husband.

In my earlier volume, I tried to give a picture of the times in which I grew up, of myself and incidentally of the people around me.* In this book, I feel the times need not be discussed by me, for over and over again, the period will be written about by historians. Yet perhaps I shall be able to give some impressions which may help in the understanding of the stream of history during these complicated years.

Many books will be written in the next few years about my husband and about the people with whom he worked. Therefore, what I have to say, if it is to contribute anything more to the understanding of his life and character and objectives, must be about him as an individual.

I do not claim that I can be entirely objective about him, but there are some things I know that I feel sure nobody else can know. Although no human being ever completely knows another human being, one cannot live for many years with a person without learning something about him. Other people may know certain sides of Franklin's char-

* This Is My Story, Harper & Brothers, 1937.

I

acter or particular facets of his personality better than I; but if I can contribute what I have learned and what I believe to be true, I may help to fill in the true picture for future historians.

The few books that have already been written about Franklin show quite plainly that everyone writes from his own point of view, and that a man like my husband, who was particularly susceptible to people, took color from whomever he was with, giving to each one something different of himself. Because he disliked being disagreeable, he made an effort to give each person who came in contact with him the feeling that he understood what his particular interest was. Frances Perkins, in her book, has drawn a wonderful picture of him that in many respects no one else could possibly have drawn. Yet even in her book, I think, there are little inaccuracies and misinterpretations, arising from the fact that each of us brings to any contact with another person our own personality and our own interests and prejudices and beliefs.

Often people have told me that they were misled by Franklin. Even when they have not said it in so many words, I have sometimes felt that he left them, after an interview, with the idea that he was in entire agreement with them. I would know quite well, however, that he was not and that they would be very much surprised when later his actions were in complete contradiction to what they thought his attitude would be.

This misunderstanding not only arose from his dislike of being disagreeable, but from the interest that he always had in somebody else's point of view and his willingness to listen to it. If he thought it was well expressed and clear, he nodded his head and frequently said, "I see," or something of the sort. This did not mean that he was convinced of the truth of the arguments, or even that he entirely understood them, but only that he appreciated the way in which they were presented.

There is another fact which few people realize: the President of the United States gets more all-round information than most of the people who come to see him, though any one of them may know his own subject better than the president does. The president, however, must have a general outlook which takes in over-all considerations; whereas other people think primarily about their own ideas, plans and responsibilities for the specific thing they hope to accomplish. This circumstance puts on a president the responsibility of gathering all possible points of view, of hearing very often conflicting ideas on a given subject, and of then making a final decision. It is one of the most difficult things a president has to do.

In addition, the fact that he can never have a personal loyalty greater than his loyalty to the nation sometimes makes it seem as though he were disloyal to his friends; but a man holding the office of President of the United States must think first of what he considers the greatest good of the people and the country.

As time went on, I think Franklin often felt that he must save himself from the strain of argument, and that his obligation to the people who came to see him was discharged when he took the time out of a very strenuous program to sit and listen. I know he always gave thought to what people said, but I have never known anyone less really influenced by others. Though he asked for advice from a great many people, he simply wanted points of view which might help him to form his final decision if he had not reached one, and which he sifted through his own knowledge and feelings. But once he reached a decision, people flattered themselves if they thought they ever changed it.

Franklin often used me to get the reflection of other people's thinking because he knew I made it a point to see and talk with a variety of people. I did not need to go on lecture trips, or go to inspect projects in different parts of the country, but my husband knew that I would not be satisfied to be merely an official hostess. He often suggested that I interest myself in certain things, such as the homestead projects. He knew that life would be very uninteresting to me if I did not feel I was accomplishing something. Therefore, for my sake, he was glad when he found that for a few weeks in spring and fall I could and did go on paid lecture trips. I knew that I would not plan such trips unless I had definite commitments and had signed formal contracts; but when they were an obligation, I arranged my time so that they were possible. The trips took me to many places throughout the country to which otherwise I might never have gone.

Naturally these lecture trips gave me more money for things I wanted to do than my husband could afford to give me. At the same time, I felt that Franklin used whatever I brought back to him in the way of observations and information as a check against the many official reports which he received.

Very often, when some matter was being fought out with his advisers, he would bring up the question at dinner and bait me into giving an opinion by stating as his own a point of view with which he knew I would disagree. He would give me all the arguments which had been advanced to him and I would try vociferously and with heat to refute them.

I remember one occasion, though the subject of the argument has now been forgotten, when I became extremely vehement and irritated. My husband smiled indulgently and repeated all the things that everyone else had said to him. The next day he asked Miss Thompson if I could have tea in the West Hall in the White House for him and Robert Bingham, who was then our ambassador to London and about to return to his post. I dutifully served them with tea, fully expecting to sit and listen in silence to a discussion of questions with which I probably would not be in agreement. Instead, to my complete surprise, I heard Franklin telling Ambassador Bingham to act, not according to the arguments that he had given me, but according to the arguments that I had given him! Without giving me a glance or the satisfaction of batting an eyelash in my direction, he calmly stated as his own the policies and beliefs he had argued against the night before! To this day I have no idea whether he had simply used me as a sounding board, as he so often did, with the idea of getting the reaction of the person on the outside, or whether my arguments had been needed to fortify his decision and to clarify his own mind.

After Franklin became president, many people told me how much they disagreed with him and how they were going in for an interview prepared to tell him so in no uncertain terms. They went in, but if

I had a chance to see them as they came out, they usually looked at me blandly and behaved as though they never had disagreed at all. Only now and then was someone honest enough to say he had not been able to put forward his own point of view—a difficulty due partly, I think, to the effect of Franklin's personality and partly to the person's awe of the office itself.

Franklin had the gift of being able to draw out the people whom he wished to draw out and to silence those with whom he was bored—and in both cases the people were greatly charmed. When he did not want to hear what somebody had to say, he had a way of telling stories and talking about something quite different. Everyone who worked with him had to learn how to handle this technique of his if they were not to find that the questions they wanted to ask, or that the opinion they wanted to state, never got into words because Franklin talked so steadily and so interestingly that they forgot what they had come to say.

Of all his intimates only a few, I think, ever really understood how it was that people sometimes thought he was in agreement with them when he was not, or had given his consent when really he had never contemplated giving it. I may have been able to help some people to this understanding. Louis Howe, I think, always understood this trait in Franklin, and Frank Walker, Edward J. Flynn, Henry Morgenthau, junior, and Bernard Baruch came to know it well. With none of these men was his own interest ever paramount. The interest of each was in my husband and in the work to be done and they could be very objective even when their own work was involved.

I was often supposed to be a great influence on my husband politically. Over and over again people wrote, crediting me with being responsible for his actions and even for some of his appointments. Frances Perkins' appointment to the cabinet is a case in point. As a matter of fact, I never even suggested her. She had worked with Franklin in New York State and was his own choice, though I was delighted when he named her and glad that he felt a woman should be recognized.

There were times when a list of names suggested for appointment, to serve as individuals or groups, would come out and there would be no woman's name on the list. Then I might go to my husband and say that I was very weary of reminding him to remind the members of his cabinet and his advisers that women were in existence, that they were a factor in the life of the nation and increasingly important politically. He always smiled and said: "Of course; I thought a woman's name had been put on the list. Have someone call up and say I feel a woman should be recognized." As a result, I was sometimes asked for suggestions and then I would mention two or three names. Sometimes they were considered and sometimes they were not.

The political influence that was attributed to me was nil where my husband was concerned, largely because I never made the slightest effort to do what I knew I could not do. If I felt strongly about anything I told Franklin, since he had the power to do things and I did not, but he did not always feel as I felt.

I have since discovered, of course, that a great many government people to whom I referred letters regarded them as a mandate requiring prompt attention. Evidently they thought that if what I suggested was not done, I would complain to my husband. As a matter of fact, all I ever expected was that they would be interested in accomplishing the things that should be accomplished, since government is supposed to serve the good of the people. I thought that every government official investigated complaints and gladly tried to correct injustices. I realize now that this was a rather naive idea, for it is apparent from what people have told me that it was often only fear of White House displeasure that set the wheels in motion. This was not true of many departments, but I suppose it is only natural that some of the older departments, where a number of civil service people feel entrenched, should not want to bother with new activities. Both Mr. Woodin and Mr. Morgenthau must have made great changes in the old Treasury Department management. The standards set, particularly after Mr. Morgenthau became Secretary of the Treasury, must have seemed alarming to some of the old types of civil service officials.

I felt very critical of civil service officials at times. When they have been in a department for a long while, they can make any change very difficult. Nevertheless, I think it is true that there are an astonishing number of people who want to serve their country and are willing to accept the modest security and low pay of a civil service employee simply because they feel that they are performing a patriotic service.

Consciously, as I have said, I never tried to exert any political influence on my husband or on anyone else in the government. However, one cannot live in a political atmosphere and study the actions of a good politician, which my husband was, without absorbing some rudimentary facts about politics. From him I learned that a good politician is marked to a great extent by his sense of timing. He says the right thing at the right moment. Though the immediate reaction may be unfavorable, in the long run it turns out that what he said needed to be said at the time he said it. I do not mean that Franklin never made mistakes; most of the time, however, his judgment was good. He could watch with enormous patience as a situation developed and would wait for exactly the right moment to act or speak. The quarantine speech, for instance, was delivered at a time when it was necessary that people be made to think. The meeting with Winston Churchill at Argentia and the announcement of the Atlantic Charter came at a crucial point in the country's life; in the same way, the D-Day prayer lifted the morale of the people at a moment when that kind of inspiration was most needed.

Franklin was a practical politician. He could always be told why certain actions or appointments were politically advisable. Sometimes he acted on this advice; on the other hand, he did many things and made many appointments against the advice of the party politicians, simply because he believed they would have a good effect on the nation as a whole. And he was almost always right. However, as a practical politician, he knew and accepted the fact that he had to work with the people who were a part of the Democratic party organization. I often heard him discuss the necessity and role of local political organizations, but he recognized that certain of them were a detriment to the party as a whole. He never got over his feeling against Tammany Hall or any boss-ridden organization, though he acknowledged that some were well administered and valuable.

Though Franklin always said I was far too impatient ever to be a good politician, and though my sense of timing is nowhere near so trustworthy as his was, I have grown more patient with age and have perhaps learned from my husband that no leader can be too far ahead of his followers. Also I think my observations of conditions and of the feelings of the average people within our country are fairly trustworthy.

CHAPTER TWO

"LIFE WAS NEVER DULL"

DURING THE years of my husband's governorship and presidency, but particularly after we were in the White House, I had many occasions to think seriously about the problem that faces the family of a man in American public life, especially a man who becomes the subject of great controversy—hated wholeheartedly by some and loved equally wholeheartedly by others. Of necessity, the attitude toward him must carry through to the members of his family and have some effect on them all. For the young the situation is extremely difficult. Special privileges are offered to them on every side. If they do not accept, they are considered ungracious and unappreciative. If they do accept, they are accused of being selfish, arrogant and greedy, and of thinking themselves important and above other people—in fact, of having all the disagreeable traits that we most dislike in the young.

I remember, for instance, when Franklin, junior, then a young college student, was arrested for speeding between Albany and Boston. Someone, thinking to be kind to his father, took him home to dinner and tried to help him escape the usual treatment given to young offenders. His father and I hoped devoutly that he would be treated as severely as possible, so that he would learn once and for all the inevitable results of breaking the law, even when the offense is not very serious. Above all we wanted him to learn that punishment for breaking the law falls inexorably on all alike in a democracy. I can remember our utter dismay at discovering that he had got off without even a modest fine. We knew only too well that the youngster had not learned his lesson; also that no one would ever believe that we had not tried to exert influence and had not asked for special consideration.

Some other somewhat similar episodes, two of which might have had serious results, occurred in the years that followed. The only reaction I discovered among the children, at the time, was a general feeling of injustice that they were always not only caught, but given much publicity—a circumstance they attributed to their father's position and not to their own misdeeds.

I spent many hours trying to explain to one of our sons, who was complaining bitterly about the hardships of their position, that everybody had some difficulties to overcome in life, and that they had the drawback of bearing a name that had been rather well known for some years before their father even thought of being in public life. The additional fact that their father was Governor of New York State at the time made it more difficult, as they might have to walk more carefully than the average boy of their age.

On the other hand, I pointed out, they had never been hungry, they had never doubted that they could have an education and that afterwards there would be opportunities awaiting them to earn a living. Many boys would give a good deal for that amount of security, and the things they complained about might well be looked upon as minor difficulties. Even as I talked I knew I might as well "save my breath to cool my porridge," for preaching never does any good and strong individuals have to learn by personal experience, which is the hard way.

Years later, one of our sons told me, after a visit to my aunt, Mrs. Stanley Mortimer, who had rented a place in Scotland for the shooting, how impressed he was because she could walk the moors all day and play poker with them far into the night, yet never appear weary. He said: "I don't know why you never told us about your mother's side of the family. We always thought all our energy came from the Roosevelt side; but we know the other side of the family now and we quite understand that we can't help having all our vitality, because we get it from both sides—the Roosevelts and the Halls. In addition, mother, remember we are Roosevelts on both sides, too, which makes it even worse."

The Delanos weren't lacking in vitality either, so perhaps the children had some reason to say that high spirits and the love of adventure came to them naturally, and we could not ask that they give us peace and quiet. Five individualists, such as our children, growing up together in a family where the father was deeply immersed in public affairs, and the grandmother, true to her Delano tradition, bent on being the head of the family, did mean that life was never dull for me.

Our trouble, of course, came not only from the way the boys were treated outside the home—given too many privileges on the one hand and too much criticism on the other—but from the fact that my husband's mother adored her grandchildren, and thought of them as her own. She often got angry with me because I seldom told them what was right or what was wrong. The reason I didn't was that I was never sure I knew myself. However, everything was always black or white to her; she had no doubts and never hesitated to tell the children what she thought. As a result, they often fooled her. The two youngest members of the family particularly, always treated her with an affectionate *camaraderie* which won from her almost anything they desired. She took them to task, but at the same time she showed how pleased she was and they knew that whatever they wanted would be forthcoming. Franklin, junior, wrecked the small car we gave him when he graduated from school, and we decided it would be a good thing for him to go without one for a while. Almost before we knew it, his grandmother, at his request, had replaced the car with a much more expensive one. When we objected, she looked at us quite blandly and said she had not realized that we disapproved. She never heard anything she did not want to hear, and this was one of the occasions when she was all ears to her grandson and deaf to the remarks of his parents.

John was more careful of his possessions and made fewer demands, being a quieter and more conservative child. He played polo in his freshman year at college, but found he could not afford it and gave it up without a murmur. He has always shown strength of character and prudence and ability in financial matters.

My husband had some very firm ideas about what children should do once they were educated. Up to the time that their education was complete, they shared in the family life and possessions, but he thought that the day the boys graduated they should go to work and live on their earnings. As I think about it now, I realize that this conviction came from his Delano background. His great-grandfather in Fairhaven, Massachusetts, who was a retired sea captain, built himself a comfortable house where he and his many children and relatives lived in what I imagine was luxury for those days. Warren Delano, the eldest son and my husband's grandfather, at the age of seventeen was driven to Boston and turned over to the Forbes family, whose ships sailed the seven seas. From that time on, young Warren was on his own and sailed in the Forbes sailing ships as supercargo. He made his own way eventually to a partnership in Russell and Company, in Hongkong, an American firm which later became a British firm. The other brothers in the family started out in exactly the same way, and all of them expected to look after their female relatives, whether they were wives, sisters or cousins!

My mother-in-law differed in only one respect from my husband in these ideas. Although she believed the children should work, she wanted them all at home under her supervision and guidance, for she had a strong feeling about holding the family together in almost matriarchal style. Consequently she disliked having any of the young members of the family financially independent of their elders; keeping them financially dependent, she thought, was one way of keeping them at home and controlling them. She was most generous in her gifts when she wanted to make any. She gave her son and me and any of the grandchildren anything she felt was essential, but she did not like any of us to have regular incomes of our own. Nor did she like extravagance of any kind, though she permitted extravagances, for some unknown reason, more readily in the younger generation. I think she always regretted that my husband had money of his own from his father and that I had a small income of my own; and when I began to earn money it was a real grief to her. When Franklin was ill, however, she offered him any money he needed without a question and longed to have him return to Hyde Park and never work again.

In spite of my mother-in-law's dejection about my earning money, I think she eventually became reconciled to it, realizing that it enabled me to do many things for which my own income was insufficient and which would have been too great a financial drain on my husband, had I depended on him. The money I had inherited from my parents' estate shrank during the depression years, and I ended with a very small yearly income. However, long before leaving New York City in 1933, I had begun to earn money through my teaching, writing and radio work. I can remember my pleasure when I first was able to give some substantial help to the Women's Trade Union League in paying off the mortgage on their club house, and to carry through some of our plans on the Val-Kill experiment.

With the first money I earned through commercial radio work, during the bad days of the depression, I established two places where girls who were unemployed and searching for work could have lunch and a place to rest. One was in the Women's Trade Union League club house, and the other was in the Girls' Service League headquarters on Madison Avenue. We gave the girls a hot lunch and snacks during the day, and provided facilities for sewing, mending, and the like. Several people became interested and helped me with supplies of various kinds, and many volunteered to cook and serve meals and to talk to the girls and advise them.

The large sums I was able to earn through radio and writing during those bad times made it possible for me not only to make contributions to organized charities but also to give work or help to individuals who could not be helped through the usual channels. I do not question that I often gave to people who were not worthy; but in those years it seemed better to take that risk than to fail those who were worthy. After a few disillusionments, however, I finally made an arrangement with the American Friends Service Committee whereby they did much of the investigating and I gave them almost all the money I earned through radio. At first I had this money paid directly to them, not receiving any of it myself. Then Hamilton Fish made an attack on me in Congress, claiming that I was evading income taxes by regarding a series of radio talks as benefits. I had, of course, obtained a ruling from the Treasury Department in 1933 that it was legal to turn the money over to a recognized charity; but as long as there was any basis for questioning my right to do this, I decided to have the money paid directly to me. I deducted part of it toward my income tax and sent the balance to the American Friends.

The money I earned from all of my radio work and some of my writing during the years I was in the White House I felt should be used not simply for charity donations but primarily to help people help themselves. Because that is also the philosophy of the Friends, I chose them to handle the money for me. I never gave a present to any of my children out of that earned money. On some occasions I had to use part of my small principal, because I had given away so much I could not meet my income tax otherwise. I did not save a single penny during those years because I thought it was not right to do so, and I left the White House with less cash in my own principal account than I had when I went to Washington.

My husband's income was never very large and he had to spend some of his principal every year he was in Albany and in the White House. As he died before his mother's estate was settled, that never was of any help to him.

At the time I married my income varied from $5,000 to $8,000 a year. Franklin knew that I had little knowledge of how to handle money, and he also knew that I had no right to disturb the existing trust arrangements, under which my money was managed largely by older members of my family and I simply received the income at certain intervals. I was invited by these family businessmen, Henry Parish and Emlen Roosevelt, to come and look at my securities and consult about them, but I was much too frightened to do so and too little interested. My grandmother, who brought me up after my parents died, had kept me on such a strict allowance until I was twenty-one that I had learned to do with what I had. It never occurred to me to try to increase my income by a change of investments; I simply accepted whatever came and managed.

When I look back on how little we spent in our early married days, I appreciate the changes in the cost of living in the last forty years. My husband and I agreed that we would put an equal amount into the house account, and we lived easily and comfortably if not luxuriously on $600 a month. He paid, in addition, the rent and the children's schooling and doctors' bills. I dressed the children and myself and we went shares on presents to our relatives and friends. We shared some charities and gave individually to others when we were able to and wanted to. In later years, our charities were our individual responsibilities, except in rare cases when we gave jointly.

These arrangements seemed to me entirely fair and equitable, and it was not until after two children were added to our family that we increased the amount we put into the house account. Even then I paid my full share and so had less to spend in other ways.

As our household expenses grew over the years, Franklin assumed more responsibility for running the home, and gave all the children modest allowances up to the time they left school. Before they were old enough to be put on an allowance, I bought their clothes, as I said, and I always bought my own; however Franklin thought that once they had an allowance, they should buy their own clothes in order to learn how to manage money. Now and then I had to rescue them by giving them useful gifts of underwear, shirts and socks. The habit has persisted and they tease me about it now.

After our daughter, Anna was married, both Franklin and his mother gave her a small allowance. I gave her little presents when I could, including my original account books, although I realized they were too antiquated to be of any value since the cost of living had already risen far above what it had been in my young married days. However, because of my husband's theory that once a male child of the family was educated he should be on his own, our two older boys, James and Elliott, were not given an allowance after they finished their schooling. They, therefore, had to begin at once to earn a living. That complicated their lives considerably, because instead of being allowed to start at the bottom and work up, they were offered jobs that gave them too high returns. And they were too young and too inexperienced to realize that they were offered those jobs only because of their name and of their father's position.

Franklin had a very strong feeling that our sons should be allowed to make their own decisions and their own mistakes. Occasionally some of his friends suggested to him that he could give the boys a little guidance, but he always said they must find things out for themselves. I think his attitude came very largely from the fact that his mother had wanted to direct his every thought and deed and that he had had to fight for independence. For instance, I doubt if as long as she lived she ever let him leave the house without inquiring whether he was dressed warmly enough or urging him to wear his rubbers or put on a sweater under his coat. The older he got, the more it annoyed him. She had her own ways, too, of making her opinion known and of getting around him. If, as sometimes happened, he did not want to see some old friends or various other people she wanted him to see, she would calmly invite them to luncheon or dinner anyway, and simply not bring them into the dining room until after Franklin was seated and it was too late for him to do anything about it.

She always complained that she never saw Franklin alone, but if they were left together by themselves for very long they often disagreed. Those two were too much alike in certain ways to be left long alone. Franklin was as determined as she was, and as the years passed he went ahead and did anything he wanted to do, in spite of the fact that he had a great respect and love for his mother. But, though out of her devotion to him she did a great many things that were difficult for her, she never accepted the fact of his independence and continued to the last to try to guide his life.

Nevertheless, I often think of how much she had to put up with. For instance, though she entertained them for his sake, she strongly disapproved of Governor Smith and some of Franklin's other political acquaintances and was unable to believe that they could have any ability. Curiously enough, I think Al Smith respected her in spite of the fact that he must have known how she felt, which only made him more self-assertive in her presence. However, she was always pleasant and one had to know her to appreciate her little barbs. I remember one time when Huey Long was lunching with us at Hyde Park and Franklin, in order to talk to him about some bill on which he wanted his support, had seated Mr. Long next to himself. My mother-in-law, who could whisper louder than anyone I ever knew when she wanted to be heard, was at the opposite end of the table. And suddenly I heard her say to the man on her right, in her piercing whisper: "Who is that dreadful person sitting next to my son?"

As a result of Franklin's long experience with his own parent, he had an almost exaggerated determination that he would not subject his sons to similar interference, and the feeling became a plan of action.

It took me much longer than Franklin to gain some measure of independence, because I had had so much insecurity in my young life. At first the sense of security that my mother-in-law and my husband gave me made me very grateful. Gradually I had to learn that to develop, one must have a certain freedom of thought and action; and because of the long and slow and sometimes painful process that I went through to attain this independence, I was almost obsessed with the idea that, once the children were grown, they should not be subjected to the same kind of control that had held such sway over me. I am afraid my daughters-in-law sometimes thought that I was not even interested in them, because I was so very anxious to have them feel that I was not in any way trying to control or interfere with their lives, nor trying to demand attention from my children when they had families of their own. I probably carried this theory too far, and perhaps still do at times.

As Franklin became busier in his public life, he found it impossible to take time for the boys' interests, which kept them from asking for advice they might have sought quite naturally had he been freer to give it. One after the other, James and Elliott learned through bitter experience, and it was a bitter disillusionment as well.

Elliott did not go to college because he disliked his years at Groton so much. He was kept at Groton because both my mother-in-law and Franklin felt that wherever he went he would resent discipline; and

Franklin believed the discipline was valuable even if distasteful, while my mother-in-law did not want to break with family tradition. As a result, he went at an even earlier age than James into earning a living and had even a harder time in consequence.

Their early marriages came about largely because they were not really rooted in any particular home and were seeking to establish homes of their own. This added to their need to make money quickly. I quite understood their dissatisfaction. Partly because my husband could never quite decide to make the break with his mother and build a home of our own and partly because he loved the old house so much, we always lived with my mother-in-law at Hyde Park. I had no feeling that it belonged to me; and while the children loved the place, felt it belonged to them, and were completely at home there, they did not feel tied to it by any responsibility. It is hard to make children feel either in the Executive Mansion in Albany or in the White House that they are living in their own home, and we had spent only a few short years in our New York City house next to my mother-in-law's. When we lived there, they were too young to have much feeling about it, and after 1928 we were never all together there for any length of time.

(My mother-in-law gave the New York houses to my husband many years before she died and he paid the insurance and taxes and upkeep on them. Soon after her death he sold them for a moderate sum to the Hillel Foundation for the use of Hunter College. He was delighted to have them become interfaith houses for the college, for he knew that his mother would have been pleased to have them used in that way. As a matter of fact, I think Franklin was much relieved not to have to continue paying out such a large part of his income for houses in which he felt he could never afford to live in the future.)

Hyde Park and later Warm Springs had come to mean "roots" to Franklin. In some ways Campobello meant more to me. Franklin had begun going to Campobello when he was two years old, and while our children were small we went there every summer. The house next to his mother's belonged to us, and some of the children have happy memories of it and of the life we lived there. Franklin was always on vacation when he came to Campobello, before he had infantile paralysis, and many of the children's happiest times were with him there.

After we went to Washington in 1913, we lived in two different houses which we rented furnished, but again they were not homes except in the sense that home is wherever the family lives together. I think our children never acquired the roots which some children are fortunate enough to gain from a feeling of attachment to a particular piece of land or a particular house.

For the two younger boys things were a little easier because, as a great concession, my husband continued their allowances until his death. Franklin, junior, went to law school after he graduated from Harvard and married, so he couldn't earn money; and John started at the bottom in the merchandising business and needed something to keep him going after his marriage. When they went into the Navy they wanted to keep on paying some share of their home expenses. Having an allowance, these two had less immediate need to earn money, so they were not put through the same experiences that the two older brothers had undergone.

Perhaps it is well at this point to clear up a story that has come back to me at various times: that our youngest son, John, was a conscientious objector and a pacifist and did not want to go into the service. Like every other young man I know, he was not, in the years before we were attacked, eager to go to war. He was working hard and getting on well and his own life absorbed him. Once we were at war, however, there never was any question for him, any more than there was for any of our other sons. Whatever had to be done for the war had to be done, and none of them dreamed of being a conscientious objector or a pacifist.

As life grew busier in the White House, my husband had less and less time for family affairs, and I can remember how resentful the boys were when they found they actually had to make an appointment to see their father, if they wanted to talk to him privately. On one occasion one of our sons had something he felt it was important to talk over with his father, so he made an appointment. My husband was always kind and gentle, and while our son talked he seemed to be listening, though he was reading a document he held in his hand. The boy asked if he heard him. His father answered "Yes," but when there was a pause in the talk, he looked up and handed the boy the paper he was holding and remarked: "This is a most important document. I should like to have your opinion on it." I imagine that seemed like a slap in the face to the boy, who thought that what he was talking about was more important than anything else in the world. He looked at the paper, commented on it and left the room.

Soon a very indignant young man came to me saying: "Never again will I try to talk to father about anything personal." It took me a long while before I could bring him to understand that he had happened to strike the wrong moment and that he would have to try again when conditions were more auspicious, and that his father had paid him a great compliment in asking his opinion on a matter of importance to the country. It was not an acceptable idea at the time.

I can remember another episode that was entirely characteristic of my husband. One of our sons was going through a crisis in his personal life, and both his father and I were anxious to keep him from following a certain course on which he was determined. My husband asked me to telephone this child, which I did. I returned to Franklin's study expecting to find him breathlessly awaiting the results of my conversation. Instead I found him deeply engrossed in going over a letter. If I remember rightly, it was his first peace note to all the nations, including for the first time the Soviet Union. When he looked up, I told him that I had been entirely unsuccessful. His face clouded for a moment, and then he said: "Well, we can not help it. Do you want to hear my first peace note to the nations?" He always accepted the inevitable and went on to the important things in hand. Philosophically this was right, but at the time I think it made the children feel that he was not so deeply interested in their concerns as they felt he should be.

Now, years later, I find that those difficulties which were so hard to bear at the time no longer seem important to the boys or to Anna, who had her troubles in other ways. They now recognize the things that were important, for their perspective and sense of values have changed; and I think their father as a public man means more to them today than he did in their earlier years.

It may seem that I have gone into a great deal of very frank detail about our family affairs and the personal life of the family. I have done so with a purpose, because I sometimes wonder whether the American public, which encourages the press to delve into the private lives of public servants and their families, realizes how much the family of a public man has to pay in lack of privacy for the fact that he is willing to serve his country in an elective or an appointive office.

In addition, I doubt if the public realizes the price that the whole family pays in curtailment of opportunity to live a close family life. Much has to be sacrificed by all to the public interest and there is little or no personal compensation for the members of the family. There are, of course, pride in the man's achievement and gratitude if he is able to help his countrymen and the world. Love is usually selfish; but when sufficiently disciplined, a family may be glad that a man has the opportunity to fulfill his heart's desire and they will work with him in every way they can to help him to achieve his objectives. But something of the personal relationship must be lost. It is the price paid for a life spent almost entirely in public service.

CHAPTER THREE

PRIVATE INTERLUDE: 1921–1927

AT THE end of the first volume of my autobiography I spoke of the Democratic National Convention of 1924, which was followed by the defeat of Mr. John W. Davis, candidate for the presidency, and the victory of Alfred E. Smith as Governor of the State of New York.

My husband again became primarily a business man. However, he could never devote himself solely to one undertaking. Politics, as they affected him personally, receded into the background for a time, but there never was a moment when he was not interested in the American people and in every detail of the political situation.

After leaving the law office of Carter, Ledyard and Milburn in 1910 and up to the time of his illness in 1921, Franklin had been more or less continuously in public life. He had been elected state senator from our rock-ribbed Republican district and had been active in the Democratic National Convention which nominated Woodrow Wilson for his first term, attracting enough attention to be appointed Assistant Secretary of the Navy in the spring of 1913. The Navy having always been one of his main interests, he was well qualified for the job. He and Secretary Josephus Daniels made a good team. Secretary Daniels was older and more experienced politically, and in relations with Congress could do what Franklin could never have done; while Franklin provided a background of naval knowledge that Secretary Daniels did not have.

Franklin's job in the Navy Department was, I believe, one of the milestones in his life. It would have been easy for him to have become just a nice young society man who, after his work in the department was over for the day, sat around in the Metropolitan Club for a while and talked with his friends. But Louis Howe, who went to Washington with us as Franklin's secretary, decided that this was a period in Franklin's life when he had better learn something new. Louis, though gnomelike and frail always, was an indefatigable worker. As a newspaperman in Albany, he had first noticed Franklin in the legislature and had made up his mind that there was a young man with a future. From then on he watched him closely. Now he insisted that Franklin find out something about labor conditions in the navy yards, which were his special province in the department, and come in contact with the men. And he succeeded in getting him interested. This was Franklin's first close contact with labor; and there is no doubt, as I have said, that it was one of the turning points in his development. Certainly it proved of value to him later, both as governor and as president. In both of those periods, of course, he increased enormously in his understanding of people and their needs, and with Louis' help gradually developed a political flair that gave him great confidence.

While he was still in the Navy Department, he at one point ran in the New York State primaries for United States senator and was defeated, and in 1920, at the San Francisco convention he was nominated for the vice-presidency, with Mr. James A. Cox as the presidential candidate. That campaign was fought mainly over the League of Nations, which the Senate had voted down the year before. In fact, President Wilson's tragic illness had come about as a result of his efforts to bring that issue before the country.

After this defeat Franklin went into business in New York City, heading the New York office of the Maryland Fidelity and Deposit Company for Mr. Van Lear Black.

When Edward Bok offered his peace award in 1923, Franklin submitted a paper on organization for peace. Esther Lape, who had been my friend since our return to New York City in 1920, became member-in-charge of the Bok Foundation. At Mr. Bok's request, I helped her to organize the committee and this work. From our past experience in the League of Women Voters, we knew that working together would be easy. We had Esther Lape's friend and partner, Elizabeth Read, who was practicing law in New York City, to count on too, so the thinking and planning proceeded smoothly.

I should like to pay a tribute here to the long friendship I have enjoyed with both Elizabeth Read and Esther Lape. Elizabeth Read was a very rare human being whose honesty and insight had been heightened by her legal training. Though she was a very able person she was without intellectual arrogance or vanity and had an extraordinary gift for friendship. Her great intellectual integrity and courage will always be an inspiration to those who knew her. Esther Lape was perhaps more brilliant in some ways, but the two intellects complemented each other, and to be with them was an experience which their friends always cherished.

In conversations with Esther Lape in later years Franklin often referred to the peace plan he submitted in the first Bok competition. I think he never forgot the ideas that he set down then. The writing of this peace plan was proposed largely as something to keep alive his interest in outside matters during the first years of adjustment to his illness, when it would have been easy for him to become a self-centered invalid. However, it served an even more far-reaching purpose, since it was the basis on which he built other plans for world peace in later years. His original plan aimed at remedying the defects that had actually been revealed in the functioning of the League of Nations; later he brought this draft up to date with new thinking.*

In January of the year following Alfred E. Smith's 1924 state victory, Franklin became a partner in Mr. D. Basil O'Connor's law firm. The firm became Roosevelt and O'Connor, an association which continued until March 3, 1933. However, from 1924 to 1928, Franklin devoted a good part of his time to finding out how far he could recover from infantile paralysis. The disease had attacked him in 1921 while we were at Campobello, and his hands and arms as well as his legs became partially paralyzed. The use of his hands and arms came back

* See Appendix i.

completely and he developed, because he used them so constantly, broad shoulders and strong arms; but his legs remained useless.

Little by little, through exercise and wearing braces, he learned to walk, first with crutches and then with a cane, leaning on someone's arm. The first braces were heavy; later, lighter ones were made. However, for the rest of his life he was unable to walk or stand without the braces and some help, though he could still swim and play water polo.

The perfect naturalness with which the children accepted his limitations, though they had always known him as an active person, helped him tremendously, I think, in his own acceptance of them. He had so many outside interests that he was always busy, and boredom was something he never experienced in his whole life.

Two things he could still enjoy—swimming and driving his own car. His car had special hand controls, since he could not use his legs. He was as good a driver as any one I have known with this specially equipped car.

Franklin's illness was another turning point, and proved a blessing in disguise; for it gave him strength and courage he had not had before. He had to think out the fundamentals of living and learn the greatest of all lessons—infinite patience and never-ending persistence.

People have often asked me how I myself felt about his illness. To tell the truth, I do not think I ever stopped to analyze my feelings. There was so much to do to manage the household and the children and to try to keep things running smoothly that I never had any time to think of my own reactions. I simply lived from day to day and got through the best I could.

In the winters, Franklin cruised off the coast of Florida in a houseboat, until a great storm wiped the boat out of existence. The only bitter remark I ever heard him make about his illness was in connection with the use of the houseboat, which was an expense that, in view of the considerable cost of bringing up a family of five children, we had to consider carefully. One day he said: "Well, I suppose I'd better do all I can to learn to move about as much as possible. I don't want to be a useless burden to the rest of my family."

We had tried so hard to ignore any handicap he labored under that I'm sure the two youngest boys had never even thought about what their father could not do; and I had taken it for granted that he himself had also come to ignore his disabilities. His bitterness was a shock, and I never forgot again that much of his gallant joking was merely a way of forcing himself to accept cheerfully what he could not help. I remember, for instance, one night in New York City, during a campaign, when he had to be carried on and off the speakers' platform. It was a difficult ordeal, but he passed it off with a smile and a joke.

In the summers up to the time he decided to develop Warm Springs, he took treatments under Dr. McDonald in Marion, Massachusetts. The summer of 1926 we had a house there, and I remember with some amusement how occasionally when my husband wished to escape visitors, and saw me sitting on the porch with someone when he drove up after a treatment, he would drive right on and stay out until the visitor grew bored with me and left.

The exercises prescribed by Dr. McDonald were strenuous, but he had an extraordinary ability to give his patients confidence. Franklin, who always learned a great deal from those with whom he came in contact, never failed to give Dr. McDonald credit in his later work with other doctors and nurses at Warm Springs.

Franklin went to Warm Springs for the first time in the autumn of 1924. It was then a very run-down southern summer resort which had seen much better days. The old hotel with its piazzas called to mind the southern belles of Civil War days. The outdoor swimming pool was the one really fine thing about the place, and the water at once seemed to justify all the praise which George Foster Peabody and Tom Loyless had poured forth. Mr. Peabody was a financier and philanthropist who came from Georgia. He knew and liked my husband and hoped it would be possible to help him; also he was eager to rehabilitate the old summer resort, in which he had a sentimental interest. Mr. Loyless was living there because his health had broken and he had had to give up his newspaper work permanently.

Mr. Loyless had told my husband he would find new hope once he began to swim in the "healing waters." These springs had been known since the days of the Indians who, even when they were at war with one another, maintained peace in that area, believing the waters had medicinal value. There is no claim made now that they have any "healing powers," but the buoyancy and warm temperature of the water make it possible for one to swim for long periods without becoming tired or chilled. My husband loved the place at once and described it enthusiastically in letters to his mother.

My grandmother, Mrs. Theodore Roosevelt, had come from Georgia. I never knew her, but her sister, Mrs. James King Gracie, who was very kind to my brother and me when we were children, had told us endless stories of plantation life in the South as she had lived it, and, through her, Brer Rabbit had become a familiar and beloved character. She had made me feel that life in the South must be gracious and easy and charming. I had never lived there, however, until we went to Warm Springs.

It was a disappointment to me to find that for many, many people life in the South was hard and poor and ugly, just as it is in parts of the North. Even though I realized how greatly many people benefited from the place, I never really enjoyed living in Warm Springs as much as my husband did. I was grateful that he got so much joy and satisfaction out of it, but I never liked keeping house there. I remember the first house we lived in and my surprise that I could look through the cracks and see daylight. I can also remember driving with Miss LeHand one day to a nearby town to buy some chickens and my perfect horror when I learned I had to take them home alive, instead of killed and dressed. At Hyde Park there were chickens in the farm yard, but that was a mile away from the house and I didn't hear them being killed. In Warm Springs they ran around in our yard, until the cook wrung their necks amid much squawking and put them in the pot. Somehow I didn't enjoy eating them!

Nevertheless Warm Springs itself was a beautiful spot, and a wonderful spirit existed among the patients.

My lasting impression is of the kindness of all our neighbors. Hardly a day passed that something was not brought to our door—wood for the fireplace, or a chicken, or flowers. Frequently the flowers came arranged in an old silver bowl or china vase that was a priceless family possession, and I would worry until the flowers faded and the container was returned to its owner.

For a number of years my husband went to Warm Springs every autumn, and I remember with a mixture of joy and sadness the Thanksgiving Day celebrations. There seemed so much happiness in the children's faces, but the complete gallantry of all the patients always brought a choke to my throat. Some of them were on stretchers, some in wheel chairs, some on crutches. Some hoped to get well, many faced permanent handicaps, but all were cheerful that one evening at least.

The newspaper correspondents who went with us after Franklin was elected governor were very kind to the patients, and Franklin's two bodyguards, Gus Gennerich and Earl Miller, used to play the piano for the children by the hour, to the great joy of them all. They were always finding kind things to do. This was equally true of the secret-service men and the White House staff who went with Franklin to Warm Springs while he was president.

Earl Miller, who at that time was a New York State Trooper, thought that my husband should learn to ride horseback again, as many of the patients at Warm Springs had, and he insisted that it would be a good thing if Miss LeHand and I rode too. Miss LeHand (Missy) had been Franklin's secretary ever since the 1920 campaign. She was young and pretty but delicate, for she had had rheumatic fever as a child. While she could ride and drive and swim, the more strenuous forms of exercise were forbidden. Though she did not come to live with us until we went to Albany, she often stayed with us in Warm Springs and in Hyde Park, and was devoted to my husband and his work.

The roads through the woods and up and down the mountains were perfect for horseback riding, and Missy was a much better pupil than I. It took me a long time to gain enough confidence to learn to ride astride, for I had always ridden sidesaddle. Even though I did not have to start from scratch, I did have to acquire sufficient courage to feel that I could sit on a horse and have some control over the animal. Finally, however, riding became a pleasure which I continued to enjoy both at Hyde Park and in Washington for several years. When Earl Miller left us, he gave me his horse, Dot; I grew fond of her and rode her until she died. After that I gave up riding because I never again could find a horse in whom I had the slightest confidence. Also, I had fallen off Dot three times, and each time it had taken me longer to recover from the slight effects of the fall.

My husband was not able to get any pleasure out of riding after he became paralyzed, though he had been a fine horseman. He rode with Earl Miller in Warm Springs and at Hyde Park, but never got over his sense of insecurity in the saddle, because he could not use the muscles necessary to balance himself on a horse. The effort proved to be a detriment rather than a benefit to his health, so he abandoned it. The only real satisfaction for him in riding would have been to reach places in the woods that were inaccessible any other way. However, he was able to get to almost any place in the woods in his small car.

In the early days of Warm Springs, Miss LeHand spent a good deal more time there than I could. I still had four children, Anna, Elliott, Franklin, junior, and John, at home during the school year, either in our New York City house or at Hyde Park with my mother-in-law. Also I was carrying on a certain amount of political activity. This political work was done largely at the instigation of Louis Howe, who had again become my husband's secretary and assistant. After Franklin left the Navy Department in 1920 their connection would probably have been severed because Louis had been offered another job and he had accepted it before he heard of Franklin's illness. However, the moment he learned how seriously ill Franklin was, he came all the way to Campobello and asked to be allowed to act as secretary. From then on, they were never separated until Louis died. This again was one of the important events in Franklin's life; for if Louis had not come back to work for him, it would have been much harder for Franklin to return to politics.

Louis paid only occasional visits to Warm Springs, but he worked unceasingly in New York; already, I think, he had made up his mind that some day my husband would enter public life again. He laid his plans accordingly, using everyone he felt could be useful. I sometimes think he used even his own family, adjusting their plans to fit whatever work he had to do. I have always felt that Mrs. Howe and their children deserved special recognition for enabling Louis to carry out his plans, for it often meant that he had a scant amount of time to spend with them. However, the fact that they all had similar intellectual interests and many outside interests probably made it possible for them to share and enjoy Louis' varied activities.

During these years before Franklin went back actively into politics, a number of the things I did were undertaken at Louis Howe's suggestion in order to interest Franklin. I was pushed into the women's division of the Democratic State Committee, not because Louis cared so much about my activities, but because he felt that they would make it possible for me to bring into the house people who would keep Franklin interested in state politics.

Mrs. Daniel O'Day was the chairman of the women's division. She was a charming woman who had come from the South as an art student, Paris-bound, and had married Daniel O'Day, who brought her to live in New York. She had a warm heart and strong convictions which she lived up to even in the face of severe criticism.

My main job was to raise money for our work. I still consider this important because, when the women's division has its own money, it can make its own plans and carry them through. I have found that sometimes work which must be done with women does not seem important to the men who head up the state committee. Besides, being vice-chairman of the committee under Mrs. Daniel O'Day and raising money for the women's division, I worked on programs to interest the women and young people of the state between campaigns. Later I edited, with Louis Howe's help, a small monthly magazine.

Altogether, I worked in the women's division of the Democratic State Committee for six years. Those were the years when I came to know well many women with whom I have often worked since— Marion Dickerman, Nancy Cook, Mrs. William H. Good, Mrs. Henry

Goddard Leach, Mrs. Norman Mack, Fannie Hurst, Mrs. Henry Morgenthau, junior, and many others.

Had Elinor Morgenthau and I not been thrown together by our common interests, the miles that separated us in Dutchess County might have remained a barrier for a long time. However, through working closely together, as we did throughout all the years I was on the committee, we became warm friends. She is a sensitive and generous person whose qualities I recognized and appreciated and our relationship developed with the years. Her wide knowledge of the theatre and music and literature made it possible for her to help with the art groups in every campaign; and long after I ceased to work at either the state or national headquarters, she continued to work hard throughout every election.

Elinor is also an excellent organizer, and even now I find echoes of our work. A short time ago at Lake Success, a young woman lawyer told me she first became interested in the political world through winning a contest for school children which Mrs. Morgenthau and I organized under the auspices of the Democratic State Committee. The prize was a visit to New York City, and we arranged some very active days for the young winners. Evidently they have remembered it, for Elinor Morgenthau has heard from some of them since, as I have, too.

We all worked hard in those state campaigns. The organizing was primarily my job and, again with Louis Howe's help, I thought up, I think, some of the best stunts that were undertaken. For instance, in the campaign of 1924 Alfred E. Smith was running against my cousin, Theodore Roosevelt, junior, who had previously been Assistant Secretary of the Navy in the Harding administration. The recent Teapot Dome scandal—with which Theodore Roosevelt, junior, had had nothing to do—had created much excitement; so capitalizing on this, we had a framework resembling a teapot, which spouted steam, built on top of an automobile; and it led the procession of cars which toured the state, following the Republican candidate for governor wherever he went!

In the thick of political fights one always feels that all methods of campaigning that are honest are fair, but I do think now that this was a rough stunt and I never blamed my cousin when he retaliated in later campaigns against my husband.

Louis also insisted that I learn to make speeches; he even went and sat in the back row when I was speaking and told me about my mistakes afterwards. Once he asked me why I had laughed at a certain point in my speech. "Why, I didn't know I laughed," I said. "There wasn't any reason to laugh." "I know there wasn't," said Louis, "so why did you give that silly little giggle?"

It was not very obvious to me at that time why making speeches was necessary, and at first it was the most painful thing I had to do. Now I can see that Louis felt that unless I learned to be useful to the party in this way, I would not get much consideration from any of the leaders.

It was during these years too that I became engaged in two enterprises with Nancy Cook and Marion Dickerman, whom I had met in my political work. Franklin was particularly interested in one of our undertakings. He helped to design and build a stone cottage beside a brook where we often went to picnic during the first years after he was paralyzed. The brook was called Val-Kill so we called the cottage Val-Kill cottage. Franklin was the contractor and the builder and, though Mr. Henry Toombs was the architect, he liked to talk over every detail. We built not only the cottage, but a swimming pool in which the children and occasionally Franklin enjoyed much sport. Later we built a more elaborate pool, but by that time Franklin was "The President" and we had to conform to the regulations set by his doctor and put in filtration machinery. I do not think we had any more fun, however, in the bigger and more elaborate pool than we had in the original small one, the building of which my husband had supervised.

The cottage was not an end in itself. It was the place in which Nancy Cook and Marion Dickerman lived and from which Miss Cook directed a furniture factory. Nancy Cook was an attractive woman who had distinct artistic ability and could do almost anything with her hands. She had long wanted to make reproductions of early American furniture. We obtained help and cooperation from the Metropolitan Museum, the Hartford Museum and from many individuals. We procured drawings and went to look at famous pieces of old furniture. Miss Cook had no desire to reproduce worm-eaten antiques; she wanted to use methods employed by our ancestors, and see whether she could find a market for furniture which, though the first processes were done by machinery, would be largely handmade and therefore expensive. Because the finishing was all done by hand, the wood looked and felt as though it had been used and polished for years.

My husband had very little interest in the production of furniture but he was greatly interested in finding some industry that could be developed in country areas such as ours, and that could perhaps furnish occupation for some of the younger men who would otherwise leave the farms. By giving them work in an industry which would yield them a fairly good income during the slack period on the farms, he thought one could keep the progressive, more active group of young people working steadily and so raise the standard of farm development in our area.

Franklin had heard the story of a small community in Vermont where the people loved their homes and the countryside, but could not quite make a living on the farms. One enterprising citizen went away for a time and on his return suggested using certain kinds of wood which could be found in that neighborhood for some industry. They put up a small factory in which, during the winter months, they made wooden handles and wooden saucepan knobs, finding an outlet through one of the large manufacturers. By producing large quantities of the little wooden knobs and handles, they raised their standard of living and held on to the farms and homes they loved.

This experiment made my husband eager to find out whether in our neighborhood something of the same kind could be done. He had a great love for the soil and wanted to see it developed; but he realized that many of the farmers around us had a difficult time holding their young sons on the land, because the return for hard and strenuous work was meager. His interest in our enterprise was therefore in the training and the employment of young men in the vicinity. Of course, we had to have a certain number of expert craftsmen, and were fortunate in finding some very fine cabinetmakers of Italian and Norwegian descent. Nancy Cook ran the enterprise and I put in most of the capital from my earnings from radio and writing and even used some of the small capital that I had inherited from my mother and father. The others, especially Nancy Cook, contributed what they could afford.

We kept the factory going all through the early depression years, when the employment of people seemed vitally important. At last Miss Cook found that carrying two jobs—she was also executive secretary of the women's division of the Democratic State Committee—was too much for her, so we closed the shop.

My husband's object was not achieved, and I think the idea has been proved impractical on a much larger scale in some of the homesteads which were started during the depression. Some have succeeded but few have returned much of the original investment. Nevertheless, in the crisis they took people off relief and gave them back self-respect and a sense of security—a considerable achievement.

We found in our shop that as soon as a young man learned a trade in which he could make more money than he could on a farm he did not care enough about farm life to want to give up for the summer the good wages and regular hours he enjoyed in his trade. It is true that during the depression years, when work was hard to find, many workers from the town and cities returned to the farms; but as soon as work in a factory or at a trade was available, the young men sought the easier life with larger financial return. In this they were usually urged on by their wives, who felt that life on the farm was hard for them as well as for their husbands.

The truth seems to be that if you farm in parts of the country where financial returns are small, you must love the life and prize the sense of security you get from knowing that you are more self-sufficient than any city dweller and less vulnerable to vicissitudes beyond your control. A farmer with a mortgage on his farm, however, does not always find this to be true, since he has to make a cash income. Consequently, the lure of wages keeps most men at their trade, just as it did the boys who were trained in our factory, and good wages still take ambitious boys to the cities.

Although this experiment was a disappointment to Franklin, he accepted the failure philosophically both in our own case and later in the case of the country-wide experiment. I think he felt regret; but, with the same acceptance of the inevitable which he showed in so many other matters, having tried the experiment and become satisfied that it did not work, he gave it up and sought other solutions. He hoped that some day it might work out. He always accepted things as they were and set such experiences aside as something to remember and perhaps use in the future.

I never made any money out of this furniture-making venture. In fact, I think I was probably one of the best customers the shop had, because I bought various pieces of furniture as wedding presents and as gifts for other occasions.

Nancy Cook and Marion Dickerman lived in the stone cottage until they moved to Connecticut in 1947. During the depression I took over the factory building and was able, through my earnings, to turn it into a fairly comfortable if somewhat odd house. Though I did not have any architectural advice, I did have the help of a friend, Henry Osthagen, who is an engineer. We used local labor entirely. Employing people seemed the best way to spend some of the money I was able to earn during those years. Part of the shop we made into an apartment for my secretary, Malvina Thompson, and I frequently went there to work quietly with her; the rest of the building became a guest cottage, which we used when the big house was overcrowded—something that often happened during the years when my husband was president. Since turning the old Hyde Park house over to the government, I have made the converted shop building my year-round home, though I keep an office in a small apartment in New York City.

Though Miss Thompson and I live in the same house in Hyde Park—she has had her apartment there since 1936—our arrangements can be entirely separate when we want them to be. "Tommy," as she was nicknamed by my daughter many years ago, has been my secretary since 1922—first on a part-time arrangement, but since 1933, when we moved to Washington, on a regular full-time basis. In all these years she has taken very few days off, because our life has always been busy. She has been with me on most of my trips—and they have been many—and though there have been many relaxing interludes, she has never been really free.

Tommy is a wonderful person to keep one living up to one's obligations, because her conscience is of the New England variety. At the same time she has a sense of humor and real wit and has pulled us through many difficult situations by her ability to see the funny side of things and her determination not to be overwhelmed by situations of any kind.

During the early years of my acquaintance with Nancy Cook and Marion Dickerman, I became associated in the Todhunter School with Miss Dickerman, who was first the assistant principal and then the principal. It was a private school for girls from the primary grades through high school. Miss Todhunter, who was British, finally sold the school to Marion Dickerman, Nancy Cook and myself and went back to England. I began teaching there in 1927. I taught only the older girls because I considered that it took less training to teach them than to teach the younger children. I gave courses in American history and in English and American literature and later we tried some courses in current events which I hope were more practical than are many of the courses given to sixteen- and seventeen-year-old girls. We visited the New York City courts, and I think many young people learned a great deal from sitting in one of the children's courts for an hour. Those whom their parents allowed to go I took to see the different kinds of tenements that exist in a city like New York, as well as the big markets and various other places. All this made the government of the city something real and alive, rather than just so many words in a text book.

In spite of my political activities and having to run the Executive Mansion in Albany, after my husband was elected governor I continued to teach for two and a half days a week, leaving Albany on Sunday evenings and returning Wednesday afternoons. It was rather strenuous when we were in Albany, but, of course, fairly easy when we were at Hyde Park, as we were there for longer periods, when the legislature was not in session. For a while, after we went to Washington, I conducted a class for graduates and their friends, first on a weekly and then on a monthly basis.

CHAPTER FOUR

BACK TO POLITICS: 1928

IN THE spring of 1928, when it looked as though Governor Smith would be the candidate for the presidency on the Democratic ticket, Mrs. Belle Moskowitz asked me to organize the women's end of the office for the national campaign.

That June my husband went with our son, Elliott, to the Democratic National Convention which met in Houston, Texas. Elliott was thrilled at the chance to be with his father, but I had no desire to take part in the hurly-burly of a convention—the 1924 convention had given me all I wanted of that type of experience. In addition, our two youngest boys, Franklin, junior, and John, were at Hyde Park and I had to stay with them. To my relief, my husband stood the Texas heat remarkably well and came home to Hyde Park completely happy, feeling that he had had a great part in bringing about the nomination of Alfred E. Smith.

Franklin and I had long supported Governor Smith politically because of his social program; we believed that he wanted the welfare of the average man and woman. Franklin remembered how after the Triangle Fire in 1911 in New York City Governor Smith had worked for better factory laws in our state. This fire had been a shocking disaster, in which a great many girls and women had been burned to death owing to the lack of fire exits and fire protection in the factory.

Because Governor Smith had spent the greater part of his life in one state and practically in one city, he had certain shortcomings; nevertheless we felt that he understood the needs of the people and that he had a genius for government; and we never doubted his integrity. His memory was prodigious and his method of talking to people during the campaigns, particularly in his own state, which he knew so well, was remarkably effective.

Franklin did not feel he could do a great deal of work in the campaign, but he came into the office occasionally, and he headed the Businessmen's Division, sat in on planning meetings and made some speeches. He assigned Louis Howe to represent him at the headquarters full time, working with Governor Smith, John Raskob, Edward J. Flynn and others.

In the early autumn of that year Franklin spent considerable time at Warm Springs, but he was glad to have me continue to help in the campaign, and pleased that I could work under Mrs. Moskowitz's direction. She was a challenge to all of us at headquarters, because she really knew whether we were working hard and achieving results. She was completely devoted to Governor Smith and to the social program which he had developed as governor of the state—and which many of us felt she had largely inspired. Indeed, Governor Smith himself always gave credit to her for the intelligent way in which much of the welfare program was planned and carried out. Mrs. Moskowitz and I worked together in full harmony from April to the end of the campaign in November, and I have always been grateful to her for the opportunity.

During that campaign, we all worked hard at what was obviously a losing fight, though none of us acknowledged it and most of us, I think, did the kind of work that usually brings success. It was not until I began to see the full alignment against us that I became doubtful of success. Governor Smith was a Roman Catholic, and the kind of propaganda that some of the religious groups, aided and abetted by the opposition, put forth in that campaign utterly disgusted me. I think by nature I am a fairly liberal person, without intense prejudice, but if I needed anything to show me what prejudice can do to the intelligence of human beings, that campaign was the best lesson I could have had.

I can remember even now some of the extraordinary questions about Governor Smith that Franklin told me people asked him while he was in Warm Springs that autumn. The questions on the subject of the Roman Catholic church particularly stand out in my memory. Franklin had learned how little the southern farmer knew about the Catholic church when he brought to Warm Springs a very remarkable nurse, Miss Helena Mahoney. She went down with Dr. LeRoy Hubbard, who had been a public health doctor in New York. Both of them had had some experience with polio. Dr. Hubbard was retired and glad to devote his time to a new experiment. Miss Mahoney was also interested in the new venture, and I hope she had no idea of the comments that were made when the people in Warm Springs discovered that she was a Roman Catholic. After she had been there for some time, and had traveled miles to a Roman Catholic church in a city for occasional Sunday worship, one of the Georgians remarked to my husband that Miss Mahoney was really a fine woman in spite of her religion! His further remarks revealed that he had fully expected her to arrive with horns and a tail and breathing fire.

It could hardly be expected that these Georgians should look with much favor on a candidate for the presidency who was a Roman Catholic. One of them asked my husband in all seriousness if it were true that, should Governor Smith be elected president, his children would be illegitimate, since his marriage of many years would be declared invalid. My husband burst into roars of laughter and remarked that he considered himself safely married even though he lived in New York State where Alfred E. Smith was the governor; but he never was sure how convincing he had been.

In 1928 I was still fairly young and could put in prodigious hours of work, but I sometimes wonder how any of us, particularly Miss Thompson, and Miss Tully, lived through that campaign. It proved that work is easier to carry if your heart is involved. Miss Thompson was interested because I was interested, and Miss Tully, who had been Cardinal Hayes' secretary, probably felt a religious interest in the campaign, in addition to her admiration for Governor Smith.

Grace Tully was young and very pretty, and had been extremely well trained by Cardinal Hayes. Our work was somewhat different from that to which she had been accustomed, but it was good preparation for her future work with my husband and Miss LeHand.

My mother-in-law went to Europe that summer, and my husband and I so divided our time at Hyde Park as not to leave the two younger boys long without one of us. When I was in Hyde Park for week ends I devoted my days to the boys and in the evenings played cards with them or read to them until their bedtime. Then Miss Thompson and I started to work, often continuing until the early morning hours.

In the fall, after school began, I did not go into the office until noon on the days I taught, but I stayed until the work was finished at night, often well after midnight. Then I went home to do my school papers and was at school the next morning at half-past eight. On the other days, I was in the office at nine o'clock in the morning and stayed until late in the evening.

We did have some diversion. Twice a week we invited visiting Democrats to a tea in one of the large rooms in the General Motors building, where we had the campaign headquarters. Our working group was very congenial: Mrs. June Hamilton Rhodes, who directed publicity for the women's work, was always gay and happy and often made us laugh and relax. Alice Disbrow, who later became Mrs. O'Day's secretary during her terms in Congress, also worked with us long hours every day.

It was during this campaign that I induced Mary W. Dewson to come in and work with us in the Democratic party. She went to take charge of the St. Louis headquarters. Her work there was so good that we knew that no future campaign should be conducted without her; nor was it, as long as she was well enough to take part.

Speaking was still something of an ordeal for me, so it was always understood that my part of the work involved simply organizing the office, handling the mail, greeting women visitors, consulting on requests for speakers—in fact, just being generally useful. Mrs. Mary Norton, congresswoman from New Jersey, as head of the women's speakers' bureau, made the arrangements for women speakers, and all requests were referred to her.

Elinor Morgenthau and Nancy Cook, who were working with the Democratic State Committee, moved with their staff to the General Motors building for the campaign. Then, in the latter part of the summer of 1928, the vice-chairman of the Democratic National Committee, Mrs. Nellie Tayloe Ross, moved into her office at the national headquarters, with Mrs. James O'Mahoney as her assistant. Mrs. Ross had served as Governor of Wyoming after the death of her husband, who had been (the previous) governor.

Her arrival at headquarters meant that we started at once to make plans for an extensive speaking trip for her, and of course, she was always in demand for many of the activities at headquarters. I am afraid we kept her pretty busy. I remember one day I had Miss Tully scurrying everywhere to find Mrs. Ross while a tea party waited to greet her. She finally was found completely exhausted, lying on the floor of our diminutive rest room, trying to regain enough energy to face shaking hands with several hundred people. We often were quite inhuman in the schedules that we planned for her, expecting her to make a speech, and write the next one while on the train between engagements. Finally she told me that that was not the way in which she could do her best work and that her schedule would have to be revised.

Since then Mrs. Ross has continued in active government work and is now the Director of the Mint in the Treasury Department. She has made a real place for herself and is always a popular speaker with women's groups.

There was one occasion, however, on which she must have been overawed by her host. Governor Smith told me of a visit she made to him in Albany while she was Governor of Wyoming. Since Governor Smith did not really feel that a woman should be the governor of a state, he gloated over the fact that he had asked her some questions which from his point of view required exact figures for a proper answer. Mrs. Ross could not give them to him, and told him as casually as I should have that she would have the figures sent to him after she went back to her home state, where they were available. To Governor Smith, who could reel off every figure that had to do with the government of the State of New York, this seemed sacrilege, and he was surer than ever that no woman could really be a good governor.

Once or twice, when speakers failed at the last minute, I had to make short trips out of the office to take their places. I remember one trip I took with Mrs. Charles Dana Gibson to New Hampshire. I was to give the facts and figures and she was to charm the audience. Mrs. Gibson carried out her part of the program. As everybody knows, she is one of the celebrated Langhorne sisters from Virginia, whose beauty and wit are famous not only in the United States but in many other countries. She had married the artist, Charles Dana Gibson, who used her as a model for his many drawings of the Gibson girl. She has always been a loyal Democrat and has taken part in nearly all the campaigns, but I do not think she found overnight jaunts as easy as I did. She rose to the occasion, however, telling southern stories aptly and well to illustrate the political points she wished to make. Everyone applauded loudly and whatever shortcomings were mine, she made up for them.

In September of that year I motored to Groton with our youngest son, John, to put him in boarding school. I had by then come to feel that once a child went to boarding school there never again could be the strong ties with and the dependence on the family that had existed up to that time. I had never been a convinced advocate of boarding school for the twelve-year-old, but it was a tradition. My husband, who had not gone to boarding school until he was fourteen, always felt that the loss of those two years were a hardship, because by the time he entered the school the other boys had already formed their friendships and he remained always a little the outsider. Our boys all went at the age of twelve, or soon thereafter. I still believe it is too early an age and a loss both to the parents and to the children. The day I took each boy to school, unpacked his clothes and settled him was always a terrible day for me, and when it came to the last child, it was particularly hard. I think I resented taking our youngest son more than the others because there was then no child left at home. My daughter, Anna, had been married to Curtis Dall, so she was already full of her own affairs. It was fortunate, I think, that I had a strenuous autumn to cope with after our youngest son went to Groton. I might otherwise have been a very disagreeable companion for my husband and my mother-in-law.

Even though I was teaching school and working in the national campaign headquarters in New York City, I attended the New York State Democratic convention in Rochester that fall. I mention this here to tell the story, as I remember it, of how my husband was finally induced to run for the governorship.

The afternoon before the nominations were finally made, John J. Raskob, then chairman of the National Democratic Committee, and Governor Smith asked me to come to talk with them. This was no surprise for I had heard that Governor Smith wanted my husband to run. However, I knew Franklin felt he should continue his treatment at Warm Springs, where he was at the time. They told me how much they wanted him to run, and asked me if I thought it would really injure his health. I said I did not know; that I had been told the doctors felt that if he continued with his exercises and swimming at Warm Springs he might improve. My husband himself once laughingly said that if he lived long enough he might be able to walk again, but progress was slow and I sometimes wondered how much more could be achieved.

Both Governor Smith and Mr. Raskob insisted that they did not want to urge anything that would injure Franklin's health. If, however, it was not simply his health, but other reasons which kept him from consenting, they would like to know it. I said I did not think any other reasons were paramount, and that I felt he thought the possibility of making further improvement in his health was worth a try. Also, having undertaken a heavy financial responsibility in Warm Springs, he felt an obligation to try to make it a success.

Franklin had put a great deal of his own capital into Warm Springs, far more than probably was wise.* Nevertheless, it was his great interest, and I never questioned anything that he wanted to do with his own

* Franklin originally lent $201,677.83 to start Warm Springs and received a demand note for this sum, dated February 29, 1928. This was paid back by the Foundation, some of it after his death. In appendix ii will be found the full account furnished me by Mr. Basil O'Connor and published with the consent of Mr. Raskob and the Ford family.

money, since I felt that was strictly his business. Mr. Raskob and Governor Smith questioned me closely about this and Mr. Raskob asked whether it would have any effect upon Franklin's decision if he were relieved of all financial anxieties. I told him I was sure it would not. Later, when Mr. Raskob talked to Franklin, he offered to lend him for a year a very large sum of money if that would relieve him and make it possible for him to run for governor.

My husband did not consider this loan, but in October of that year Mr. Raskob gave $25,000 to Warm Springs. In March of that same year, Edsel Ford had given $25,000 for the patients' swimming pool. He had visited some friends there, Mr. and Mrs. Lynn Pierson, who evidently succeeded in interesting him. Many other people gave large and small amounts in those early days, but the list before me gives only the sums donated generously by Mr. Raskob—an additional $50,000 in 1929 and, at different times during 1931, sums amounting to $38,000 more.

Finally, after Governor Smith, Mr. Raskob and I talked over the situation, they asked me if I would be willing to try to get my husband on the telephone and ask him to run for governor. They had been trying all day to reach him and had not been able to. I answered that I would not ask him to do anything he felt he should not do, let alone run for office. I never felt it was right to try to influence decisions of this kind, I told them, and I certainly did not feel it was right at that time. I insisted that he must make his own decisions, but I said I would be willing to try to get him on the telephone.

We parted for a few hours. They put in a call to my husband for me early in the evening and found that he had gone to Manchester, Georgia, to make a speech and could not be reached until he returned to Warm Springs. Time wore on, and it looked as though I would not get him on the telephone before I had to take a train to New York City with Miss Dickerman. She had come up to the convention with Miss Cook to help with any work the women's division of the state committee might have, but we both had to be at the school teaching our classes the next morning. I finally succeeded in getting Franklin on the telephone at the Foundation after his return. He told me with evident glee that he had been keeping out of reach all day and would not have answered the telephone if I had not been calling. I had just time enough to tell him that I had called because Mr. Raskob and Governor Smith begged me to, and that I was leaving him to Governor Smith because I had to catch the train. Then I ran. I can still hear Governor Smith's voice saying: "Hello Frank," as I hurried from the room to gather up my belongings and catch the train. I did not know until the following morning when I bought a newspaper that my husband had been persuaded finally to accept the nomination. I never heard him say later whether he regretted his decision or not. Having decided, he put any other possibility out of his mind.

I sometimes wonder whether I really wanted Franklin to run. I imagine I accepted his nomination and later his election as I had accepted most of the things that had happened in life thus far: one did whatever seemed necessary and adjusted one's personal life to the developments in other people's lives.

The children were interested in their father's campaign, but on the whole they were so occupied with their own lives—at that time all the boys were either in Groton or at Harvard—that it had less interest for them than the later campaigns, when they were old enough to take some part. They were accustomed to their father's concern with public affairs and appeared to accept his governorship without much excitement. It seemed a routine matter, and at first they thought it would not affect their own lives very greatly.

Louis Howe was not happy about Franklin's candidacy. He always thought in terms of the future, and he had planned that Franklin should be a candidate four or eight years thence. Louis feared that if Governor Smith lost nationally, it might not be possible for Franklin to carry the state for the governorship, which might spoil any chance he had for future political office.

I used to laugh at Louis and say one could not plan every move in this world; one had to accept circumstances as they developed. That was one thing that Louis hated to do. He liked to feel that he dominated circumstances and, so far as it was humanly possible, he often did.

Comparatively speaking, I knew very little about the 1928 campaign for the governorship. Since I had started to work in the national office, Franklin felt I was obligated to continue there, and that took the greater part of my time. I did go to hear him speak occasionally, and he made a very complete campaign throughout the state. I think he did not expect to carry the state if Governor Smith lost the presidency, and when we left the state headquarters at a very late hour on election night, we were still uncertain of the outcome. The next morning, when the final figures were in, my husband was governor-elect by a very narrow margin. I think he had a feeling that it was a great tribute to him to have been elected when Governor Smith, who had such a large following in the state, had been defeated.

On that election night I visited the national as well as the state campaign headquarters and I thought that Governor Smith accepted his defeat very gallantly. It must have been hard for him to have had Franklin elected, while he himself was defeated, but he never showed it in any way. He went back to work in the state and on January 1, 1929, he received us when we went to Albany.

CHAPTER FIVE

THE GOVERNORSHIP YEARS: 1928–1932

MANY PEOPLE have suggested to me that when Governor Smith asked my husband to run for the governorship, when he himself was running for the presidency, he even then had it in mind that he still would be able to direct the work of the governor.

I doubt very much whether that was true. I think he felt, as most men do when they are running for office, that he was going to win, and he could not have expected to watch very closely what went on in the state if he were in Washington.

However, after his defeat I think he may have expected to remain in close touch. One of the ways in which he undoubtedly expected to keep his hold on the state government was through Mrs. Belle Moskowitz. He suggested a number of times to my husband that she would be invaluable to him, and each time Franklin replied that while he had great respect for Mrs. Moskowitz's ability and knew what her advice and help had meant to Governor Smith, he felt it would be unwise for him to retain her in his own close administrative circle. The reason for his feeling was very simple. He thought it impossible for anyone to transfer loyalty after working so long and so closely with someone else.

Governor Smith, had asked Franklin to nominate him for the presidency and to run on the state ticket as governor because of the fact that Franklin would bring him needed strength. However, I think that Governor Smith did not have much confidence in the Harvard man, a man who had had a different kind of education and who cared about many things which meant little or nothing to Governor Smith.

There are two kinds of snobbishness. That of the man who has had a good many opportunities and looks down on those who lack them is usually recognized by all. The other kind of snobbishness is rarely understood, yet it is real. It is that of the self-made man, who glories in his success in overcoming difficulties and admires greatly people who have achieved the things he considers of importance. Governor Smith, for instance, had a great deal of respect for material success. He admired men who, like John Raskob, had made a success in business through their own efforts or who in some other way had made a name in the world in spite of modest beginnings. But he tended to look down on a man who had not met and conquered the situations he himself had—a man like Franklin, who was content not to make a great deal of money so long as he had enough to live comfortably. Franklin had always been moderately wealthy, but Governor Smith couldn't believe that he could be as able as if he had been self-made. The fact that Franklin would spend money on a picture or on the first edition of a book but would economize on food and clothes and entertainment was hard for him to understand. Governor Smith always wore expensive clothes, because they indicated material success; he liked to eat in well-known restaurants; he liked good food and specially prepared dishes. When we went to Albany, the domestic staff in the Mansion was troubled because they felt they could not cater adequately for us. For instance, they had always had to make monumental desserts for the Smiths, and thought we would expect even grander dishes. They were greatly relieved when they learned that we ate very simple food—like our traditional scrambled eggs for Sunday-night suppers.

Franklin could see no sense in spending money in a restaurant when he had a home to eat in, and he had a lot of little economies. For example, he never paid more than two dollars for a shirt, and boasted when he found he could get one for $1.50, and he never would buy more than two pairs of shoes, though he bought those and other things in England, as his father had. When we were first married, he asked me one day what I had done with a pair of his shoes, and I said I had sent them to be soled. He thought I meant "sold" and was very angry. Not long ago, when I was cleaning out the big house after his death, I found a suit, which I gave to Jimmy, that his grandfather had bought in London and which had been kept all those years simply because it was "too good to throw away."

Governor Smith did not understand that kind of economy. I always felt strongly that he had a defensive attitude, which arose, of course, from his consciousness that he lacked breadth of knowledge, for he was too intelligent not to know that he did not have a certain kind of cultural background. It often seemed to me that he said things which were contemptuous of academic knowledge simply to bolster his own sense of security.

In those days I think that in some ways I understood Governor Smith better than Franklin did, because during my intensive work with the Democratic State Committee while Franklin was ill I had had more opportunity to observe him from different points of view. While he and Franklin had known each other for a long time, they were never really intimate. Franklin thought only of his ability as an administrator, as a campaigner, as a statesman and as governor, and he had the greatest admiration for his knowledge of government. I agreed that he had an extraordinary flair for government and that his memory and his knowledge of New York state were phenomenal. Indeed, I believed in him and considered him a great man in many ways, and I worked for him. I thought that had he been elected president, he would have chosen his cabinet well, even though his knowledge of the country as a whole was slight and his advisers in the state knew little of the nation. However, I never felt he could have handled our foreign relations or gauged what was happening in the world as a whole. Also, I thought him less of a humanitarian than most people did, crediting Mrs. Moskowitz with the social welfare plans for which he was generally acclaimed, and which he carried out, I thought, largely because he knew they were politically wise. I think he always felt that since he had risen from modest beginnings, others could be expected to do the same thing. He was a deeply emotional person who was not always able to control his emotions, and certain kinds of discipline he did not understand. Nevertheless, he had fine qualities; he was loyal, and completely devoted to his church, his family and his friends, and he fiercely resented any criticism of those he loved. Once, I recall, when someone asked Mrs. Smith to take off a few strands of pearls for a campaign photograph, he turned swiftly and commanded: "Leave Katie alone!"

Feeling as I did about him, I was not greatly surprised when after his defeat it became evident that he thought he was going to retain a behind-the-scenes leadership in the state. It would not work; and he soon discovered that it would not work and left Albany for New York City.

He was disappointed and probably felt that he was not being treated fairly by the man he had brought into office—an emotional reaction which he could not control. It was natural for him to feel that he was responsible for Franklin's success in politics, since he had urged my husband to run for governor. Franklin himself, however, felt that his success stemmed from his own action in accepting. The request to run had been made to help Governor Smith, not Franklin D. Roosevelt, and it was on that basis and that basis alone that the appeal had been considered.

In many ways Governor Smith did not know my husband. One of Franklin's main qualities, which Governor Smith was apparently unaware of, was that he never assumed any responsibility that he did not intend to carry through. It never occurred to Franklin that he was not going to be the Governor of New York with all the responsibility and work which that position carried. That ended the close relationship between my husband and Governor Smith, though there was no open break, so far as I ever knew.

Franklin had some very clear ideas about state government. He studied the reorganization plans that had been initiated under Governor Smith and I think he approved practically everything that he had done. His attitude toward the objectives that later were developed on a national scale was apparent in his approach to questions in the state.

He pushed old-age pensions, for instance. I can remember one letter, similar to many others which came to me while I was in Albany, which started: "I am the farmer's wife who wrote you two years ago asking the status of old-age pensions. You told me then that the Legislature had not made its final decisions. Will you please tell me what I am entitled to now?" The "farmer's wife" was one of the many who wrote, and their numbers greatly increased when a comprehensive social security bill was being considered in Washington.

As governor, Franklin also showed his interest in labor and his belief in labor's rights. He felt that they should receive the same consideration that management's rights received; and when times became hard, the theory that government had a responsibility toward the people was incorporated in the state policies. Franklin has been accused of giving labor too much power, but his effort was simply to equalize the power of labor and capital. As a close student of history, he knew how great and unhampered capital's power had been during some previous administrations.

His particular personal interest was in soil conservation and forestry. However, his interest in the development of water power, in the Indian problem, transportation problems generally, education, and finally in relief and general welfare was also stimulated by his experience in the first place as the administrator of a state. All these objectives, as well as his understanding of them, were expanded during the presidential years. And because he had traveled so extensively even before he was president, he knew how different the problems were in different areas of the country. All this was excellent preparation for the years ahead.

Once back in public office, Franklin's political interests and ambitions reawakened. I am sure that when he found he could again play an active part in politics he took a satisfaction in the purely political side of the struggle, in achieving new office. It is hard to disassociate his ambition and enjoyment of the science of politics for its own sake from his desire to achieve through political action real gains for the people, first of the state and then of the nation, and finally of the world. The objectives grew as circumstances developed the need for them, and the horizons broadened as time went on and we, as a nation, were swept into a position where the world was depending on us.

The work in Albany was, of course, invaluable as background for the work that was to come. There he had the experience of working with legislative groups in which his political party was in the minority. Later, in Washington, I often wished that it were possible for him to carry out with the Democratic representatives there—even though the party was in the majority—the kind of educational work he had done in Albany with the Democratic legislators. Judge Rosenman was his counsel and sat in with him, and there were occasional meetings when all the legislation backed by the administration was talked over and explained and the entire campaign mapped out. As the sessions progressed, there would be further meetings, so that there never was a time when the Democrats were not entirely familiar with the governor's thinking and when he did not have a finger on what was being done in the Legislature. I spoke of this a number of times after we got to Washington, but my husband always said the group in Congress was too large and he did not see how it was possible to hold the same type of meeting.

The years in Albany cast their shadow before them. Frances Perkins was in the New York State Labor Department, Harry Hopkins was doing a job on relief and welfare, Dr. Thomas Parran was Commissioner of Public Health, Henry Morgenthau, junior, was Conservation Commissioner. Many experiments that were later to be incorporated into a national program were being tried out in the state. It was part of Franklin's political philosophy—and over and over again I heard him expound it—that the great benefit to be derived from having forty-eight states was the possibility of experimenting on a small scale to see how a program worked before trying it out nationally.

It is quite probable that Franklin derived this concept of the forty-eight states as experimental laboratories from his study of Justice Brandeis' writings and opinions, for he knew the Justice and had a deep respect for him. Another great and learned man who also had his influence on Franklin was Justice Holmes. Franklin had known him quite well when he, Franklin, was Assistant Secretary of the Navy, and he often joined the Sunday-afternoon meetings that Justice Holmes held with some of the young men in Washington at that time. President Wilson, too, had a profound effect on Franklin's thinking and political philosophy. Franklin admired him greatly, I know, and believed deeply in his ideas and ideals. He realized that Wilson had certain weaknesses—for instance, an inability to put himself across with people as an individual—but he also realized how well Wilson gauged public opinion and how far reaching was the influence of what he wrote and said in his public speeches. There is no question in my mind but that all three of these great men had an effect on Franklin that was evident in his actions both as governor and as president.

My own life during those governorship years was a full one. In my teaching I really had for the first time a job that I did not wish to give up. This had led to my planning to spend a few days every week in New York City, except during school vacations. I realize now that it was a foolish thing for me to have done, since while I probably fulfilled all the obligations that went with my position as the wife of the governor and hostess in the Executive Mansion, I did not have much time to make real friends or to see much of the Albany people outside of the official routine. There were many interesting people in the government circle there and some "old inhabitants," most of them charming and interesting people of Dutch ancestry, with traditions and attachments which went far back into Hudson River history, whom I should like to have known better.

I did see some old friends. Mr. and Mrs. Edwin Corning, Mr. and Mrs. Frederick S. Greene, and Mr. and Mrs. Charles Fayerweather became close friends. Mr. and Mrs. William Gorham Rice, friends of my husband's mother, had been kind to us when we lived in Albany during my husband's terms as state senator, and now welcomed us warmly again. Mary Hun (now Mrs. Charles B. Sears) was an old friend of Franklin's, and Mr. and Mrs. Parker Corning and some of the other congressmen and their wives came occasionally to the Mansion.

A number of newspaper people who later became close friends were very soon in our circle of acquaintances. Mr. and Mrs. Walter Brown were perhaps the first. Later Walter Brown became secretary to Governor Lehman. Many newspaper men who were later in Washington, such as Ernest Lindley, Fred Storm, Francis Stevenson, Eddie Roddan, Louis Ruppel and John Boettiger, we first knew in Albany. James Kieran was also in the Albany group, but he did not go to Washington. James Mahoney, who was chief clerk at the Executive Offices under Governor Smith, stayed on with my husband and we often saw him with his wife and children at the Mansion. Lieutenant Governor and Mrs. Lehman, Judge and Mrs. Rosenman, and Mr. and Mrs. Henry Morgenthau, junior, were all people whom I could have seen more often, however, if I had not stuck to teaching, though we did see something of each other. Fortunately the Morgenthaus were our neighbors in Dutchess County so we were able to see them there as well as in Albany. Herbert Lehman was a good running mate for Franklin because of his long business experience, which proved most valuable in solving financial situations. As a lieutenant governor, he had built himself the fine reputation which he later reinforced as a successful governor.

My husband, who loved being on the water, found that the State of New York had a very small boat used by state officials for canal travel on inspection trips. He decided to use it himself during the summers for the same purpose. Captain Harry Pratt, one of the nicest men I ever knew, was in command. Franklin found these trips restful, and we sometimes took some of our boys with us. The state automobile, driven by Montford Snyder, a young man from Rhinebeck who remained with us all through the years in Albany and in Washington, would follow us from point to point along with state police. During the day we would leave the boat and visit various state institutions. This was valuable training for me. I had paid occasional visits to state prisons, insane asylums or state hospitals for crippled children, but never with the intention of looking into the actual running of any institution and gauging its good and bad points.

The head of the institution that we were visiting usually got into the car with my husband and drove around the grounds, pointing out what new buildings were needed and where they should be built. In this way Franklin gained a personal knowledge of the exterior of the institution, which helped him when he met with the legislative appropriations committee.

Walking was so difficult for him that he could not go inside an institution and get a real idea of how it was being run from the point of view of overcrowding, staff, food and medical care. I was asked to take over this part of the inspection, and at first my reports were highly unsatisfactory to him. I would tell him what was on the menu for the day and he would ask: "Did you look to see whether the inmates actually were getting that food?" I learned to look into the cooking pots on the stove and to find out if the contents corresponded to the menu; I learned to notice whether the beds were too close together, and whether they were folded up and put in closets or behind doors during the day, which would indicate that they filled the corridors at night; I learned to watch the patients' attitude towards the staff; and before the end of our years in Albany, I had become a fairly expert reporter on state institutions.

In the summer of 1929, we made an inspection trip on the canal which eventually brought us out to a point from which Franklin went down the St. Lawrence River to discuss the St. Lawrence Waterway with Canadian and United States officials. He had decided that I should take the two youngest boys, who never had been to Europe, on an educational jaunt that summer. Elliott had finished Groton but had no desire to go to Europe, and was more or less in conflict with us as to what he would do, since he had failed some of his college entrance examinations and quite frankly admitted that he had failed them on purpose because he did not want to go to college. He spent a good part of the summer with his father while the other boys and I were in Europe, and almost persuaded him to let him enter at once on some work connected with travel to foreign countries.

When I returned from Europe, I felt so keenly that he should at least pass his college examinations that we compromised on a year at the Hun School, where he did extremely well, both in scholarship and in athletics. He not only passed his college board examinations with flying colors, but also was offered a sports scholarship in two of the major universities. He was outraged by this and it fixed his determination not to go to college. Since we could not persuade him to change his mind, he started at once to earn a living.

The two youngest boys and I made the canal trip with Franklin, and in Montreal we were met by my friends, Nancy Cook and Marion Dickerman, who were to go on the European trip with us, taking their car with them. During the few hours in Quebec we drove about the city and loved it as much as on our previous stay there. The long boat trip to the mouth of the St. Lawrence was smooth and a good introduction to the sea, so the boys found no difficulty in adjusting to life on shipboard, and they loved the voyage.

At one point, I received a wire from Franklin: "Hope you have a good trip. What shall I do with your casket?" I puzzled over this for some time and it finally dawned on me that I had forgotten one piece of my luggage—a lunch basket! It was, of course, a typographical error, but that message remained a family joke for many years, and we told my husband he was preparing for any contingency.

I had, at Franklin's suggestion, engaged a car to meet us in Liverpool to drive the boys and myself while we were in England. When we left England another car was to meet us to drive us on the Continent. Miss Cook and Miss Dickerman were to drive their own car throughout the trip. I hoped that this would be a little easier way of travel for the boys, realizing that a summer spent moving constantly from one sightseeing spot to another was not going to be an ideal vacation for them, at thirteen and fifteen, or for me.

The ship stopped for a short time in Northern Ireland, where James was spending his vacation. He met the boys there and took them to the Dublin horse show, which was one of the things they desired above everything else to see, while I went on to Liverpool.

While the boys were in Ireland, I motored up to spend a few days with Miss Cook and Miss Dickerman, who had left the ship at Glasgow, and in our separate cars we toured the Lake Country. I enjoyed that trip very much because the poets and writers of the lake district have always seemed familiar friends, and seeing their country brought them even closer.

Then I went over to Ireland to collect my two sons. I think I spent one day at the horse show. I lunched at the American Legation and met one of the Indian princes who had presented the cup that was being competed for on that particular day. I remember him rather vividly because someone whispered to me to keep my gloves on, explaining that the Prince kept his own on and did not shake hands with anyone except when thus protected from direct contact. I noticed too that all the leather-covered furniture had been removed because the gentleman objected to the use of leather, the cow being a sacred animal in his native land. (Luckily my gloves were cotton!) I decided then and there that entertaining foreigners whose religious customs needed so much consideration might give rise to complications and I hoped fervently that this duty would never fall to my lot. However, when it did come my way, I found that once I knew what people's habits and customs were, it was quite easy. The essence of all hospitality lies simply in being kind and in giving your guests the surroundings that will make them comfortable.

We crowded in attendance at the dog races and a ride in a jaunting cart, and then I took the boys off on what was intended to be a more educational trip than visiting horse shows.

In London, Franklin, junior, developed for the third time that year a curious illness which we came to call "Franklin pox," but the doctor insisted that it was German measles. It was over in two days and did not interfere very much with our sight-seeing. The thing the boys most wanted to do was to go down the Rhine, because they had heard it was like the Hudson River. When you go away from home, you always want to see anything that reminds you of what you left behind!

So we took a small steamer up the Rhine from Cologne to Coblenz and while the boys liked the scenery, they did not like being in Germany, largely because they had never learned the language. This trip taught them one thing—if they wanted to enjoy a country it was well to be able to speak its language. They could not wait to get back to France where they could make themselves understood.

In every city where we stayed, we climbed bell towers, and I tried to walk my sons in the evenings. I wanted them to be so weary that they would not start roughhousing before they went to bed, since roughhousing usually turned into a battle royal and I got my exercise separating two very angry brothers. I realized that I was a poor person to be taking on a trip two youngsters who needed good, hard physical exercise daily, and many times I wrote to my husband how glad I should be to get home and how nervous the full responsibility for making plans and keeping the boys well and happy made me. The accounts, passports, and so on, weighed on me particularly, for I had never been entirely responsible for these before. Above all else I dreaded not being able to keep within the sum of money that we had allotted for the trip, and I put in a good many anxious hours wondering if I would come out with enough to get us home. I accomplished this successfully, but I never again wanted to take active youngsters traveling, either on pleasure or education bent.

My husband had particularly wanted me to show them the fronts over which our men fought in World War I, Quentin Roosevelt's grave, and some of the cemeteries. I had already pointed out to them in the little villages of England the monuments to the men who had been killed in that war. The cemeteries, with their rows and rows of crosses, made an impression on the boys, but they were, of course, entirely unable to gather the significance of the new buildings in the old French villages and towns. To young Americans, new buildings were not strange, and while I was impressed by the way nature had covered her scars in the woods and fields, I pointed out to the boys the whitened stumps and the fact that the trees were so young, showing that whole forests had been mowed down just a few years before. In the fields, I pointed out the ditches, which had been dug by soldiers for protection, and the curious holes made by bursting shells, now covered with grass.

My older son said to me one day: "This is a funny country. There are only boys our age and old men coming out of the fields. We've seen young men in uniform doing maneuvers but there don't seem to be any men of father's age." That, of course, was simply another proof that the war had taken from France a very heavy toll of her young men from 1914 to 1918.

This same sense of the loss of a generation came to me very vividly at the first organizational meeting of the United Nations in London, in 1946. So many of the Europeans were older men who had made the effort with the League of Nations and were a little doubtful about a second international effort to keep the world at peace. The loss of a generation makes itself felt acutely twenty to twenty-five years later, when many men who would have been leaders are just not there to lead.

We experienced in Paris some of the hottest weather I have ever known, and I took the boys under protest to the Louvre and other galleries. Visiting my mother-in-law's sister, Mrs. Forbes, in her apartment on the Avenue George V, was cooler, but even there we panted.

James joined us for a few days in Paris and we went to the Eiffel Tower, which was attractive largely because it was cooler at the top than anywhere else. I remember seeking entertainment in the circus and in the theatre, but we were all glad to go to Mont-Saint-Michel, which I remember for its beauty and also as the scene of one of our most violent roughhouse battles.

Finally we had a day on the beach before boarding our ship. On the way home John developed an earache, and I was extremely anxious, until he recovered. Franklin, junior, had a pleasant trip. On landing I breathed a sigh of relief and made a vow that never again would I take a trip on which I had to be responsible for the young.

Back in Albany, I became immediately submerged again in the busy routine of my life as mother, governor's wife and teacher, and there were few breaks until the state campaign of 1930. That was a very easy campaign, and I think it was a satisfaction to all of Franklin's supporters that he won the largest vote cast for any Democrat up to that time in a gubernatorial election. This circumstance had the double advantage of making Franklin strong in the state and strong as a potential candidate for the presidency. That prospect did not interest me particularly but it did interest his political supporters.

During his terms as Governor of New York he attended many of the Governors' Conferences, because he always felt that they were important. Whenever possible he wanted the advantage of contact with other governors, for the discussion of problems was enlightening. Sometimes I went with him. I remember particularly one of the last Governors' Conferences, at which President Hoover started to make an address. The wind blew away his papers and he was so completely dependent on them, since he was speaking over the radio, that he had to end his speech. It must have been a surprise to the radio audience and a great disappointment to the men at the conference.

In the course of that conference, which was at Richmond, Virginia, all the governors were invited to dine at the White House. My husband was already considered one of the strongest possible candidates for the Democratic nomination for president. I was familiar with the way in which guests had to stand in the East Room at a state dinner before they were received by the president and his wife, so I was a little worried about Franklin, who had to have somebody's arm and a cane. In addition, he became rather tired if he stood without support for any length of time.

We arrived a little ahead of time, since we knew we should have to walk rather slowly down the main hall to get into line, and then we stood and waited. Twenty minutes passed and the President and Mrs. Hoover did not appear. Every kind of rumor flew about the room. It was said we were waiting for some of the governors, two of whom never appeared. My husband was twice offered a chair, but he evidently thought that if he showed any weakness someone might make an adverse political story out of it, so he refused each time. It seemed as though he were being deliberately put through an endurance test, but he stood the whole evening very well, though the one-half hour before President and Mrs. Hoover appeared was an ordeal.

This idea may seem preposterous but in political life you grow suspicious. The strategists on both sides weigh how far they can go without awakening in the people a feeling that the rules of fair play have not been observed. You hear a whisper of this or that, but the whispers are never brought to the attention of the candidates and no official recognition is ever given them.

I can hardly remember a campaign in which, in our village of Hyde Park, scurrilous things were not said about my husband and his mother and myself, and even about the children. Some of my friends came to me in anxiety because they had heard a story that my husband did not have infantile but had some other disease which was progressive and would eventually attack the brain.

During the 1932 campaign Louis Howe heard that the Republicans planned to issue a statement claiming that infantile paralysis was a progressive disease which eventually affected the brain. Louis immediately asked Dr. George Draper, a leading authority on polio, who with Dr. Lovett, had taken care of Franklin, for a counterstatement which he could use if necessary. Dr. Draper gave him a full statement, from the medical point of view, refuting any such ideas. He noted that Sir Walter Scott had had infantile paralysis when he was a small boy, and no one could point to any impairment of his brain. The opposition never used that statement openly and Louis never used Dr. Draper's. Evidently it was thought that such an attack might prove a boomerang.

In a later campaign there was one particularly ludicrous story, which I remember well. A lady, who was never identified by name, had been a guest in the White House over night, it was said, and she told "someone" of the unspeakable things she had heard—my husband shrieking like a maniac in the middle of the night and people rushing to control him. We were never able to find out who the lady was or what she thought she heard, or whether the whole story was pure fiction. Certainly she never heard my husband, for he was a very controlled person and never raised his voice even when he was angry. He very rarely was angry, though I have seen him moved to righteous wrath. When that happened he went to lengths he never went to at other times in telling people exactly what he thought of them, but even then his voice was never raised; it was just cold and cutting. Though I often entirely agreed with him and was glad that he had felt strongly and had spoken out, I could not help being sorry for the people, who usually withered under his wrath.

I remember vividly coming back to the White House one day and finding Franklin shaken with anger after an interview with an ambitious and intriguing man who, through his gossip, had caused a fine public servant to resign because, true or false, the gossip and publicity would have hurt his family. The ambitious gentleman—call him X— had come to see Franklin to ask when he was going to be appointed to the new position he coveted. Franklin, deeply angry, said: "X, if I were St. Peter and you and Y came before me, I would say to Y, 'No matter what you may have done, you have hurt no one but yourself. I recognize human frailties. Come in.' But to you I would say, 'You have not only hurt another human being, but you have deprived your country of the services of a good citizen; and for that you can go straight to Hell!" The man turned and left the room and they never met again. When I saw Franklin shortly after this episode, he was still white with wrath.

My husband's mother was never very happy about the gossip and rumors concerning her and her son and her grandsons. Disagreeable letters upset her very much, and the statement that she was paid by the government for the use of her house at Hyde Park as a summer White House distressed her above everything. She was proud of her home and extremely happy when her son and his family and friends could be with her, and nothing would have induced her to accept money from any source. In any case, there was at no time a suggestion of government pay, and after her death my husband continued to pay the expenses of the house and grounds out of his own pocket.

All people in public life are subject to this type of slander. Circumstantial evidence can almost always be produced to make the stories that are circulated about their private lives seem probable to the people who want to believe them. A man who chooses to hold public office must learn to accept the slander as part of the job and to trust that the majority of the people will judge him by his accomplishments in the public service. A man's family has to learn to accept it also. In my husband's case, even his little dog, Fala, came in for his share of false accusations.

In 1931 my mother-in-law, who in spite of her years still loved to go to Europe, went off on one of her annual visits and developed pneumonia in Paris. My husband was so very anxious about her that he made a hurried trip over, accompanied by Elliott. It was Elliott's first trip abroad and I am sure he found it valuable and interesting, though he was one of the children who always said he preferred to travel in his own country before traveling anywhere else. As I remember, the whole trip took only about three weeks, but Franklin's presence gave his mother just what was needed to accelerate her recovery, and he left her well on the way to regaining her strength.

Franklin believed that it was right to let people, as they grew older, do the things that they want to do and therefore he never interfered with anything his mother really had her heart set on. When people suggested to him that she should not go abroad he said: "After all, the place where you die and where you are buried is of little importance."

CHAPTER SIX

THE FIRST PRESIDENTIAL ELECTION: 1932

FRANKLIN did not tell me when he decided to run for the presidency, but I knew from Louis Howe that he, Louis, had decided and had long been working in his own way to prepare the ground. For a year or more, everything that Louis had undertaken for my husband had been with the idea of broadening his acquaintanceships and knowledge of conditions throughout the country. This little man was really the biggest man from the point of view of imagination and determination I have ever known; his body was weak but his mind never stopped working for a second. He made few personal friends and he judged most of those by their loyalty to "The Boss," as he called my husband. He was one of the few people who never said "yes" when he meant "no." He had Franklin's full confidence and respect, and though it took me a long while to appreciate him, I came to admire his loyalty and great ability to manipulate people and events to achieve his ends. During the years when Franklin was ill he wrote innumerable letters for him to people all over the country. Many years later, these letters were often brought out to be shown me with pride, which proved that Louis gauged well how to build friendships even between people who had never met.

It was Louis Howe who mapped out the preconvention campaign. The strategy and the choice of men were left largely to him and though he talked his plans over with Franklin, he really "masterminded" the whole campaign. He knew the limitations his physical strength and his gnomelike appearance placed on him and he knew, too, that staying in the background and pulling the strings was what he enjoyed. He loved the sense of power and though he wanted a few people to know he had it, on the whole he preferred anonymity. It was he who chose Edward J. Flynn and James Farley, to play their important roles, though Franklin of course liked and trusted them both and they were both worthy of his trust. Ed Flynn came to understand much that my husband believed in and worked for, believing himself in many of the same things. Jim Farley, as certain types of men do, believed in the man for whom he worked, but was not so much concerned with the ideas and ideals for which that man stood. Many times, in connection with the work of the women's division of the National Democratic Committee, he told me that if I thought a thing should be done, he would do it, though I would know quite well that he was not really convinced and perhaps had not even bothered to understand what it was all about. He trusted me as a person, I think, in connection with the work of the women, and he trusted Franklin. Jim Farley had a marvelous gift with people; he could do a prodigious amount of work, and he carried his share of the burden at that time just as magnificently as did Louis and Ed Flynn. What happened later is another story.

There were many other devoted and loyal men who believed in my husband and who, contributing generously of their time and money, worked directly in the campaign. Among them were Frank Walker, the Henry Morgenthaus, senior and junior, W. Forbes Morgan, and Bernard Baruch. These men gathered about them other men who became active in planning to meet future problems. The men who formed the so-called brain trust were picked chiefly by Louis Howe and Sam Rosenman. They were a group with whom Franklin consulted in laying plans to meet the problems that all of us were aware had to be met by whoever was elected president in 1932. There were lawyers, professors, politicians, all gathered together to think out ways and means of doing specific things. The original "brain trust" consisted of Professor Raymond Moley, Professor Rexford G. Tugwell, and Judge Samuel I. Rosenman. Later Adolf Berle was brought in, and on certain occasions Dr. Joseph McGoldrick and General Hugh Johnson were consulted.

Throughout the whole of Franklin's career there never was any deviation from his original objective—to help make life better for the average man, woman and child. A thousand and one means were used, difficulties arose, changes took place, but this objective always was the motive for whatever had to be done. In the end, in spite of all his efforts to prevent it, a war had to be fought, because the inexorable march of events showed that only by war could fascism be wiped out. The persecution of the Jews was only the beginning of the persecutions that would have been inflicted upon all those who differed from the fascist leaders. All freedom for the average man would have gone, and with its going, the objectives that Franklin and all other men in democratic nations believed in would have been lost.

While Franklin's desire to make life happier for people was paramount, mixed with it, as I mentioned earlier, was his liking for the mechanics of politics, for politics as a science and as a game which included understanding the mass reactions of people and gambling on one's own judgment. Always in Franklin there was evident a sense of humor, which could turn the most serious subject into an object of fun at times when he thought those around him needed a little break in the tension or perhaps a reminder that they were not so important as they thought; for one can reach a point where one's importance looms so great that one simply cannot carry the responsibility. This was at the bottom of many jokes that he sometimes aimed at himself, as well as at others.

Franklin always felt that a president should consider himself an instrument chosen by the people to do their bidding, but that he should also consider that as president he had an obligation to enlighten and lead the people. I think he felt guided in great crises by a strength and a wisdom higher than his own, for his religious faith was simple and direct. Franklin knew that it would be foolish to think of himself, an individual, as a fountain of wisdom to which all men must turn; nevertheless he had to make the ultimate decisions, and in some cases that would have been well-nigh impossible without faith in spiritual guidance.

I have never known a man who gave one a greater sense of security. That was because I never heard him say there was a problem that he thought it was impossible for human beings to solve. He recognized the difficulties and often said that while he did not know the answer, he was completely confident that there was an answer; that somewhere a man could be found who could give the answer, and that one had to try until one either found it for oneself or got it through someone else. He never talked about his doubts. When he was planning something he consulted many people and took the best advice he could get, but once he had made his decision he wasted no time in worry. I remember very well a day when he was still governor and the country was going through the bank crisis. Franklin, who had come up from Warm Springs, was conferring with Louis Howe and Lieutenant Governor Lehman, and Mr. Lehman, worried and nervous, kept pacing the floor. The telephone rang, and as Louis, who had been sitting quietly on the couch the whole time, got up to answer it, Franklin, in what was nothing in the world but reaction to Herbert's restlessness, exclaimed: "Louis, will you please sit still and stop moving about so much!" After Mr. Lehman left, Franklin said: "Herbert is not going to be able to work tomorrow. But we've made our decision and I cannot see why he must continue to worry."

That was characteristic of Franklin. I never knew him to face life, or any problem that came up, with fear, and I have often wondered if that courageous attitude was not communicated to the people of the country. It may well be what helped them to pull themselves out of the depression in the first years of his administration as president. He knew quite well he could not pull them out with the best policies in the world unless the people themselves made those policies work. But he believed in the courage and ability of men, and they responded.

Without the ability to be gay and to treat serious things lightly after the serious thinking is done and the decisions reached, I doubt whether any man could long carry the job of being President of the United States. It takes a combination of many and varied attributes to carry

Mrs. Roosevelt watching one of the craftsmen in the Val-Kill furniture factory, 1927.

(Photo by J. T. Halloway)

Franklin D. Roosevelt at Warm Springs, Georgia, November, 1928.

A Family Christmas party at Hyde Park, 1930. Anna, with Buzz on her lap; Eleanor Roosevelt; Governor Roosevelt, holding Sistie; and Mrs. James Roosevelt.

MR. AND MRS. ROOSEVELT WITH MISSY LEHAND, AT THEIR SWIMMING POOL AT HYDE PARK.

PRESIDENT ROOSEVELT INSPECTING A NEW CAR, 1933. IKE HOOVER IS AT EXTREME RIGHT; MISSY LEHAND AND SECRET SERVICE MAN IN BACK SEAT; MRS. ROOSEVELT AND ANOTHER SECRET SERVICE MAN BESIDE THE CAR.

MRS. ROOSEVELT WITH TWO OF THE PARK RANGERS WHO ACCOMPANIED HER ON HER CAMPING TRIP IN THE HIGH MOUNTAINS, YOSEMITE NATIONAL PARK, 1934.

MRS. ROOSEVELT BROILING STEAK ON A GRILL ON THE PORCH OF THE HYDE PARK COTTAGE.

President Roosevelt attending the Gridiron Dinner, Washington, D. C., December 8, 1934. From left to right: Louis Howe; President Roosevelt; Gus Gennerich, Personal Bodyguard to the President; and Warren Delano Robbins, U. S. Minister to Canada.

Mrs. Roosevelt inspecting a slum in the Caribbean area, 1934.

PRESIDENT AND MRS. ROOSEVELT AT THE CORONADO HOTEL, OCTOBER, 1934.

(Acme)

THREE GENERATIONS OF ROOSEVELTS: FROM LEFT TO RIGHT: ANNA ROOSE-
VELT BOETTIGER, ELEANOR ROOSEVELT, SARAH DELANO ROOSEVELT, AT
FRANKLIN FIELD, PHILADELPHIA, JUNE, 1936, WHERE THEY HEARD PRESIDENT
ROOSEVELT DECLARE WAR ON "ROYALISTS OF THE ECONOMIC ORDER" IN HIS
SPEECH ACCEPTING THE NOMINATION.

(Acme)

PRESIDENT ROOSEVELT WAITING WITH GENERAL EDWIN M. WATSON, HIS
MILITARY AIDE, WHILE MRS. ROOSEVELT INTRODUCED HIM FOR HIS ADDRESS
TO MEMBERS OF THE NATIONAL EDUCATION ASSOCIATION ON THE WORLD'S
FAIR GROUNDS, JUNE, 1938.

Mrs. Roosevelt and the President in the Oval Room, second floor of the White House.

great responsibilities, recognize them and still enjoy life. It is a combination that is almost essential for leaders of nations in times of crisis.

From the personal standpoint, I did not want my husband to be president. I realized, however, that it was impossible to keep a man out of public service when that was what he wanted and was undoubtedly well equipped for. It was pure selfishness on my part, and I never mentioned my feelings on the subject to him. I did not work directly in the campaign, because I felt that that was something better done by others, but I went on many of the trips and always did anything that Franklin felt would be helpful.

The nominating convention was held in Chicago, with Senator Thomas J. Walsh as permanent chairman. In any final analysis, Franklin owed much to him for his skillful handling of the convention. I stayed in Albany, but some of the children went to it.

Alfred E. Smith was also a candidate for the nomination and had many ardent supporters. I think he felt strongly that gratitude should have compelled Franklin to withdraw in his favor, since he had been instrumental in getting Franklin to re-enter public life four years previously. In the meantime, however, my husband had acquired a feeling of complete political independence; and I think he believed that he could meet the tremendous crisis the country was facing better than anyone else in the party. A man must have this confidence in himself or he could never undertake the heavy responsibilities of leading a nation. People used to comment to me on the egoism of my uncle, President Theodore Roosevelt. I know many people felt that Franklin D. Roosevelt had the same quality. Undoubtedly he did to a certain extent; a man could not carry the burdens of the presidency otherwise.

I always felt that my husband's religion had something to do with his confidence in himself. As I have said, it was a very simple religion. He believed in God and in His guidance. He felt that human beings were given tasks to perform and with those tasks the ability and strength to put them through. He could pray for help and guidance and have faith in his own judgment as a result. The church services that he always insisted on holding on Inauguration Day, anniversaries and whenever a great crisis impended were the expression of his religious faith. I think this must not be lost sight of in judging his acceptance of responsibility and his belief in his ability to meet whatever crisis had to be met.

The regular machinery of the Democratic National Committee, which handled the tickets to the convention, was, of course, favorable to Smith, and refused to give a fair proportion of tickets to our convention committee, though they had promised a fair share to all the potential candidates. The day after my husband made his acceptance speech, however, a large carton of convention hall tickets was sent to our suite in the Congress Hotel!

As each state delegation to the convention was pledged to support my husband's nomination, that state was painted red on a large map of the United States which hung just outside the Franklin D. Roosevelt headquarters in the Congress Hotel. One morning it was discovered that during the night someone had pasted a large sign over the map: "It's votes not acres that count!" The Smith supporters were suspected.

The night before my husband was nominated, we sat up until morning in the Executive Mansion. All the newspaper people, among them Lorena Hickok, whom I was later to know well, spent most of the night in the garage. Finding them still there the following morning when I came down, I invited them to come in and have breakfast with me on the porch. I knew they had had no dinner, and nothing to eat except the eggs I had cooked for them in the middle of the night.

Two days later, my husband, John, Elliott and I flew to Chicago where Franklin was to accept the nomination. We had with us Miss LeHand, Miss Tully, and Franklin's two bodyguards, Gus Gennerich and Earl Miller. For Earl Miller this was the last trip with my husband. When Franklin left Albany, Earl Miller went into the Department of Correction and became personnel director.

The plane trip was something no candidate had ever before undertaken and it created considerable excitement. Previously, the candidate had not been officially notified of his nomination until later in the summer, which meant long trips for the members of the notification committee. Franklin thought that in times as serious as those of

1932 this was an unnecessary expense. Louis Howe met us when we arrived in Chicago and we proceeded through crowded streets and cheering crowds to Convention Hall.

In the days when there had been a lapse of several weeks between the nomination and the official notification, there had been no need to write an acceptance speech in advance of the nomination, but my husband's decision to fly to the convention made the writing of a speech, or at least an outline of it, necessary.

Mr. Raymond Moley has stated that he wrote that acceptance speech. I feel sure he was never aware of some of the things that happened in connection with it. There were two versions of the speech. Quite evidently they were somewhat alike, and thus the confusion must have come about. The fact is that my husband wrote one speech himself. It was dictated to a stenographer in Chicago over the (long distance) telephone from Albany, Franklin, Miss LeHand, Miss Tully and Judge Rosenman taking turns at dictating. That speech as it was thus dictated, together with one that Mr. Moley and Mr. Tugwell wrote as an improvement on it, were brought by Louis Howe when he met us at the Chicago airport. As he started to hand both versions to my husband, Franklin said: "Oh, I've revised it and have a new draft in my pocket. I have been working on it on the plane." The one in his pocket was the one he read at the convention, though he read through the others and consented to include one or two things that Louis felt were especially important and that were not in Franklin's own revised draft.

Governor Smith and his family and supporters did not wait to congratulate Franklin but left Chicago immediately. The other candidates stayed and felt less bitter.

In September, Franklin started on a long campaign trip across the country. Some of the children accompanied him but I did not join him until he reached Williams, Arizona, on the way home. Fortunately one or more of the children were always able to be with him on all the campaign trips, for he loved having some of the family with him. They not only helped to entertain people on the train, but also kept him amused, for we made it a family practice to look for funny incidents to make him laugh.

Exhilarated, as always, by contact with people, Franklin came home from the 1932 campaign trips with a conviction that the depression could be licked. He had an extraordinarily acute power of observation and could judge conditions in any section from the looks of the country-side as he traveled through. From him I learned how to observe from train windows: he would watch the crops, notice how people dressed, how many cars there were and in what condition, and even look at the wash on the clothes lines. When the CCC was set up, he knew, though he never made a note, exactly where work of various kinds was needed. Franklin saw geography clearly. For example, years later, Prime Minister Peter Frazier told me how he had gone to talk with Franklin about a little island off New Zealand, which he thought could be used for war purposes. For a minute Franklin had looked puzzled; then his face cleared and he said: "Oh yes, but I think perhaps such and such an island would be better." That stumped Mr. Frazier, who had to look up where that other island was.

On the 1932 campaign trips, Franklin was impressed by the evidences of our wastefulness, our lack of conservation, our soil erosion; and on what he saw he based his plans for action. But the thing he felt most strongly was that there was a vitality in the people that could be salvaged. I believe it was from his faith in the people that he drew the words of his first inaugural address: "The only thing we have to fear is fear itself."

The campaign speeches and later the fireside chats, as they came to be known, entailed a great deal of work on Franklin's part. In the campaigns, the subjects were carefully chosen, the places and times to speak discussed with many advisers. Then the research began. Franklin expected the people assigned to this to bring him arguments on both sides of the question and as much information on the subject as it was possible to gather. He went over all their material carefully and picked out the facts that were to go into the speech; then he gave it, after considerable discussion, to those whom he entrusted with the writing of the first draft. When they brought this back to him, he worked over it with them two or three times.

I have known him, even after a draft had been submitted for literary criticism to the best person who had been asked to help from that point of view, to read the final copy over and over again, put in words or take them out, transpose sentences and polish it until he knew it by heart and it completely represented his own thought. The final process of cutting a speech is difficult and Judge Rosenman was particularly adept at it. The essentials in an important speech must remain, because it is necessary to get in everything that will clarify the subject; yet it must not be complicated by the addition of even one unnecessary word. As many as ten people might work on a speech, but in the last stages, two or three would do the paring.

I have, however, known Franklin to take a speech that had almost reached the final stages and tear it up and dictate it from the beginning, because he felt the others had not made it clear enough for the layman to understand. Franklin had a gift for simplification. He often insisted on putting in simple stories, drawn from conversations with visitors or friends in Warm Springs or Hyde Park, where his opportunity was greatest for close contact with people who talked to him as a human being and not as a public official. These illustrations I think helped him to give many people the feeling that he was talking to them in their own living rooms, and that they knew and understood the complicated problems of government.

I have sometimes been asked what role I played in connection with my husband's speeches. The answer is that I played no role at all. It is true he sometimes used parts of letters or paragraphs from articles I gave him to look at; and I often read his speeches before he actually delivered them. But that was the extent of it. If I liked his speech after he delivered it, I always said so; if for any reason I disapproved of it, I said nothing. But I never expected him to pay any attention to my ideas—he was much too good a speaker to need any advice from me.

His voice lent itself remarkably to the radio. It was a natural gift, for in his whole life he never had a lesson in diction or public speaking. He had debated from the time he went to school and perhaps when he was young had singing lessons, because at college he liked to sing. But that was the extent of his training in the use of his voice. His voice unquestionably helped him to make the people of the country feel that they were an intelligent and understanding part of every government undertaking during his administration.

The night of election we were in New York City, and I circulated between the State Committee headquarters and those of the National Committee. I brought my mother-in-law down and later managed to get my aunt, Mrs. Douglas Robinson, through the crowds when she came to congratulate Franklin.

There was one young reporter I had come to know fairly well since he had been assigned to Albany by the Chicago Tribune after my husband's nomination. He had traveled up and down from Hyde Park for week ends and had been on the campaign trips. His name was John Boettiger, and he was later to marry our daughter and to become one of the people for whom I have a very special and personal feeling. I used to tease my daughter by saying that I knew John before she knew him.

That Election night, amidst all the rejoicing after the results were known, he came to me and said: "I wish I knew what you are really thinking and feeling." He showed in that question great perspicacity, for one would naturally expect the wife of a man who had just been elected President of the United States to be completely overjoyed.

I was happy for my husband, of course, because I knew that in many ways it would make up for the blow that fate had dealt him when he was stricken with infantile paralysis; and I had implicit confidence in his ability to help the country in a crisis. Naturally he had wanted to win, and he wanted this opportunity to serve his country in public life.

But for myself, I was probably more deeply troubled than even John Boettiger realized. As I saw it, this meant the end of any personal life of my own. I knew what traditionally should lie before me; I had watched Mrs. Theodore Roosevelt and had seen what it meant to be the wife of the president, and I cannot say that I was pleased at the prospect. By earning my own money, I had recently enjoyed a certain amount of financial independence, and had been able to do things in which I was personally interested. The turmoil in my heart and mind was rather great that night, and the next few months were not to make any clearer what the road ahead would be.

Life began to change immediately. As soon as my husband's election was established, the secret service assumed responsibility for his protection. Our house in 65th Street was filled with secret-service agents, and guests were scrutinized and had to be identified when Franklin was in the house.

Herbert H. Lehman had been elected governor. We turned the Executive Mansion over to him and Mrs. Lehman on Inauguration Day, January 1, 1933, and drove to Hyde Park. The work of the governorship was very familiar to Mr. Lehman, so he took over with complete confidence.

I had grown very fond of many of the people who worked for us in the Mansion. The major-domo, Harry Whitehead, was very able, and we kept in touch with him at Christmas time every year until he died in 1946. One of the drawbacks to living in a public house is that the people who serve you and work with you have to remain when you leave, although you feel there has come to be a personal tie between you and them. That is true, of course, of the personnel in the office as well as in the house. Franklin was sorry to say good-by to the people who had worked with him at the state capitol, though he knew they would find Governor Lehman the kind of leader for whom they could work wholeheartedly, just as I knew that Mrs. Lehman would appreciate in the staff the same qualities that had meant so much to me.

Soon after the New Year my husband paid a visit to Washington. President Hoover asked him if in the interim before inauguration he would take joint responsibility for certain policies, but Franklin felt that until he had the control, he could not share the burdens.

Later in the winter I paid the customary visit to Mrs. Hoover and decided how, on moving in, I was going to use the rooms. She showed me some of the rooms herself, but when I asked to see the kitchen, she turned me over with relief, I am sure, to the housekeeper and to Ike Hoover, the chief usher in the White House, whom I had known in President Theodore Roosevelt's day. He had expressed a desire to talk to me about the arrangements for Inauguration Day.

I remember that trip very clearly. I had gone down with Lorena Hickok, who was then a reporter for the Associated Press and assigned to "cover" me, and had spent the night at the Mayflower Hotel. In the morning we walked down Connecticut Avenue and then parted. I hurried across Lafayette Square, for I was afraid I was late, and walked up to the White House portico with considerable trepidation. I thought of the days when my husband was Assistant Secretary of the Navy and I used to drive by the White House and think how marvelous it must be to live there. Now, I was about to go there to live, and I felt it was anything but marvelous.

I assigned rooms for the various members of our family, and left it to Ike Hoover to plan the ceremonies at the White House, since he knew much more about them than I did. I emphasized that they must be simple. Talking to Ike was like talking to an old friend, so I clung to him. To find him still there gave me a great deal of reassurance.

After my visit to the White House, I went back to 49 East 65th Street, New York City, and proceeded with plans for packing and moving. Only once did I try to solve some of the questions that seethed in my mind about what I should do when I lived in the White House. I tentatively suggested to my husband that perhaps merely being hostess at the necessary formal functions would not take all my time and he might like me to do a real job and take over some of his mail. He looked at me quizzically and said he did not think that would do, that Missy, who had been handling his mail for a long time, would feel I was interfering. I knew he was right and that it would not work, but it was a last effort to keep in close touch and to feel that I had a real job to do.

I had no way of knowing then that I would have more mail of my own than I could handle without spending hours and hours far into the night on it. Neither did I know how much the ability to help people would mean, nor what a steadying effect the beauty of the house and gardens, the dignity and serenity of the place, would have on the souls of its inhabitants. The opportunity to meet and to come to know the interesting men and women of the world was also a compensation I had not yet thought about.

Inauguration of 1933 was not a light-hearted occasion, for the man going out of office or for the man coming in or for the people of the country as a whole. President Hoover had been through a very trying period. His great anxiety had been reflected in his inability to preserve his equanimity in his daily contacts with the people in the White House. We were told afterwards how difficult it had been for him even to say good-morning or smile at the people of his household.

I have often thought with sympathy of what he went through and what it must have meant to the members of his family to watch him bear that heavy burden and grow wearier and wearier, and more and more depressed, facing insoluble problems, having to tell the public that prosperity was just around the corner and having to hold to the belief that this was so. He was a victim of circumstances and of economic and political beliefs that could be changed only by a complete crisis and courageous new actions. He had served the country well during World War I, and there is no question but that during his term of office he wanted to do what was best for the country. He has, since those unhappy days, rendered service to his country and the world on numerous occasions.

My husband often told me of his drive with Mr. Hoover from the White House to the Capitol and of how he, Franklin, tried to keep up a cheerful conversation in the face of a very silent companion. Crowds were cheering and unconsciously my husband responded, until he suddenly realized that beside him Mr. Hoover was sitting motionless. There was hope in my husband's heart and mind, but he realized that could not be the state of mind of the man sitting next to him. Finally, as they reached one of the government buildings which had been begun during Mr. Hoover's administration, my husband found himself pointing to the steel structure and remarking on the "lovely steel." It must have sounded inane, but it indicates how desperate he was in his search for small talk.

My own trip to the Capitol with Mrs. Hoover has left me with few recollections, though I remember asking her whether there was anything she would particularly miss in leaving the White House. She told me that no longer to have the feeling of being taken care of, and of never needing to make train reservations or to plan anything for herself, would make a great difference to her. I decided then and there that that was something I must not allow myself to become dependent on. Later I knew that what I should miss most was the abundance of flowers and the pleasure of being able to share them with my friends. It is a luxury I have never experienced anywhere except in the White House. However, that pleasure disappeared when the greenhouses were demolished to make room for a highway and we had flowers enough only to decorate the White House. I admit I also found that traveling with Franklin was made very comfortable; anything I wanted was always easy to get. It was a convenience, too, to be able to visit exhibitions at times they were not open to others, and thus avoid the crowds; and, though it may sound like a small thing, I particularly enjoyed meals out on the south portico and in the rose garden under Andrew Jackson's magnolia tree.

After the inauguration ex-President and Mrs. Hoover left immediately by train for New York City. I was sure that though they probably had no confidence in the future, they were relieved to be shedding their responsibilities.

Soon after the inauguration ceremonies Lorena Hickok, to whom I had promised an interview, came up to my sitting room. Both my husband and Louis Howe had agreed to the interview because she was the outstanding woman reporter for the Associated Press and they both had known her and recognized her ability in New York. In fact, she was probably the only woman reporter whom either of them knew at that time. I do not remember what I told her, but I do remember that we were interrupted so often that we finally retired to the bathroom to finish the interview.

I am sure Miss Hickok wrote a friendly and discreet story. She was an excellent reporter whose sense of duty to the news was always paramount; still we had become warm friends and I felt that she would always be fair and truthful.

The sudden death of Senator Thomas J. Walsh just before inauguration had caused us to cancel most of the ceremonies planned for that day at the White House, although we had a simple buffet lunch for a few personal and political friends, and a reception in the afternoon.

The condition of the country was so serious on that Inauguration Day, March 4, 1933, that very little time was given to purely social amenities. Almost at once my husband began calling meetings, and the first thing that happened was the bank holiday. I was a little concerned because we had been staying at the Mayflower Hotel for two or three days and I had no extra cash. I went to my husband and asked him what would happen if we needed some money, particularly since the boys, some of them, had to leave very soon. He smiled and said he thought we should be able to manage whatever was absolutely necessary. I began to realize then that there were certain things one need not worry about in the White House.

CHAPTER SEVEN

I LEARN TO BE A PRESIDENT'S WIFE

In the first days of his administration, my husband was much too busy finding ways and means of meeting the financial crisis in the country to be bothered with anything else, so I went to work to organize the household and the secretarial side of the office which did the work for the president's wife.

The inauguration was on a Saturday. The following day, after all our guests had left, Miss Thompson and I went over the White House from basement to attic, looking into closets and generally inspecting the entire house. After President and Mrs. Hoover had removed all their personal belongings, the White House staff had furnished the family rooms with what they could find in the warehouses. We had, of course, sent down a great many of our own belongings, some furniture, many books and pictures, and so on.

Unconsciously I did many things that shocked the ushers, especially Ike Hoover. My first act was to insist on running the elevator myself without waiting for one of the doormen to run it for me. That just wasn't done by the president's wife.

Whenever I move, I am impatient to get completely settled at once, so Monday morning following the inauguration, I started moving furniture about, having decided the day before just how I wanted things. My bed was in the very large room that I afterwards turned into a sitting room and office. It took me so long to move from bed to dressing table to wardrobe that I decided I was wasting good time, so I had my bed moved into the small adjoining dressing room.

Mrs. Hoover had furnished what we called the West Hall as a solarium, with birds, wicker furniture and plants. I decided to use that end of the wide hall as an extra sitting room, and in order to hurry things along, I helped with the moving and placing of the furniture, much to the horror of the household staff. We cleared out all the greenhouse effects and found some old leather-covered chairs and sofas in the warehouse. For these I had cretonne slip covers made, and we used them until the budget allowed for the purchase of new furniture.

I had asked for a telephone on the desk in my sitting room. Two days went by and no telephone. I made inquiries and found that the telephone men had not been able to get into my room because I did not leave it long enough—and it wasn't considered proper to have men working while the president's wife was in the room. I quickly remedied that by insisting that I was quite accustomed to having workmen around.

In one of the second floor sitting rooms, Mrs. Hoover had put some furniture that dated back to President Monroe's day. It was very lovely and everyone admired it, but it looked to me too fragile for my husky sons, and I had visions of its being broken. Consequently I had it returned to the museum, putting a few of the less fragile pieces in the middle hall on the second floor. In the Monroe Room, as it was called, I put good, substantial furniture and never worried about breakage. I hung my grandfather Theodore Roosevelt's portrait in that room, along with the portraits of President and Mrs. Monroe. Thinking we might rent our New York house when we moved to Washington my husband had said: "You can't rent your grandfather, take him with us."

When I inspected my husband's bedroom, I discovered that the brass bed which had been put in there was too short for him, so Miss Cook had made in the Val-Kill shop a four-poster bed of extra length, which he used all the years we were in the White House. Finding that my own bed was also too short, I ordered a new one for myself as well, and later had an extra-long one made for the room which our youngest son usually occupied when he came home.

Almost at once, even though the times were so serious, there were some festivities for the young people. I remember how very angry one of our sons was when he returned from a dance at a late hour in a borrowed, ramshackle car, and was stopped at the gate. He had no identification with him, and it was a long time before anyone was found who recognized him and he was allowed to come in and go to bed. The next morning he said: "What kind of a place is this anyway, where you can't get in when you are living here?" This led us to the discovery that every time a member of the family came in or went out the time of departure and time of return was noted in the usher's log. A similar record was made for anyone who came in, whether for a short or a long visit.

Like most American children, mine had been in the habit of raiding the icebox whenever the pangs of hunger were noticeable. The first time they discovered that the icebox was kept locked at night they had another cause to upbraid me.

Soon after we moved into the White House, Anna and her two children came to live with us, for she was separated from her husband though not yet divorced. Franklin, junior, and John were still in college. James was married and living in Boston. Elliott was separated from his wife and left soon after the inauguration to look for a new job in the Southwest, stating firmly that he had no use for the East and never wanted to live there again. His first marriage had been a quick disillusionment. He had found no community of interests with his wife and realized rather soon that he had mistaken a feeling of sympathy for love. They were both too young to know that a successful marriage requires more than a desire to marry and a warm feeling for someone who has gone through experiences similar to one's own.

As I saw Elliott and another young man who had attached himself to Elliott start off on this trip, my heart was heavy. I did not doubt that he would find a job, but I had a feeling of separation and of uncertainty about his future. I realized that my husband was far too busy with the problems of the country to be really concerned, or even to have personal problems drawn to his attention.

Fortunately for me, Miss Thompson had been willing to go with me to Washington. She had lived in New York while my husband was governor and had made only occasional trips to Albany. Until now Miss Tully had helped me as well as Franklin, but from the time we went to Washington she worked only for him.

Long before Inauguration Day, Mrs. James M. Helm had offered to help us out at the White House on a voluntary basis for "a few days," until we learned our way about. Mrs. Helm, the daughter of an admiral and the widow of an admiral, had lived in Washington for many years and knew all those formidable people called the "cave dwellers," a term applied to the few people who really live in Washington and are not birds of passage. Franklin and I had seen her with the President and the second Mrs. Wilson in Paris, when Mrs. Helm was Mrs. Wilson's secretary, and again on the ship coming home. Franklin liked her very much, so we were all equally grateful for her offer of assistance.

Mrs. Helm, Miss Thompson and I have laughed many times about the first week or so that we were in the White House. Miss Thompson and I were taken on a fast trip through the house and the executive offices. We were introduced to many people, but no one told us what their respective duties and functions were. Mrs. Helm, who had just come to be on hand for consultation and questions, had brought her Red Cross sewing with her. We have always doubted whether she ever finished that particular piece of work, for we kept her busy.

The mail kept piling up around Miss Thompson's desk—letters, books, gifts and various other packages. She tried to cope with it single-handed, because no one had told us we had a staff to help us, until finally Edith Helm could stand it no longer and mildly said: "Why don't you give that mail to Mr. Magee? He is sitting downstairs doing nothing and he is there with his staff to help you." After that we worked out a system which operated very well, and we were always complimented on the fact that all the mail was answered in a fairly short time after it was received.

Later Edith Helm's volunteer work developed into the permanent position of social secretary. Miss Thompson soon found that handling the mail and doing my personal work was all she could possibly manage, and she had as little interest in mastering the intricacies of Washington social life as I had.

From the beginning I made it a habit to breakfast in the West Hall at eight or half-past. My husband breakfasted in bed and I always went to his room as soon as his breakfast tray was brought up. I stopped only to say good-morning, for he liked no conversation at this hour, which he devoted to reading all the newspapers. Some of them he merely scanned, but many articles he read in full. He was more careful about reading the opposition than he was about reading what his supporters had to say. Certain columnists I could never get him to read, however; for, once he decided that a man was insincere or lacking in traits of character which he considered essential, he regarded anything the man wrote as valueless. I remember one man to whom I had given a number of letters of introduction when he and his wife went to Europe for the summer. He returned from Germany convinced, as were the owners of the paper for which he wrote, that naziism was good. That, of course, indicated to both my husband and to me either that he was completely insincere or had a warped and twisted mind. From then on Franklin gave his writings no further consideration.

The grandchildren were the only ones allowed in Franklin's room while he ate his breakfast and occasionally I had to rescue him from the little darlings. Once I heard much noise and calls for help and, on going in to his room, found two little girls, Sara and Chandler, jumping up and down on his bed, shouting at the tops of their lungs: "He's my grandfather!" "No, he isn't, he's mine!" Franklin sat trying with one hand to protect his breakfast tray from being swept off the bed, and holding the telephone in the other. "Wait a minute, Hacky," he was saying desperately to the operator. "I can't talk to Paris just yet."

After breakfast each morning I went to my desk in my sitting room to see in turn the housekeeper, the usher and the social secretary.

My grandmother and my mother-in-law had taught me how to run a house and I assumed, in accordance with their teachings, that all good housewives made out their own menus, put away and gave out the household linen, bought the food and gave all the orders for the day.

In the White House, I learned this was done under the housekeeper's supervision, so I felt that as far as the house was concerned, I had no work and little responsibility.

The housekeeper who served President and Mrs. Hoover had left and I had brought down Mrs. Henry Nesbitt, who had worked with me in Hyde Park in the League of Women Voters. She had had experience in managing a tea shop and a small food-selling business. Her husband came down with her to do the bookkeeping. She herself did the buying, prepared the menus and generally supervised the household. She was the first person who came to see me after breakfast every morning, with her menus prepared for the day. I tried to tell her approximately how many people were expected for meals, but we soon discovered that the number frequently changed at the last minute, so she had to be prepared for any contingency.

Franklin had never been difficult to please about food, but he seldom went out to meals when he was in Washington and food prepared by even the best cook becomes monotonous without change. His trips provided a welcome break, but as the years went on and he became less robust, Mrs. Nesbitt and the White House cooks and I found our task increasingly difficult. After his mother died in September, 1941, we installed her cook on the third floor of the White House in a small kitchen which had been put in for use in case of illness. The two meals a day she cooked for Franklin gave him some variety. She also went to Hyde Park when he did. On the rare occasions when he was able to go to Warm Springs after he became president, he always had the same cook, Mrs. Daisy Bonner, who had served him there for many years previously. He also took McDuffie, his valet, and Mrs. McDuffie. Later he took Prettyman, who became his valet when McDuffie had to leave.

Year by year, however, Franklin took less interest in his food. I shall always be especially grateful for the gifts of game, cheese, fish, turkeys, and the like, which kind friends sent him, for they seemed to arouse his interest and he would eat with more relish.

In the Hoover administration the housekeeper lived on the third floor of the White House, but Mrs. Nesbitt preferred to have her own apartment and come in early in the morning. Miss LeHand took the housekeeper's apartment in the White House and lived with us as she had in Albany. Only toward the end of her last illness did she return to her home in Somerville, Massachusetts, where her sister and nieces lived. She remained with them until her death.

I was rather surprised to find how inadequate the arrangements were for the household help in the White House. A few of them had rooms on the third floor and stayed at night. Most of them came in by the day, as they do in most southern communities, but the arrangements for changing their clothes, as well as their dining room facilities, were extremely inadequate. I tried to organize things a little more comfortably, but I never was happy about it until extensive changes were made on the basement floor. During the remodeling of the kitchens, I remember, the cow trough that was used in Jackson's time was unearthed outside the building. It was carted off by the contractor, whose sense of history was not as keen as my husband's, but we heard about it, and Franklin immediately told me to get it back. Thereafter it stood in the south grounds, filled with flowers.

Some aspects of housekeeping in the White House might be of general interest. For one thing, I think few people realize what the expenses are of a man who holds a public office such as the presidency or even a governorship. Both New York State and the federal government pay the wages of the household help, but whatever it cost to feed them came out of my husband's own pocket. In Albany we had eight to ten regular household employees and in the White House usually about thirty. I have always thought that the government of both the state and the nation should pay for their food. In the White House, the yearly thousands of visitors meant that we had to employ many more people than we should otherwise have needed, simply to keep the public rooms clean. In addition, the Christmas parties that we gave every year for the guards and all the people working in the White House, on the grounds and in the garage, were always paid for by my husband. Formal parties and state dinners were paid for by the government from a contingent fund, but if Franklin and I had any of

our children or personal friends at a formal dinner, we had to pay their
pro rata share of the cost. Then, of course, the requests for contributions were countless—and a president is always expected to give more
generously than anyone else. Every president, I am sure, leaves the
White House poorer than he was when he went in.

All this made the bookkeeping and the housekeeping complicated
jobs. There were also complications and difficulties about purchases
made for the White House. Nothing that is worn out and discarded
can disappear. It must be produced when you say you have bought
something to replace it. As a result, warehouses are filled with old
furniture which is only now and then disposed of, when there is no
longer a square foot of room left. If the housekeeper has to buy even a
new tea strainer, for instance, the old one has to be kept in case she is
asked to produce it to show that she had to buy a new one.

Everything is used until it is worn out. Any items no longer usable
are destroyed in the presence of witnesses. Anything of historical interest, such as the gold piano and the old elevator cage, is placed in the
Smithsonian Institution. Obviously there is very little danger of waste-
ful purchases out of the White House budget.

The replenishing of curtains and rugs and the recovering of walls
and furniture in the formal rooms have to be seen to carefully and
constantly, because a house that is always on exhibition should look its
best at all times. Mrs. Hoover told me that some visitor wrote her that
one of the curtains over the large staircase window had a darn in it,
which had surprised and annoyed the observant visitor. She did not
realize that the height and size of the windows make new curtains a
great expense.

I had many comments on the service. I remember an occasion
when one of the ladies of a group I was receiving, a Democratic group
at that, dashed up to me and complained about the service in the
White House. It was a very large reception and small tables with refreshments had been placed even in the corridors. But because at one
of the tables the refreshments did not arrive quickly, the lady suggested
that she be allowed to go into the pantry and correct the situation! I

restrained her, telling her gently that the staff was doing its best but the numbers of guests were taxing even the maximum staff which was on duty that day.

The Fine Arts Commission has to be consulted on all new purchases for the formal rooms and on gifts which are to be accepted for the White House. Gifts must also be approved by congressional act. A special committee was appointed by President Coolidge to help in refurnishing the formal rooms. The members of this committee help the wife of the president and have given many lovely pieces to the White House. On that committee two of the most interested people have been Mrs. Harold Irving Pratt and Mr. William Delano, the well known architect.

Every morning after Mrs. Nesbitt and I finished our discussion of the relevant housekeeping matters, the usher would come to my sitting room. His purpose was primarily to check over the comings and goings of guests and members of the family. He also had to have a list of any people who were coming to see us, because otherwise they would not be admitted.

Then Edith Helm would arrive with her lists of invitations to public functions, of receptions I should hold, or whatever else she thought I ought to do. These three interviews took comparatively little time. I think Edith Helm often felt I did not take enough interest in the social side of the White House duties, but at that time they seemed to me rather unimportant. Indeed there never came a point when I felt the world was sufficiently stable for us to take time to think very seriously about purely social matters. Certain duties, however, which I thought at first were useless burdens, I later grew to realize had real meaning and value.

For instance, the teas. It seemed to me utterly futile and meaningless to receive anywhere from five hundred to a thousand people of an afternoon—none of whom I would probably ever see again—shake hands with them and then have them pass into the dining room to be given a cup of tea or coffee by Mrs. Helm and Miss Thompson.

We had fun over this "pouring" of tea and coffee. Mrs. Helm served coffee and Miss Thompson, tea. One day the Chief of Protocol in the

State Department came to Edith Helm in glee, with a letter from a Washington hostess asking whether tea or coffee took precedence, since she wanted to honor one of her guests by giving her the more important beverage to pour. There was a good-natured feud between Mrs. Helm and Miss Thompson thereafter and they never changed their beverages.

After receiving the tea guests, I would walk into the state dining room and have a few desultory conversations; then I would go upstairs and the party would come to an end. At first I did not realize that I had to leave the room before anyone else, and the ushers, who wanted people to leave within a given time in order to get ready for whatever was next on the calendar, always had to remind me. It was hard for me to remember that I was not just "Eleanor Roosevelt," but the "wife of the President."

I soon discovered that, particularly to people from out of town, the White House has a very deep significance. I was only a symbol, as wives of presidents had always been and would always be. The White House is a place where the people's hospitality is dispensed to the representatives of other countries; and in a way, it is with a sense of ownership that citizens of the United States walk through the simple, but dignified and beautiful rooms. I think to many people the White House, in itself, symbolizes the government, and though standing and shaking hands for an hour or so, two or three times a week, is not exactly an inspiring occupation, still I think it well worth while. I did it regularly, three times a week during the winter months. We also came to think that the small amount of formality and pageantry furnished by the ushers and the junior aides was valuable.

My husband used to tease me and say he had two aides while I had twenty. All of them were young men from the Army, Navy and Marines, assigned to White House duty. They could be called on to fill a place at dinner at a moment's notice, regardless of any personal engagements they might have had. This applies to anyone invited to the White House for a meal, unless he is on an informal footing and can explain if he does not feel he can change a previous engagement.

The young aides were trained in their duties by the senior aides. At the formal functions both the senior and junior aides were required to be present, but only a few of the junior aides had to come to my receptions, so they rotated.

The young men who stood at attention facing my husband and me during the evening receptions gave me some useful hints on "how to stand and not grow weary." One of them said, after a long reception, when I complained that I could not bend my knees: "Oh, you should not stand so rigidly. Just bend your knees a little, frequently. No one will notice and you will be much less tired."

At the first few receptions of each season, my arms ached, my shoulders ached, my back ached, and my knees and feet seemed to belong to someone else. However, I soon grew accustomed to it, and I was lucky in having a supple hand which never ached.

My husband found the formal receptions very tiring, since standing for a long period of time with braces on was something of an ordeal. He tried never to have more than a thousand people to greet and after the reception was over he went upstairs at once. Now and then I would send up to his study a few people with whom he wanted to talk, but only on special occasions, because there usually was work awaiting him before he could go to bed.

There is a little ceremony that is always carried out before and after these formal receptions which both my husband and I liked to have people see. We have rather few traditions or traditional formalities in this country, so I think it is interesting and important to preserve those that we have. Just a few minutes before the president goes down for one of the big receptions, a color guard comes up to his study in the White House. Here on either side of the fireplace stand two flags—the flag of the United States and the president's flag. The color guard enters the room under orders, faces the flags and salutes. The flags are taken out of their standards and the guard marches down the stairs with them and places them at the door of the room where the president receives. The flags are not returned until after he comes upstairs. Then this same little ceremony takes place again, except this time the guard lines up and salutes after they have replaced the flags. We always invited the people who dined with us before these receptions to come up to the president's study and watch the ceremony; if people went up to talk to the president after the reception, they stood at attention while the flags were returned to their standards.

Speaking of traditions reminds me of a boy of about thirteen who once lunched at the White House. When his lunch was served, he said: "This pains me—this eating up taxpayers' money." The woman sitting beside him assured him that he was eating food which the president paid for, and to go ahead and enjoy it. To make conversation she said: "Isn't this a beautiful room?" referring to the state dining room. Whereupon the young man said: "Perhaps, but it's just like the lobby of any large hotel." A little annoyed, she said: "But think of the things that have occurred here, and our traditions." The response was: "Oh, do we have any traditions?" I gathered later that the conversation ended there.

At my receptions, as well as at the large, formal ones, I came to be very much interested in the faces of the people who went by. This turned occasions that might have been boring into a valued opportunity to get a picture of the type of people who make up our country. That in itself seems to me one of the worth-while experiences to be gained from living in the White House. After a reception for one of the women's organizations, I received a letter which so amused me that I am quoting it here:

"I want to thank you for a lovely experience last week when you received our group at tea. After I went through the line and shook hands with you, I stood and watched you. I wondered what you were thinking as you shook hands with each woman. Did you notice a funny hat, or a smart dress, or were you looking for a familiar face? In other words, do you shake and think, or do you just stand and shake?"

In my reply I told the woman that I tried to concentrate on faces and to recognize as many as I could, because being a little deaf I never really heard names. Of course, when you look at people carefully, you have various reactions: you think "what a pretty and intelligent face," or "what a kind face," and so on. However, when there are a great many people, toward the end faces become blurred. Once I walked into the dining room after the receiving was over and saw two old friends. "Where did you come from?" I said, and they told me they had gone through the line and that I had shaken hands with them warmly.

Another letter amused me too:

"Instead of tearing around the country, I think you should stay at home and personally see that the White House is clean. I soiled my white gloves yesterday morning on the stair-railing. It is disgraceful."

That dear lady did not realize that the stair-railing was wiped off every fifteen minutes, but the hundreds of people who visit the White House every day that it is open to the public make keeping it clean a little difficult. After closing hours every day, a thorough cleaning job is done in all the rooms open to the public, and they need it!

Another time, someone wrote taking me to task for the fact that the squirrels in the White House grounds did not look well. I sent for the man at the zoo who knew about squirrels, and he said they were getting too many peanuts, because everybody fed them. He advised supplemental food, which Mrs. Nesbitt thereafter bought for them.

Edith Helm was invaluable in bringing me to see the necessity of protocol. All protocol was foreign to me, and until I learned that it was really required for two purposes—protection and orderly procedure—I resented it deeply, as do most Americans. One Congressman's secretary, in replying to a formal invitation for him, addressed the envelope to "The Chief of the Proletariat" instead of to "The Chief of Protocol," which indicates how little protocol means to the average American.

No other place in this country considers protocol except in the deference shown to people because of age or personal achievement, but Washington lives by a very rigid schedule. Some of it I still think unnecessarily complicated, but by and large, I know it is necessary. The foreigners living in Washington would understand no other procedure. Also, the importance that most Americans attach to the posts they hold, whether elective or appointive, is probably justified; for in prestige most public servants find their only return. Certainly the financial returns are slight in comparison to what the majority of them could earn in business or in a profession. The kudos that goes with public office is essential to obtain good men. In a way it is a recognition of the sacrifices that men or women who enter public service must make. In addition, it maintains respect for the office itself.

Mrs. Helm had the State Department to help her on all questions of protocol. This was a great advantage and relieved me of all responsibility. I never had to seat a formal dinner table, except to make suggestions about the ends of the table where our children or personal friends might be seated. They could be placed where I thought they would most enjoy themselves. Everybody else sat according to precedence, and personal enjoyment had nothing to do with it. This meant, of course, that the same people sat next to each other at countless dinners.

On talking with Mrs. Helm soon after the inauguration of 1933, I found that most of the formal entertainments for the season were already over. There were some traditional garden parties which would have to be held, especially the garden party for the veterans, and of course, one could never tell what organizations would be holding conventions and ask to be received. However, I had time to settle down before any of the larger entertainments fell to my lot.

I added a few parties to the social calendar of the White House—a so-called Gridiron Widows' party, and teas and a garden party for the women who held executive or administrative positions in the government.

Every year the newspaper men invite the president to the Gridiron dinner, which the men in the newspaper field consider a most important event. Women are never allowed to attend—not even the women of the press. I decided it would be fun to have an evening party for the women on the same night—not only newspaper women but wives of newspaper men, and the cabinet wives, since the secretaries usually attended the Gridiron dinner with the president. We had this party every year until the war caused us to give up all entertaining that was purely for pleasure. Every other year the press women provided the entertainment and on alternate years it was provided by some of the cabinet wives, my daughter when she lived with us, and some friends. Elinor Morgenthau was wonderful in planning and staging our skits, and Louis Howe gave us expert suggestions and direction and helped us with make-up. One year he made me up as an old apple woman and no one recognized me. Our parties lasted longer than the men's, so Franklin was usually home and in bed before I went upstairs after bidding my last guest good-night.

As for the teas and the garden party for the women executives, I had discovered that a great many women who held rather important positions in the government had never been to the White House or met the wives of the secretaries heading their departments. I had one large garden party in the spring and a series of teas during the winter season for these women, and I invited the wives of the cabinet members to receive with me. I am sure the women enjoyed the breaks in their work, but the war ended these parties too.

Each year before the winter social season really started, sometime fairly early in the autumn, I invited the cabinet wives to lunch with me to decide how many days "at home" each one should have, and the dates, so that there would be no confusion. In the spring we gave one joint reception for the wives of the members of the House of Representatives. For the wives of the senators we had a buffet luncheon, to which each of us contributed some special dish.

Every year I went once, and I am sure that most of the cabinet wives, as well as Frances Perkins, went at least once, to the weekly luncheon meetings of the senators' wives. These meetings, at which they did work for the Red Cross, produced over the year an astounding amount of work, for the women were very faithful in their attendance. A different group of women was in charge of each meeting, and I always looked forward to the delicious luncheon they managed to serve under rather crowded conditions, as well as to the conversation and the opportunity to meet interesting women from all over the country. I also went to a luncheon meeting every year at the Congressional Club.

I am including here a sample of my social calendar for one week. I think you will see that a president's wife is not exactly idle.

Monday
1:00 P.M.—Lunch with Mrs. Hull
4:00 P.M.—Tea for 175 guests
5:00 P.M.—Tea for 236 guests

Tuesday

1:00 P.M.—Lunch with Mrs. Garner

4:00 P.M.—Tea for members of Delaware Democratic Club

4:30 P.M.—Tea for foreign diplomats' wives

7:00 P.M.—Dinner for 22

9:00 P.M.—Judicial reception

Wednesday

4:00 P.M.—Tea for 266 guests

5:00 P.M.—Tea for 256 guests

Thursday

1:00 P.M.—Formal luncheon for 52 guests

4:00 P.M.—Tea, Women's Division of Infantile
                  Paralysis Foundation

5:00 P.M.—Tea for Executive Board of the
                  Federation of Women's Clubs

Friday

1:00 P.M.—Lunch for wives of cabinet members

8:00 P.M.—Diplomatic dinner—94 guests
                  197 additional guests for music after dinner.

I am also giving some figures on the number of people who visited the White House in normal years as well as the number who had tea, lunch or dinner, or evening refreshments at the White House.

During the year of 1939:

4,729 people came to a meal

 323 people were house guests

9,211 people came to tea

14,056 people were received at teas, receptions, etc.; all of them had some light refreshments.

1,320,300 people visited the public rooms of which 264,060 had special passes from their Congressmen to see the state dining room, the Red Room, the Blue Room and the Green Room.

The average attendance at the Easter Egg Rolling was 53,108. The record shows that 180 children were lost and found; two people were sent to the emergency hospital; six people fainted and twenty-two had to be treated for small abrasions.

At the end of the day after the Easter Egg Rolling the grounds were really a shambles but, thanks to the men who took care of them, by nine o'clock the next morning they were as neat and tidy and beautiful as ever.

It can be readily seen that during these years the formal entertainment gave me quite a heavy program; so it was fortunate that I was practically always well. I can remember only a very few occasions when I had to call on Dr. McIntire. Once, a little while after Christmas, I had an uncomfortable attack of sinus, but a few days at Hyde Park cleared that up for me. One other time I had some kind of fever and pain, and no one ever did discover exactly what was the matter. For a few days everyone was much worried, but I managed to dictate my column every day and, while I did not want to talk to anyone unless I had to, I recovered in a remarkably short time.

Only once did I come near having to give up an official entertainment. Before dinner on the night of one of the big receptions I began to feel very strange—cold and nauseated—but between dinner and the start of the reception I thought I had pretty well got myself in hand. I was wrong, however, and after I had shaken hands with about two or three hundred people, I had to ask my husband to stop the line, because everything was black before my eyes. I went upstairs for a little while, felt better, and came down again. The next time I felt ill, we had to stop the line for only a few minutes; and the pause passed as the usual interval which my husband took to rest. I sat in a chair and wondered whether I was going to be able to stand and shake hands with the rest of the people. However, I managed it, and after my husband and I went upstairs, I came down again, according to my custom, and walked through the rooms once. I knew if I did not, the newspaper women would think I was seriously ill. After a good night's sleep, I was well enough the next morning to start with Elinor Morgenthau on a motor trip down into Virginia, doing the driving myself.

After I finished the morning routine of seeing the three people I have already mentioned, Mrs. Nesbitt, Mrs. Helm and the usher, Miss Thompson came into my sitting room to begin work on the mail. We had had to work out a completely new system for handling the correspondence.

Consulting with Ralph W. Magee, head of the correspondence bureau, we had found that most of the mail in former administrations had been answered by form letters; he even had copies of forms used in President Cleveland's administration. Whether a correspondent asked for a handkerchief for a church bazaar or for a white elephant, she or he was told: "Mrs. —— has had so many similar requests, it is not possible to accede to your . . ."

I decided that the times were too serious and the requests too desperate to have mail answered in that way, so none of my letters was answered by form number so and so. Miss Thompson and I worked out a memo which I quote here:

"All of the mail as it is received is to be put on Miss Thompson's desk unopened. Miss Thompson will go through the envelopes, picking out personal mail, letters from government officials and any letters that look as though they might need immediate attention.

"The mail will then go to Mr. Magee to be opened, read and classified—invitations to speak, appeals for contributions, etc., are to be put in separate piles. Letters which can only be answered by the various government departments are to be routed to them for preparation of a reply.

"After the mail has been sorted and classified, it is to be returned to Miss Thompson's desk, together with any letters to be signed."

Miss Thompson read the mail and prepared answers for all those she could handle, sometimes for her own signature and sometimes for mine. Letters of special interest to me and letters that she did not feel she could answer were put in a basket for me. Letters for me to sign were put on my desk before Miss Thompson went home or just before dinner if she happened to be staying for the evening. My personal letters were always given to me unopened. Because of Miss Thompson's long association with me, she could recognize the handwriting and addresses of my family and personal friends.

After I had fulfilled my obligations to my guests, whether at formal or informal parties, I signed the mail, and read such letters as I had not seen before, wrote on other letters an outline of what I wanted said in reply and laid aside those that I had to dictate answers to. This often kept me busy far into the night. Before I went to bed, I returned these baskets to Miss Thompson's desk, so she could work on them in the morning. As soon as she came to my desk in the morning, we attended to the letters which had to be dictated.

Personal work, such as my column, articles, books, radio scripts, and the like, was always done on over-time for which I personally compensated Miss Thompson so that there could be no question of her using time that belonged to the government for work that was purely personal. This work was done in the evenings and on Saturdays and Sundays.

In all the years we were in Washington, I could never drive Miss Thompson away for a holiday, so she had much accumulated leave which she never used and which, under civil service rules, she could not claim when we left Washington.

Ralph Magee, who had been in the White House for many, many years, was head of the bureau which had handled the mail for the president's wife for several administrations. I have always had a great sympathy for government people who have to face so many changes in the people who direct their work.

Miss Thompson and Mrs. Helm both had offices in the White House, although their staffs were first in the executive offices and later in the east wing when that was built. Mrs. Helm and Miss Thompson became warm friends and worked together harmoniously, so I never had to stop to think about whether I was giving something to Mrs. Helm that I should have given to Miss Thompson, or vice-versa. They simply exchanged anything I gave them in a hurry that was not within the scope of their work.

The people in my office, and that includes those under Mrs. Helm's direction as well as those under Miss Thompson's, worked hard and efficiently. When we first went to the White House, William Rockwell was head of the social bureau, and after his death Adrian Tolley succeeded him. If there was urgent work to be done, these people worked willingly on Sundays, holidays or in the evening. I shall always be grateful to them for all they did to make my own work possible.

As the years went on, I knew some of them better than others. Irene Orndorff and Dorothy Dow (now Mrs. Robert Butturff) spent many summers at Hyde Park, working hard and long and taking a great interest in everything that I was interested in. There were many changes in personnel over the years, but these two women remained with us as long as we were in the White House.

As time went on, we developed our system further. Many people send gifts to the president and his wife. At first I was naive enough to think they were all without strings, but one experience made me more cautious. A woman sent me a handmade quilt, which I gave to a church which had asked for a donation. Several months later the donor wrote me that she had meant the quilt as a gift but since sending it she had had bad luck, and would I please send her fifty dollars. Since the quilt had been given away, I had to send the fifty dollars. No one would have money enough to buy all the things that are offered for sale—paintings, etchings, handwork of all sorts. After the quilt episode we put the items sent in as gifts in large bins, marked with the month they were received. We kept them for about two years, then gave them to someone who could use them if we could not use them ourselves. The room called the Oddities Room at the Library in Hyde Park is filled with a variety of gifts sent to my husband, and they are of great interest to many people.

The table beside my desk was always piled high with manuscripts sent to me to read and criticize, with government documents and reports to keep me up to date, and with countless other material. I made it a practice, if I found anything interesting in my reading or in my mail, to put it on the table next to my husband's bed, so that he could look at it at night. I learned to save anything I wanted to tell him till he was in bed, for that was likely to be the only quiet time in the whole day.

As conditions changed for the better, my mail dropped off; but if anything disturbed the public, it immediately increased. From March, 1933, to the end of the year, I received 301,000 pieces of mail. The year before the 1940 election I received about 100,000 letters. The campaign for a third term, the draft, and various other administration measures caused it to increase. During the war it assumed large proportions but was, of course, of an entirely different character than it had been during the depression years.

The variety of the requests and the apparent confidence that I would be able to make almost anything possible always worried me a little. Many of the requests, of course, were not honest. I tried from the beginning to find people in various communities to whom I could refer letters that sounded desperate. I had good contacts in many places, which I used until the relief administration was established and I could refer cases to them.

Often I found that people wrote on the chance that they might get some money, however little, with which to buy a new rug or something like that. One woman wrote me that she would like to adopt a baby and would I please find one for her. Before my answer could reach her, she wrote again to say that if I got the baby she would need a cow and if she had both the baby and the cow, she would need an icebox in which to keep the milk!

Another woman wrote me, or thought she had written me, a real sob story. At the same time she wrote to a friend, telling her that she had written to me asking for money. If the money came, would the friend please hold it for her and corroborate her hard luck story if any inquiries were made, because she had used the friend's address. Unfortunately for her she put the letters in the wrong envelopes and I received the letter intended for her friend.

From California came a pathetic letter telling the story of twenty dollars in dimes of a certain year, which my correspondent said her father had given to her stepmother. Naturally her stepmother treasured them, and when she went off on a visit charged this woman to guard them carefully. However, while she was gone, the woman, who was going to have a baby, spent the money. Now, fearing her stepmother's anger, she asked me to get her twenty dollars worth of dimes of that particular year, promising to send me twenty dollars in return. She painted herself as young and helpless, with a husband who earned very little. As was my practice, I sent this letter to a friend, who on investigation discovered that it was a complete hoax. The woman was middle-aged; her husband made an adequate salary; she had a comfortable home. Over the radio she had heard an announcement that dimes of that year were worth from twenty-five to fifty cents and thought she had found an easy way of making a little money.

Miss Thompson was always accusing me of being too soft-hearted, but I caught her once about to send money for a dress and shoes and underclothes to a young girl who wrote that she was going to be graduated from high school, was to be the valedictorian of her class, and had only her brother's overalls and shoes to wear. She too thoughtfully, I felt, included a page from a mail order catalogue with sizes, colors, prices, and so on, all carefully written in. I was suspicious and asked someone to investigate and we found that the whole story was untrue. The child's parents were fairly comfortably off, and she was not valedictorian of her class—she wasn't even graduating. Apparently she simply wanted some new clothes.

Sometimes the mail—or telephone—brought requests for personal interviews from people who thought I could help them in one way or another, and when I could I tried to make time for them. Once, very shortly after we went to the White House, Mrs. Florence Kahn, representative from California, asked me to see a man. I talked to him and then referred him to someone in one of the government departments. After that person had seen him he called Tommy to ask if I knew that the man was crazy. When Tommy telephoned Mrs. Kahn's office to report this discovery, she was told that they had suspected it, but sending him to me was the only way they could get rid of him.

In all the twelve years I cannot remember that my office made any mistakes that caused either my husband or me embarrassment. For that I pay tribute to the meticulous care with which the work was always done.

One incident that merely amused me caused the staff great worry, however. A large tea of about three hundred and seventy-five people was scheduled for an afternoon. At five o'clock only about ten people had arrived. Time went on and still there were only about ten people. We investigated and learned that in rechecking the list of people to be invited, someone who was fairly new in the office had assumed that certain check marks meant the invitations had been sent, and accordingly filed the list. The few people who came had been invited on separate lists. I sent the food to one of the institutions in the District and assured everyone that I was not in the least annoyed, but on the contrary delighted to have an unexpected free hour.

In addition to the regular duties I have already mentioned, there were my press conferences. I had soon discovered that the women reporters in Washington were living precariously as far as their jobs were concerned. People were losing their jobs on every hand, in every field, and unless the women reporters could find something new to write about, the chances were that some of them would hold their jobs a very short time.

Miss Hickok pointed out many of these things to me, because she felt a sense of responsibility for the other women writers. My press conferences were her suggestion. I consulted Louis Howe and he agreed that I should hold them regularly for women reporters.

I knew that the society reporters who covered the White House were given handouts from the ushers' office about formal functions, and were invited to attend many of the state functions and to come in and look at the table before a state dinner. I was told, however, that they used many devious methods to get information, even bribing people in the house. Therefore, I decided that everything that was legitimate news should be given out by me. I began to wonder, too, if there was anything besides the purely social doings that might be of special interest and value to the women of the country and that the women reporters might write up better than the men. I realized that I must never trespass on my husband's prerogatives, that national and international news must be handled by him in his press conferences; nevertheless it seemed to me that there were many things, even connected with my own activities, which might be useful and interesting if well written up. It was new and untried ground and I confess I was feeling my way with some trepidation.

I shall never forget my first press conference. It was held in the Red Room on the first floor of the White House. I could feel the disapproval of the ushers as I went in with fear and trembling, trying to cover my uncertainty by passing around a large box of candy to fill in the first awkward moments. Most of the women facing me were total strangers, although I had met Ruby Black, who represented the United Press, and Bess Furman of the Associated Press. I only hope they did not know how terrified I was in entering this untried field. I had often seen my husband hold press conferences and I had given interviews to many individual writers, but a press conference of my own was new to me. I knew, too, that many people around my husband were doubtful whether I could handle press conferences without getting myself and him into trouble. Louis Howe and my husband alone seemed unworried.

Louis Howe was responsible for my confidence in newspaper reporters. He had a very high regard for his own craft and insisted that newspaper people were the most honorable group in the world. I took it for granted that the women would be as honorable as the men, and my confidence was very seldom betrayed. As I look back over the years, I think I have a great deal for which to thank the newspaper women. Every press conference was a battle of wits, and at times it was not easy for me, or for them, I imagine. For instance, when they were trying to find out whether Franklin would run for a third term, they asked all sorts of trick questions, such as: "Will the social season next winter be the same as usual?" or: "Where would you hang all these prints in Hyde Park?" Usually I was able to detect the implications of the question and avoid any direct answer. Louis Howe had trained me well. My press conferences did not bother me or my husband as much as they seemed to worry other people. I believe the reporters and I came through with mutual respect, though there were one or two occasions when I was indignant at things that occurred.

I was particularly annoyed once when a woman reporter quoted me as having said that we would not feed Europe after the war was won. I had replied to a question about our ability to produce enough food to feed Europe by saying that we alone would not feed her. I then pointed out how much food could come from Canada, South America and other countries. Fortunately for me, Miss Thompson always took notes of anything I said at these conferences; one of the women reporters took shorthand notes and another was extremely quick in her notes. We therefore had a verbatim record of the conference that confirmed my own version. Since there existed a White House women's press association with its own rules, I could leave it to the newspaper women to insist that more care should be used in the future, and without any refutation from anyone I could deny this story which had been written either through carelessness or by intention.

One other incident that annoyed me very much at the time was in connection with a dance for young people which we gave during the Christmas holidays one year. The press was not invited, since it was a private party and had nothing to do with public entertainment. One of the women reporters who attended my press conferences, when she found she was not entitled to go to the party, requested an invitation for her young daughter. The invitation was sent and we assumed that the young lady was coming as a guest to spend a pleasant evening. The next day her mother wrote a long, inaccurate and rather disagreeable story based on information that her daughter brought home. Her scoop caused great annoyance among the other newspaper people, both men and women. I never again really wanted to ask that lady to anything at which she was not officially entitled to appear.

During all the years I held press conferences in Washington, one member, Elizabeth May Craig, who writes for a chain of Maine papers, fought valiantly to have men as well as women admitted. She believed in equality between the sexes and was so well established that at no time was her job in jeopardy. She is one of the best known and wisest of the Washington correspondents, men or women, and she has made a valiant and consistent fight along many lines for the rights of women. I have great respect for her point of view, but I never quite agreed on this question or changed my decision on my press conferences. I felt, as I have said, that I could not in any way encroach on my husband's side of the news.

I succumbed to this pressure once when I held my first press conference on my return from the Southwest Pacific. A good many men attended, but not one asked a question. I could not help smiling at May Craig as they left.

The fact that I held press conferences in Washington seemed to suggest that I should hold them wherever I went. Consequently, on my lecture trips or visits to different parts of the country, I was always immediately asked to see the press. These press conferences outside of Washington were attended by men and women reporters in the locality and often by high school students of journalism who asked to be allowed to attend.

As we traveled about the country, some amusing incidents occurred in connection with these conferences. Miss Thompson and I arrived in one of the middle western cities about half-past six in the morning. We were met at the station by a woman reporter, who drove to the hotel with us. She asked me many questions which I was glad to answer, and when we reached the rooms at the hotel, Miss Thompson told her I would see her again at half-past nine at the scheduled press conference. The lady replied that her editor had told her not to leave Mrs. Roosevelt for a minute during the day, and she assumed that she was coming into our rooms with us. Miss Thompson held different views, knowing that I wanted some free time to get ready for a strenuous day, and the lady was left on the outside of the room when the door was closed. In the afternoon paper there was a nice story about me, the last sentence of which read: "Mrs. Roosevelt was accompanied by her secretary, a grim middle-aged woman in a plain tailored suit."

In a southern city several high school students attended the press conference. At the lecture later in the evening one of the ladies of the lecture committee told Miss Thompson how much her daughter had enjoyed the conference and how sweet and charming and kind Mrs. Roosevelt's secretary had been. Then looking at Miss Thompson, she said: "That secretary didn't come tonight, did she?" Miss Thompson thought it would be simpler if she said "no" and let it go at that, though she was the only secretary with me.

On one occasion when we were flying back from the west coast she herself was interviewed at one of the stops in the middle of the night by a young woman reporter who thought she was Dorothy Thompson. Only with the greatest difficulty could she convince the young lady that there was a mistake in identity.

At another place, in Kentucky, I was asked to see the press before breakfast. I agreed, and discovered that the girl and boy were either too inexperienced or too nervous to ask questions, so I both asked and answered the questions for that interview.

By and large, I think my weekly meetings with the women of the press were one of the most rewarding experiences of my White House life. Out of them I gained some friends whom I value very highly.

CHAPTER EIGHT

THE FIRST YEAR: 1933

DURING THE early White House days when I was busy chiefly with getting settled and organizing my side of the household, my husband was meeting one problem after another. I think it had a most exhilarating effect on him. Decisions were being made, new ideas were being tried, people were going to work and businessmen who ordinarily would have scorned government assistance were begging the government to find solutions for their problems, willingly accepting almost anything that was suggested.

What was interesting to me about the administration of those days was the willingness of everyone to cooperate with everyone else. As conditions grew better, of course, people's attitude changed, but fundamentally it was that spirit of cooperation that pulled us out of the depression. Congress, which traditionally never has a long honeymoon with a new president, even when the political majority is of his party, went along during those first months, delegating powers to the president and passing legislation that it would never have passed except during a crisis.

All this meant, however, that Franklin was very busy and had no time for any personal interests. Consequently very soon after we went to Washington I realized that if I wanted friends and members of the family to visit us in the White House I would have to take the initiative. My husband, I knew, would be delighted to see them and would never question whom I invited, or when they came, but they could not be permitted to interfere with the work he had to do, and their comfort and pleasure would have to be solely my responsibility.

I planned all the family reunions and parties and tried to remember to invite to the White House old friends and other people to whom I thought it would mean a great deal to come at least once into that historic mansion. This applied not only to those who came to stay, but to those who came to meals. If anyone was neglected or overlooked, the blame is wholly mine. Franklin arranged his own times for seeing the people who worked with him, but except for the purely formal, official entertainments to which people came by right of position, the social invitations were always left to me.

As Miss LeHand lived in the White House she very often, when I was not there, invited people she thought my husband would enjoy, or whom she personally wanted, but he never gave this type of social gathering a thought.

Soon after the inauguration of 1933, however, we began to have a succession of visitors whom after dinner Franklin would take upstairs to his study, where he expected not to be disturbed, unless he specifically asked us to join him.

There were two very simple reasons why these particular people were invited to the White House these first years. One was that the economic and political situation in the world made it necessary for him to establish contacts with the leaders of other countries; the other was his desire to build new contacts for better understanding in this continent and abroad.

The routine of the visits was always similar. Sometimes we had a quiet family dinner, after which Franklin took the visitor or visitors up to his study in the oval room for a talk. Later there was usually an official dinner, and when there was a lady in the visiting party we included the ladies of the cabinet or the wives of the government officials whom we were inviting. If the guest was a man alone, Franklin had an official stag dinner or an official stag luncheon.

For the heads of nations, Franklin worked out a reception which he thought made them feel that the United States recognized the importance of their government. On rare occasions we went together to meet people in the presidential reception room at the railroad station; then drove in two cars, he with the gentleman and I with the lady or ladies, back to the White House. More often the Secretary of State met the visitors. If they were heads of states, they drove up to the south portico of the White House, where an honor guard and military band, assembled on the lawn, paid them military honors. My husband greeted them in the diplomatic reception room and received the members of their party; then he introduced them to the cabinet members and such Supreme Court Justices, senators and representatives from the Foreign Affairs Committee as were present.

When no military honors or immediate receptions were scheduled, Franklin and I together sometimes met the guests at the front door; but whether Franklin could or not, I always made it a point to greet the guests at the door, and to see them off when they left.

If the guests arrived in the afternoon we had tea for the entire party; afterward, all but the most important guests went to a hotel or to their own embassy. Later Blair House across Pennsylvania Avenue was acquired by the government and arranged for the use of important visitors. The head of a government spent one night in the White House, accompanied by his wife if she was with him. There usually was a state dinner with conversation or music afterwards. The following morning Franklin and his guest would often have another talk before the guest went over to Blair house or to his embassy.

On one or two occasions important visitors came when I could not be there, and Franklin had to do all the honors. However, visits were as a rule planned far enough ahead for my schedule to be arranged accordingly. Most of my plans were as flexible then as they have been the rest of my life. Only when I had signed a contract to speak or had made an engagement many weeks beforehand, did I feel I could not change them.

One of our first guests in 1933 was Ramsay MacDonald, who came with his daughter, Ishbel. We enjoyed meeting him, but even then we sensed in him a certain weariness. The loss of his wife had been a great blow to him. On leaving, he gave me a little book he had written about her. In many ways his daughter was a more vivid and vital person than he; she did everything with zest. I remember on one occasion when we were returning from a trip down the Potomac, she boarded a Gloucester fishing boat with me and helped me bring a large fish ashore as a gift to my husband.

Louis Howe, who never paid attention to any one whom he had not already met and known for many years, liked Ishbel MacDonald so much that they sat and talked together for hours, and even exchanged letters after the visit. This showed in her a rather rare perspicacity because most people did not on short acquaintance recognize the qualities that made Louis Howe a really interesting person. Ishbel has been in Parliament in her own country for some years now, and is the real influence in public affairs that we felt she some day would be.

I think Franklin believed even then that it was most important for the English-speaking nations of the world to understand each other, whether the crisis was economic or, as it was to be later, military. This did not mean that he always agreed with the policies of these other countries; but he recognized the importance to us and to them of good feeling and understanding and cooperation.

The Prime Minister of Canada also came to stay with us that first spring, so that he and my husband and the Prime Minister of Great Britain could more or less coordinate their common interests.

In the same period Edouard Herriot, the French statesman, also arrived in Washington. I remember that twenty-five French news correspondents came to tea while he was there. As I look over the lists of what seems now an almost unbelievable number of guests that first year, I find that we received an Italian Mission, a German Mission, and a Chinese Mission, and even a Japanese envoy who came to lunch. Other guests of perhaps special interest included the Governor General of the Philippines, Frank Murphy, later on the Supreme Court, who brought with him Manuel Quezon; the Prime Minister of New Zealand, who came with his wife to lunch; and His Highness Prince Ras Desta Dembe, special Ambassador of the Emperor of Ethiopia. He presented us with a photograph of the Emperor and two lion skins, one of which remained on the floor of the oval room where it was my husband's pride and joy.

During that first year the President of Panama also paid us a visit. He was not the only guest from our own hemisphere. There was a stag dinner for the Brazilian Delegation in early May; we received a special ambassador from the Argentine; the Mexican envoy came to lunch; and the Brazilian envoy returned, after a trip through the country, to report on his travels.

Franklin had a deep conviction that we must learn to understand and to get on with our neighbors in this hemisphere. Though they belonged to the Latin races, he felt sure we could find some common ground. He believed it was up to us, who had been to blame in many ways for a "big brother" attitude which was not acceptable to our neighbors, to make the first effort. So even at that early date he was beginning to lay down through personal contacts the policy of the Good Neighbor, which was to become of increasing importance.

Another outstanding guest of that year, although she was in a different category, was Marie Dressler, whose visit still brings back a warm memory. My husband had a vivid recollection of one of her speeches during World War I, when a railing broke and she nearly flattened him out as he tried to keep her from falling backwards! On this occasion she came to tell him that she thought a cure had been found for cancer. He had some misgivings about that, but he had great admiration for her spirit and the remarkable come-back which she had made on the screen. I do not think I have ever known a kinder person. Her maid told her that some of the White House staff would love to see her in person and get her autograph, so she went from the kitchen to the attic just to give them all pleasure. When she left there was regret throughout the household and a real appreciation that a very warm and vital person had been with us.

From the time we moved to Washington in 1933, Louis Howe became more and more of an invalid. At first, however, he was able to be in his office and to keep his finger on much that was going on, and the second bonus march on Washington by the veterans of World War I, he handled personally.

The first march, which had taken place in Mr. Hoover's administration, was still fresh in everybody's mind. I shall never forget my feeling of horror when I learned that the Army had actually been ordered to evict the veterans from their encampment. In the chaos that followed, the veterans' camp on the Anacostia flats was burned and many people were injured, some of them seriously. This one incident shows what fear can make people do, for Mr. Hoover was a Quaker, who abhorred violence, and General MacArthur, his Chief of Staff, must have known how many veterans would resent the order and never forget it. They must have known too the effect it would have on public opinion.

When the second bonus march took place in March of 1933, I was greatly worried for fear nothing would be done to prevent a similar tragedy. However, after talking the situation over with Louis Howe, Franklin immediately decided that the veterans should be housed in an old camp and be provided with food through the relief administration. Louis spent hours talking with the leaders. I think they held their meetings in a government auditorium and were heard by the proper people in Congress. As a result, everything was orderly.

Although Louis often asked me to take him for a drive in the afternoon, I was rather surprised one day when he insisted that I drive him out to the veterans' camp just off Potomac Drive. It did not take long to get there. When we arrived he announced that he was going to sit in the car but that I was to walk around among the veterans and see just how things were. Very hesitatingly I got out and walked over to where I saw a line-up of men waiting for food. They looked at me curiously and one of them asked my name and what I wanted. When I said I just wanted to see how they were getting on, they asked me to join them.

After their bowls were filled with food, I followed them into the big eating hall. I was invited to say a few words to them—I think I mentioned having gone over the battle fronts in 1919—and then they sang for me some of the old Army songs. After lunch I was asked to look into several other buildings, and finally we came to the hospital which had been set up for them.

I suppose I did not spend as much as an hour there; then I got into the car and drove away. Everyone waved and I called, "Good luck," and they answered "Good-by and good luck to you." There had been no excitement, and my only protection had been a very weary and gnomelike gentleman, Louis Howe, who had proceeded to sleep in the car during my entire visit.

Louis seemed pleased that I had done as he suggested, and I think it had a good effect. Afterwards several people inquired what protection we had had, and seemed a little horrified when I answered, "None." The camp had simply been the destination of one of the rare drives which Louis thought did him some good at that period.

Most of us who watched Louis could tell, however, that he was failing. He sat a good deal of the time in his room, surrounded by newspapers, but up to the last few months his advice was still valuable. He died on April 18, 1936, in the Naval Hospital in Washington. He had lived in the White House until a short time before his death. Mrs. Howe, who came down to be with him, stayed with us at the White House and later, just before the end came, his daughter and son joined her.

I always felt that the loss of Louis' influence and knowledge and companionship was a great blow to my husband. Louis had seemed to have a very acute sense of the need for keeping a balance in Franklin's appointments, making sure that my husband saw a cross-section of people and heard a variety of points of view. While Louis was alive, I had fewer complaints from various groups that they were excluded and kept from seeing Franklin than ever again. Considering how many people want to see the president and how hard it is to keep some semblance of balance, I think Louis did a remarkable job. As long as he worked in the executive office of the White House, he was head of the secretariat and if he felt that some one should see Franklin, they saw him. I do not think he purposely brought in people who particularly agreed or disagreed with Franklin, but he did try to see that all points of view reached him, so that he would make no decision without full consideration.

I can remember several occasions after Louis' death when people told me that this or that person was hurt because the president had not been able to see him, and, that therefore the president could not count on his vote. I always told my husband, and he would wearily say: "I wish there were more hours in the day and that I had the strength to work longer hours at night." As he grew busier and busier, this complaint was made more often, and Franklin's answer was increasingly truthful and sad.

Louis had a wonderful secretary whom he always called "The Rabbit." Her real name was Margaret Durand. Why he gave her that nickname I never heard him say. Perhaps it was because she always scurried around like a rabbit when Louis wanted anything, and she had a gentle and defenseless air. She was devoted to Louis, and after his death carried on in the presidential campaign of 1936 with many of the people who had worked with him in 1932. She later died of tuberculosis. All of us have a very warm memory of her devotion to Louis Howe and to the ideas for which my husband stood. Franklin always appreciated all that she did.

I think this same thing should be said of many of the other women who worked in the office. I do not have to speak in detail of Missy LeHand and Grace Tully, for everyone knows how much they meant to the smooth running of the office and in Franklin's daily life and work.

Missy was young and pretty and loved a good time, and occasionally her social contacts got mixed with her work and made it hard for her and others. To me she was always kind and helpful, and when I had to be away she took up without complaint the additional social responsibilities thrust upon her.

Grace Tully also was young and very pretty and an able helper. Later, when Miss LeHand retired, she took her job and filled it well. She too liked a good time, and was popular among many groups; but since she did not live in the White House her difficulties with those who wished to use her were not so apparent.

There were others, like Miss Louise Hackmeister, who first worked with us in the 1932 campaign. Her introduction to Louis Howe was rather startling. He picked up his phone and said: "Find the Rabbit," and then hung up. "Hacky," as she was affectionately called, was completely puzzled and asked Miss Thompson what on earth Mr. Howe was talking about. She said she thought she was working in a political campaign headquarters, not in a zoo.

My husband considered Hacky the most remarkable telephone operator he had ever known. She recognized everyone's voice after once hearing it; and he said if he told her to find Mr. Jones in St. Louis, for instance, she always got the right Mr. Jones in a very short time. She is still in the White House, and I think innumerable people have come to listen for her cheerful voice and word of recognition with pleasure and real warmth of feeling.

Among the others in the office were Roberta Barrows, Mary Eben, Paula Tully Larabee, Toi Batcheldor, Dorothy Brady Jones and Lela Styles. Katharine C. Blackburn did not actually work in the White House, but she did an excellent job of compiling a brief summary of the news; she and her staff read hundreds of newspapers and clippings every day. Of course, everyone who works in the White House or in any department of the administration, works directly or indirectly for the president; only through their devotion and loyalty can he accomplish his best work.

My husband was fortunate in having Steve Early and Marvin McIntyre as his secretaries. The two men had been friends for many years. Both had been with Franklin on his first campaign trip when he was running for vice-president and we had had many reunions between 1920 and 1933. I have always wanted to say that I know it meant a financial sacrifice for them, and others, to stay on as White House secretaries, but they made possible the work my husband did. Because they functioned as a team of men who knew one another, many things were done in the first days of the administration that I doubt could otherwise ever have been accomplished. Franklin knew he could count on their loyalty and support, even when they did not agree with him. As the years went by, certain jealousies grew up among those who worked around Franklin. That is bound to happen, I am afraid, in any president's entourage, but as far as Steve and Mac were concerned, it never affected their genuine interest in their work and their devotion to my husband.

Admiral Ross T. McIntire was my husband's doctor for all the years he was in the White House, and my children and I are deeply grateful for the care and attention he gave him, as well as for his friendship and loyalty. Lieutenant Commander George Fox was equally devoted and gave of his time and strength cheerfully; we owe him also a deep debt of gratitude.

General Edwin T. Watson was Franklin's military aide almost from the beginning and later one of his secretaries. They became warm friends and my husband always enjoyed having him around. His friendly and genial manner endeared him even to disappointed visitors.

The permanent staff in the executive offices of the White House, which continues regardless of changes in the administration, is invaluable to any president. Rudolph Forster, and after his death, Maurice C. Latta, really ran the office, watching every paper that went out so that no mistakes would be made. This is a very important and ticklish business for a little mistake can bring very serious results.

I should include in my appreciation everyone else who worked in the White House executive offices, as well as the ushers, the men in the garage, the men who worked on the grounds, the maintenance men, the florists—in fact everyone who in any way served the president. They all contributed to making his work possible.

I do not know whether my husband ever told any of these people in the way they wished to be told that he appreciated their work; there was no question but that he knew what their work meant and was deeply grateful for all they did. I am sure he always meant to tell them when his terms of office were over and he had the time. It is perfectly human for people to want recognition for their work, especially when it requires sacrifice and unselfishness. I sometimes urged my husband to give a little more time to writing to these people or seeing them in connection with their daily work. He always looked sad and said: "If I do those things, I will not have time to do the really pressing things. One must risk having people think one unappreciative because it is impossible to do everything. Life moves too fast at present and one can only do so much in a day."

Franklin never expected great formality from those about him and I think a general spirit of friendliness prevailed which kept people from being in awe of him. Many a time someone would go into his office for no more important purpose than to tell him a new joke. He always enjoyed it.

During the early years when life was not so strenuous, Franklin saw movies two or three times a week, for there was complete equipment in the White House. They helped him to forget temporarily the cares of his office. He always had a *Mickey Mouse*, which amused him greatly. Though he rarely asked for a particular movie, he hated a picture to be too long, and it must not be sad. Occasionally he saw a government movie on housing or forestry or agriculture, but usually he wanted entertainment. He did not, I remember, want to see *Gone With the Wind*, but one evening after he had gone to bed, Franklin jr. showed the movie at a party he was having. The screen at that time was on the second floor, outside Franklin's door, and he woke to the sound of pain and strife. The next morning he announced decidedly that he did not understand how anyone could want to see that kind of picture. He did read the story, however. He had an amazing ability to skim through any kind of book and get everything out of it. When I gave him *Gone With the Wind* to read, he handed it back to me in a very short time. He couldn't possibly have read it so quickly, I was sure, and I told him so—but I couldn't catch him out on a single point.

Franklin always read a great deal, chiefly biography and history, but occasionally a detective story; and one of his favorite little games was trying to figure out ways you could disappear with $50,000. For other diversion, he worked on his stamp collection, did crossword puzzles, played solitaire, and now and then other card games. He particularly enjoyed playing poker, and was good at it. And of course, he swam when he could.

Soon after we moved to the White House a fine swimming pool was installed through a public subscription started by the *New York Daily News*. Once things settled down a little, Franklin tried to get in a swim after work in the late afternoons, and then went to his room for a rubdown and rest. He tried in this way to keep up some of the exercises which he would have been getting at Warm Springs, had he ever been able to go there for more than a few days at a time. At one period he was walking in the water quite well, and I think his health really improved during the first few years. This was his only real exercise and physical recreation. After the rubdown (usually given him by George Fox, who went with him everywhere) he read the evening papers, just as many as he read in the morning; then we all joined him in his study before dinner and enjoyed a short period of rest and informal conversation.

Franklin was given a number of dogs, but I am sorry to say most of them came to an untimely end. I had brought with me to the White House a big police dog and a female Scottie. The police dog grew progressively worse in disposition. He was so zealous in protecting me and my room that he let no one cross the threshhold. Following me unnoticed into the Red Room one day when I was saying good-bye to the Prime Minister of Canada, he lunged out from behind me and took a firm hold of the gentleman's leg. The serious upheaval came, however, when he bit someone who, trying to make friends with him, put a hand through the fence surrounding the grounds of the White House. Finally he chased one of the maintenance men, and that was the last straw. I sent him back to the police barracks in New York State from which he came. At about the same time, my little Scottie, who was deaf, bit one of the newspaper women in the lip. I took the lady to the hospital and sent the dog to the veterinary to be done away with. That was a sad day for me and no one thought it wise to say too much to me about dogs for a long time.

Later Anna and John Boettiger left their two dogs, red setters, with me for a time. They had very good dispositions, but even they began to be a little affected by the atmosphere of the public house. I finally decided that while I lived in the White House, I would have no more dogs.

I remember giving one puppy that had been sent to Franklin to the ten-year-old son of a friend who came to Congress that first year,

Mrs. John Greenway. When we asked the boy if he would like the puppy, which was going to grow into a very large dog, he was delighted. Mrs. Greenway was busy and told her son to arrange for a kennel for it. Much to our amusement and surprise, he had the kennel made by the Corcoran Art Gallery, having drawn the design and given the specifications himself.

No dog was completely happy in the White House until Fala came, and he became a really satisfactory part of Franklin's life.

My own relaxation I found principally in riding horseback and that first spring in Washington I frequently rode before breakfast, often with Elinor Morgenthau. Occasionally Missy LeHand joined us. If I could not get in a ride before breakfast, I went usually around ten or eleven o'clock and got back before lunch.

There was always one young Army officer from Fort Myer, chosen by my husband's senior military aide, in charge of the stables where we kept our horses. Usually he rode with me unless I was riding with friends. If anything interfered so that he could not ride at the time I wished to go, he chose as a substitute some other young officer who was a good horseman.

I remember frightening almost to death one poor young man, who had been detailed to ride with me. My horse, Dot, was beautifully trained in many ways, but she had an objection to flying paper. One day I saw a piece lying ahead of us on the road, but I had no way of knowing that the wind would come along and lift it up just as we reached it. It blew up under Dot's nose, she shied across the road and I went off. Luckily I did not lose my reins. After I found and replaced my stirrup, I got on and finished my ride. I tried to reassure the poor young man but for the rest of the ride he looked very worried and could not believe that I was entirely unhurt.

Another time, when I was riding with Elinor Morgenthau and Missy LeHand, Dot slipped in a puddle, went down on her knees, and I found myself in the puddle beside her. I got up promptly and got on again. I thought the episode had gone unnoticed and intended to say nothing about it. I was sitting at breakfast in the West Hall about an hour later when Steve Early came in, looked at me curiously and said: "I knew it couldn't be true. I was just called by the Associated Press and told they had a report that you had fallen off your horse down by the Potomac, and I said it wasn't true or I would have heard about it." Shamefacedly, I had to say it was true, and asked: "How on earth did any one get word so quickly to the Associated Press?" I was enlightened then and there: anyone telephoning in an interesting news item was paid for it; consequently many people were on the watch for any occurrence such as this. In this case, a man driving by had seen me fall.

Aside from this one recreation, riding, my time was entirely taken up with the life of the White House. The president's wife does not go out informally except on rare occasions to very old friends. Now and then in the spring Elinor Morgenthau and I stole away in my car or hers, and stopped in at some little place for lunch or tea.

Driving my own car was one of the issues the Secret Service people and I had a battle about at the very start. The Secret Service prefers to have an agent go with the president's wife, but I did not want either a chauffeur or a Secret Service agent always with me. I never did consent to having a Secret Service agent, but during the last years at the White House, life became so busy that I did less and less driving myself and took fewer and fewer trips by automobile, either for pleasure or for business. I always had my own car, however, and during the first years I covered a good many miles driving myself.

After the head of the Secret Service found I was not going to allow an agent to accompany me everywhere, he went one day to discuss this very serious question with Louis Howe. Finally he plunked a revolver down on the table before Louis and said: "Well, all right, if Mrs. Roosevelt is going to drive around the country alone, at least ask her to carry this in the car." I carried it religiously, and during the summer I asked a friend, a man who had been one of Franklin's bodyguards in New York State, to give me some practice in target-shooting so that if the need arose, I would really know how to use the gun. After considerable practice, I finally learned to hit a target. I would never have used it on a human being, but I thought I ought to know how to handle a revolver if I had to have one in my possession.

I told this story once in front of a small boy when I was on a lecture trip. The story became very glamorous under the small boy's repetition, and he was reported to have said he had seen the gun. This created great excitement, because in the city where I was going next to lecture, it was against the law to carry firearms, and an official of that city threatened to arrest me on arrival. Our son, James, who was at that time one of his father's secretaries, called me from the White House and I had to explain that since I was not driving, I did not have the gun and therefore would not be arrested. The Secret Service, feeling I should be protected against such possibilities, gave me a badge to carry everywhere which entitled me to have a gun as part of my luggage. Needless to say, I never had to use it. Episodes like this used to bother my friends much more than they did me. So far as I was concerned, they were simply part of the whole picture.

When all my formal duties in Washington were over that first spring, I went off on a motor trip with Miss Hickok. Someone had told me how beautiful it was to drive around the Gaspé Peninsula, and since I could still drive without having people recognize me, I had been looking forward with a great deal of pleasure to this holiday. My husband and I had lent our Campobello house to some friends and I planned to stop there for a few days.

Miss Hickok and I drove to Quebec, where we stayed for a night or two, and then went on through Murray Bay to Rivière Du Loup, where we were the last car to be taken on the ferry that day. We spent the night in a hotel which has the atmosphere of an inn in some little provincial town in France. That to me is the most interesting thing about the Province of Quebec. It has apparently kept itself free from the influence both of its neighbor to the south and of the British; not only do the people speak French, but the whole landscape and atmosphere are those of a French countryside. The villages always seem to be dominated by the church, and as we went along I realized that advice of every kind had to come from the padre. He is not only the doctor for the soul, but often the only doctor for the body to be found for many miles and he must act as lawyer and financial adviser as well.

In many places at that time the church provided the only drama and color in the people's otherwise drab and monotonous lives. Today, of course, there may be movies and shops and modern roads on the Gaspé Peninsula, but in the summer of 1933 there were none of these. The only road was a good dirt road, frequented by comparatively few people.

I was intrigued by the people I met on the road, and amused at the difficulty I had in understanding their French, though they seemed to be able to understand mine.

Outside every house there was a little conical mound which I discovered was the oven in which they baked their innumerable loaves of bread. I was told that the chief diet of the local people was a loaf of bread, cut in half, hollowed out and packed with flaked smoked fish over which was poured a good, dark molasses from the West Indies. I think it was a balanced diet, but it struck me as none too attractive as day-in-and-day-out food. On the whole, however, the people looked very well fed.

Our first night we stayed in a hotel on the banks of the St. Lawrence River, with no other inhabitants anywhere near. We were practically the only people in the hotel because it was early in the season. We had a swim and lay on the beach, and then enjoyed a good dinner and a comfortable night.

The next day we had an amusing encounter. We stopped to look at a little church which was built right down by the road near the water; as far as we could see there was no parish near. A woman was mending some of the church vestments and we asked if we might go into the church after we had looked at some of the stones in the churchyard. The padre appeared and asked if we would like to lunch with him, since he was going to have a fresh fish which he knew we would enjoy. He led us up what seemed like an impossible bank to climb and there perched high above the church, surrounded by trees, was the rectory. More surprising than anything else, was a trailer with a Texas license plate. When I asked the padre if he had been in the United States, he told us that he had been back from there only a short time. For many years he had lived in different parts of the States, chiefly in Louisiana and Texas, but his health had failed and he had come back to his native village to try to recuperate.

There seemed to be a great many people in the house. I discovered that they were all helping him because recently a fire had burned down most of the house. They showed us everything with great pride, and finally, after what seemed time enough to catch the fish, lunch was announced. We ate alone with the padre because, as I learned later, he did not have enough china for the relatives to eat at the same time.

Finally the padre asked me my name and when I gave it, he asked: "Are you any relation to Theodore Roosevelt? I was a great admirer of his." I smiled and said, "Yes, I am his niece." I was delighted to find that no recent history seemed to have penetrated to this part of the world; he apparently had no idea that my husband was at that time in the White House.

That night we stopped at a little inn in a fairly large fishing town. As the next day was Sunday, we attended service in the big Roman Catholic church which dominated the town. They prayed for us by name, which was kind but a little embarrassing. When I came out, my Buick open roadster was invisible. I had parked it in the square in front of the church and it was now completely concealed by all the small fry, as well as some of their elders, who were examining it with care.

The countryside was suffering from a drought and we saw a colorful procession, led by the priest, going to a shrine by the sea to pray for rain. We were impressed by the beauty of the scene as, after a long climb, we came again to a view of the open sea. Below was the Percé Rock. That night we stayed in cabins just before crossing the United States border.

The following day was dreary driving. There had been a forest fire, and for miles and miles we drove through burnt-over country with wretched little shacks here and there. It looked as though people might be trying to establish homesteads, but since there were few signs that any farming was being done, I decided that fishing and trapping must be their real source of livelihood.

It was a relief when we arrived at the most fertile of all Maine counties—Aroostook. We stayed at a farmhouse that night. I was interested in finding out what conditions were, so I bought a paper which told me a good deal about the potato situation. I found an opportunity to start the farmer talking about how long he and his family had been on the land and what he grew, and so on. I aired the small local knowledge which I had just acquired. He seemed much surprised that I should know the price of potatoes or any of the problems of that region, and when I told him that my husband was interested in farming, he finally asked who I was. I had a feeling that no Maine farmer would look with favor on the wife of a Democratic president, but he was kind enough to say that he was keeping an open mind. He added, however, that I had better not mention who I was to some of the neighbors; if I did, they might not want to show me their farms and he was arranging to take me around so I could see them the next morning.

The news spread, nevertheless, since I think he could not help telephoning to some distant friends and relatives to come over early in the morning. In spite of my politics, the farmers in the neighborhood were kind enough to let me see their farms, so we spent a most interesting morning learning about farming in that area.

We drove on to the next town to find to our horror that word of our coming had preceded us. They were having a procession, to which they added my car. I shall never forget how Miss Hickok looked; she was badly sunburned and had covered herself with sun-tan cream. I doubt if I looked very much better, but there was no time to think of appearances. Miss Hickok said I used some unbecoming language as I tried to drive properly in the crowd and still wave with one hand. Luckily the procession did not last long, and after being greeted by a group of Indians, we were able to go on our way.

I discovered that Uncle Ted's old guide lived in that region and was reminded of the fact that my uncle had taken many hunting and fishing trips in that part of the country.

Finally we reached one of the summer theatre places where Miss Hickok's friend, Jean Dixon, was playing in summer stock. She had asked us to spend a night or two with her. We had a pleasant visit, after which we drove to Lubec and spent a week at Campobello. The car was left in a garage in Lubec and we were met by a boat. It was

Lorena Hickok's first encounter with the long and slippery steps which at low tide make the descent to any boat a matter for some consideration.

Always, when my husband and I met after a trip that either of us had taken, we tried to arrange for an uninterrupted meal so we could hear the whole story while it was fresh and not dulled by repetition. He had always asked me questions, even before the Gaspé trip, but now his questions had a definite purpose.

After this trip he asked about life in northern Maine, and very quickly the pattern for reporting on future trips evolved. It was extremely good training for me, though my trips with Franklin during his governorship had already given me some experience as a field reporter. That I became, as the years went by, a better and better reporter and a better and better observer was largely owing to the fact that Franklin's questions covered such a wide range. I found myself obliged to notice everything. For instance, when I returned from the trip around the Gaspé, he not only wanted to know what kind of fishing and hunting was possible in that area, but what the life of the fisherman was, what he had to eat, how he lived, what the farms were like, how the houses were built, what type of education was available and whether it was completely church-controlled like the rest of the life of the village.

When I spoke of Maine, he wanted to know about everything I had seen on the farms I visited, the kinds of homes and the types of people, how the Indians seemed to be getting on and where they came from. I told him I thought they were of the same tribe as old Tomah Josef, who used to visit Campobello Island for many years. That interested him.

Franklin never told me I was a good reporter nor in the early days were any of my trips made at his request. I realized, however, that he would not question me so closely if he were not interested, and I decided this was the only way I could help him, outside of running the house, which was very soon organized and running itself under Mrs. Nesbitt.

The rest of that first summer, to the best of my recollection, I spent in Hyde Park and on a short vacation in the Adirondacks. Franklin had to stay the greater part of the time in Washington, though he tried to go to Hyde Park whenever he could.

I went back to Washington when Ike Hoover died in September. He had been the head usher in the White House for so many years that his death was a shock to us all. To me it was a real sorrow, for I thought of him as an old friend whom I could count on for help, even though he did not always approve of the freedom with which I acted. He was never quite certain that some of the things I did were compatible with the dignity of the president's wife.

In the autumn I was invited by the Quakers to investigate the conditions that they were making an effort to remedy in the coal mining areas of West Virginia. My husband agreed that it would be a good thing to do, so the visit was arranged. I had not been photographed often enough then to be recognized so with one of the social workers I was able to spend a whole day going about the area near Morgantown, West Virginia, without anyone's discovering who I was or that I was even remotely connected with the government.

The conditions I saw convinced me that with a little leadership there could develop in the mining areas, if not a people's revolution, at least a people's party patterned after some of the previous parties born of bad economic conditions. There were men in that area who had been on relief for from three to five years and who had almost forgotten what it was like to have a job at which they could work for more than one or two days a week. There were children who did not know what it was to sit down at a table and eat a proper meal.

One story which I brought home from that trip I recounted at the dinner table one night. In a company house I visited, where the people had evidently seen better days, the man showed me his weekly pay slips. A small amount had been deducted toward his bill at the company store and for his rent and for oil for his mine lamp. These deductions left him less than a dollar in cash each week. There were six children in the family, and they acted as though they were afraid of strangers. I noticed a bowl on the table filled with scraps, the kind that you or I might give to a dog, and I saw children, evidently looking for their noon-day meal, take a handful out of that bowl and go out munching. That was all they had to eat.

As I went out, two of the children had gathered enough courage to stand by the door, the little boy holding a white rabbit in his arms. It was evident it was a most cherished pet. The little girl was thin and scrawny, and had a gleam in her eyes as she looked at her brother. Turning to me she said: "He thinks we are not going to eat it, but we are," and at that the small boy fled down the roar clutching the rabbit closer than ever.

The pathos of poverty could hardly have been better illustrated. It happened that William C. Bullitt was at dinner that night; and I have always been grateful to him for the check he sent me the next day, saying he hoped it might help to keep the rabbit alive.

This trip to the mining areas was my first contact with the work being done by the Quakers. I liked the Quaker people I met, Clarence Pickett particularly, and I liked the theory of trying to put people to work to help themselves. There was a chair factory which was equipped with some of the most remarkable makeshift machinery I had ever seen, but it taught the men to do something in addition to mining and it also bolstered their hope. The men were started on projects and taught to use their abilities to develop new skills. Those who worked on chairs made furniture for their own scantily furnished homes. The women were encouraged to revive any household arts they might once have known but which they had neglected in the drab life of the mining village.

This was only the first of many trips into the mining districts but it was the one that started the homestead idea. The University of West Virginia, in Morgantown, had already created a committee to help the miners on the Quaker agricultural project. With that committee and its experience as a nucleus, the government obtained the loan of one of the university's people, Mr. Bushrod Grimes, and established the Resettlement Administration. Louis Howe created a small advisory committee on which I, Mr. Pickett, and others served. It was all experimental work, but it was designed to get people off relief, to put them to work building their own homes and to give them enough land to start growing food.

It was hoped that business would help by starting on each of these projects an industry in which some of the people could find regular work. A few small industries were started but they were not often successful. As I said in a previous chapter, only a few of the resettlement projects had any measure of success; nevertheless I have always felt that the good they did was incalculable. Conditions were so nearly the kind that breed revolution that the men and women needed to be made to feel their government's interest and concern.

I began to hear very serious reports of conditions in Logan County, West Virginia, where for many years whole families had been living in tents because they had been evicted from company houses after a strike. All the men had been blacklisted and could not get work anywhere; they were existing on the meager allowance that the state of West Virginia provided for the unemployed.

For many years I had been sending a small contribution to this area through the Women's Trade Union League, but I had never seen what the conditions were. I began to hear that the tents were worn out, that illness was rampant and that no one had any medical care. Finally Mrs. Leonard Elmhirst and I established a clinic to take care of the children. When I told my husband of the conditions there he told me to talk to Harry Hopkins and to tell him that whatever should be done must be done, and that these families must be out of tents by Christmas. It was done; and for two years, out of my radio money and Mrs. Elmhirst's generosity, we tried to remedy among the children the effects of conditions which had existed for many years.

I came to know very well a stream near Morgantown called Scott's Run, or Bloody Run because of the violent strikes that once occurred in the mines there. Some of the company houses, perched on hills on either side of the Run, seemed scarcely fit for human habitation. In one place the Quakers had established a self-help bakery and a nursery school.

I took many, many people to see this village of Jere, West Virginia,

along Scott's Run, for it was a good example of what absentee ownership could do as far as human beings were concerned. The coal mines
of West Virginia are owned largely by people not living in the state.
The money goes out and does not come back, leaving the state poorer
in cash and in personal interest than before. Most of the people living
along the Run, which flows into a broader stream below, worked no
more than two or three days a week. Some of the children were sub-
normal, and I often wondered how any of them grew up.

The Quakers tried to improve conditions by getting the children off
the floors at night. It was quite usual to find all the older children
sleeping on bags or rags on the floor and the mother and father and
youngest children in the only bed, which might or might not have a
mattress. Sometimes there was just a blanket over the springs. The
WPA mattress project helped considerably, as did the building of
sanitary privies. The welfare commissioner who authorized them, Miss
Alice Davis, nearly landed herself in jail because they were built on
private mine-owned property and she had not known it was against
the law to improve privately owned property.

However, breaking rules or even laws saved a good many lives.
Every spring and every autumn in this area there had been an outbreak of typhoid fever; only after several people died would the company doctor appear and inoculate the rest of the population. No
efforts were made to eliminate the cause of the disease. The Run in
Jere, like all the others that ran down the gullies to the larger, main
stream, was the only sewage disposal system that existed. At the bottom of the hill there was a spigot from which everyone drew water.
The children played in the stream and the filth was indescribable.

You felt as though the coal dust had seeped into every crack in the
houses and it would be impossible to get them or the people clean.
When you walked into a kitchen, you were struck by the scarcity of
cooking utensils. Though the families were almost always large, it was
rare to see more than two or three cups and plates on the shelves, most
of them chipped or broken.

Some of the older miners still could speak only enough English to
understand the orders given by the mine boss. Nobody had taken the

trouble to help the adults, who were going to live and work in this country, learn English and understand our government. The children went to school when they had clothes. Unexplained absences could often be attributed to the fact that if one child in the family went to school, the other children had to stay at home because there was only one dress or one pair of pants or one pair of shoes in the family, although shoes did not matter much since all the children went barefooted most of the time.

Where there was a company store every family always owed a bill; as they were thus kept permanently in debt, they could never move away.

After the homesteads were started, I persuaded many people to go down to visit them. On all my early visits I stayed at the home of the project superintendent, Mr. Glenn Work, who had been a mine foreman and knew the conditions under which the miners and their families lived. The homestead project started near Morgantown was called Arthurdale and took in people from all the near-by mining villages.

One of the first people to go to Arthurdale was Bernard M. Baruch, who helped me to establish the original school and always took a great interest in the project, even visiting it without me on some occasions. I have always hoped that he got as much satisfaction as I did out of the change in the children after they had been living on the project for six months.

Miss Elsie Clapp, a fine teacher and a follower of Dr. John Dewey, whom Mr. Pickett knew, was asked to come and start the school. Once before she had done a similar job of creating a community where none had existed, and she now rendered a remarkable service to Arthurdale. Later the state of West Virginia took over the school. Though for some time we continued the nursery school, we finally realized that the kind of experimental school which Miss Clapp established was really not satisfactory to the people. It did its job of creating a community feeling by drawing the people together, but it was a new idea and the people wanted what other communities had. Eventually Miss Clapp moved on and the school became completely state supported.

I remember one gentleman, whose home is in New York City, whom I took into one of the houses along Scott's Run. He came out very rapidly indeed, having found two of the children sick in bed and living conditions such as he had never seen before. When I joined him outside he said: "I will give you any money you want to help remedy these conditions, but please do not ask me to go into any more houses. I feel contaminated and it makes me really ill."

Some of the people who went with me during these years were Mr. Baruch, Mrs. Henry Morgenthau, junior, Mr. and Mrs. Frederick B. Adams, Mr. and Mrs. Allee Freed, Mr. and Mrs. George T. Bye, Mrs. Henry Goddard Leach, Mr. and Mrs. Robert Deans and Major Henry S. Hooker. All of them, at one time or another, helped some specific project, but our most constant helpers were Mr. Baruch, Mrs. Morgenthau and Mr. and Mrs. Freed. After Mr. Freed's death, Mrs. Freed still maintained her interest.

The homestead projects were attacked in Congress, for the most part by men who had never seen for themselves the plight of the miners or what we were trying to do for them. There is no question that much money was spent, perhaps some of it unwisely. The projects were all experimental. In Arthurdale, for instance, though the University of West Virginia recommended the site, apparently nobody knew what was afterwards discovered—that there was a sub-stratum of porous rock which finally caused great expense in making the water supply safe. Nevertheless, I have always felt that many human beings who might have cost us thousands of dollars in tuberculosis sanitariums, insane asylums, and jails were restored to usefulness and given confidence in themselves. Later when during the last war I met boys from that area, I could not help thinking that a great many of them were able to serve their country only because of the things that had been done to help their parents through the depression period.

At the time of an act, one is not likely to realize its future ramifications. My trips into this area, as well as my lecture trips, turned out to have an unsuspected value when I visited the men in hospitals during the war. Frequently a boy in a hospital bed would say: "I come from ――. You made the commencement address at my school."

Then I would try to remember something about his town, because a lonely boy in a hospital bed in some far off place will often feel better about the world if somebody remembers the town square or the court house in his home town.

Nothing we learn in this world is ever wasted and I have come to the conclusion that practically nothing we do ever stands by itself. If it is good, it will serve some good purpose in the future. If it is evil, it may haunt us and handicap our efforts in unimagined ways.

I have been getting rather far away from my original story, but perhaps what I have said will help make clear why Arthurdale and the other homestead projects held so much interest for me for so many years. I shall never be able to forget some of the people or some of the things I saw there.

For instance, just before Christmas Day after the first people moved into their houses, I went to call on a young woman who had just had a baby. Her two other children were perhaps four and six years old, little girls. The baby was a boy. As I went in I remarked that I was afraid it was going to be difficult for her to do much about Christmas. She looked at me, her face alight, and said: "This will be a wonderful Christmas. Do you know what Christmas last year was like? We were in rooms which had no windows; the only light came through the door. We did not dare tell the children it was Christmas but when they went out they came back and said: 'Mother, it must be some kind of a day, some children have new toys.' All we had for Christmas dinner was some raw carrots for them to chew on. This year they will each have a toy and we have a chicken, one of our own, that we are going to eat. It will be wonderful."

There was another family, a family of thirteen. The father worked in the furniture factory which the Quakers had started. He made most of the furniture for his own house on his own time, including a table large enough for the whole family of thirteen to gather around. One morning when I went to see them at about nine o'clock, I found the house in immaculate order and smelling of freshly baked bread. The mother told me she and her husband were going off for the week end, and she was up early baking bread because she did not want her eldest daughter to have to do it while she was away. This couple were among those who particularly seemed to enjoy the square dances; the woman looked young in spite of her eleven children. I have heard good things of their sons' war service and I hope they now own their house and land.

There was one elderly man whom I particularly liked. He was rather a problem because his wife was old and sick and the only person he had at home to help him was a grandson of about thirteen. The old man worked as janitor of the administration building, kept himself and his house and grounds clean, and took care of his wife like a trained nurse.

Oh, yes, the human values were most rewarding, even if the financial returns to the government were not satisfactory.

Years later after the Social Security Act was passed, I saw how it worked in individual cases in this area. There was a mine accident in which several men were killed, and my husband asked me to go down and find out what the people were saying. One man received the Carnegie medal posthumously because he had gone back into the mine to help rescue other men. His widow had several children so her Social Security benefits would make her comfortable. In talking to another widow who had three children and a fourth about to be born, I asked how she was going to manage. She seemed quite confident and told me: "My sister and her two children will come to live with us. I am going to get Social Security benefits of nearly sixty-five dollars a month. I pay fifteen dollars a month on my house and land, and I shall raise vegetables and have chickens and with the money from the government I will get along very well. In the past probably the mine company might have given me a small check and often the other miners took up a collection if they could afford it, but this income from the government I can count on until my children are grown."

Two other events of that first autumn in Washington stand out in my mind. On November 17, 1933, Henry Morgenthau, junior, was sworn in as Under-Secretary of the Treasury in the oval room in the White House, thus starting on his long and arduous labors in the

Treasury Department. When Secretary Woodin resigned, Henry Morgenthau succeeded him and held the office until shortly after my husband's death, when he also resigned and left Washington.

On that same day my husband and Mr. Litvinoff held the final conversations on the recognition of the Soviet Union. There was considerable excitement over the first telephone conversation between the two countries; it took place between Mr. Litvinoff in the White House and his wife and son in Russia. The ushers noted it in their daily record book because while there had been overseas conversations with many other European countries, this was the opening of diplomatic relations with Russia.

My husband used to speak often of one particular point in these negotiations, which dealt with the freedom of religious practice in Russia. He had insisted that when any recognized religious group had more than a certain number of members, it should be permitted to have a pastor, minister or priest as the case might be, to carry on religious services and perform whatever church rites were desired. He obtained assurance that this permission would be granted, though at first there was some hesitation.

Needless to say, among some of my husband's old friends there was considerable opposition to the recognition of Russia. His mother came to him before the announcement was made to tell him she had heard rumors that he was about to recognize Russia, but that she felt this would be a disastrous move and widely misunderstood by the great majority of their old friends. My husband told me this with amusement, adding that he thought his mother was entirely correct and that probably many of his old friends were going to have to put up with a number of shocks in the years to come. This was a truth that proved itself many times over during his presidency. Not only with his old friends but with various other people he had frequent run-ins over the new theory that government had a responsibility to the people. I remember that when Senator Carter Glass insisted that Virginia needed no relief, Franklin suggested he take a drive with him to see some of the bad spots. The Senator never accepted his invitation.

The opening of diplomatic intercourse with Russia and our relations in this hemisphere were the administration's first points of attack in our foreign policy, but the major emphasis in those early years was and had to be on questions of domestic policy and our internal economic recovery.

As I look back over the actual measures which were undertaken in this first year, I realize that the one in which my husband took the greatest pleasure was the establishment on April 5, 1933, of the Civilian Conservation Corps camps. The teen-age youngster, the boy finishing high school, the boy who had struggled to get through college, all were at loose ends. For years Franklin had talked in desultory fashion about the value of out-of-door work and knowledge for boys, and he had always wanted to run a school at Hyde Park which would give young people a mixture of manual and intellectual exercise. I think these ideas were in the background of his mind when he began to plan the CCC. Certain of the arrangements, of course, were a matter of necessity. There was, for example, no organization except the army that had the tents and other supplies essential for a set-up of this kind, which was why part of the program was promptly put under its jurisdiction. Franklin realized that the boys should be given some other kind of education as well, but it had to be subordinate to the day's labor required of them. That phase of the program was never as well planned as the physical work program. Franklin did not have time to do it himself and left it to other people, who found the problem of divided authority difficult to solve. Nevertheless the Civilian Conservation Corps had a triple value: it gave the boys a chance to see different parts of their own country, and to learn to do a good day's work in the open, which benefited them physically; also it gave them a cash income, part of which went home to their families. This helped the morale both of the boys themselves and of the people at home. The idea was his own contribution to the vast scheme of relief rehabilitation planning. Because it helped the young men of the nation, and because the work they did held a deep and abiding interest for him, the CCC was one of the things he felt might well have become permanent.

This was followed on June 16th by the National Recovery Act, with General Hugh Johnson in charge. The basic importance of the NRA was that it made it easier for the industrialist who wanted to do the right thing. The chiseler and the man who was willing to profit by beating down his labor could no longer compete unfairly with the man who wanted to earn a decent profit but to treat his employees fairly. The NRA was declared unconstitutional almost two years later. I thought that was unfortunate, for it seemed a simple way to keep bad employers doing what was right. I have always felt it had a very good effect.

The Public Works Administration, which came into being on the same day, made it possible for the government to plan and undertake public works during this period of depression. It helped to take up the slack of unemployment by lending money to the states for projects that they could not finance by themselves.

Five months later in November, 1933, the Civil Works Administration was set up and in time put four million unemployed to work.

In my travels around the country I saw many things built both by PWA and by CWA. I also saw the results of the work done by CCC. The achievements of these agencies began to dot city and rural areas alike. Soil conservation and forestry work went forward, recreation areas were built, and innumerable bridges, schools, hospitals and sanitation projects were constructed—lasting monuments to the good work done under these agencies. It is true they cost the people of the country vast sums of money, but they did a collective good and left tangible results which are still evident today.

The old story of the men who leaned on their shovels and shirked was, of course, true here and there, but on the whole the United States can be proud of its efforts. They pulled the country out of the depression and made it possible for us to fight the greatest and most expensive war in our history.

Perhaps the most far-reaching project was the Tennessee Valley Authority. That was Senator George Norris' greatest dream and no one who witnessed the development of the Authority will ever forget the fight he put up for something that many people ridiculed. The development had been begun during World War I, but at the end of that war most of the work was stopped. Nothing further was done until my husband, who well understood Senator Norris' vision, supplied an impetus at a time when it could accomplish the maximum results for the country. With the demands of a possible war in mind, Franklin insisted on pushing work on the TVA as rapidly as possible. He believed even then that under certain circumstances, war might come soon, and he knew if that happened we would need everything the TVA could make available.

In the campaign of 1932, my husband and I had gone through some of this TVA area, and he had been deeply impressed by the crowds at the stations. They were so poor; their houses were unpainted, their cars were dilapidated, and many grownups as well as children were without shoes or adequate garments. Scarcely eight years later, after the housing and educational and agricultural experiments had had time to take effect, I went through the same area, and a more prosperous area would have been hard to find. I have always wished that those who oppose authorities to create similar benefits in the valleys of other great rivers could have seen the contrast as I saw it. I realize that such changes must come gradually, but I hate to see nothing done. I wish, as my husband always wished, that year by year we might be making a start on the Missouri River and the head waters of the Mississippi. Such experiments, changing for the better the life of the people, would be a mighty bulwark against attacks on our democracy.

CHAPTER NINE

THE PEACEFUL YEARS: 1934–1936

As I LOOK back, the years from 1934 to 1936 seem to me the quietest and least anxious of any of the years we spent in the White House. The reforms instituted were beginning to put the country back on a more even keel; good feeling existed generally between capital and labor and between the president and Congress; and in our family life we had gradually managed to adapt our private traditions and habits to the exigencies of the White House, setting the pattern for the years that followed.

In the spring of 1934, Franklin suggested that I make a trip to Puerto Rico. General Blanton Winship, the governor of the island at that time, was faced with great difficulties. Labor conditions were bad, and there was not enough food for the constantly increasing population. The sugar companies owned large tracts of land and, because the work was seasonal and the wages pitifully small, the workers practically starved in off-seasons. Rexford Tugwell, who was then in the Department of Agriculture, was going down to make a study of what could be done in that field, and my husband thought if I went, too, it might show the people that he was really interested in conditions there.

Because it was my first trip of this kind, the newspapers sent some women correspondents to cover it. They were all members of my press conference: Emma Bugbee of the *Herald Tribune;* Bess Furman of the Associated Press; Ruby Black of the United Press, and Dorothy Ducas for the International News. There was one press photographer, Sammy Shulman, whom I had known for some time. Lorena Hickok, who was working for WPA, also went to observe and report back to Harry Hopkins. All of them proved the best and most helpful of traveling companions.

We flew via Miami, stopping at Haiti and San Domingo on the way. In Puerto Rico I stayed at La Fortelesa, the governor's old house and once a fortress of sorts, a lovely pink stucco building that dominates the bay.

Following the very careful program laid out for me, I visited a number of rural schools, some of which were trying to improve the quality of education offered the children. I also saw the homework done by the women. Some of it was beautiful embroidery, but often it was done on material that was not worth the work. I am sure if the women of the United States knew the conditions under which those handkerchiefs, nightgowns and slips were embroidered they would want to boil them before putting them on or using them. Factory wages were very low and the amount paid for homework unbelievably small. Little girls sat all during their lunch hour in school embroidering handkerchiefs in order to add a few pennies to the family income.

The conditions in rural homes were unsanitary enough, but in the towns they were even more shocking. I remember going down a street, looking into the houses of factory workers. Most of the houses consisted of two rooms; the back room had no light, and practically the only light in the front room came through the doorway. There were no screens and, of course, no plumbing or other modern conveniences in these old brick buildings. Many of the women cooked out of doors, and I wondered how they could produce their meager meals on the little stoves they used.

The real slums were actually worse, I thought, in the capital city. Huts made of bits of tin and scrap iron and wood picked up after the last hurricane were built out over the water. We walked on duck boards placed precariously over the piling, and the water came up under every house. There was also a slum which clung precariously to the side of the cliff. Here goats and other animals lived under the houses. Again there was no sanitation, and typhoid was common. If it had not been for the climate and the diet of rice and beans, bought from the United States, there probably would have been a great deal of rickets on the island. Tuberculosis took a heavy toll. Every year more and more children were born, which made the question of population on that little island a matter for serious thought. The Catholic church taught the girls to do beautiful embroidery, and the nuns did all they could to make the lives of the children a little better.

From Puerto Rico we went to the Virgin Islands where, bad though some of the conditions were, they seemed at that time slightly better than in Puerto Rico. Efforts were being made there as well as in Puerto Rico to put up some new houses, but the people had to be taught how to use them. They did not know how to live decently even under better physical conditions, because the circumstances under which they had been forced to live had made cleanliness almost impossible.

If the Virgin Islands were allowed to retain more of the tax revenue from what they produce and sell, their problem would be easier to solve. Also, if shipping and air facilities were developed the islands would have great possibilities as vacation spots, and could derive considerable revenue from the tourist trade.

On my return I begged my husband to send down some labor people and industrialists to look over the situation. Some of my friends have since gone there to develop new industries, among them Adrian Dornbush, who had worked on the WPA Art and Crafts programs in Washington. He developed a number of uses for the Puerto Rican bamboo and I think has several small industries going successfully. When Mr. Tugwell later became Governor of Puerto Rico, he tried to carry out many of the ideas he had thought, on his first trip, might help, but the islands still remain a difficult problem and one which the United States is far from having solved satisfactorily.

The Puerto Rican people love their island. Its scenery, hills, beaches and sea are beautiful. Precautions must be taken for ocean bathing, but as soon as swimming pools and beaches are available and hotels begin to improve and transportation becomes easier, I think people will find it a very satisfactory and accessible spot.

In the summer of 1934 my husband decided to make a trip through the Caribbean and the Panama Canal and out to Hawaii, taking with him our two youngest sons, Franklin, junior, and John. The newspaper men traveled on a separate ship, visiting Franklin every now and then. I remember his telling me with gleeful chuckles that he had had to provide the newspaper men with the historical background of most of the places where they stopped—he was particularly interested in Cartagena—and I can well imagine that he insisted on lecturing them on all points of historical interest. Though this was a very good thing for our sons too, they clearly did not let it prevent them from having a good time. Their tales to me were usually about the wonderful parties they went to, and their drives with the daughters of the officials who greeted their father.

Franklin was an extremely good traveler, and if he had not already known the history of all the places he visited, he would have taken great pleasure in reading it. His knowledge of geography, stimulated by his stamp collection, was phenomenal and grew with the various trips he took. He had a keen interest, too, in the ship's navigation and I think always felt a certain responsibility, even though he was only a passenger.

He had been through the Panama Canal many years before with my brother, and he noted every difference on this trip. Though he did not, I think, stop at Galapagos Islands, he marked them in his mind for a future cruise. He went there later, taking several Smithsonian scientists who wished to study some peculiar animals that could be found nowhere else. I think, too, he later urged Vincent Astor, with whom he cruised on several occasions, to take another trip for scientific study to these islands.

Once they reached Hawaii, he and the boys had a wonderful time. He enjoyed meeting the native Queen and eating poi, which very few members of the party really liked.

While Franklin was gone I went west. Lorena Hickok had arranged

to take her vacation at the same time and met my plane at Sacra-
mento. Evading the newspaper people with some difficulty, we drove
her car by slow stages to the ranch where my daughter and her two
children were spending the summer, near Reno, Nevada. Mr. and
Mrs. William Dana, who had been kind enough to take them in,
also managed to give Miss Hickok and me a room. I was delighted
to find the children and Anna so well taken care of, and since I was
still able to ride horseback, I enjoyed myself very much.

The Danas had a wonderful old character to take care of their
horses. His name was Bar Francis and they told me he had been a
"bad man" and later a sheriff, which is a wonderful combination. By
the time I met him he was oldish and very respectable, and my interest
in him was in his ability to train horses. His own horse followed him
around and did anything Bar Francis told him to do. He would lie
down, look for something to eat in his master's pocket, and let Bar
Francis do all kinds of tricks, like leaning from his back to pick up a
handkerchief on the ground. He would even dance in time to music
which Bar Francis hummed. Bar Francis let me ride him as a great
favor, and when I mounted from the ground he said: "You are mighty
spry for a lady of your age."

I have no idea whether Bar Francis is still alive, but I had the
greatest respect for him. Anyone who is trusted by animals, though
he may lack the superficial virtues, is bound to be a fine person fundamentally.

On leaving the Dana ranch, Lorena Hickok and I drove by a back
way into the Yosemite and were met by the rangers, with horses. We
took a trail high up into the mountains where the rangers were restock-
ing some pools with fish. The days we spent there were for me days
of enchantment, but I was worried about Lorena Hickok. I learned
that nobody who smokes a great deal and whose heart is not strong
should try to camp above 10,000 feet. She more or less panted throughout the days we were there, while I climbed easily to 13,000 feet and
looked down on other pools, and rode to picnic places and got up early
to watch the head ranger catch the trout that kept eluding me. I finally
agreed that I would clean the fish, since I was quite incapable of catch-
ing them.

We sat around the camp fire at night and the men told stories. They had carefully prepared a tent for us, but I put my sleeping bag out of doors under the stars and the pines. One night I woke with a start to feel something sniffing at my feet. I thought of all the stories I had heard of bears coming to the camp to find food, and when I could stand the uncertainty no longer, I flashed on my light and sat up suddenly, only to find that the head ranger's dog had broken away from his home miles off, found his master's trail and was now going from one sleeping bag to another in an effort to find his proper place!

On the way down, after fording a stream at a camp where we were going to desert the horses for automobiles, I suddenly looked back and, to my horror, saw Lorena Hickok's horse lying down in the ford. Luckily he gave her time to slide off before he rolled over. She was soaked but unhurt, and we had to take her to one of the cabins to get dried out before we could continue down to the inn on the floor of the valley. We stayed at the inn until we had visited all the sights, then motored on to San Francisco, where, I recall we found it not only difficult but impossible to evade the newspaper reporters. After one night in San Francisco, we started on the drive through the Red Woods along the Pacific—one of the most beautiful trips that I know of. We took time out to go to Crater Lake and to make the boat trip to the curious volcanic islands. From there we drove to Portland, along the Columbia River Highway, and I had my first glimpse of the power development there.

In Portland we found my sitting room literally filled with flowers; neither of us had ever seen such a display before. "Hick," who has a macabre humor at times, said: "All you need is a corpse." I realized for the first time that Portland is really the City of Roses.

Miss Hickok and I parted in Portland and I was joined by Miss Thompson, Louis Howe and Steve Early, who had come out to meet my husband and go back by train across the country with him. Louis had expected to meet Lorena Hickok and me in San Francisco and was very indignant with us for going on without making any effort to get in touch with him, but I finally made my peace. After my husband arrived, we all listened to wild tales of pleasure in Hawaii and wonderful days at sea.

We spent one day on the way back driving through a portion of Glacier Park, where Franklin and Secretary Ickes were taken into an Indian tribe at one of the lodges and given wonderful names. When my turn came, the Indians called me, I think, the Medicine Pipe Woman, which amused me since I don't smoke as a rule. When we first went to the White House, I often took a cigarette and lit it after lunch in order to make the women who did smoke feel more comfortable, but I dislike the taste it leaves in my mouth.

The boys decided that they were going to swim in the lake at Glacier Park and induced me to go with them. As I stood, hesitating and wondering whether I could bear the icy water, one of the boys gave me a push and I found myself gasping and swimming back as quickly as possible. The Indians stood watching us silently, as much as to say, "What fools these mortals be." When I was safely back on the float I decided the Indians were right and ran to the cabin to get warm again.

The boys left us at different stops on the way home to fly to various destinations, but I recall one dinner we had together on the train before they left, at which a number of cabinet officers were present. They looked so horrified when they heard the boys arguing violently with Franklin on a number of points that I finally felt impelled to explain that in our family the boys had always been encouraged to express their opinions. I did not add what was soon evident: that their father always waited while they expressed themselves loudly and forcefully and until each one had had his say, and then demolished them with a few well chosen arguments of his own.

In the winter of 1936, Louis Howe finally moved from the White House to the hospital. We kept telling him and ourselves that he was going to improve and come back again, but suddenly word came that he had died. I think it was one of the greatest losses that my husband sustained. He was to have others and all were hard to bear, because in public life you can have no private time for sorrow. Duties must be performed and your own feelings must be suppressed. Louis' death deprived my husband of a close relationship and the satisfaction of having someone near to whom he could talk quite frankly, whose advice he might not always follow but whose presence was stimulating.

The loss of companionship had come more or less gradually, since during the previous autumn and winter Louis could not be counted on. He, himself, however, had been so sure he could carry on at least until after the 1936 election that he had planned to be moved to New York City and to direct the campaign from his bed in the hotel.

Franklin arranged for the funeral service to be held in the East Room. He seemed to feel that if you lived and worked in the White House, this was a last tribute to which you were entitled. When his loyal bodyguard, Gus Gennerich, died, Franklin insisted that he have this tribute paid him; in the same way when my brother died at Walter Reed Hospital in the autumn of 1941, Franklin insisted that I arrange the funeral service at the White House. My brother had lived with us after we were married and, since he was six years younger than I, we always felt as though he were one of our children.

Louis Howe's death left a great gap in my husband's life. I have always felt that if Louis had lived the number of people drawn closely but briefly into the working and social orbits of Franklin's life would have been fewer. For one reason and another, no one quite filled the void which unconsciously he was seeking to fill, and each one in turn disappeared from the scene, occasionally with a bitterness which I understood but always regretted. There are not many men in this world whose personal ambition it is to accomplish things for someone else, and it was some time before a friendship with Harry Hopkins, somewhat different but similar in certain ways, again brought Franklin some of the satisfaction he had known with Louis Howe.

What worries we had in those two years from 1934 to 1936 were largely such personal ones as this. In fact, we approached the campaign of 1936 with a feeling that on the whole the country was getting back on its feet. I did no formal work in that campaign, though I visited the campaign headquarters and went with Franklin on some of his trips. To tell the truth, I never felt it was good taste to go out and electioneer for my husband, so in none of the campaigns did I take any particular part in the political activities unless I was specially asked to for some specific reason.

I remember vividly the trip into Rhode Island, Massachusetts, and Connecticut, when we drove through miles of small towns where the streets were lined with people. Very little local preparation had been made, for the authorities did not believe there would be much of a crowd, but even on the country roads people had gathered to stand and watch the president go by. As we progressed the Secret Service men got more and more worried and finally, at their insistence, the states assigned troopers and National Guardsmen. Boston Common was a seething mass of people who had waited for a long time for Franklin's arrival. I was in the first car with him. He managed to remain confident that everyone was being taken care of, but I became conscious of the fact that behind us the crowds were closing in and that there was real danger that people might be run down, or that some of our party would be cut off.

Occasionally someone would try to throw flowers into the car, or to reach the car and shake hands with my husband; but the Secret Service men were very efficient and the poor person would find himself pushed gently out of the way while the car kept on and the Secret Service man ran to catch up with us. This had to be done for safety's sake, but I never was happy about it. To this day, I look back on those trips, triumphal in that they augured well for the election, as nightmares of anxiety not for myself or Franklin, but for the people in our party and in the crowds. No matter what your fears, however, you must smile and bow; and if you stop to receive flowers, or some remembrance of the place, you must appear to be enjoying yourself, and carefree.

On this trip my husband spoke in a hall in Worcester, Massachusetts, to a very large audience. One of the people in our party, who was sitting on the platform behind my husband, heard one of the women next to her say to a friend: "I know they built an extension on this platform to accommodate all the people, but I do hope it is strong enough so that it won't cave in." One could feel sure that the Secret

Service men had inspected every inch of the building but at each little creak or noise, those who had heard the remark worried.

The final day of the trip my husband rode in the first car, with some of the politicians and the rest of us following behind. We were supposed to rejoin the train at Stamford, Connecticut. Fortunately for the women in the party, we had some strong, tall newspaper men with us. Fred Storm, of the United Press, I remember particularly on that occasion. We attached ourselves to his coat tails while he fought his way through the crowd and got us on the train. Without him, I think we should have been left behind or trampled to death as the crowd tried to get a glimpse of the president, who was already on the train.

When the returns came in election night Maine and Vermont were found to be still in the Republican fold. My husband said with a wicked twinkle in his eye: "I knew I should have gone to Maine and Vermont, but Jim wouldn't let me."

There was no uncertainty or waiting for the returns this election. As usual we were at Hyde Park, where the dining room on election night was always turned into what seemed to me the nearest thing to a newspaper office. The machines on which news came in were set up in a little room off the dining room, Franklin himself had telephones, long dispatches were handed to him by relays of people, and everybody made out averages. I was expected to show interest in the returns, but also to be with his mother in the library to help entertain the guests and keep them out of the dining room, except for a few favored individuals. The newspaper people would come and be given refreshments, and finally, when the returns came in, the people in the village of Hyde Park would have a torch light parade and come to greet my husband. We would go out on the porch and listen to a few words from him, usually shivering in the cold.

Now as I look back, I realize that I was a very unsatisfactory person on these occasions. I always worried about whether anyone was being neglected and whether there was enough food, or whether something else might be wrong. I never was able to forget about things, to take them naturally and enjoy myself, and to let other people worry. It would I am sure have been just as effective.

That has been one of my bad habits all my life, even where my children were concerned. Instead of enjoying them, most of the time I was disciplining them or worrying about their health or trying to give them pleasures that their father's illness prevented them from enjoying with him. I never was really carefree. It is a pity that we can not have the experience that comes with age in our younger days, when we really need it. We certainly would enjoy life more and I am sure that somehow the responsibilities would all be taken care of quite as well.

I remember that our youngest son, John, happened to be at Hyde Park one week end when Miss Thompson and I were busy putting on a picnic for some royal visitors at Franklin's cottage on top of the hill. There was no furniture in the cottage, and no water, so my husband's decision to hold the picnic there entailed considerable work. Walking in on us in the middle of the preparations my son said: "Why mother, I thought these things just happened. I never knew anyone worked at them!" Then and there I realized how badly I had brought up my sons. As far as they knew things did just happen; however, they probably would have happened just as well if I had not fussed about them quite so much, and I would have been a more agreeable hostess. I am quite sure many a person wished for a less busy hostess.

When we went back to Washington in 1936, Franklin was received with great acclaim, and his second term of office began very auspiciously. He had carried with him a big Democratic majority in the Congress, and the party members felt so secure that they began to believe they could do anything they wanted to. That is a bad attitude for any group of people to adopt, particularly when they are responsible for the smooth running of a country that has only just become stabilized after a great depression.

Throughout all those early years in Washington, one of Franklin's major interests was in changing the bad feeling that existed between us and our Latin-American neighbors. He had always felt, as I said, that our attitude was that of a rather objectionable big brother and that we would create better feeling by a wiser and more neighborly policy. After the November elections, he made a personal effort to implement this policy by attending the Inter-American Conference for the Maintenance of Peace, held in Buenos Aires, in 1936. He wanted to take our son, James, with him as his aide, partly because James had worked hard in the campaign, and partly because James understood how to help him get about in crowds. Franklin always liked to have one of the boys with him, if it did not interfere too much with something else they ought to do.

The question of Jimmy's rank arose. At that time he was a reserve officer in the Marine Corps, but in order to serve as his father's aide, he was given the rank of lieutenant colonel. Later he asked to be demoted to captain again because he did not want the rank that had been given him for a specific occasion to put him permanently where he did not belong.

I was particularly thankful that Jimmy was with his father on this trip, because Gus Gennerich died suddenly while they were in Buenos Aires. His death was a real sorrow to my husband, and of course, a shock to the whole party. To us at home it brought real grief, too, for Gus was a dear and faithful friend.

Franklin was deeply touched by the evident enthusiasm that his trip created and particularly happy that he seemed able to inaugurate the good feeling that he so greatly desired to see grow.

This trip and all other trips that had diplomatic significance were planned in consultation with Secretary Hull and the State Department. Sumner Welles, Franklin's able Undersecretary of State, was not only particularly well informed about South American affairs but also very much in sympathy with what Franklin was trying to do there in Latin-America, and he supported the Good Neighbor policy wholeheartedly. Franklin found him an excellent co-worker and counted on him for help with detailed background information at every step. I think, however, that Franklin's own good will toward the governments and people of these countries was an important aid to the State Department in making our policy effective.

On the way home, Franklin stopped in Uruguay. He always liked to tell the story of his greeting by the president of that country. When they met, he assured Franklin that he need not worry about anything happening to *him,* but since he, the President of Uruguay, had been threatened, Franklin must not be surprised if there were some shots. However, the President of the United States would not be the target. My husband got into the car and drove around, but in telling about it afterwards he said he could not helping wondering if he might not get hit by mistake, even though he was not the target. However, no one was shot that day.

From Uruguay they went to Brazil, and Franklin again was very much pleased by the enthusiasm that his visit called forth. It was there that he was given the gifts for me that created so much comment in one of the newspaper columns and in radio broadcasts some time ago. For this reason I think it wise to tell the whole story here.

Undersecretary Welles was asked by President Vargas and his wife if they might send some gifts to me, for they knew the rule that no President of the United States or any government official could accept personal gifts from a foreign government while in office. Madame Vargas sent me a beautiful hammered-silver tea set and she and her husband together sent me, from their collection, a very large aquamarine, one of the biggest and most perfect stones in the world. My husband presented me with these gifts on his return and I was deeply impressed by them, but realized that only in the White House or at some official gathering could such a large tea set be used. The stone was kept in my safe in the White House.

After Franklin's death, I gave the tea set to the airplane carrier, U.S.S. "Franklin D. Roosevelt," and I hope that the Brazilians were pleased to see it on the ship when she made a good will visit there shortly after being put into commission.

I could not quite decide what I should do with the aquamarine, for I no longer had a really safe place in which to keep it. I gave it to Bernard Baruch in order that he might make some inquiries about its value. I had tried to have it appraised, but no jeweler seemed able to tell me its exact value. At that time, Drew Pearson, the columnist, announced that I was about to sell this stone; that it had been given to my husband and not to me, and that it was valued at $25,000. I was appalled at the thought that I might suddenly be accused of having kept out of my husband's estate something that had actually belonged to him; so I immediately asked James, who was with his father when these gifts were presented, if he remembered about them. He promptly responded that they had been handed to him to give to me. Although I realized that my own son's testimony would not be considered very good, I could think of no other way of proving the point; my husband was dead, and Mr. Pearson kept insisting that the present Foreign Minister of Brazil had told him that the stone had been given to Franklin. I suppose the Foreign Minister had no idea what the difference was between giving it to my husband and giving it to me.

I had not wanted to give this stone to the Franklin D. Roosevelt Library because I felt it had very little connection with any of my husband's collections. I hoped to do something with it that would in some way benefit the Brazilian people. Fortunately, I discovered that Mr. Welles knew all about the presentation of this gift to my husband for me, and he told me that it would give great pleasure to the Brazilian people if the stone were placed with Franklin's other collections in the Library at Hyde Park. It is there now. I think it does interest people and perhaps does serve a good purpose by symbolizing the kindness and generosity of Brazilian feeling toward our country.

My husband knew me so well that on this trip he bought me a very small aquamarine pendant, which I sometimes wear. In giving it to me he said: "I have brought you this inconspicuous gift because I feel quite sure that you will never wear the large stone."

It used to annoy him that when he asked me what I would like for my birthday or Christmas I always wanted utilitarian things such as towels, sheets and pillow cases. My only interest in jewelry is a sentimental interest in having something that has belonged in the family or that has been worn by someone I really care about or that is given to me by someone I love. I like beautiful things, but it would never occur to me to go out and spend money on jewelry to wear when there is already so much in the family. The younger people in the family generally prefer more modern pieces even though for purely sentimental reasons they will treasure things that belonged in the family.

As a matter of fact, I have enjoyed what frivolous gifts Franklin occasionally gave me, and I am sure that just because he chose them they will mean something to the children to whom I give them now or in the future.

Franklin himself was easy to buy gifts for, because he always had a long list of first editions and prints which he wanted. And after he built the cottage at Warm Springs and the one in Hyde Park, there were countless things he needed and wanted for those houses.

While Franklin was in South America, Miss Thompson and I went on my first real lecture trip. In the spring I had undertaken four lectures in the middle west and I had not felt happy about them; this was to be my first trip under the W. Colston Leigh Lecture Bureau. Any paid lectures I have given since have been under his direction, and the relationship with Mr. Leigh has been increasingly satisfactory from both the business and the personal standpoint. Lecturing grew easier as time went on, but I still never get up to speak without nervousness, though as I talk it vanishes. I use notes for long lectures but never follow a manuscript, because I find it easier to think on my feet and be effective when I am not reading.

These trips gave me a wonderful opportunity to visit all kinds of places and to see and get to know a good cross section of people. Always during my free time I visited as many government projects as possible, often managing to arrive without advance notice so that they could not be polished up for my inspection. I began to see for myself some of the results of my husband's actions during the first hundred days of his administration, and in meeting and talking with people all over the country I got the full impact of what the new programs had meant to them. It was evident that the home and farm loans, for example, had saved many a family from outright disaster.

Of course I always reported to Franklin upon my return, but aside from any value my reports may have been to him, I had another, more personal, reason for wanting to make these trips. All the years that I lived in Washington I was preparing for the time when we should no longer be there. I did not want to give up my interests in New York City, because I always felt that some day I would go back. I never anticipated that so many years would pass before I left Washington. There was much to do while we were there, and I had many enjoyable privileges, but I kept expecting to leave at the end of every four years and I did not want to be spoiled by enjoying the privileges too much or to lose my interest in activities that might be continued after I left the White House. This seems to me ridiculous as I look back upon it now, but I might as well record the fact that it was one of my constant preoccupations.

Because I was under contract for the lecture trips, I had to keep to my schedule. That meant work and discipline—and I felt I needed both. In addition, I really did enjoy getting away to less formal surroundings, though I was to find that going on lecture trips did not always mean that I succeeded in being "unofficial." On occasion, I was more guarded and watched over than in Washington. Late one night in Detroit when we opened the door of our suite in the hotel to go out and drop some letters in the mail chute, three men rushed out of the adjoining room and asked what was wrong. We discovered that they were plain-clothes men assigned to watch over me.

In another city, Little Rock, Arkansas, the mayor assigned two big, husky motor-cycle policemen to escort me during the day. In the morning I decided to have a shampoo, so made an appointment at a hairdressing shop. I was escorted by the policemen, but fully expected they would leave me at the door. To my surprise they came right into the shop with me and sat where they could watch the whole operation, much to the amusement and perhaps annoyance of the other customers.

In New York City I could go about without having much attention focused on me. After our son, James, moved into our New York house for a while, I took a small apartment downtown in a house that was owned by my old friends, Elizabeth Read and Esther Lape. Later my brother had a small apartment in the same building. It was a great contrast to the White House, and I think for that reason I enjoyed it. Miss

Thompson and I were very comfortable there and could work with little interruption, and we particularly enjoyed the opportunity of seeing our old friends.

The theater was one of the things which drew me to New York City, for in Washington the opportunities for seeing good plays are rather rare. In those early years, whenever possible, I got Franklin to go to any play that came to the National Theater which I thought he would like. Usually I asked the cast to come back to the White House for supper afterwards. Franklin always enjoyed this too, but the opportunities for these pleasures grew rarer as he grew busier.

Each year during the March of Dimes campaign, a play was brought down from New York City for a benefit performance in the District of Columbia and at first Franklin attended these performances. On these occasions, too, we always had a supper party afterwards, even when later he did not go. The year that "Life With Father" was put on, Franklin was greatly entertained by the small boys who played the Day children. One of them, the youngest, I think, was much interested in the White House as I took them through it. He was particularly impressed by the story of how, when the White House burned during the War of 1812, Dolly Madison saved the portrait of George Washington by cutting it out of the frame and rolling it up and escaping just as the British arrived. The youngster exclaimed: "What kind of a knife did she use?" I doubted if Franklin had ever thought of that, and wickedly I felt that at last I had a question to stump him, so I said sweetly to the boy: "I don't know, but I am sure the president will tell you. Let's go and ask him." We did, and with only a moment's pause, Franklin said: "Why, the kitchen knife, of course!"

My husband's birthday was always a busy day for all of us. The movie stars took part generously in the celebrations held for the benefit of the victims of polio, and it was great fun to have them lunch with us. For their part they all enjoyed, I think, the tour of the house on which I always took them, with the help of whichever children were at home, and they were most generous in giving their autographs to the White House staff.

In the evening I made the rounds of the hotels where birthday balls were given, and usually came back to the White House in time to hear my husband broadcast, in the company of many of the stars. I know how touched and deeply grateful for their cooperation Franklin was and how glad that his birthday could be made the occasion for helping the victims of polio.

In our pre-White House days Louis Howe, who was a versatile person, had always spent a great deal of time and thought on my husband's birthday parties; as long as he was able to direct them, they were always amusing. He wrote special songs and poems for them and assigned everyone some particular stunt.

My husband always planned my birthday parties. As he knew I did not like much fuss, he usually simply gathered for a dinner the friends I especially cared about, but I was always glad when I ceased to be the center of attention. A left-over from my early shyness I imagine!

In our early years in the White House we felt that it was important to spend as many of the holidays as we could, particularly the Christmas holidays, in Washington. Franklin's mother and his half sister-in-law, Mrs. James R. Roosevelt, always came down for Christmas and we tried to maintain our home traditions, besides following those that had been established in the White House.

As a family we had always tried to be together at Christmas, until the children married and moved away. It was part of our tradition to have stockings for everyone in our bedroom Christmas morning, and as soon as the children awoke, they woke us and everyone else. Our Christmas tree was usually ready Christmas Eve, the older children helping to trim it. Franklin always directed the placing of every ornament or string of tinsel, even after he had polio, and never, as long as he lived, would he hear of our using anything but real candles. For all his advanced political theories, he clung to the old-fashioned traditions in many curious little ways.

At Hyde Park we lit the tree on Christmas Eve for the party to which we invited all the people on the place. Christmas afternoon at about four o'clock we lit it for our own children and put all the presents in piles around it. When our children were young, Christmas dinner was in the middle of the day. As they grew older we had it at night, and then as grandchildren came along and joined us, we went back to the midday meal. After we went to the White House, we kept the same routine as far as the family was concerned, adding to it whatever had to be done officially.

In the morning, the day before Christmas, my husband and I had a reception for the White House clerical staff and the Secret Service men, at which he gave each a small remembrance and wished them all a happy Christmas. In the afternoon we had a party for the household staff, chauffeurs, maintenance men, and police. To this afternoon party each employee was asked to bring his immediate family if he cared to do so. The children under twelve years old received a personal gift and each employee a money present and a cornucopia of candy. We usually gave the police guards a tie or a handkerchief, a fruit cake, and a cornucopia of Christmas candy.

Of course, this meant a great deal of organizing and planning beforehand. During the year when I saw anything in my travels that I thought I could give as a Christmas gift, I bought it and had it sent to the White House. We had a closet on the third floor which we called the Christmas closet, and here the items were stored as they arrived.

I bought toys by the dozens, ordered the candy and cakes and ties or handkerchiefs well ahead of time. The lists of employees and their families, with the names and ages of the children, were furnished me by the housekeeper and the ushers. Early in the fall, the gifts for the children were wrapped in tissue paper and the Christmas cards with the money enclosed addressed for each person. This was really a big job and had to be done carefully, for I wanted no one to be overlooked through inadvertence. At first Mrs. Mollie Somerville and Mrs. Muriel Lund were responsible for this part of the work. After Mrs. Somerville left, Mrs. Lund and Mrs. Dorothy Butturff and, later, Miss Catherine Heffron carried on until we left Washington. At first these young women, who were accustomed to making only their own purchases of wrappings and ribbons, were appalled at the amount of paper and ribbons, tags, and so on, that they had to get for me, but they soon took it for granted that they had to buy in large quantities.

In addition, of course, I had my personal Christmas gifts to prepare, and I often stood on my feet until the small hours of the morning doing a task which I always enjoyed. When friends came to stay, I often asked them to spend an evening helping me wrap packages in the Christmas closet. Some of them still mention it as the Christmas season approaches.

The White House was always beautifully decorated by William Reeves, the head gardener for over forty years, and his staff. The big tree in the East Room, trimmed in white and silver, was the loveliest tree I have ever seen.

On the day of the party, several long benches were lined up along the east side of the big East Room. The toys and gifts were laid out alphabetically; the cornucopias of candy were put on a near-by table, the envelopes with money on another, the cakes on still another, in a regular assembly line. After each family was greeted by my husband and me and any members of our family who were at home, they went around the room and were given their gifts by the people assigned to each table. If any of my children were home, they always helped.

When our two youngest sons were still at home, before they reached boarding school age, I began giving a Christmas party at the Women's Trade Union League clubhouse in New York City for children whose fathers were ill or injured and unable to work. I felt that our boys ought to know that all children were not so fortunate as they were. Usually there were thirty-five or forty children there, for whom I had bought warm gloves, sweaters and roller skates or dolls or some toy. My boys were hosts at the party. Of course, we had ice cream and cake and cocoa and oranges and apples, knowing that to children no party was a real party without them. At one of the parties a little girl asked Franklin, junior, for a gift to take home to her sister, who had not been able to attend because they had only one coat and dress between them. They had drawn lots to see which one would come. He was shocked to learn such conditions existed and came to me with the most unhappy expression on his face, asking me not only for the presents but to please see about the clothes. In his world everyone who needed clothes got them.

I gave these parties every year, even after my sons were grown, until employment was at its peak in 1941. We found then they were not needed, so I gave them up and have never resumed them.

The week before Christmas I usually went to Hyde Park for a day to distribute our gifts to the people who lived on the place or who worked for us. If we happened to go up immediately after Christmas, we gave a party in the big house for the people on the place. Later, after the Military Police School was established at Hyde Park, we held two evening parties in the library for the soldiers who were stationed there. Franklin was much amused by some of the new recruits who, when they saw him for the first time, often completely forgot how they had been taught to salute and found new and original ways to hold their guns.

These parties all began with our singing Christmas carols together. The men had a glee club of their own and always serenaded us one of the evenings we were at home. After the carols everybody went up to the tree and received a cornucopia of candy and some little remembrance, and then we had dancing and light refreshments. Through the good offices of John Golden there was usually some kind of entertainment, which not only the soldiers but my husband and the family also enjoyed. I remember one astounding gentleman, Mr. Frank Paxton, who could tell us facts about any place in the United States we could name. The soldiers got great pleasure out of trying to stump him on their home towns. Even my husband tried unsuccessfully to catch him.

One very stormy evening neither the entertainers nor the music, nor even the girls who were invited to the dance, arrived until very late because of the snow and ice; so after we had sung carols for a while, I asked my husband to talk to the men, to tell them some stories of the First World War and anything he felt he could tell about World War II. He talked, and they had such a good time and asked him so many questions that when the music and the girls arrived they were disappointed at having to end the conversation.

Christmas Eve in Washington was usually a busy day for me. I started by going to a party for underprivileged children, given by the welfare council at the National Theater. Then I joined my husband to wish all the people in the executive offices a merry Christmas.

Usually at lunch time I had to be at the Salvation Army headquarters, where we had a service just before the food baskets were given out. I am afraid that during the depression years these services had an un-Christian effect upon me; because invariably before receiving their baskets, the poor wretches were told how grateful they should be. I knew if I were in their shoes I would be anything but grateful. From there I went to the Volunteers of America for the same sort of service and giving of food baskets, returning home in time for the afternoon party in the East Room.

After the party my husband and I and any of the family that was with us went to the lighting of the Community Christmas Tree, where my husband broadcast a Christmas message. Then he would return to the White House while I went on to a Christmas tree in one of the alleys (the slums of Washington), where again we sang carols. As I looked at the poor people about me I could not help wondering what Christmas could mean to those children.

Returning home I would find my husband reading Dickens' Christmas Carol to any of the family that was gathered together. From year to year he varied the passages which he read in full and the passages he skimmed over, but I think the part he enjoyed most was the story of Fezziwig and the Christmas party. He always read that with relish. He also loved the part where old Scrooge wakes up Christmas morning and calls out the window to the boy and tells him to get the turkey for Bob Cratchit's family. And of course, having a great sense of the dramatic, he always put a good deal of drama into his reading of the parts about the ghosts. In fact, whenever he read anything aloud like this, he acted it out straight through, which was why he held the attention of the little children so well, even before they could understand the meaning of the words. He usually finished reading The Christmas Carol after dinner. Then there were stockings to be filled, and finally Miss Thompson and I nearly always went to midnight services at St. Thomas Church.

There were two Christmases when I had to leave the family, but in each case everything was organized before I went away. Once it was for a hurried trip to Boston, where our son, Franklin, junior, was in the hospital. He was a guinea pig for the use of the sulfa drugs and we were anxious about him for some time. It was a long while before he was quite well again.

The other time my daughter had had an operation, and because I knew that she was not strong enough to see her family through Christmas I flew out to Seattle. It was a nerve-wracking trip. I kept wondering whether I would be prevented by weather from getting there in time to be useful and would have to spend Christmas in a hotel somewhere along the line. However, everything went well, and I was there in time to keep her from doing as much as she might otherwise have done.

The last two years during the war we went to Hyde Park for Christmas; the grandchildren who were staying with us while their fathers were away preferred it to being in Washington.

As soon as the holidays were over, we went back to Washington. My husband liked to be in the White House on New Year's Eve. We always gathered a few friends, and at midnight in the oval study the radio was turned on and we waited with the traditional eggnog in hand for midnight to be announced. Franklin always sat in his big chair, and, as the president, would raise his glass and say: "To the United States of America." All of us stood and repeated the toast after him. Somehow the words were especially meaningful and impressive in that house and gave a touch of solemnity to the personal greetings that followed.

CHAPTER TEN

SECOND TERM: 1936–1937

FRANKLIN DID not talk a great deal about the work that he was doing, either at meals or in private family conversation. Most of us felt that when he was with his family he should have a respite from the concerns of his office. However, if a subject came up when people were present whose opinion he wanted to ask, we would learn something of how he felt and of the arguments advanced by those with whom he worked.

When an administration bill was up before Congress, we often found that the number of Congressmen coming to his study in the evenings increased. I had to learn very early that I must make an evaluation of the bills on which he had to get support. He calculated votes very closely on what was known as the administration policy, which was considered "must" legislation.

Only bills that were "must" legislation got full administration support. In the first years these were largely economic or relief measures; later on they were measures for defense. While I often felt strongly on various subjects, Franklin frequently refrained from supporting causes in which he believed, because of political realities. There were times when this annoyed me very much. In the case of the Spanish Civil War, for instance, we had to remain neutral, though Franklin knew quite well he wanted the democratic government to be successful. But he also knew he could not get Congress to go along with him.

To justify his action, or lack of action, he explained to me, when I complained, that the League of Nations had asked us to remain neutral. By trying to convince me that our course was correct, though he knew I thought we were doing the wrong thing, he was simply trying to salve his own conscience, because he himself was uncertain. It was one of the many times I felt akin to a hair shirt.

I also remember wanting to get all-out support for the anti-lynching bill and the removal of the poll tax, but though Franklin was in favor of both measures, they never became "must" legislation. When I would protest, he would simply say: "First things come first, and I can't alienate certain votes I need for measures that are more important at the moment by pushing any measure that would entail a fight." And as the situation in Europe grew worse, preparation for war had to take precedence over everything else. That was always "must" legislation, and Franklin knew it would not pass if there was a party split.

People do not realize how much pressure is brought to bear on a president, and how the various pressures sometimes loom so important that the real desires of the man himself must be subordinated. War hysteria, for example, had an effect not only on some of the campaign speeches but on administration policies.

Often people came to me to enlist his support for an idea. Although I might present the situation to him, I never urged on him a specific course of action, no matter how strongly I felt, because I realized he knew of factors in the picture as a whole of which I might be ignorant. I would do all I could for the people who came to me, short of stating what my husband might think or feel, and he never asked me to refrain from speaking my own mind. For that very reason, I suppose, in spite of my protests to him, I frequently was more careful than I might otherwise have been. As I said, I felt he was in a position to evaluate the essentials of his program and that I had no right to endanger that program by any action of mine.

One of the ideas I agreed to present to Franklin was that of setting up a national youth administration. Harry Hopkins, then head of the WPA, and Aubrey Williams, his deputy administrator and later head of the National Youth Administration, knew how deeply troubled I had been from the beginning about the plight of the country's young people, for I had talked to them about it a number of times. One day they said: "We have come to you about this because we do not feel we should talk to the president about it as yet." They went on: "There may be many people against the establishment of such an agency in the government and there may be bad political repercussions. We do not know that the country will accept it. We do not even like to ask the president, because we do not think he should be put in a position where he has to say officially 'yes' or 'no' now."

I agreed to try to find out what Franklin's feelings were and to put before him their opinions and fears. I waited until my usual time for discussing questions with him and went into his room just before he went to sleep. I described the whole idea, which he already knew something of, and then told him of the fears that Harry Hopkins and Aubrey Williams had about such an agency. He looked at me and said: "Do they think it is right to do this?" I said they thought it might be a great help to the young people, but they did not want him to forget that it might be unwise politically. They felt that a great many people who were worried by the fact that Germany had regimented its youth might feel we were trying to do the same thing in this country and they might not look upon the move with favor. Then Franklin said: "If it is the right thing to do for the young people, then it should be done. I guess we can stand the criticism, and I doubt if our youth can be regimented in this way or in any other way."

I went back to Harry Hopkins and Aubrey Williams the next day with Franklin's message. Shortly after, the NYA came into being and undoubtedly benefited a great many young people. It offered projects to help high school and college youngsters to finish school, and provided training both in resident and non-resident projects, supplementing the work of the Civilian Conservation Corps in such a way as to aid all youth.

It was one of the occasions on which I was very proud that the right thing was done regardless of political considerations. As a matter of fact, however, it turned out to be politically popular and strengthened the administration greatly.

As time went by, I found that people no longer considered me a mouthpiece for my husband but realized that I had a point of view of my own with which he might not at all agree. Then I felt freer to state my views. However, I always used some care, and sometimes, for example, I would send Franklin one of my columns about which I was doubtful. The only change he would ever suggest was occasionally in the use of a word, and that was simply a matter of style. Of course, this hands-off policy had its advantages for him, too; for it meant that my column could sometimes serve as a trial balloon. If some idea I expressed strongly—and with which he might agree—caused a violent reaction, he could honestly say that he had no responsibility in the matter and that the thoughts were my own.

Though Franklin himself never tried to discourage me and was undisturbed by anything I wanted to say or do, other people were frequently less happy about my actions. I knew, for instance, that many of my racial beliefs and activities in the field of social work caused Steve Early and Marvin McIntyre grave concern. They were afraid that I would hurt my husband politically and socially, and I imagine they thought I was doing many things without Franklin's knowledge and agreement. On occasion they blew up to him and to other people. I knew it at the time, but there was no use in my trying to explain, because our basic values were very different, and since I was fond of them, I thought it better to preserve the amenities in our daily contacts.

One afternoon, I remember, I gave a garden party at the White House for the girls from the reform school in Washington—most of them were colored. Steve thought that was very unwise, politically, and I did get some bad publicity in the southern papers. Steve felt the same way about my work with the members of the American Youth Congress. Franklin, however, never said anything to me about it. I always felt that if Franklin's re-election depended on such little things that I or any member of the family did, he could not be doing the job the people in the country wanted him to do.

I know Franklin felt the same way. Many of his political advisers, as well as some of the family, were deeply troubled over Elliott's and

Leaving the Church in Nahant, Mass., after the wedding of John Roosevelt and Anne Lindsay Clark, June, 1938. From left to right: James Roosevelt, Mrs. Franklin D. Roosevelt, Mrs. James Roosevelt, Sr., President Roosevelt and Elliott Roosevelt.

President and Mrs. Roosevelt with some of the young patients at the Warm Springs Foundation, April, 1938.

(Acme)

THE HOME CLUB PICNIC, AT HYDE PARK, N. Y., AUGUST, 1938. FROM LEFT TO RIGHT: MRS. FIORELLO LAGUARDIA, CAROLINE O'DAY (IN CAR), MAYOR LAGUARDIA (ON RUNNING BOARD), PRESIDENT ROOSEVELT, MRS. ROOSEVELT.

(From the Franklin D. Roosevelt Memorial Library)

PRESIDENT ROOSEVELT WITH THREE OF HIS SECRETARIES, NOVEMBER, 1938. FROM LEFT TO RIGHT: THE PRESIDENT, MISS MARGUERITE LEHAND, MARVIN MCINTYRE AND GRACE TULLY.

PRESIDENT ROOSEVELT, MRS. ROOSEVELT AND HARRY HOOKER, AFTER
THE EASTER SERVICE AT ST. THOMAS' EPISCOPAL CHURCH, WASHING-
TON, D. C., APRIL, 1938.

HARRY HOPKINS, PRESIDENT ROOSEVELT AND MRS. ROOSEVELT LEAVING
WARM SPRINGS, GEORGIA, FOR WASHINGTON, D. C., APRIL, 1938.

PRESIDENT AND MRS. ROOSEVELT WITH THE PRESIDENT'S MOTHER,
MRS. JAMES ROOSEVELT, LEAVING THE POLLING PLACE AT HYDE PARK,
N. Y., NOVEMBER, 1938.

MRS. ROOSEVELT AND PRESIDENT ROOSEVELT BEING INTERVIEWED AT
WARM SPRINGS, GEORGIA, NOVEMBER, 1938.

PRESIDENT ROOSEVELT SIGNS DEED FOR GIFT OF PROPERTY FOR THE
MEMORIAL LIBRARY AT HYDE PARK, 1939, AS MRS. ROOSEVELT AND
FRANK WALKER LOOK ON.

PRESIDENT ROOSEVELT, WITH MRS. ROOSEVELT, LAYING THE CORNER-
STONE FOR THE FRANKLIN D. ROOSEVELT MEMORIAL LIBRARY, NOVEM-
BER, 1939.

(Acme)

FROM LEFT TO RIGHT: MRS. ROOSEVELT, CROWN PRINCE OLAF OF NORWAY,
MRS. JAMES ROOSEVELT, CROWN PRINCESS MARTA AND PRESIDENT ROOSE-
VELT, SEATED ON THE PORCH OF THE ROOSEVELT HOME AT HYDE PARK,
MAY, 1939.

(Acme)

RECEIVING THE KING AND QUEEN OF ENGLAND AT UNION STATION, WASH-
INGTON, D. C., JUNE, 1939. FROM LEFT TO RIGHT: KING GEORGE, PRESI-
DENT ROOSEVELT, GENERAL EDWIN M. WATSON, MRS. ROOSEVELT, QUEEN
ELIZABETH.

(Acme)

QUEEN ELIZABETH WITH MRS. ROOSEVELT IN WASHINGTON, JUNE, 1939.

(Acme)

PRESIDENT AND MRS. ROOSEVELT WAVING GOODBYE TO KING GEORGE AND
QUEEN ELIZABETH FROM THE PLATFORM OF THE HYDE PARK STATION, AS
THE ROYAL COUPLE LEFT FOR CANADA, JUNE, 1939.

(Bachrach)

Mrs. Roosevelt in the Monroe Room at the
White House

(Bachrach)

Mrs. Roosevelt, on the south portico of the
White House, after returning from a ride in
1940.

Anna's divorces, feeling that they would react unfavorably on my husband's political career. In each case, Franklin had done what he could to prevent the divorce, but when he was convinced that the children had made up their minds after careful reflection, it never occurred to him to suggest that they should subordinate their lives to his interest. He said that he thought a man in politics stood or fell by the results of his policies; that what the children did or did not do affected their lives, and that he did not consider that their lives should be tied to his political interests. He was quite right. I think the majority of the people in the country regretted that he had to undergo any anxiety of this kind, but realized that his family was much like other families. And many families, during this period of uncertainty, experienced stresses and strains which were, perhaps, a part of the times.

It is possible that sometimes Franklin carried his disregard of criticism too far. I was appalled when, in 1937, he asked James to come to Washington as one of his secretaries. James of course was delighted, for he had always been interested in politics and thought the opportunity to help his father a great chance to learn much and be really useful in the administration. I, however, could foresee the attacks that would be made on his father for appointing him, and on James himself, and I could imagine all kinds of ways in which, through his necessarily political activities, he might get himself and his father into trouble. I protested vehemently to Franklin and told him he was selfish to bring James down. I talked to James and tried to persuade him not to come, but he could see no objections. Finally I was silenced by my husband's saying to me: "Why should I be deprived of my eldest son's help and of the pleasure of having him with me just because I am the president?" It did seem hard, and what he said had a point. Nevertheless, I was unhappy, and I think my fears were justified by what actually happened.

Jimmy did a good job and it meant a great deal to Franklin to have him, but he was more vulnerable to the jealousies and rivalries than were the other secretaries, and he did get into trouble when he began to work with people in Congress. As a result of the work and anxiety, he developed ulcers of the stomach and eventually had to go out to the Mayo Brothers hospital for an operation. Franklin, with his usual necessary entourage, arrived the morning of the operation. He was very calm, as he usually was in a crisis, and chatted as though nothing were on his mind. I can be calm and quiet, but it takes all the discipline I have acquired in life to keep on talking and smiling and to concentrate on the conversation addressed to me. I want to be left alone while I store up fortitude for what I fear may be a blow of fate. However, I have learned to feel one way inside at such times and outwardly to go on like an automaton. I still remember waiting through the operation that morning and then waiting some more until the doctors came with the laboratory report and said nothing malignant had been found. They told James the nervous strain was bad for him, and he accepted their advice not to return to his duties at the White House.

In 1937, about the time he brought Jimmy to Washington, Franklin became much troubled over the decisions that the Supreme Court was rendering. His advisers were divided, some of them feeling that it was very unwise to have any change made in the court. Franklin, felt, however, that if it was going to be possible to pass progressive legislation only to have it declared unconstitutional by the Supreme Court, no progress could be made. He also felt that people became too conservative as they grew older and that they should not be allowed to continue indefinitely to wield great power.

The defeat of the Supreme Court bill seemed to me to be a real blow to Franklin, but he spent no time in regrets and simply said: "Well, we'll see what will happen." Later he was able, little by little, to change the complexion of the court. He remarked one day that he thought the fight had been worth while in spite of the defeat, because it had focused the attention of the public on the Supreme Court and its decisions, and he felt that aroused public interest was always helpful. He had a firm belief in the collective wisdom of the people when their interest was awakened and they really understood the issues at stake.

Though I had been in complete sympathy with what he was trying to do, I used to think that he might have saved himself a good deal of trouble by just waiting a while, since it was death and resignations that really gave him the opportunity to appoint new people to the Supreme Court. However, if he had not made the fight, perhaps fewer people would have resigned.

As we neared the congressional election in 1938 I could see that Franklin was again troubled. The way he had felt about the Supreme Court was in line with the way he felt about reactionary legislators. He believed it was essential to have liberal congressmen if his liberal program was to continue. The fact that the Democratic party had a large majority had not unified it as a fighting group, but rather had divided it into factions; at times it seemed that within the Democratic party there was to all intents and purposes a group of people who might work better with the more conservative Republican party. This situation led to a division among the presidential advisers and within the cabinet, and resulted finally in what was known as the purge.

If there were political mistakes in this campaign, some of them, I think, might have been avoided if Louis Howe had been alive. After Louis' death, Franklin never had a political adviser who would argue with him and still give him unquestioned loyalty. Louis gave Franklin the benefit of his sane, reasoned, careful political analysis and even if Franklin disagreed and was annoyed, he listened and respected Louis' political acumen. Whether he ignored Louis' advice or not, at least all the reasons against the disputed action had been clearly stated and argued. Once Franklin made his decision, Louis loyally tried to help him achieve his objective, even though he might feel the methods or even the objectives were unwise.

In Harry Hopkins my husband found some of the companionship and loyalty Louis had given him, but not the political wisdom and careful analysis of each situation. Louis, as I said, would argue until he felt Franklin had seen all sides of a question. Harry would not do this. He gave his opinions honestly, but because he knew Franklin did not like opposition too well—as who does?—he frequently agreed with him regardless of his own opinion, or tried to persuade him in indirect ways. He would wait for what seemed to him an auspicious moment to bring up a subject, and if it was one he was not too familiar with, he would bring in other people to back him up with their opinions, until he felt Franklin was completely won over to his point of view. This was not as valuable a service as forcing Franklin, in the way Louis did, to hear unpleasant arguments.

One difference between the two advisers was that Louis Howe had been older than Franklin, and because he had helped him so greatly in so many ways during his early political life, could be more independent than Harry Hopkins. Franklin, in turn, shaped Harry; he widened his horizons and taught him many things about domestic politics and foreign affairs. Consequently Harry's opinion did not carry the weight with Franklin that Louis' had.

Jim Farley would argue with Franklin, but never very effectively, because his reasons for advocating a course were always those of political expediency. Ed Flynn told him the truth as he saw it and argued fearlessly but he was not always on hand. Consequently, after Louis' death, Franklin frequently made his decisions without canvassing all sides of a question.

In the main, I think that in the case of the purge Franklin would have followed much the course that he did follow, no matter what might have been said, because his basic reason was a feeling that he must have in Congress people who understood and would work for his objectives. Without such men, he knew he would have to resort to time-taking effort to persuade people against their will, using pressure to bring them into line so that the Democratic party would stand together as a fighting unit. This takes thought and time which the chief executive of the United States can well spend in other ways.

Much, of course, can be done by the vice-president, the speaker of the House, the party leaders in both the Senate and the House, and the cabinet members, if they develop strength in Congress. In the last analysis, however, the president is the one responsible for the action of his followers; when they do not follow him he feels that his leadership has been weakened. Of course, it is impossible to have one hundred per cent agreement within a party, especially when that party has a comfortable majority in Congress, but the larger proportion of it must be united to be effective.

Of course, Franklin did **not expect** Congress to go down the line on every occasion. From his life-long study of American history and from his own experience, he keenly appreciated the value of the checks and balances etsablished in our government by the Founding Fathers. He realized that the willingness of Congress to vote whatever powers were necessary to meet an emergency was not a situation it was especially desirable to perpetuate in a democracy. He knew that very often a crisis was required to get new things tried, but he was aware also that in trying them out you sometimes found that they failed. Then you knew that your methods or objectives must be modified. Franklin never resented constructive criticism from the members of Congress. What he did resent was the refusal of certain congressmen to understand the over-all needs of the country, the narrow point of view which let them pit their local interests against the national or international interest. Once crises were past, he never expected blind acceptance of his programs. He always listened to the people and wanted to get their reactions, for he was convinced of their fundamental wisdom. This conviction is, I think, the basis of true leadership in a democracy. Franklin always said that no leader could get too far ahead of his followers, and it was because he felt that Congress was close to the people that he had a healthy respect for its reaction to any of his proposals.

Franklin's activities in the campaign of 1938 were thought by many people to have been a political mistake. I am not a good enough politician to know, but I have tried here to set forth the reasons that I think actuated him. I know that when the purge failed, he did not waste time wishing he had not tried it. He never started anything without envisioning the possibility that it might be a mistake, and he was always ready to begin again when something did not work out. When, after the purge, people told him he had made a mistake, he would say: "Well, that is water over the dam now. If I made a mistake, I thought I had good reasons for what I did. Now we will try to have my past actions do as little harm as possible to the programs which we must consider for the next two years." I never knew anyone who had a more confident and hopeful attitude.

Some of the people who worked closely in the administration with my husband during this second term were brought in through Missy LeHand's efforts to find someone to help in the way that Louis Howe had. Louis himself had brought in Raymond Moley. Stanley High and Thomas Corcoran came later as close advisers, and for a time William C. Bullitt was given important positions and was frequently consulted.

I think none of them ever meant a great deal to Franklin. I also think they exploited Missy's friendship, believing her more interested in them personally than in what they could contribute to Franklin's work. In that they were mistaken; she was deeply interested in seeing that the best possible results were achieved in whatever work my husband was doing, and though occasionally someone fooled her for a time, I always waited for enlightenment to come, with confidence born of long experience.

For my part, I did not know well many of the people working with Franklin in the government. It has never been easy for me to make real friends, and since I was brought up in an age when one did not call people casually by their first names, I always remained on a more or less formal footing with most of the people around Franklin. However, in one way or another during these years I came to know a few of them fairly well.

Archibald MacLeish, the Librarian of Congress, was someone whom Franklin enjoyed, and I too had a warm admiration for both him and his wife. Justice Felix Frankfurter was also a trusted adviser. Naturally, after he went on the Supreme Court bench he could not be called upon in the same way that he had been when he was head of the Harvard Law School. I always admired Mrs. Frankfurter and thought she did many fine things, especially when during the war she took into her house a family of British children. It was not an easy thing for anyone to do.

I have said before that of the cabinet people Henry and Elinor Morgenthau were the two closest to us; and Mrs. Morgenthau and I had many interests in common. For one thing, we were both much interested in the woman's prison at Alderson, West Virginia, where a remarkable woman, Dr. Mary Harris, was the superintendent. She was doing notable work with the women, many of whom had been committed for being drug addicts or for helping their husbands to run stills in the mountains. The training was largely in housework, all of which in the prison was done by inmates, but they were given opportunities to learn to read and write. We found many women who, having come in with practically no education and no knowledge of how to live decently, were appreciative of the chance to return to their families better equipped to cope with the responsibilities of a home. Many of them, particularly the mountain women, had not only a husband but a large number of children as well.

Once when Dr. Harris told her cook that I was coming, the cook asked her how many soldiers were coming with me and if she had to prepare enough food for them. When Dr. Harris told her that no one but Mrs. Morgenthau was coming with me, the cook said: "Lawdy me, does that man in the White House trust us down here enough to send his wife alone?"

I was introduced to a very gentle-looking colored woman who was mowing the lawn, and when I asked later what her offense was, I was told she had committed a murder and was in for life. Of course, murder that is committed from an emotional impulse does not necessarily indicate criminal tendencies; it may not even mean that the person is likely to murder again. In any case, this particular woman was one of the most trusted inmates, and I never heard that she showed any further signs of violence. Years afterward I came to know quite well, and to count as a friend, a woman who had been in this prison for mailing drugs to another drug addict. She had known one of the cabinet wives, and wrote asking if she could come to see me to talk over conditions in Alderson and similar prisons for drug addicts. She pointed out to me that the sentences imposed on the prisoners were much too short to effect real cures and that the drastic measures used in abruptly removing the drugs to which they were accustomed were particularly hard on women.

On one occasion, Elinor Morgenthau and I drove in my car down into Virginia where, somewhere near Williamsburg, we met Sanford Bates, who was then head of federal prisons. He took us over a number of prison camps where he was trying to introduce industries under moderate security conditions to provide for the inmates an intermediate step between regulated prison life and the business of earning a living in normal society. We also visited the prison in Richmond and were shocked to find how poor were both the educational system and the opportunities for keeping the men busy.

I am reminded here of a story Miss Thompson tells about the time during the war when I visited one of the prisons in Baltimore with Mr. Maury Maverick who was in charge of prison industries during the war and wanted me to see the salvage work being done there. In order to fit the trip into my schedule, I had had to leave the White House very early without saying good-morning to Franklin. On his way to the office, he called to Tommy and asked where I was: "She's in prison, Mr. President," Tommy said. "I'm not surprised," said Franklin, "but what for?"

Another old friend in the cabinet was Frances Perkins, in whose work I was extremely interested. Notwithstanding the very unfair treatment meted out to her by the press and many other people— especially some women's groups—who should have known better, it was a remarkable achievement.

Harry Hopkins, of course, was still another person whom I knew well, because the appeals for help which had poured in during the early years of the depression had brought me in close contact with the people administering the relief programs. Harry threw his whole heart and all of his abilities into organizing relief on a national scale. He was a man whom I not only admired but came to have a deep trust and confidence in.

When his second wife died, Jimmy and Betsy, who had known her better than we had, were quick to take his little girl, Diana, into their home and to do all they could for her. He had a number of friends who were deeply interested in her as well as devoted to him, like Mrs. Florence Kerr and others. Not long after Barbara Hopkins' death, his own health began to worry him, and I told him that I should be glad to do anything I could for Diana. Consequently she stayed with us more and more often, as Harry also did, at first just off and on, but finally at my husband's invitation coming to the White House to live.

Later I began to see a side of Harry which I had not known before.

It is a natural development, I imagine, to seek entertainment and diversion when your life is lonely. What surprised some of us was the fact that Harry seemed to get so much genuine pleasure out of contact with gay but more or less artificial society. People who could give him luxuries and the kind of party in which he probably never before had had the slightest interest became important to him. I did not like this side of Harry as much as the side I first knew, but deep down he was a fine person who had the courage to bear pain and who loved his country enough to risk the curtailment of his life in order to be of service, after all chance of fulfilling any personal ambition was over.

Although Harry Hopkins was not so wise a friend to Franklin as Louis Howe had been, he was completely loyal and, as I have said before, he did give Franklin some of the satisfactions of companionship which had been sadly missing since Louis' death.

Another person I saw often was Aubrey Williams. He was an idealist who, I think, never lost his sense of values as Harry, in certain ways, did. A fine administrator and organizer, he was not always politically wise. On one occasion when we were both attending a meeting in Birmingham, Alabama, he said some things to the newspaper reporters which he felt so miserable about afterwards that he came to my suite in the hotel and asked if I thought he should resign. I told him I did not believe my husband would think that he had made too serious a mistake. While Franklin often wished that people would think before they spoke, he understood that it is a habit hard to acquire, and his only remark about this particular incident was: "Of course I don't want Aubrey to resign. He's much too valuable. He'll learn and this will blow over." It did.

The meetings of the Southern Conference of Human Welfare in Birmingham were attended by both colored and white people, although they were segregated in the meeting places. Aubrey and I were late at one session and dashed into the church where the meeting was being held and sat down on the colored side. At once the police appeared to remind us of the rules and regulations on segregation. I was told that I could not sit on the colored side. Rather than give in I asked that chairs be placed for us with the speakers facing the whole group. At a later meeting word came to us that all the audience was to be arrested and taken to jail for breaking one of Birmingham's strongest laws against mixed audiences. However, nothing happened and the meetings for the rest of the day went off well.

Two women of whom I am very fond and whom I am always happy to see now are Mrs. Florence Kerr and Mrs. Ellen Woodward, who worked on relief with Harry and later in Social Security, doing remarkable work in spite of the handicap of being women. Other women in government service whom I came to know and to admire were Katharine Lenroot, head of the Children's Bureau, Dr. Martha Eliot, her associate, Hilda Smith, whose life's work has been in workers' education, Mary Anderson, head of the Bureau of Women in Industry, and the late Mrs. Mary McLeod Bethune, educator and head of the Negro Youth Division of the National Youth Administration. And there were many others. I think of them all with affection and am happy when our paths cross now.

In my work with Farm Security I came to know Dr. Milburn L. Wilson very well and to have a great admiration for him as a person and as an able government official. Dr. Thomas Parran did remarkable work in the Public Health Service, on one or two occasions bringing wrath down upon his head by daring to touch on certain tabooed subjects that no one before had dared to speak of openly. By speaking out, he did a great service to our men in the military forces.

I made one or two rather fruitless efforts to work with the wives of the cabinet members outside the purely official social functions. One attempt I remember very well. I had from the first been interested in housing conditions in the District of Columbia, feeling that improved housing was basic to all other efforts for better living conditions. At one point in the early years I asked the cabinet wives whether they would come and listen to a talk by someone who was an authority on Washington housing and then go with me to see some of the alleys and slums. I suggested that it might be a good thing if they and I could leave behind us as our contribution some improvement in living conditions in the capital city.

We went on our housing trip, but I could see that they had no great enthusiasm for any contact with slum conditions. The women who drove with me politely got out of the car and observed the conditions, but those with Elinor Morgenthau stayed in the car and suggested that she report to them since "she was accustomed to seeing such conditions." When we met again I was told that their husbands took a great deal of time and that, after all, the care of her husband and her official duties were a wife's most important job. They were busy with the social life of Washington and they did not feel they could undertake any work of this kind, and besides their husbands would not approve. I never made any further effort to work with the cabinet wives on anything but our joint social duties. They were most cooperative in that field, which they felt was safe and correct.

Though I liked all these women, I never came to know many of them well. That, I think, was largely because I had reached an age when making real friends was becoming more difficult; also my preoccupation with young people and many other problems, as well as the amount of time I had to spend on my own social obligations and my mail and writing, made it difficult for me to arrange the kind of everyday contacts that might have drawn us closer together.

I have never known what it was to be bored or to have time hang heavily on my hands. It has always been difficult to find time to do the things I want to do. When I was young I read a great deal, but during these last years I have had to read so many things that those I should like to read are too often neglected. Sometimes I think it would be delightful if an afternoon or evening could actually be given to uninterrupted reading for pure pleasure. In the White House I often left a movie in order to work on my mail and went back just before the end, hoping that my guests did not know I had deserted them in between. I practically never found time to go to the movies outside the White House, and life is not very different even now. I never have time to listen to the radio except to news broadcasts morning and evening, and now and then to a program which holds some special interest.

I always saw a great many people, perhaps more than was necessary or wise, but usually they were people who for one reason or another felt I could be helpful to them and rarely people I was seeing for pure pleasure. This is not to say that I have not had a great deal of pleasure in such contacts or that I have not made some friends outside of official life in Washington. Nevertheless, business and pleasure have almost always been mixed. I would find it hard even now to separate the two!

During two winters before the war, Miss Thompson and I took a house in Florida for a month and had different friends visit us. We ourselves never stayed more than two weeks, turning the house over to some friends for the rest of the month. We always had the mail sent down, so though it was a period of greater holiday freedom than I was accustomed to, it was not a holiday in the usual sense of the word.

During these years there were a certain number of the kind of personal crises that are bound to occur in any large family and that disrupt life temporarily. For example, the telephone rang between four and five o'clock one winter morning and I recognized our son Franklin's voice saying, "Ethel and I have had an accident. We ran into the back of a car parked without lights and because of the icy condition of the roads, I was unable to stop. We are both in the hospital." They were down in Virginia and Franklin, junior, wanted me to come down and get them. I called the garage and left in half an hour. When I reached the hospital a few hours later Franklin, junior, who was then in bed, had no recollection of having called me and could not imagine how I happened to be there. He had had a concussion and his action was probably subconscious—a reassertion of the childhood habit of turning to one's mother automatically when one is in trouble.

I had had another car driven down and he and Ethel were taken back to Washington, where everything was ready for them. Mr. and

Mrs. DuPont had been notified and came down to make sure that their daughter was not really injured seriously. Fortunately they were both on the road to recovery in a short time.

I was rather well conditioned to coping with family crises; for my grandmother's code was something like that of the actors who believe that "the play must go on." It probably served me on many occasions when other people might have gone to pieces. I could not afford to do this because Franklin simply could not be worried more than was absolutely necessary. Since there was nothing any of us could do about the problems and situations that he had to face politically and in public life, we all did our best to soften any blows that were purely personal.

Meanwhile my own work had to go on regardless of anything else. When I first went to Washington I had been writing a weekly column and a page in the *Woman's Home Companion,* as well as a great many articles for other magazines. Louis Howe was then more or less my agent, but after I was in the White House, I began to get so many requests that it became necessary for me to work through a literary agent, because Louis was busy otherwise. I shall always be grateful that I affiliated with George T. Bye, who was my agent from that time till very recently. He and his wife became my friends besides, helping me in many ways. However, it was Louis Howe who kept encouraging me to write, as he had from the beginning.

The weekly column seemed a very dull affair, and finally an enterprising gentleman, Monte Bourjaily of the United Feature Syndicate, had an idea that he thought would vastly increase its interest. He said he felt sure that if I would write a daily column in the form of a diary it would be of great interest to the people of the United States, who were curious about the way anyone who lived in the White House passed their time, day by day. At first I thought it would be the most dreadful chore; but I was so dissatisfied with what I was doing in the way of writing that in January, 1936, I decided to sign a five-year contract with the United Feature Syndicate for a daily column, which would be shorter and perhaps for that reason easier to do. I felt I ought to be able to find something in my everyday activities that would be interesting to the public. From that time on I have written a column six days a week, and only once failed to get it in on time. I write Sundays through Fridays, which means that I have Saturdays off. When I go on trips I sometimes have to write a number of columns ahead, because it may be impossible to send them in in the usual way. Otherwise I write the column during the morning or at noon every day, though occasionally, if the following day looks like a very busy one, I write it in the middle of the night before. It must be in by 6 P.M. Writing this column has become so much a habit that when people remark that it must be difficult to do, I am always a little surprised. I think I should really miss what seems to my friends a difficult chore.

When I told my husband I was considering writing a daily column, he thought it would be too much to undertake with all the other work I was carrying. However, aside from groaning over what he thought would be a terrific job, he was entirely agreeable to my trying to do it. Some time later, when he was annoyed with certain columnists, he made a disparaging remark at his press conference about all columnists. One of the reporters reminded him that his wife was writing a column. Without hesitation he said: "She is in an entirely different category; she simply writes a daily diary."

The column has been written in many places and under many conditions; and it means that a portable typewriter is a permanent part of my baggage. I dictate it directly to Miss Thompson, who takes it on the typewriter; then I correct it and she makes a final copy and sends it off by wire. If Miss Thompson is not with me, it takes a little longer, because I feel that with anyone else I have to read the final copy. With Miss Thompson I never have to, since she reads it herself for errors and is familiar enough with the kind of thing I would say not to make any real mistakes. We have written the column while sitting on rocks, eating a picnic lunch, in a slowly moving automobile, on trains, in planes and on ships, once even on a destroyer. One time we were in a hotel room in rural Kentucky where there was no flat surface except the bed! All the while we were working with the typewriter on the bed and Miss Thompson on her knees, someone kept coming to the door to ask if we were through. Finding a telegraph office in order to file the copy is often as difficult as getting it written.

When I went to the South Pacific in 1943 on a five weeks' trip, I did not take anyone with me to act as secretary. Every night, after a long day of hard work, I painfully typed my own column unless I had been able to do it on a flight during the day. I learned to type many years ago but, not having had much practice, I am slow, and it took me a long time to write about what I had done during the day.

On the whole I think I have been a satisfactory contributor and not too much trouble to the syndicate. The five-year contract was renewed with a provision that after I left the White House we could drop the column if we found it was not profitable for either of us. It has proved even more profitable, however, and when I do anything of special interest, like making a trip abroad, there is always an increase in the sales. The greatest increases came during the visit of the King and Queen of England and when I went to England in 1942. But I found that even during the difficult times when newsprint has been hard to get my column has done very well. It cannot, of course, compete with some of the popular writers like Mr. Winchell, Mr. Pearson, Mr. Lippmann, Mr. Welles, Mrs. Anne O'Hare McCormick and Mr. Krock.

On one occasion I submitted my contract with the United Feature Syndicate to my own lawyer, who was not familiar with contracts of this kind. He was very funny about it; he said: "My dear, it is worse than a marriage contract. You can't get out of this one." I made this contract with Mr. George Carlin, who, like George Bye, became a friend as well as a business associate, and I decided I would trust his judgment on it. He was most helpful to me and I grew to have complete confidence in him and to admire him greatly. Through our business contact I came finally to know his family and the personal association became close and warm. Once the whole family, including a little girl who was five years old, came to visit us in Washington, providing us with one of our nicest stories about the Lincoln Memorial. The little girl stood at the bottom of the statue, looking up, and as they came closer she said to her father: "Daddy, he looks as though it would be nice to sit in his lap."

Our sadness was deep when George Carlin died in the fall of 1945. It seemed such an untimely death, for there was so much for him to do in the world. His successor, Mr. Laurence Rutman, has been more than kind, so I have been very fortunate in my contacts with the United Feature Syndicate.

The *Ladies' Home Journal* page, which I wrote from 1941 until the spring of 1949, when I moved over to *McCall's*, was an experiment which was suggested to me by Mr. and Mrs. Bruce Gould and Mr. Bye. Here again I was fortunate in having a pleasant and friendly relationship. The page turned out to be a very successful feature and is something that I really enjoyed, though I was much amused by some of the questions. Occasionally they are rude and personal, but on the whole, I think, they come from people sincerely seeking information or asking for help. At first unable to believe that people would really ask some of the questions which were sent me, I accused the editorial staff of making them up. As a result they always sent me the letters on which the questions are based. Frequently they took a number of letters which had questions on similar subjects and made one composite question.

When I was in Washington, I was often asked for information about government policies, which it was then easy for me to obtain. Now it is more difficult, though I still can get a good deal of information that other people would find it hard to get, because I have friends in such a wide field of interests and activities. When I do not know the answer to a question and cannot find it, I say so frankly.

Occasionally the magazine sends me letters from people which they do not think should be included in the questions but which they think I might like to answer personally. Usually I do.

When I left the White House I thought I would shortly have very little mail. I have less, it is true, but I still receive a considerable quantity, because people seem to think that I am still able to do things which I can no longer do, not having government agencies to appeal to. I send a number of deserving letters on to the appropriate agencies, but only if the agency becomes interested will the letter be answered. I try to answer letters which seem important, but I can no longer keep the staff to do the kind of job that I did in the White House, nor do I think it would really be valuable if I could.

CHAPTER ELEVEN

THE ROYAL VISITORS

THE ARRIVAL of the Swedish crown prince and princess in the United States in the summer of 1938 marked the beginning of a series of visits from members of Europe's royal families. It was evident that the people of Europe were deeply troubled by the general feeling of unrest and uncertainty on the continent, and were looking for friends in other parts of the world—hence their sudden interest in the United States.

The Swedish crown prince and princess were making a trip through the country to visit the various Swedish settlements, and on July first came to stay at Hyde Park, where we had a dinner for them. In May the following year, the day after a dinner and musical for the president of Nicaragua and Senora de Somoza, we entertained the crown prince and princess of Denmark at tea. In June we had another South American guest when the chief of the Brazilian Army paid my husband a visit, and later that same month the crown prince and princess of Norway arrived and came to tea. They, like the other pairs of royal guests, visited the settlements of their countrymen here, later coming to us at Hyde Park for a short time.

In each case we had a few people to meet them at dinner and a picnic at Franklin's newly built stone cottage on top of the hill. There are a number of Norwegians living near us at Hyde Park who asked to put on a show for the crown prince and princess of Norway. I shall always remember that as one of our pleasantest parties. Mrs. Nelly Johannesen, our neighbor, prepared some Norwegian dishes for the picnic and then our Norwegian neighbors sang and danced on a platform against a background of miles of rolling country and hills. Other guests who came from up and down the Hudson River to meet these young royal visitors seemed to enjoy the parties. We were to come to know Princess Marta and Prince Olaf and their children very well, for during the long years of the war, though the prince was here only occasionally, the princess with the children lived in this country.

At the time of his visit our impression was that the Danish prince was more interested in his holiday than in the serious questions of the moment, and had perhaps less realization of the menace of Hitler than we had expected of one in his position. I remember an amusing conversation I had with him about the fact that members of the government in our country could not travel incognito, as members of the royal families could in Europe when on their holidays. He seemed to regard it as an affront and an extraordinary invasion of privacy that anyone should dare to recognize you if you wished to call yourself by another name. I decided that it would be quite impossible to explain to the prince that in our country, where official positions were not inherited, people did not feel that you had changed much because you suddenly had an official position, and they were likely to expect you to behave just as you had always behaved before.

My husband welcomed these visits and I think encouraged everyone to come here whom he had any chance of persuading. Convinced that bad things were going to happen in Europe, he wanted to make contacts with those he hoped would preserve and adhere to democracy and prove to be allies against fascism when the conflict came.

That same spring the king and queen of England decided to visit the Dominion of Canada. It was quite evident that they too were preparing for the blow that might fall and knew well that they would need the devotion of every citizen in their dominions throughout the world. My husband invited them to come to Washington largely because, believing that we all might soon be engaged in a life and death struggle, in which Great Britain would be our first line of defense, he hoped that their visit would create a bond of friendship between the people of the two countries. He knew that though there is always in this country a certain amount of criticism and superficial ill feeling toward the British, in time of danger something deeper comes to the surface, and the British and we stand firmly together, with confidence in our common heritage and ideas. The visit of the king and queen, he hoped, would be a reminder of this deep bond. In many ways it proved even more successful than he had expected.

Their visit was prepared for very carefully, but Franklin always behaved as though we were simply going to have two very nice young people to stay with us. I think he gave some of the protocol people, both in the State Department and in the entourage of the king and queen, some difficult moments.

There was one person, however, who looked on the visit as a very serious affair—William Bullitt, then our ambassador to France. He sent me a secret memorandum, based on experience gained from the king and queen's visit to Paris the year before, in which all the smallest details were noted. I still keep that memorandum as one of my most amusing documents. Among other things, he listed the furniture which should be in the rooms used by the king and queen, told me what I should have in the bathrooms and even the way the comfortables on the beds should be folded! He admonished me to have a hot-water bottle in every bed, which I did, though the heat of Washington must have made them unbearable. One thing that was listed and that I was never able to find was a linen blanket for the queen's couch. Nobody I asked on this side of the ocean knew what it might be.

I always wanted to ask Mr. Bullitt whether, when he stayed in the White House, he had not found in the bathrooms some of the things he listed as essential, like soap, a glass, towels, and the like.

Mrs. Charles Hamlin presented to the White House some very lovely old English prints for the rooms to be used by the king and queen, and they still hang in there today.

One of the funny episodes of that visit arose from the concern of a firm which felt that the king and queen would not enjoy their tea unless it was made with the same kind of water that they used in London. The company had the London water analyzed and tried to reproduce it in this country, and sent me a number of bottles of it. The doctor insisted on analyzing it again, and I think it was finally decided that even if the tea did not taste so good to them it was safer for their majesties to use Potomac River water.

The Scotland Yard people had to stay in the house, of course, and outside the king's room and outside the queen's room was a chair where a messenger always sat. It seemed a little foolish to me, since their rooms were just across the hall from each other and their sitting room was down only a couple of steps. Not until 1942, when I spent two nights in Buckingham Palace and saw how large it was, did I understand the reason for the messengers. There they wait in the corridors to show guests where to go, and to carry any messages one wishes to send.

One day before the visit, I invited Lady Lindsay, wife of the British ambassador, to tea and asked her if she was being given any instructions which might be helpful to me. Lady Lindsay was an American whom I had known a long while, and we looked at things from more or less the same point of view. Her sense of humor was keen and she looked at me rather wickedly when she said: "Yes, Sir Alan Lascelles has been to stay with us and he has told us that the king must be served at meals thirty seconds ahead of the queen. He added that the king does not like capers or suet pudding. I told him we did not often have suet pudding in the United States and that I really had not expected the king to like capers. My husband sensed that I was saying something naughty and so I had to become serious and stop playing with words. I explained to Sir Alan that we rarely have boiled mutton and therefore capers were not much used in a sauce." I read her my memorandum from abroad, which amused her as much as it did me, and we parted with the promise that we would share any instructions we received in the hope that we would succeed in having everything as it should be.

For these very formal occasions we were always given beforehand a complete layout by the chief of protocol of the State Department.

To show how easy everything was made for us, I am reprinting in the appendix the one that covered the king and queen's visit to Washington.

In the White House there are in the dining room two special, high-backed armchairs, one for the president and one for his wife, and no one else ever sits in them at meals. They presented a great problem for the household on this occasion. Should only the king and the president have the armchairs? That did not seem respectful to the queen, but we could not take his chair away from the president. Finally Franklin solved the difficulty by inquiring quietly: "Why don't we buy two more armchairs identical with those we now have?" This was done and all was well.

I told Franklin that British protocol required that the head butler, Fields, stand with a stop watch in his hand and, thirty seconds after he and the king had been served, dispatch a butler to serve the queen and myself, and I inquired what was to happen about the White House rule that the president was always served first. He looked at me with firmness: "We will not require Fields to have a stop watch. The king and I will be served simultaneously and you and the queen will be served next."

Then came another serious question: Should the president sit with the king on his right and the queen on his left and me on the right of the king? Or should we follow our usual custom? This was a little more difficult, but Franklin finally decided we would follow the usual custom of the United States—the king would sit on my right and the queen at Franklin's right. The reason for this decision was that since the king and queen were going to see a good deal of us, it did not seem quite fair to box the king in between us when he had so little time in which to meet and talk with other people. Franklin later explained this to the king, who accepted every arrangement in the most charming and delightful manner.

Mrs. Helm's work for these big formal occasions was really a very serious undertaking and necessitated much running back and forth between the State Department and her office. Miss Thompson was kept quite as busy in her way, because to her office came the many letters and gifts addressed to me, sent in by people from all over the United States, to be presented to the king and queen. Others, of course, were sent to the president, and kept his secretaries busy. For those few days Miss Thompson's office was the catch-all, and it was difficult for anyone to get in or out of it.

Our preparations for the big formal dinner and the reception which was to follow provided us with considerable amusement, because most people thought we should have singers from the Metropolitan Opera, at the very least, whereas my husband and I thought we should try to give the king and queen something they would not have at home. The opera would be nothing new to them; and we thought it would be interesting to entertain them with some of the American folk arts. For the same reason we tried to give them American food while they were with us. I called in the young friend whom I mentioned in an earlier chapter, Adrian Dornbush, who had been doing some work with the Arts and Crafts section of the WPA, and much to the horror of Mr. Henry Yunge, who arranged all the regular White House musical programs for Steinway and Sons, we planned a sort of folk festival. This did not mean, of course, that we would not have some well-known artists. Lawrence Tibbett was to sing several songs; Kate Smith was to sing "The Moon Comes Over the Mountain," which was one of the things the king wanted to hear; and Marian Anderson consented to sing some Negro spirituals, besides some other songs. But we also arranged for ballad singers and dancers from the south.

My husband got his news of the Canadian trip mostly from the prime minister of Canada, who like others, hoped that this visit would be of great value to the king. In talking and writing to my husband he probably emphasized the more important aspects of the trip—the questions that they must have opportunity to discuss with the king. However, the newspaper reports, which were excellent, had many human interest stories which touched the people of our country and whetted their curiosity. When the train arrived bringing their majesties to Washington, the interest was at its height.

The secretary of state and Mrs. Hull with their party had met the members of the royal party at Niagara Falls, and accompanied them on the train to Washington. There was much pageantry about their arrival and the procession to the White House. That was something my husband always enjoyed, for he liked to put on a show. I dreaded it. At the appointed time we went down to the station and, with the government officials who were members of the reception committee, stood waiting in the president's reception room for the train's arrival. Franklin had arranged for some of the members of our immediate staff at the White House to be in inconspicuous places where they could watch this reception and take part in the procession back to the White House.

After the presentations were over, my husband and I escorted the king and queen through the Guard of Honor, which was drawn up in front of the station. The British National Anthem and "The Star-Spangled Banner" were played, and there was a twenty-one-gun salute. Then the inevitable photographs were taken and finally my husband and the king, and the queen and I got into our respective cars and started with military escort on the slow drive to the White House. There were crowds all along the way and I was fascinated watching the queen. She had the most gracious manner and bowed right and left with interest, actually looking at people in the crowd so that I am sure many of them felt that her bow was really for them personally.

Sometime before this the International Wool Growers of Australia, South Africa, New Zealand and the United States had combined and through my friend, June Hamilton Rhodes, had presented to the queen and me some thin woolen material from which we were to have dresses made to wear at our first meeting. I had mine made and wore it, but the day was so warm I took it off as soon as I could. The queen could not bear to wear hers that morning, for she was already suffering from the unusual heat which can come to Washington even in early June.

In spite of the heat, however, a light cover had been placed by her footman over her knees when she got into the car. She sat upon a cushion which I afterwards discovered had springs to make it easier for her to keep up the continual bowing. The same arrangements were made for the king.

We drove into the White House grounds by the southeast gate and in through the south entrance. Immediately on our arrival, what is known as a Diplomatic Circle was held in the East Room for the heads of all the diplomatic missions and their wives. At that time the British ambassador, Sir Ronald Lindsay, was dean of the diplomatic corps, so he presented the chiefs of missions and their wives to the king while Lady Lindsay presented them to the queen. My husband and I were not present at the Diplomatic Circle. When it was over, the king and queen went to their rooms for a few minutes of quiet before we assembled for an informal luncheon. At the luncheon besides the king and queen and my husband and myself, were Prime Minister Mackenzie King of Canada, Lady Katherine Seymour, Sir Alan Lascelles, Lieutenant Colonel Piers Leigh, Missy LeHand, James, Elliott, Franklin, junior, and their wives.

After lunch the king and my husband in one car and the queen and I in another drove about Washington. Our route was given out beforehand, so that people could have an opportunity to see their majesties. It meant, of course, that we had very little chance to talk except when we were driving where people could not line up on the sidewalks. At one point, the queen endeared herself to me by saying suddenly: "I saw in the paper that you were being attacked for having gone to a meeting of the WPA workers. It surprises me that there should be any criticism, for it is so much better to allow people with grievances to air them; and it is particularly valuable if they can do so to someone in whom they feel a sense of sympathy and who may be able to reach the head of the government with their grievances."

We visited the Lincoln Memorial, the Cathedral Church of St. Peter and St. Paul, Rock Creek Park and other points of interest. We returned to the White House in time for the king and queen to dress, and at a quarter before five, they left the White House through a line of Boy and Girl Scouts drawn up on South Executive Place, to attend the garden party at the British embassy. While they were gone, my husband rested.

The garden party created much excitement among the newspaper women, all of whom wanted to be invited and some of whom were not. Like so many things that happen in Washington, this tempest in a teapot caused almost more comment than many much more important things.

While we were out some amusing things had happened at home. The housekeeper, Mrs. Nesbitt, was harassed and when she was harassed she usually went to Miss Thompson. The fact that the many servants quartered in our servants' rooms were requiring as much attention as she had expected to give to everyone combined, was in itself a burden she found difficult to handle; and Miss Thompson was her refuge. Even in this country, where people had shed their blood to be independent of a king, there is still an awe of and an interest in royalty and in the panoply which surrounds it. The first intimation of any real difficulty between our staff and the royal servants came when the housekeeper reported to Miss Thompson that the king's valet was making unreasonable demands from her point of view and did not like our food and drink. Miss Thompson has a certain decisiveness, besides a sense of humor, so when Mrs. Nesbitt said: "What shall I do?" Miss Thompson answered: "If you think you have done all you should do, just say so." Even the ushers were not having an easy time, in spite of all their experience, for they were not accustomed to having protocol hold good among the servants. As the queen's maid was walking down the middle of the second floor hall on her way from the queen's room to the elevator, one of the ushers asked her if she would tell the lady-in-waiting that the queen wanted her to come to her room. The maid drew herself up and said: "I am the queen's maid," and swept down the hall toward the elevator. The usher, who by this time was exhausted with the heat and the extra work, could think of nothing but a bit of good American slang and said: "Oh, you're a big shot, hey?"

One story Miss Thompson will never forget concerns one of the messengers in the White House who had a yen for drawing, and who had made an almost life-sized, black-and-white portrait of the queen, which was not very good. He asked one of the maids to put it on the queen's dressing table with a note requesting her autograph and opinion of it. When the queen discovered it she evidently sent for her lady-in-waiting to remove it; the lady-in-waiting sent for one of the ushers, who immediately recognized the artist, showed it to Miss Thompson, and went off. When he came back he said: "If that man ever again utters the word autograph, it will curdle in his throat."

After the garden party the king and queen in some miraculous way managed to change and looked completely unhurried when the dinner hour arrived. I was fascinated by the queen, who never had a crease in her dress or a hair out of place. I do not see how it is possible to remain so perfectly in character all the time. My admiration for her grew every minute she spent with us.

The dinner and the party afterwards went very well, though there were a few harrowing moments. First of all, Marian Anderson was loath to sing Negro spirituals, but we discovered it in time to persuade her that people coming from England would want to hear the music that above all else we could call our own. Once we had to slow up the receiving line because the heat and the exertion of the day made the queen feel faint. Then Kate Smith thought she was going to be late for her broadcast, so we had to rearrange the program and let her sing first!

One of the young men who had been asked to sing some folk songs had been reported to the FBI as a communist or bolshevik and likely to do something dangerous. The charge was completely untrue and made by someone who wanted to be disagreeable, but when the FBI reported it to the secret service men they had to be true to their traditions and follow the tip through. When the young man came in after dinner he was "frisked" by our secret service men and then by the Scotland Yard people, and apparently was so frightened he could hardly sing. I hoped fervently he would not reach for his handkerchief during the performance, because I was sure both the secret service and Scotland Yard would jump on him.

When everyone finally got to bed that night, they must all, including the king and queen, have breathed sighs of relief.

The next morning before their majesties left the White House, they walked down a line of newspaper women and greeted them, then went to the British embassy, where they received members of the British colony, and from there to the Capitol. At the Capitol they were received by the vice-president and by Speaker Bankhead, and escorted to the rotunda where they received members of the Senate and the House. After that they met us on the U.S.S. "Potomac" and we had lunch on the way down the river. At Mount Vernon the usual ceremony was observed and the king laid a wreath on Washington's tomb. Time was growing short, and some people who had driven out there were presented to the king and queen as they hurriedly got a glimpse of the old Mount Vernon house and grounds.

On the way home we stopped at Fort Hunt to visit a Civilian Conservation Corps camp. My husband, of course, could not walk with the king and queen, but I have a vivid recollection of that visit; it taught me a great many things.

The king walked with the commandant of the camp towards the boys who were drawn up in two lines in the broiling sun. A large bulletin board had been put up with pictures of the various camps throughout the country, showing the different kinds of work done by the boys, but he did not stop to look at it then.

As we went down the long line, the king stopped at every other boy and asked questions while the queen spoke to the intervening boys. I, of course, walked with the queen. At the end of the first line, the commandant was prepared not to go down the second one, but the king turned automatically and started down. He asked really interested questions, such as whether they were satisfied with their food, what they were learning and whether they thought it would help them to obtain work and lastly, how much they were earning. He had explained to us beforehand that for a long time he had had a summer camp where boys from the mining areas of Great Britain went. He had been deeply troubled to find that many boys had no conception of doing a full day's work, because they had never seen their fathers do a day's work, many of Great Britain's miners having been on the dole for years. This spoke volumes for the condition of the mining industry in Great Britain, but the king seemed interested chiefly in the effect it had on these young men; he wanted to set up something as useful as the CCC camps in Great Britain.

When we reached the end of the second row of boys, the commandant said: "Your Majesty, the day is so hot that, while the boys have prepared their barracks and mess hall for your inspection, we shall all understand if you do not feel it wise to cross the field in this sun." The king responded: "If they expect me to go, of course I will go." That was a kind of noblesse oblige that I had not often seen in our own officials with whom I had inspected CCC camps and NYA activities and other projects.

The queen and I followed slowly across the field in the hot sun, and I saw one of the most thorough inspections I have ever witnessed. They looked at the shelves where supplies were kept, and when they heard the boys made their own equipment, they had tables turned upside down to see how they were made; they looked into the pots and pans on the stove, and at the menu; and when they left there was very little they did not know. In the sleeping barracks the king felt the mattreses and carefully examined shoes and clothes.

Finally we trudged back across the field and when we reached the bulletin board with all its pictures, the queen murmured gently in my ear that the heat had made her feel very peculiar and did I think she could return to her car. I assured her that no one would mind and we went back and sat in the car while the king examined every picture.

After arrangements were made to send him a full set of pictures, the motor cavalcade started off for Arlington Cemetery, where the king laid a wreath on the Tomb of the Unknown Soldier. Anyone who lives in Washington must be familiar with that simple and impressive monument, with the sentries always pacing back and forth. From the monument we went to the Canadian Cross, where he laid another wreath, and then back to the White House, where a tea party was waiting for us in the garden. Mrs. Helm and Miss Thompson poured, and we had hot tea for our British guests and iced tea for the Americans, if they preferred it.

My husband had carefully coached me for this party, for he said the king had particularly asked to meet the heads of all the agencies which were contributing to the recovery and doing new things in the government. As I introduced each agency head, I was supposed as briefly as possible to outline the work that person was doing, and then give the man or woman, as the case might be, about three minutes alone with the king, then take him over to the queen and present the next person to the king. I had rather dreaded trying to engineer this and wondered how I was going to condense the introduction into a brief enough explanation, but I soon found that my explanation could be very short, for the king seemed to know at once, as I spoke the name, what that person was doing, and he started right in with questions. I had expected to have a hard time keeping the line moving; I had watched my husband's secretaries struggling with him and it was impossible, if he got interested, to pry anyone away, but the king proved much more amenable. Better training, I commented inwardly, but I've since thought it was probably complete exhaustion.

The party seemed to go off successfully for all concerned. I was so impressed with the king's knowledge that at the next meal at which I sat beside him, I asked him to tell me how he knew what work every person in our government did. He told me that before he came he had made a study of the names and occupations of everyone in the government; that the material had been procured for him, and was part of his preparation for this trip to Washington.

In the course of the day, I had had a chance to tell the queen that little Diana Hopkins, aged eight, whose father they had met, was very excited because the only kind of a queen she knew anything about was a fairy queen, and therefore she felt this queen must be a fairy queen. The queen had at once suggested that Diana be in the hall as she and the king left for dinner, so Diana and I sat in the second floor hall waiting for them to come down on their way to the British embassy for the formal dinner there. The king was resplendent in his uniform, but Diana had eyes only for the queen, who wore a white, spangled dress and a jeweled crown. She looked like a fairy queen and the illusion was so perfect that when I presented Diana she curtsied to the queen and ignored the king. Both of them said a few kinds words to her and then went down in the elevator. A few minutes later Diana and I went down to the ushers' office and I turned over to Harry Hopkins a starry-eyed little girl who will never forget, I hope, what a fairy queen really looks like. She said: "Oh, Daddy I have seen the Fairy Queen."

My husband and I followed the king and queen to the British embassy and after dinner they went to their train. They were to be taken to Red Bank, New Jersey, ferried to New York City, and the next day were to visit the World's Fair, first driving through crowded New York City streets with Mayor Fiorello LaGuardia, and finally were to drive to Hyde Park.

After they left we took a train to Hyde Park, where we had the day to prepare for the twenty-four hours which the king and queen were to spend with us there. My husband always loved taking people he liked home with him. I think he felt he knew them better once they had been to Hyde Park.

The day in New York City was interesting but completely exhausting, for Mayor LaGuardia had filled every minute to overflowing. As the day advanced the king and queen realized they were going to be late reaching us; but they were not told how late they were until they actually started, whereupon the king insisted on stopping and telephoning at intervals along the way.

We sat in the library in the Hyde Park house waiting for them. Franklin had a tray of cocktails ready in front of him, and his mother sat on the other side of the fireplace looking disapprovingly at the cocktails and telling her son that the king would prefer tea. My husband, who could be as obstinate as his mother, kept his tray in readiness, however. Finally the king and queen arrived and I met them at the door and took them to their rooms. In a short time they were dressed and down in the library. As the king approached my husband and the cocktail table, my husband looked up at him and said: "My mother does not approve of cocktails and thinks you should have a cup of tea." The king answered, "Neither does my mother," and took a cocktail.

I remember how impressed I was when two of our neighbors who were presented to the king and queen made deep court curtsies. I should have found it entirely impossible to make them without falling down.

Two very startling things happened at dinner. They seem funny now, but they caused my mother-in-law much embarrassment. We had brought up the colored butlers from the White House. My mother-in-law had an English butler who, when he heard that the White House butlers were coming up to help him, was so shocked that the king and queen were to be waited on by colored people that he decided to take his holiday before their majesties came, in order not to see them treated in that manner!

Just exactly what happened to our well-trained White House butlers that night, I shall never know. My mother-in-law had had the extra china that was needed put on a serving table that was not ordinarily used, and suddenly in the middle of dinner the serving table collapsed and the dishes clattered to the floor. Mama tried in the best-bred tradition to ignore it, but her step daughter-in-law, Mrs. James Roosevelt Roosevelt, from whom she had borrowed some plates for the occasion, was heard to say, "I hope none of my dishes were among those broken." As a matter of fact the broken dishes were part of a set my husband had been given; none of the old family china suffered.

One would think that one mishap of this kind would be enough for one evening, but just after we had gone down to the big library after dinner, there was a most terrible crash as the butler, carrying a tray of decanters, glasses, bowls of ice, and so on, fell down the two steps leading from the hall and slid right into the library, scattering the contents of the tray over the floor and leaving a large lake of water and ice cubes at the bottom of the steps. I am sure Mama wished that her English butler had stayed. I wrote about this in my column at the time because I thought it was really funny, but my mother-in-law was very indignant with me for telling the world about it and not keeping it a deep, dark family secret.

Dinner had been so late that the evening was soon over and we all retired, leaving Prime Minister Mackenzie King and the king to talk with Franklin. It seemed so late when they came upstairs I felt sorry for them, but the next day Mackenzie King told my husband that the king had knocked on his door and asked him to come to his room and talk; he added that the king had said: "Why don't my ministers talk to me as the president did tonight? I felt exactly as though a father were giving me his most careful and wise advice."

The next day after we had all been to church, people from far and near came to Franklin's cottage for a picnic. I had corralled two friends to cook hot dogs on an outdoor fireplace, and we had smoked turkey, which their majesties had not tasted before, several kinds of ham cured in different ways from different parts of the United States, salads, baked beans, and a strawberry shortcake with strawberries from Henry Morgenthau's farm in Dutchess County. I had also provided a little entertainment by two American Indians. The gentleman I had not met before, but Princess Te-Ata, who is a real princess from an Oklahoma tribe, I knew well and I felt sure that her charming songs and stories would be of interest to our guests.

The people who had worked on our place for many years, as well as all our guests had an opportunity to meet their majesties, and then when the picnic and the hand-shaking were over, my husband invited the king to swim with him in the pool. I hoped the queen would also feel she could relax in the same way, but I discovered that if you are a queen you cannot run the risk of looking disheveled, so she and her lady-in-waiting sat by the side of the pool with me while the men were swimming.

In the meantime Mrs. Helm and Miss Thompson had gone to the other cottage and were trying to brew some tea to offer the swimmers. In view of the fact that practically every pot and pan had been taken to the top cottage, this job was a little difficult, but they finally managed to produce both hot and iced tea. Miss Thompson was better in the household arts than Mrs. Helm, who quite frankly said she had never done any cooking or serving in her life.

After a very quiet dinner, we took the king and queen to join their train at the Hyde Park station. Their luggage and all the rest of their party were on board. Their majesties had said good-bye to everybody and were about to get on the train when the queen suddenly came back to me and said: "Where is the man who has driven the king? I want to thank him." I found my husband's chauffeur, Monte Snyder, and the queen thanked him for the care with which he had driven. Again I thought: "How kind and thoughtful, and what training this must take."

The royal couple stood on the rear platform of the train as it pulled out, and the people who were gathered everywhere on the banks of the Hudson and up on the rocks suddenly began to sing "Auld Lang Syne." There was something incredibly moving about this scene—the river in the evening light, the voices of many people singing this old song, and the train slowly pulling out with the young couple waving good-bye. One thought of the clouds that hung over them and the worries they were going to face, and turned away and left the scene with a heavy heart.

CHAPTER TWELVE

THE AMERICAN YOUTH CONGRESS

MANY PEOPLE may have forgotten how very worried we were about the young people in our country during the early days of the depression. In that critical period growing up was surely much more difficult than it had been at any previous time any of us could remember. How deeply the young men and women were troubled was shown by the fact that many of them felt it necessary to leave their homes, because they could not find jobs and could not bear to eat even a small amount of what little food their families had.

I felt that in any efforts they made to help themselves or one another the young people should have all the consideration and assistance their elders could possibly give them. My deep concern led to my association with various youth groups and to my meeting with many young people who either were brought by their elders to Washington, or came through an organization of their own.

I believed, of course, that these young people had the right to be heard. They had the right to fight for the things they believed in as citizens of a democracy. They had come to maturity during a period in which, because of the economic situation, their political and civil rights seemed of secondary importance. It was essential to restore their faith in the power of democracy to meet their needs, or they would take the natural path of looking elsewhere to secure what seemed to them their fundamental rights and freedoms.

199

One of the most prominent young people's organizations of this unsettled time was the American Youth Congress. It spread all over the country and worked closely with other youth groups, such as the Southern Youth Council and the Negro Youth Congress.

During one of their meetings in Washington, the leaders of the AYC came to see me and told me what they were trying to do. Gradually I began to work with them, for it seemed to me a good way to find out what was happening to young people and what they were thinking. They asked me to do various things for them, and sought my advice on many questions. I tried to get speakers for their meetings, went to the meetings myself, and I also gave them some money.

In time I came to know some of them quite well. I like all young people and those in the American Youth Congress were an idealistic, hard-working group. Whether they were communist-inspired from the beginning, I have never known. After I had been working with them for a time accusations began to be made, and I had a number of the leaders come to my sitting room in the White House. I told them that since I was actively helping them, I must know exactly where they stood politically. I knew well that the accusations might be false, since all liberals are likely to be labeled with the current catchword, whatever it may be. When I was young it was anarchist, later on it was bolshevik, and now it is communist.

I told the young people in the group that if any of them were communists I would quite understand, for I felt they had grown up at a time of such difficulty as to explain their being attracted to almost any ideas that promised them better conditions. However, I felt it essential that I should know the truth. If we were going to work together, I must know where we really agreed and where we differed. I asked each one in turn to tell me honestly what he believed. In every case they said they had no connection with the communists, had never belonged to any communist organizations, and had no interest in communist ideas. I decided to accept their word, realizing that sooner or later the truth would come out.

Probably some of these young people were the ones whom a recent book has mentioned as being a matter of worry to the Secret Service.

I must say that they never worried me or my husband; we knew quite well they would do no harm to anybody but themselves.

The first direct contact that Franklin had with the American Youth Congress came after I was fairly sure that they were becoming communist-dominated. Their speeches and actions were conforming more and more closely to the party line, and a few little incidents had made me suspicious. Ordinarily, of course, Franklin had very little time to devote to individuals or even to particular groups. Now and then, however, at my request he might see some of them to discuss a particular subject. On February 10, 1940 the American Youth Congress organized a parade and a meeting in Washington, and I thought it advisable to ask Franklin to speak to them. It was arranged that he would talk to them from the south portico of the White House. It rained that day, and it was a very wet group that stood out in the south grounds, most uncomfortable, and, I am sure, expecting to be patted on the back. Instead, Franklin told them some truths which, though they might be unpalatable, he thought it wise for them to hear, so they would realize how other people, even sympathetic people, felt about their activities. Franklin's intent to be kind and understanding was evident, but he felt obliged to say some pretty harsh things about their responsibilities and attitudes towards life.

The young people were in no mood for warnings, however kindly meant, and they booed the president. Although I could see how the young people felt on this occasion, I was indignant at their bad manners and lack of respect for the office of President of the United States. I felt certain that the communist group were the principal offenders. My husband, however, took it calmly. He smiled at me genially and said: "Our youngsters are always unpredictable, aren't they?"

It was at this time that I began to know Joseph Lash, who was to become one of my real friends and stand-bys. When the leaders of several youth organizations were summoned to appear before the Dies Committee, Joe Lash was among them. He had been an organizer and executive secretary of the American Student Union. Actually he had been voted out of office by the communists, who had gained control in his own organization; but since he had not yet been replaced, there was no one else to represent the Student Union, and he was obliged to appear before the committee. I have rarely seen anyone more unhappy. It was his responsibility to defend a group from which he had just been ousted by a well-organized minority. Even after his unsuccessful fight, he felt that the majority were probably not communist. At the hearing, he took refuge in being rather flippant. This earned for him the dislike and reproof of the committee, but because I understood the situation, my respect for him was not changed.

It was a difficult period for Joe Lash. He had been close enough to the young people's problems and to the communist groups to know the appeal that communism could have in these difficult times, and he had decided that communism was not the answer. He came to know me and to trust me, but because he could not go back on the other young people, he was careful never to tell tales about them. However, on some occasions when they were with me his irritation gave me a clue to what was really going on. He would ask them why they did not tell me certain things, or would ask them pointed questions; and he often put me on my guard by his expression of sheer unhappiness.

I sat through most of the hearings of the Dies Committee, because I had heard that when they had people before them who seemed to have little influence or backing, their questions were so hostile as to give the impression that the witness had been haled before a court and prejudged a criminal. If there is one thing I dislike, it is intimidating people instead of trying to get at facts. At one point, when the questioning seemed to me to be particularly harsh, I asked to go over and sit at the press table. I took a pencil and a piece of paper, and the tone of the questions changed immediately. Just what the questioner thought I was going to do, I do not know, but my action had the effect I desired.

Because I dislike Gestapo methods in this country, I have never liked that kind of congressional committee. I do not think such methods are necessary. I doubt that they ever harm the really powerful, but they do harm many innocent people who are unable to defend themselves.

On one occasion my husband and I were given a confidential list of organizations which were considered communist or subversive or un-American, a list compiled by the FBI for the use of the Dies Committee. People who belonged to any group on that list or who had even contributed to any of them were *ipso facto* under suspicion. We found that among those listed as contributors to two or three of these "questionable" organizations were Secretary Stimson, Secretary Knox and my husband's mother, Mrs. James Roosevelt. Franklin and I got particular amusement out of the inclusion of her name; we could picture her horror if she were told that the five or ten dollars she had given to a seemingly innocent relief organization put her among those whom the Dies Committee could easily call before it as belonging to subversive organizations.

I knew of a case where the Dies Committee insisted that a young man be dismissed from government service, because they claimed he had been affiliated with a subversive organization in Seattle. The young man replied that he had never been in Seattle and that it was a case of mistaken identity. Luckily, he worked for a man who believed him, and he was able to prove the committee to be in error. If his superior had not been a fair person, the damage would have been done, and the Dies Committee would have felt no responsibility.

I once asked the Dies Committee and the FBI point blank what evidence they had on any of the young people they were talking so loosely about. They told me they had none. A recent book written by a woman in Washington states that Mr. Dies offered me information which I refused to read. The fact of the matter is that I invited Mr. Dies to lunch and asked specifically for information; he never sent the information to me or showed it to me.

The American Youth Congress, of course, was violently opposed to "imperialistic war" and any preparation for war, and when Russia became an ally of Germany their insistence on peace became more and more vociferous. Consequently, after one of their meetings I sent for their leaders and said that on foreign affairs we were evidently coming to the parting of the ways. They had condemned everything that meant help for the countries fighting Germany.

Shortly after that I invited some of the leaders to come to Hyde Park for a night and I then told them plainly that I was no longer able to work with their organization. I promised, however, to give them a small monthly contribution for their work among dispossessed share-croppers. It happened that Elliott came to Hyde Park that same evening in the summer of 1940 to tell me he was going to enlist in the air force because his conscience urged him to do so. After I had talked over some family questions with him, he joined the group and a fast and furious argument ensued—Elliott defending his position, they arguing for theirs.

After my decision to part from them, the young people of the Youth Congress accused me of having been "sold down the river to the capitalists," and some of them picketed the White House with a peace group.

When news was received that Germany had invaded Russia, however, the Youth Congress held another mass meeting and clamored for cooperation with Russia, and for greater preparation for war. They even sent me a telegram saying: "Now we can work together again." The war was suddenly no longer an imperialistic war, and the pickets were called off at the White House.

Of course, I never worked with the Youth Congress again. I could not trust them to be honest with me.

Many of these young men entered the services, and I was interested to follow their careers. As was probably to be expected, some of them had a hard time, though others got on very well. Joe Lash was one who did well, but certain of his difficulties were typical of those that attended this whole group. He was always under suspicion and was closely watched by Army intelligence. One reason for this was that earlier he had spent a short time in Spain with the Loyalists. Fighting in Spain, of course, was an outlet for many young, altogether idealistic liberals, as well as for actual communist party members. Yet service in Spain was taken to mark a young man permanently as a communist. Another reason Joe Lash was under suspicion was because he was known as a friend of mine and came often to visit us at the White House. Many people thought that knowing me was a sort of open sesame to almost anything. Actually it was often more of a detriment than a help.

NEXT MONTH

Modern Arms and Free Men

by Dr. Vannevar Bush

Russia with an atomic bomb in her hand—what does that actually mean to you, your children and your nation? Is it reasonable to fear wholesale annihilation of life and the destruction of our civilization by atomic energy or manufactured disease? The world's greatest scientist in the field of armaments answers these questions for us plainly and fully. And because his replies are forthright and expert, he dispels unreasoned fear in this book, just as a physician ends vague terror by a candid diagnosis of our physical ills.

SEE Book-of-the-Month Club *News* FOR COMPLETE REVIEW

OOK-OF-THE-MONTH CLUB, Inc.
345 Hudson St., New York 14, N. Y.

LEASE DO NOT REMIT IN CURRENCY OR STAMPS

Mr. O. C. Steede
203 28th Ave.
Hattiesburg, Miss.

November Selection
THIS I REMEMBER

    (Incl. Mailing Expense)

PLEASE NOTIFY US OF ANY CHANGE OF ADDRESS
Note: TO FACILITATE BOOKKEEPING, THE CLUB MAKES A SMALL UNI-
FORM CHARGE FOR POSTAGE AND SHIPPING EXPENSE ON EACH PACKAGE
OF BOOKS SHIPPED, NO MATTER HOW MANY BOOKS ARE ENCLOSED. THE
ACTUAL SHIPPING COST TO THE CLUB, WHICH INCLUDES BOOK POSTAGE,
CARTONS, HANDLING, ETC., SUBSTANTIALLY EXCEEDS THIS SMALL SUM

Detach this part
which bears your
account number
and return with
your remittance

YOUR ACCOUNT
NUMBER

F-423 884

NOV.

$4.04

F

PRINTED
IN
U.S.A.

BILLS PAYABLE
WITHIN 10 DAYS

As I look back over my association with the Youth Congress and try to summarize it in my mind, I am reminded that the experience was often a trying one. Certainly one of the most difficult meetings of the congress was a convention held in Washington at a time when the young people thoroughly disapproved the administration's policies. At an early session Joe Lash spoke in favor of the government's policies, and was booed for fifteen minutes before he could continue his speech.

I had agreed to speak on another day, and knew that I would be in the same position. John L. Lewis was then having one of his early differences of opinion with my husband. The Youth Congress was consequently courting him as a great labor leader and he was to speak after me. When I rose to speak, I was greeted with boos, but that made no difference to me. I waited until I could be heard and then remarked that since they had asked me to speak and I had listened to all the other speakers, I thought in return they had an obligation to listen to me. When it was over, I said, they could express their feelings in any way they chose. When John Lewis came to the platform they cheered him vigorously—probably in order to show how they really felt!

I wish to make it clear that I felt a great sympathy for these young people, even though they often annoyed me. It was impossible ever to forget the extraordinary difficulties under which they were growing up. I have never felt the slightest bitterness toward any of them and, as a matter of fact, I am extremely grateful for my experience with them. I learned what communist tactics are. I discovered for myself how infiltration of an organization is accomplished. I was taught how communists get themselves into positions of importance. I understand all their methods of objection and delay, the effort to tire out the rest of the group and carry the vote when all their opponents have gone home. These tactics are now all familiar to me. I know that no defeat is final. In fact, I think my work with the American Youth Congress was of infinite value to me in understanding some of the tactics I have had to meet in the United Nations!

CHAPTER THIRTEEN

SECOND TERM: 1939–1940

DURING THE summer of 1939 we spent a great deal of the time at Hyde Park, which I always enjoyed being able to do. My aunt, Mrs. David Gray, stayed with us for a while. My mother-in-law went abroad and our youngest son, John, and his wife, were also abroad. John and Anne had lost their first baby early in the spring, and I had taken a hurried trip to Boston to be with John and to see Anne, whose mother fortunately was with her. It is a terrible blow to any young parents to lose their first child, and I felt deeply for them both. I found myself living over again the sorrow we had all felt when my brother and his wife lost their first baby and when we lost one of our own babies at the age of six months.

The fact that John and Anne were abroad that summer made Franklin more comfortable about his mother. While he felt he could not prevent her from going abroad, he had worried a great deal when she went on these trips ever since the time she had been taken ill in Paris. This, as it turned out, was her last trip, because the war broke out in September, and she returned on the ship with John and Anne. It was a great relief to my husband and me when the family was safely back home.

Franklin's aunt, Mrs. Forbes, who lived in Paris most of the time, refused to come home, although Franklin and Ambassador Bullitt kept urging her to return. She barely got out of Paris before Hitler's army came in.

When the news finally came that Hitler's troops had gone into Poland, Franklin called me at Hyde Park. It was about five o'clock in the morning. Mrs. George S. Huntington, an old friend of mine, was staying with me at the time, and she and Miss Thompson and I could not go back to bed, for a sense of impending disaster was on us. The thing we had feared had finally come, and we seemed to know that sooner or later we would be dragged into the vortex with all the European countries. I do not think Franklin ever felt that war was inevitable, and he always said he hoped we could avoid it, but I had a feeling that once the war started, there was not much chance for any part of the world to escape it, though in the meanwhile one hoped for some miracle.

All that September day, I could not help remembering the good-bye to the king and queen and the lump that had come into my throat as they stood on the back platform of their departing train. Now their people faced the final hour of decision. I remember going over in my mind some of the things I had felt in World War I—my foreboding that my husband might leave the Navy Department in spite of being urged to stay; my anxiety when he actually did go across in the summer of 1918; my knowledge that if the war went on he would undoubtedly resign and get into active service; my thankfulness that my children were too young to be involved; and my desire to do all I could at home since I could not leave the children and yet could not help feeling I should be doing something in the actual danger zone. All the old conflicts and anxieties passed through my mind like the fragments in a kaleidoscope.

I had no idea what this war would bring. All our sons were old enough to take an active part, and again it looked as though I should be sitting the war out comfortably in Washington. You feel a kind of rebellion when those you love are in danger, or may be in danger, and you must sit safely and idly by. However, it was a long time before one by one the real things began to happen. We were to go through another election, and to begin to take in a number of refugees from occupied countries; all of us, as individuals, were to grow accustomed to the realities of war in other countries and to prepare gradually for our own catastrophe.

As I look back over that whole year of 1939, it seems to me that my husband's major efforts were bent on trying to avert total war in Europe and to awaken us here to the need for preparation. Perhaps he might have saved himself the trouble of these various efforts, yet one would not like to feel that the president of this country had not done all he could to try to change the threatening course of history. His actions during this year and the next were only a continuation of the line of action he had begun to follow as far back as 1936. Immediately after the failure of the London Naval Conference, for instance, he had secured from Congress money to construct additional battleships and air plane carriers. The following year, in his quarantine speech in Chicago, he warned the country of the worsening political situation abroad and of the dangers it held for the United States; and he tried to persuade the people that this country should make a definite and positive effort to preserve the peace. The opposition this speech aroused was so great that Franklin realized the people were not yet ready to go along with any drastic steps toward international cooperation. All through the Czech crisis in 1938 he continued his attempts to save the peace, through appeals to Hitler and the heads of other countries. After Munich, he blamed Neville Chamberlain for weakness, but said that England had let her defenses go down so much that there was perhaps nothing else the prime minister had felt he could do. To insure that our country would never be found similarly unprepared was now Franklin's greatest concern.

In January he asked Congress for funds to expand our air force and construct new naval air bases. In April, he warned the country of the approach of war in Europe and sent a personal message to both Hitler and Mussolini, appealing for a ten-year pledge not to attack or invade other countries. In late August, Russia and Germany signed their non-aggression pact. Franklin, who was on a fishing trip off Canada aboard the "Tuscaloosa," returned hurriedly to Washington and sent a peace appeal to Hitler, King Victor Emmanuel of Italy, and President Mos-cicki of Poland, urging settlement of the Danzig-Polish Corridor issue. On the following day he sent another message to Hitler. Then Hitler invaded Poland. Convinced that further peace efforts would be un-successful, Franklin on September 21 urged Congress to repeal the embargo on the shipment of arms under the Neutrality Act, which he had signed very reluctantly in 1937, at the time of the Spanish Civil War. In December Franklin appointed Myron Taylor as his special representative at the Vatican.

The letters between my husband and the Pope, which have been published, seem to me to indicate that this appointment was one of the wise preliminary steps in our preparation for war, although it created a certain amount of difficulty among some of our Protestant groups. On the whole, however, it was well received. Mr. Taylor was well known and respected, and I think most people felt that the Pope could be a potent force for peace at this time and that we should have some direct tie with him. I do not think Franklin regarded this appointment as creating a permanent diplomatic post, but he thought it a necessity during a period of emergency.

Sandwiched in with the constant preoccupation with war and the effort to prepare the country were some pleasanter duties, too, that year. On April thirtieth Franklin opened the World's Fair. I had the good fortune to visit the Fair a number of times, and have always been glad that it was held before the outbreak of war, when it was possible to have a wide participation and to see the products and the art and culture of many countries. I enjoyed the different restaurants with their varieties of foods, and still remember with pleasure dining on the terrace of the French restaurant, watching the fountains with the multicolored lights playing on them.

The day after he opened the Fair, Franklin dedicated the Rhinebeck post office, which stands next to what it is claimed is the oldest hotel in New York State, the Beekman Arms. The post office is a simple little gray fieldstone building which already looks old and as though it had always stood there. Olin Dows, the artist, a member of one of the old Hudson River families, did the murals in both the Rhinebeck and the Hyde Park post offices, weaving the history of the neighborhood into paintings that will be historically and artistically an asset to both these villages.

Franklin was interested in all the public buildings of the towns and villages around Hyde Park, and he always urged that in Dutchess County they be built of the gray fieldstone that he loved. The schools and post offices in our neighborhood are a proof of his feeling about this type of building.

During this year Franklin had persuaded his mother to deed, with him, to the United States Government a piece of their property on the Post Road. Frank Walker headed a committee, made up of a number of other friends, to collect the money to build a library at Hyde Park. The war had its influence in this, too. For a long time Franklin had felt that it would be a great advantage if the important papers and collections of a country were not all crowded together in one building. He was conscious of the fact that in case of war, the European countries would have to scatter their collections, since one bomb could completely destroy the historical records of a whole nation. In particular, he realized that Congress was never likely to give the Congressional Library sufficient appropriation for the continuing flow of public papers to be brought rapidly up to date and made available to those who wanted to study them. He also thought it would be easier to deal with a particular period if all the records relating to it were in one place. Intending to give his own papers and many other interesting things to the library, he believed he could persuade other people who had been active in the life of the period to do the same thing.

I shall never forget his pleasure and pride in laying the cornerstone of the library on November 19 that year. It was a very simple but moving occasion. His strong feeling for history added greatly to his pleasure in knowing that here, on his own land, there would be gathered in one building the record of the period of his country's history in which he had had a part.

The next year, 1940, had the disadvantage that all election years have; everything that happens seems of necessity to have a political slant. Though the war in Europe was moving inexorably on and Hitler seemed to be sweeping all before him, some people were concerned only with the effect that any move of Franklin's would have on the chances of the Democratic party for success in the next election.

Nevertheless, throughout the year he took additional steps which, though each one in itself seemed unimportant, together tended to prepare the country for the ordeal before it. In February he urged the immediate purchase of strategic war materials; in April the combat areas were defined; and in May he asked for an additional appropriation of over one billion dollars for defense. These moves were justified, since Hitler was moving fast.

Dunkirk was a sad and anxious time for us in the White House as well as for the people of Great Britain. When the full story was told, the heroism of all the people on that embattled island and the way the Royal Air Force defended the country called forth admiration from everyone in the United States. We understood the kind of courage and tenacity that Winston Churchill was beginning to put into words, words that expressed the spirit of the British people in the months following Dunkirk.

I think it was this admiration for good sportsmanship that made my husband so bitter against Mussolini when he came into the war against France. The familiar phrase, "stab in the back," which some of his advisers begged him to leave out of his Charlottesville, Virginia, speech and which he put back in on the spur of the moment, was largely a tribute to the spirit which he recognized in the people of Great Britain and which he felt the leadership of Mussolini never fostered in the Italian people.

The occasion for that speech was the commencement at the University of Virginia Law School, where Franklin, junior, was graduating. It was a curious trip: we were all there; a trip to one's son's commencement is normal; but that was not a normal and happy occasion. The times were fraught with promise of evil. Franklin's address was not just a commencement address; it was a speech to the nation on an event that had brought us one step nearer to total war.

Immediately after the speech I went to Hyde Park, leaving my husband and Franklin, junior, in Washington. I knew by that time that those who thought the war inevitable had persuaded Franklin that he could not refuse to run for a third term if he were nominated.

So much has been said about the third term issue that I can contribute only my own impressions. I never questioned Franklin about his political intentions. The very fact that I, myself, had never wanted him to be in Washington made me doubly careful not to intimate that I had the slightest preference concerning his decision on this subject.

Many people around him worried, some because they were afraid he would run, others because they were afraid he wouldn't; and the atmosphere as they came and went was sometimes rather tense. People on both sides came to me about it, but I refused to say anything, for a man is entitled to plan his own life, particularly in matters as serious as this.

Franklin particularly enjoyed the Gridiron dinner that year; he was portrayed as the Sphinx, with a long cigarette holder in his mouth. That papier-mâché bust is still in the Oddities Room of the Memorial Library at Hyde Park.

Although I never asked my husband what he himself really wanted to do, it became clearly evident to me, from little things he said at different times, that he would really like to be in Hyde Park, and that the role of elder statesman appealed to him. He thought he would enjoy being in a position to sit back and offer suggestions and criticisms. There were innumerable things that all his life he had meant to do—write on naval subjects, go through his papers, letters, and so on. He had the library at Hyde Park, and had even agreed on a job which he would take on leaving the White House. As I remember, he was to write a longish editorial or article at stated intervals for one of the large New York magazines. He had built a small stone cottage to which he could retreat when too many people came to the big house; and while he was furious when the papers called it his "dream house," nevertheless it was part of his dream.

I had, therefore, every evidence to believe that he did not want to run again. However, as time went on, more and more people came to me saying that he must run, that the threat of war was just over the horizon and no one else who might be nominated and elected had the prestige and the knowledge to carry on through a crisis.

I had been deeply troubled by the fact that I saw no one actually being prepared to take Franklin's place, and on several occasions I asked him if he did not think he should make a definite effort to prepare some one. Franklin always smiled and said he thought people had to prepare themselves, that all he could do was to give them opportunities and see how they worked out. I felt that he, without intending to do so, dominated the people around him and that so long as he was in the picture, it was very hard for anyone to rise to a position of prominence. Finally, however, I came to realize that, after all, this was something that people had had to do many times before and that no man could hand another more than opportunity.

I do not mean that Franklin did not think seriously about a successor, for he did, fully agreeing that any one had a right to aspire to the office of president. In spite of Harry Hopkins' bad health, Franklin encouraged his ambitions till his illness proved too great a barrier. I think he finally decided that Secretary Hull would be the wisest choice. In domestic matters they had not always agreed; but the future, it seemed, would take knowledge of and experience in foreign affairs, and here Mr. Hull was pre-eminent. Besides, he knew Congress, and people respected his character and integrity.

I heard many other people discussed as possible candidates, their virtues and failings clearly set forth—not always by my husband—but as the time for the convention drew nearer, I could see that it was going to be extremely difficult to have anyone else nominated. First, the Democratic party had not found anyone else it thought could keep it in office, and second, serious-minded people were worried about the war.

Before the convention actually opened it was evident that Franklin was going to be nominated and would run; I think he had been persuaded that if he were nominated, he could not refuse. I believe he did not honestly want the nomination. If he had not been nominated, he would have been completely satisfied and would have lived his life very happily; and yet when you are in the center of world affairs, there is something so fascinating about it that you can hardly see how you are going to live any other way. In his mind, I think, there was a great seesaw: on one end, the weariness which had already begun, and the desire to be at home and his own master; on the other end, the overwhelming interest which was the culmination of a lifetime of preparation and work, and the desire to see and to have a hand in the affairs of the world in that critical period.

Nothing is ever completely black or white, I decided many years ago, and sometimes one is at a loss oneself to know just how one feels.

Finally I said to Franklin: "You have made up your mind you will not go to the convention even if you are nominated but that you will speak over the radio, and that means, I hope, I do not have to go?" He said very firmly that it was his definite intention that neither he nor I should go. I told him in that case I would go to Hyde Park and stay at my cottage and get the big house ready so that when the convention was over, he could come up for a time.

Miss Thompson and I went to Hyde Park, where we were joined by one of our young friends. Life was going very placidly when suddenly one day the telephone rang. Frances Perkins was on the wire. She said: "Things look black here; the temper of the convention is very ugly. The president should come to Chicago if he wants Mr. Wallace nominated; but if he won't come, I think you should come." I told her I thought it utter nonsense for me to go, but I thought she ought to tell my husband her feeling and that he ought to go if anyone went. I felt there was nothing I could do. Miss Perkins rang off, saying she would talk to Franklin. When she called him, he told her he was not going to the convention, but that if he were nominated he wanted Henry Wallace as his running mate.

The next day Frances Perkins called me again and said that my husband had told her he would be quite willing to have me go if she felt it was essential. I said: "Franklin may be willing, but how do I know how Jim Farley feels about it? I certainly am not going out there unless he invites me. I know there is bad feeling because Harry Hopkins has been more or less running things and perhaps has not

been very tactful, and I am not going to add to the hard feelings."
She then wanted to know whether I would go if Jim asked me to, and I
said I should have to ask my husband first. After she had finished
talking, I called Franklin and told him what Frances Perkins had said
and asked him what he wanted me to do. He said: "It might be very
nice for you to go, but I do not think it is in the least necessary." I
said: "If Jim Farley asks me to go, do you think it would be wise?"
He replied: "Yes, I think it would be."

Then I waited, and later in the morning the telephone rang and
Jim Farley asked me to come out. Since he was in rather a hurry, he
asked me, when he was through, to talk to Lorena Hickok, who was
then working with Charles Michelson on publicity for the Democratic
National Committee. She told me she felt it was very important for me
to come and that Jim Farley really wanted me.

I called Mr. C. R. Smith of the American Airlines and asked him
if he were going to Chicago. He said he was going the next day and
I asked if I might go with him. He told me he would send a cub plane
for me to the Wappingers Falls airport, about fifteen miles from Hyde
Park. Then I called my husband and told him what I had done. He
said that Franklin, junior, who was staying with him during the convention, would come to New York City and go with me to Chicago.
I said that I thought that unnecessary, and we left it open.

Listening to the convention proceedings over the radio, we heard
my husband nominated by acclaim; but I, at least, felt as though it
were somebody else's excitement and that it had very little to do
with me.

The next day I went to the Wappingers Falls airport, and the little
plane landed. The pilot, who was Mr. Smith's own pilot, allowed me
to fly the plane for a while, following the Hudson River, which gave
me a real sense of exhilaration. On landing in New York City, I saw
my young Franklin coming toward me, and I must say I was very
glad to have him along. We met Mr. Smith and left immediately,
landing in the late afternoon in Chicago. Jim Farley met me at the
airfield. The newspaper women were in the airport he said, and he
asked me to see them at once. I told him I had nothing to say, but he

thought I had better see them, so I got through the interview as best I could, saying as little as possible.

Then Jim Farley and I drove alone into Chicago. On the way he told me that Franklin had not talked to him since the convention opened and had never told him who was his choice for vice-president. I was horrified to realize that things had come to this pass between these two men, because I always had a feeling of real friendship for Jim Farley. I listened while he told me why he thought that Jesse Jones or William B. Bankhead or Paul McNutt, or some other candidates, should get the nomination. He also told me that Elliott, who was a resident of Texas at that time and a member of the delegation from that state, was planning to second Jesse Jones's nomination.

I said that before anything happened he should talk to my husband. I went directly to the hotel where Jim Farley had his offices and called Franklin. I told him what Jim had said. I also told him I had just learned he had not talked to Jim and I suggested that he talk to him and tell him how he felt. I expressed no preference for any candidate; and I think the account of the convention which Jim Farley gave in his book, as far as my part is concerned, was his impression of what I said rather than what I actually said. He quoted me as saying to my husband: "I've been talking to Jim Farley and I agree with him, Henry Wallace won't do. I know, Franklin, but Jesse Jones would bolster the ticket, win it business support and get the party contributions." Jim Farley had said these things to me and I repeated very carefully what he had said, but I never expressed a preference or an opinion on matters of this kind, and I am sure I did not change my habits on this occasion.

When Jim Farley got on the telephone, my husband evidently told him that Mr. Wallace was the person he wanted. Jim argued with him rather halfheartedly and Franklin finally said it must be Wallace. He evidently felt at that time that Wallace could be trusted to carry out our policies on foreign affairs if by chance he, Wallace, found himself hurled into the presidency. Franklin's feeling then was so strong that he was willing to insist on his running mate and thereby give him a chance to prove his ability. It was then that Jim Farley said: "You're the boss. If you say so I will do all I can to nominate Wallace, but I will have to work fast." He turned to me and said he would have to get hold of Elliott, because he was about to second the nomination of Jesse Jones; that Paul McNutt was strong too, and we would have to get to the Convention Hall as quickly as possible. We drove there immediately and I could see that Jim was much disturbed.

As soon as we got to the Convention Hall he turned me over to Frances Perkins and Lorena Hickok, and disappeared. I went to my seat immediately, got hold of Franklin, junior, and told him to find Elliott, because I was most anxious that he should not nominate anyone and so appear to be in opposition to his father's desires. Elliott came over and we talked for a minute; and I found that Jim Farley had already reached him with the information, so he did no nominating.

I saw Ed Flynn and a number of other people walking about, and many of them spoke to me briefly. Suddenly in the midst of the turmoil and confusion, Frank Walker came over to me and said: "We think now is the time for you to speak."

I made up my mind that what I said would be brief. I had prepared nothing, but I decided to base my short speech on the conversation I had heard in the hotel. If Franklin felt that the strain of a third term might be too much for any man and that Mr. Wallace was the man who could carry on best in times such as we were facing, he was entitled to have his help; no one should think of himself but only of the job that might have to be done.

The only way to accomplish my aim was to persuade the delegations in the convention to sink all personal interests in the interests of the country and to make them realize the potential dangers in the situation we were facing. While I spoke there was complete silence. It was striking after the pandemonium that had existed.

Then the balloting began. Franklin, junior, and I kept tallies on the roll calls, and for a while Mr. Wallace did not do very well. The convention was decidedly out of order; the galleries were packed with special groups favoring different candidates, and confusion was rampant. Word began to get around, however, that Mr. Wallace was to be the candidate. Mrs. Wallace sat beside me. I doubt if she had ever tried to follow a roll call before. She looked very unhappy and asked: "Why do you suppose they are so opposed to Henry?" I did not have time to explain that probably most of the people had been sent in purposely to demonstrate for someone else.

As soon as Henry Wallace's nomination as Franklin's running mate was announced, I left Convention Hall, asking Mrs. Wallace to congratulate her husband for me. I drove directly back to the airfield and got on the plane. As we started to taxi down the field someone waved at us frantically. We stopped and I was told to come back, that my husband was on the telephone. He told me he had listened to my speech and that I had done a very good job. Harry Hopkins was on another wire, waiting to speak to me, and he said practically the same thing. Then I dashed back to the plane and we took off.

The next morning my car was waiting for me at LaGuardia Field and I drove straight to Hyde Park, where I found myself in time for a nine o'clock breakfast. I felt as though it had all been a dream with a somewhat nightmarish tinge. I had to come down to earth quickly, however, and write my daily column just as though the last eighteen hours had not seemed the longest I had ever lived through.

When Franklin and I next met we talked the whole thing over. I told him that he should not leave Jim so uninformed, though I realized that the rift had become deep and that he had simply hated to call him. Franklin always insisted, however, that Harry Hopkins had had no headquarters and no official authority. Harry had simply gone ahead and acted on his own. I believe it was one of those occasions when Franklin kept hands off because to act was so disagreeable to him; only when he was forced to act by the way things were going did he do so. My going out, talking to Jim, and calling Franklin forced him to say definitely what he wanted, but he never told me this in so many words. On several occasions he said to others: "Her speech was just right." I think he thought that people should know by their own feelings when they had done well.

All this was in July. The campaign really began in September. On the 2nd of September Franklin spoke at the Chickamauga Dam celebration, near Chattanooga, Tennessee, which gave him an opportunity to drive into the Great Smoky Mountains for the dedication of the National Park. He enjoyed it very much. I had been there before in the spring and had told him about the beautiful wild flowers, but on this visit the park was different though equally beautiful. On the way home we stopped at Charlestown, West Virginia, to visit a defense plant.

The next day Franklin announced the agreement to send Great Britain fifty of our overage destroyers in exchange for naval and air bases in Newfoundland and the West Indies; and about two weeks later, on September 16, he signed the Selective Service Act. Then I began to feel that war was very close. It had already come close to us personally, for Elliott had enlisted. He had had some aviation training, and hoped to get into the air force. His eyes were very bad, but triumphantly he told me that a new kind of lens which he had just acquired enabled him to take off and land an airplane, and he had his civilian-pilot's license.

A little while later he was commissioned captain and sent to Wright Field. Inevitably, he was attacked in the 1940 campaign because he had been made a captain. It was one of the many issues used by the opposition in the hope of defeating Franklin. It always seemed to me completely unfair that Elliott should have to suffer because his father decided to run for a third term, but fairness does not enter into political strategy. Franklin and I had long since learned to accept such personal attack; but Elliott was extremely bitter, because he saw other people appointed to the same rank in exactly the same way, frequently with less background and fewer qualifications than he had.

I resented criticisms of this kind very deeply for him and for our other children, but I kept telling myself that these were the things that made one stronger if one learned to take them well. It is useless to resent anything in this world; one must learn to look on whatever happens as part of one's education in life and make it serve a good purpose in the formation of character. At the same time I could be amused at the attacks on me personally, especially the large campaign buttons announcing "We don't want Eleanor either," which many women wore.

Neither Franklin nor I ever minded the disagreeable things my cousin Alice Longworth used to say during the various campaigns, though some of the people around Franklin resented them bitterly. When the social season started after the third campaign, in which she had been particularly outspoken, she was invited as usual to the diplomatic reception. General Watson, Franklin's aide, wondered if she would have the face to come; in fact, he was sure she would not. Franklin was equally sure that she would be there, so he and Pa Watson made a bet on it. On the night of the reception, when Alice was announced, Franklin looked at Pa with a grin, and said in a loud voice: "Pa, you lose!"

It was during this campaign that the "guru letters" were brought to light, and there was great excitement about the chance of their being used against Mr. Wallace. I did not know Henry Wallace well, but my feeling was that he had simply been carried away by his intellectual curiosity. He was not realistic enough to appreciate how these letters would look to people who did not have the same kind of curiosity. I think that is one of his chief troubles: he cannot keep his feet on the ground, and therefore cannot gauge the reactions of the average person. Mr. Wallace is perhaps too idealistic—and that makes him a bad politician.

When it came to Mr. Wallace's renomination in 1944, the men who went out through the country to get the feeling of the people reported back that there was a strong belief that Wallace was too impractical and wouldn't help the ticket. Franklin's faith in Wallace was shaken by that time anyway; he said that Wallace had had his chance to make his mark, and since he had not been able to convince the party leaders that he was the right person for the job, it was not possible to dictate again who was to be the candidate. Franklin had a fatalistic feeling that if there was work for him to do he would be here to do it. If not, he believed the leaders should have a man of their own choice with whom to carry on.

Franklin had intended to make no speeches in this campaign except over the radio, but he finally was persuaded to make a few. He liked Wendell Willkie very much: he never felt the bitterness toward him that he felt toward some of his other opponents, and I do not remember his ever saying anything derogatory to him in private conversation.

This does not mean, however, that he did not feel the Democratic party should remain in power. I myself thought Mr. Willkie courageous and sincere, and I liked the way he stood for certain principles.

The campaign trips that year were extremely short. On October 10, Franklin left for Pittsburgh, Pennsylvania, and Youngstown and Dayton, Ohio, returning to the White House on the 13th. On October 23 he went to Philadelphia, and on October 27 to Newark and New York City, where, on the 28th, he spoke at Madison Square Garden. On the 29th he went to Boston and returned the 31st, only to leave on November 1 for Brooklyn, Rochester, Buffalo and Cleveland. He returned to Washington on November 3 and left for Hyde Park that night. As usual, we spent election day at Hyde Park.

Franklin was always fairly confident of success, though he said one could never be sure until the votes were counted. However, this was the election he was least certain of winning, not only because Mr. Willkie was a strong candidate but because he thought the third term issue would be a greater hurdle than it proved to be. As usual, I wanted him to win, since that was what he wanted, and I would have been sorry for his sake if he had been defeated. I always knew, though, that if he lost he would go on living a perfectly good and full life, for as I have said, he was a philosophical person who accepted and made the best of whatever happened.

CHAPTER FOURTEEN

THE COMING OF WAR : 1941

THE EARLY part of 1941 seems to have moved along much as usual. In February the Grand Duchess of Luxembourg came to stay and we had the customary parties. In that month, too, Harry Hopkins was sent to England to maintain personal contact between Franklin and the British government, for Ambassador Kennedy was about to resign and the new ambassador had not been appointed. I recalled Harry's disgust with some of our career diplomats during a previous trip he had made to observe living conditions in various European countries. He had said to me on his return: "They're so busy socially that they haven't time to find out anything about working or agricultural conditions." On this trip in 1941 he himself was a semi-diplomat, and one of the objects in sending him was to convince him of what our role in the war might have to be.

Mr. Willkie came to see my husband one day and the household was so anxious to get a glimpse of him while he sat waiting in Franklin's study on the second floor of the White House that suddenly many people had errands that took them down the hall. I would have gone myself, but I didn't hear of his visit until Franklin told me of it later.

In March Miss Thompson and I went to Florida from the 6th to the 16th, while Franklin went on a cruise off the coast. I think it was the last one that he was allowed to take, because once the threat of war was really close, he was not permitted to cruise for pleasure in dangerous waters.

On the way home from the cruise he stopped at Fort Bragg in North Carolina and I met him there. The size of this camp took my breath away; it brought home to me the fact that war was drawing near.

In the midst of a short lecture trip I flew out to Los Angeles for one day, April 14, to attend the wedding of James and Romelle Schneider. On my return, I had just enough time between planes to dictate my column in the automobile at the Washington airport and send it to be filed before Miss Thompson and I took off for North Carolina. The last part of the trip was made by private plane, because I could not have kept my engagement in Charlottesville otherwise. When we arrived, relief was written all over the faces of the people waiting for us, for everyone had been nervous about my flying with a private plane and pilot.

June was a difficult month, because Missy LeHand was taken ill—the beginning of her long, last illness. However, life in the White House had to go on just the same. On the 17th, Crown Princess Juliana of the Netherlands and her husband, Prince Bernhard, came to stay, and throughout the summer we had a number of other visitors, including in August the Duke of Kent, and in October Lord and Lady Mountbatten. Later the Duke and Duchess of Windsor came for lunch with my husband, though I had to be away to keep a long-standing engagement.

In June and July I did have some pleasant interludes when I went to Campobello Island to get our cottage ready to turn over to an institute which the International Student Service was running. Four of us worked hard, but also had a very pleasant time, between June 18 and 29, and I went back twice that summer. When I went up in early July my mother-in-law, who wanted to get to her house on the island, went with me. I drove her up in my own little car and her maid and chauffeur followed with the bags in her car. Miss Thompson and I were worried about her because she did not seem very strong, and we spent two nights on the way. The day after our first night in Boston she stopped to see John and Anne's little boy at Nahant, Massachusetts, and Franklin and Ethel's little boy at Beverly. We stopped the second night at a summer place in the outskirts of Bath, Maine, and I ordered a light supper for her. I was rash enough to order lobster for the rest of us and was concerned when my mother-in-law insisted on eating the lobster as well as the light supper I had ordered. We reached Campobello with no apparent ill effects. When I went back to Campobello in August, however, I felt she really was not well, and the doctor advised her to return to Hyde Park.

Early in August, my husband, after many mysterious consultations, told me that he was going to take a little trip up through the Cape Cod Canal and that he wished to do some fishing. Then he smiled and I knew he was not telling me all that he was going to do.

I had already learned never to ask questions when information was not volunteered, and it became almost an obsession with me as the war went on. I was conscious of the fact that because I saw a great many people I might let slip something that should not be told, so I used to beg my husband to tell me no secrets. Many times it was impossible not to know something was afoot, but if I made no effort to find out what, my knowledge was pretty vague.

Franklin invited some friends to go with him for the first few days of this Cape Cod cruise, and the trip was well covered in the news. He was seen by crowds of people from the shores of the canal and then—blank! Later he himself loved to tell the story of how he changed from the presidential yacht to the U.S.S. "Augusta," which steamed up the coast and into the harbor of Argentia, where he met Prime Minister Churchill.

The story of that meeting has been told often and Franklin, junior, and Elliott, who were there, could describe their part in it far better than I. To both boys the meeting with their father came as a pleasant surprise. Elliott had already been doing exciting work. After he enlisted he had been sent to Wright Field for training and then assigned to a group going to Gander Lake Field. From long experience at Campobello Island and on salmon fishing trips with his father, he had a pretty good idea of what that part of the world would be like in April, but the boys who had never been there and went straight from their training in Florida did not realize that they were going to meet cold, snow and sleet. It was a very unpleasant experience for them. There was no flying field, so they had to start building one. One railroad train a week brought in the necessary oil for the field. There was a small Canadian camp adjoining, but nothing else in the way of civilization. These combined circumstances produced a good deal of unhappiness and considerable illness. I had some depressed letters from Elliott at that time, and he was jubilant when the commanding officer sent him down in early May or June to sit in somebody's office in Washington until he had acquired the necessary medical supplies and recreation equipment. We had a glimpse of him on that trip, and he went back feeling much better, knowing that if the boys could not get away at least they would have some kind of recreation in camp.

After that, he was with a group that did reconnaissance for emergency flying fields. They discovered a range of mountains which had not been mapped before, and had some other interesting experiences. The pictures which Elliott showed us later were some of the best I have ever seen of that part of the world.

Because he was in that area, he was ordered to Argentia in August when his father and Prime Minister Churchill met to discuss the Atlantic Charter. Elliott had no idea why he was being hauled off the job he was on and sent to Argentia, and when he saw all the ships lying in the harbor he was a most surprised young man.

The same surprise awaited Franklin, junior. Being in the Naval Reserve, he had been called into the Navy before we were in the war and was executive officer on a destroyer, convoying merchant ships to England—and a most unpleasant job it was. It can be very cold in the North Atlantic in late winter and early spring, so he had been beseeching all the family to send him warm clothes, and told tales of coming into Portland, Maine, practically encased in ice. Because of this duty, however, his ship had the good luck to be assigned to guard the president and the prime minister. Arriving in Argentia, he received word that he was to report to the commander in chief on board "such and such" a ship. He was considerably uneasy and thought to himself: "What have I done now?" It never occurred to him that the commander in chief was not Admiral King, so when he walked on board and saw his father it was a most pleasant surprise and a great relief.

On his return, Franklin seemed happy that the Atlantic Charter had been agreed upon and announced, and that he and Mr. Churchill had had the chance to begin to know and like each other. He had met Mr. Churchill before, but had not really known him. He felt that this meeting had broken the ice and said he knew now that Churchill, who he thought was typical of John Bull, was a man with whom he could really work.

The fact that he had pulled the trip off without being discovered gave him a keen sense of satisfaction. He used to chuckle as he told of the presidential yacht sailing quietly through the Cape Cod Canal for a whole day with a gentleman more or less like Franklin in size, wearing a cap pulled well down over his eyes, sitting on the deck waving. Franklin loved little mysteries of this kind, and of course the story was a perfect one for a good raconteur, which he was. He used such stories to make conversation when he did not want to talk seriously. Once the incident was all over, no harm could come from sharing it with guests.

There were times when I felt that Franklin was indiscreet: he would recount things he had said to other people, or tell about something that had happened in a cabinet meeting perhaps; and he seemed to trust his guests never to repeat what they heard at his table. However, I came to realize that he had his own reasons for doing it—it was a way of testing people—and that in any case he never told anything that could do real harm. If a story got out, he would know pretty well who had repeated it. Very often the identity of the newspaper correspondent who got the story would be clue enough, and while it might not matter on that particular occasion, it was well to know who was likely to be tempted to talk.

To appear to be on the inside and know more than others about what is going on is a great temptation for most people. It is a rare person who is willing to seem to know less than he does or who is honest enough to say: "I saw the president and he told me nothing that had the slightest significance." Somehow, people seem to feel that it is belittling to their importance not to know more than other people.

When I found people caught by this very human frailty I would remember Louis Howe, who always went on the assumption that it was better to appear stupid, because then people left you alone and you were not in danger of divulging anything you shouldn't. As the years went on I was more and more careful to know as few secrets as possible, and Miss Thompson, whose office was off the main hall near the elevator on the second floor, became practically a recluse, making it a point to tell everybody that she knew nothing about my husband's business.

Even in my press conferences I established the fairly well understood pattern that affairs of state were not in my bailiwick but were dealt with by my husband in his news conferences. Occasionally, when I was asked for my personal opinion on some matter I would give it, and later I would be told that a good correspondent could not afford to miss my press conferences because I often foreshadowed my husband's point of view. As a matter of fact Franklin and I would rarely have discussed the subject, and only when it was one on which I felt justified in expressing my own point of view did I answer questions on affairs of state. I suppose long association makes people think along the same lines on certain subjects, so these coincidences were not so very extraordinary.

After he came back from Argentia, Franklin was increasingly busy; but fortunately he decided to go to Hyde Park for the week end of September 4, because his mother, who had seemed to pick up after her return from Campobello and to be well again except for a slight cold, took a turn for the worse. On September 7, she died. It was a great sorrow to my husband. There was a very close bond between them in spite of the fact that he had grown away from her in some ways and that in later years they had often not been in sympathy about policies on public affairs.

Franklin's mother had always wanted to die in her own room at

Hyde Park and to be buried simply in the churchyard, with the men who had worked for her on the place for many years carrying the casket. Her wishes were carefully observed.

After she died we found memoranda asking us to arrange the room in which Franklin was born the way it had been at that time, moving her furniture out of the room she later occupied back into that room. We did this, of course. I think her request showed that she realized that sooner or later the house which she loved would be a museum. She had fought the idea during her lifetime and kept trying to make me promise that I would live there; nor did she see anything strange in the idea that all my children with their families should live there with me. We never gave her any promises because, while I felt that Franklin would always want to live there, I was quite sure that if he died before I did, I should never want to live in such a big house. I was realistic enough to know that I could not count on any of the children being willing to give up their homes and live with me!

The same night that my mother-in-law was dying my brother, G. Hall Roosevelt, who had a little house not far from my cottage at Hyde Park, was taken very ill. We took him to Vassar Hospital in Poughkeepsie, and the day of my mother-in-law's funeral I had him moved to Walter Reed Hospital in Washington at his insistence. Having been there for treatments made necessary by his service in World War I, he wished to go back to the same doctors.

As soon as we could after my mother-in-law's funeral was over, we returned to the White House, and the next few weeks I spent watching my brother die. He was so strong that his heart kept him alive long after most people would have peacefully sunk into oblivion, and now and then he would recognize me when I went into his room. On September 25 he died and the funeral was held in the White House. Franklin and I took his body to Tivoli, New York, to be buried in the Hall family vault there.

The loss of a brother is always a sad breaking of a family tie, but in the case of my brother it was practically like losing a child. He had come to live with us when we were first married and from then on

Franklin and I had been his closest family; whatever happened to him, in spite of his great desire for independence, he always came to us. I had watched with great anxiety a fine mind gradually deteriorate. He had such a strong physique that he was sure he could always regain his self-control, even though he voluntarily relaxed it for a while. You could never convince him that it is very hard to shake a habit you have once let get hold of you. Fundamentally, I think Hall always lacked self-control. He had great energy, great physical strength and great brilliance of mind but he never learned complete self-discipline. Whenever his responsibilities became irksome he tended to thrust them aside and to feel that it was unfair that he should be asked to make any concessions to circumstances that he did not wish to make. As a result of this attitude, his first marriage went on the rocks; while there were undoubtedly many contributing factors, I always felt that a major one was his lack of discipline and his unwillingness to compromise or make adjustments in the light of other people's needs. In fact, he saw only with great difficulty any point of view but his own and then only when his respect for a person's strength of character was deeper than his instinctive desire to attain his particular objective.

He was one of the most generous people in the world, as far as this world's goods were concerned, and when he got his first divorce he turned over everything he inherited to his wife and children and started life again for himself. He did not lack self-confidence, and where he really cared he gave great loyalty and devotion, but it was not greater than his weakness. By the time he realized that he could not stop drinking whenever he wanted to, he had been through so much that he no longer wanted to stop. He made his second wife unhappy and left her with three little girls to bring up and very inadequate material provision. I think the differences between them were not all his fault, but though it is often hard to see that there is any blame on either side, in this case his inherent weakness was again a contributing factor.

As I look back on the life of this man whom I dearly loved, who never reached the heights he was capable of reaching, I can not help having a great sense of sorrow for him, knowing that he must often have felt deeply frustrated and disappointed by his own failure to use the wonderful gifts that were his.

Hall was a warm friend to many people; he loved children and I think missed his own. As they grew older he was devoted to them, a feeling that those of them who came to know him returned. All his life his relationship to me was a close and rewarding one for us both, though it caused me many heartaches and many moments of grave embarrassment and anxiety. He did some remarkably good work in the social service field, and Justice Murphy would have agreed, I am sure, that Hall's administration of relief in Detroit at the time that the late Justice Murphy was Mayor of Detroit was a brilliant achievement. Characteristically, he lived at one time on the same allowance that was given to the relief clients, because he wished to know exactly what they had to go through. Material things meant very little to him unless he needed them for some one else; then he was impatient if he could not acquire them with great ease and rapidity.

My brother had a kind heart and a most generous spirit, and he was often exploited by people who knew how to use him. Though he could be suspicious and skeptical about people around me, his trustfulness where he himself was concerned and his desire to be helpful often got him into trouble.

Sorrow in itself and the loss of someone whom you love is hard to bear, but when sorrow is mixed with regret and a consciousness of waste there is added a touch of bitterness which is even more difficult to carry day in and day out. I think it was in an attempt to numb this feeling that I worked so hard at the Office of Civilian Defense that fall.

On September 22, a few days before Hall died, I had agreed to take charge for Mayor LaGuardia of the activities that were not strictly defense activities but allied and necessary for the protection of the civilian population as a whole. I could not have been very useful to him for the first week, but I went to work in earnest after I returned from my brother's funeral.

Elinor Morgenthau volunteered to work as my assistant. I soon found that every activity which Mayor LaGuardia did not want in his part of the program was thrust into my division. His work as mayor of New York City prevented him from giving his full time to organizing civilian defense. The few group meetings we had left me with an impression of great hurry and a feeling that decisions were taken which were not carefully thought out. Frequently heads of divisions, including myself, were unable to discuss with him some of the things we hoped to get settled. I could not help realizing that the mayor was more interested in the dramatic aspects of civilian defense—such as whether or not cities had good fire-fighting equipment—than in such things as building morale.

One day while I was staying in my small apartment on Eleventh Street in New York, I invited Mr. LaGuardia to luncheon with me, for there was something I particularly wanted to talk with him about. I planned a simple lunch, but in the midst of the preparations my maid, who had worked for me, off and on, for years, went to Miss Thompson completely upset and said she could not cook lunch. When Miss Thompson asked her why, she said: "The mayor, the mayor, I can't cook for the mayor." Miss Thompson reminded her that she had cooked for the president and that the mayor was an easy person to please. It took a little time and some help to get the lunch ready. After lunch the mayor, as he was leaving, said: "My wife never asks me where I have been, nor whom I saw, nor what I did, but she always asks me what I have had to eat. Today I can truthfully say I did not have too much!"

I put in many hours every day at the Office of Civilian Defense, carrying on all my own work at home by toiling late every night. In the White House someone makes the rounds every hour to see that all is well. One morning my husband said to me: "What's this I hear? You didn't go to bed at all last night?" I had been working on my mail without regard to the time, and when suddenly it began to get light, I decided it was not worth while going to bed. The man patrolling the house had seen my light under the door, heard me moving about and had reported it to the household, and some one told my husband. I did not do that very often, however.

I soon discovered that the very thing I had feared was true: that

I could not take a government position, even without salary or paid expenses, without giving ample opportunity for faultfinding to some members of the opposition in Congress and even to some of our own party people who disagreed with certain policies. I did not much mind what they said about me, but when I found that anyone I appointed was in trouble merely because I appointed him, I did mind. For instance, I appointed a young dancer, Mayris Chaney, whom I had known for some time, to develop a recreational program to be used for children in shelters in case of bombing. I had seen similar activities in Great Britain. It required a knowledge of rhythm and motion and a real understanding of children to find appropriate activities that could be carried on in the confined space of a bomb shelter. She was immediately attacked, entirely unjustly, and from the clamor that arose, one might have thought Congress considered dancing immoral. When Melvyn Douglas volunteered to do a job he was amply qualified for, he was attacked as being a communist, which was an outrageous accusation.

I hope that despite these troubles, at least the trip I made with Mayor LaGuardia the night after Pearl Harbor was helpful. If I was able to give impetus to the work on the west coast and, by the mere fact of going out there, to quiet many of the rather hysterical fears prevalent at that time, then the country benefited and the trip justified my short term of office in the OCD.

Pearl Harbor day began quietly. We were expecting quite a large party for luncheon and I was disappointed but not surprised when Franklin sent word a short time before lunch that he did not see how he could possibly join us. He had been increasingly worried for some time and frequently at the last moment would tell me that he could not come to some large gathering that had been arranged. People naturally wanted to listen to what he had to say, but the fact that he carried so many secrets in his head made it necessary for him to watch everything he said, which in itself was exhausting. In addition, anxiety as well as the dampness had made his sinus bad, which necessitated daily treatment of his nose. I always worried about this constant treatment for I felt that while it might help temporarily, in the long run it must cause irritation. Sometimes Franklin decided to eat alone in his study; sometimes he had Harry Hopkins or a secretary eat with him, or some person with whom he wished to talk privately.

There have been many accounts written about Pearl Harbor day and one or two of them vary slightly, but this fact, that Franklin did not come to lunch with us, I clearly remember. His cousins, Mr. and Mrs. Frederick B. Adams (she was Ellen Delano) and their son and daughter-in-law and their young daughter were spending the week end with us and I knew they would miss not having him there.

Harry Hopkins ate with Franklin in the study that day and there were thirty-one of us at lunch. By the time lunch was over the news had come of the attack on Pearl Harbor, but we did not hear it until we went upstairs, when one of the ushers told me. The information was so stunning that there was complete quiet, and then we took up our next occupation in a kind of vacuum. I saw my guests off, and waited till Franklin was alone to slip into his study, but I realized he was concentrating on what had to be done and would not talk about what had happened until this first strain was over. So I went back to work.

A few minutes after three o'clock the secretaries of war and navy, Admiral Beardall, my husband's naval aide, secretaries McIntyre and Early, and Grace Tully were all in Franklin's study on the second floor of the White House. They were soon joined by General Marshall and the secretary of state. Later, when my husband and I did have a chance to talk, I thought that in spite of his anxiety Franklin was in a way more serene than he had appeared in a long time. I think it was steadying to know finally that the die was cast. One could no longer do anything but face the fact that this country was in a war; from here on, difficult and dangerous as the future looked, it presented a clearer challenge than the long uncertainty of the past.

It is curious how at such times one's anxiety for the nation and one's personal anxiety merge as one goes over and over all the things that have happened and may happen. For a woman, the personal side comes more strongly to the fore. In the White House, however, I knew that the personal side would have to be subordinated, and I began to wonder whether I should go out to the west coast for the Office of Civilian Defense. That decision was made for me, at very short notice, by Mayor LaGuardia.

The afternoon wore on, and though I stayed in my sitting room and did mail and wrote letters, one ear was alert to the people coming and going to and from my husband's study. He went down to the doctor's office in the late afternoon to have his nose treated, and at seven o'clock Charley Fahey came to see him for a short time. Again in the evening he had supper in his study, with James, who was then a captain in the Marines, Harry Hopkins, and Grace Tully, and all through the evening until after midnight the vice-president, the members of the cabinet and congressional leaders kept coming in. Undersecretary of State Sumner Welles spent an hour with Franklin, and his last visitors were Ed Murrow and Colonel William Donovan, who left long after midnight.

The next day was a busy one for us all. I went to the Civilian Defense office that morning at nine o'clock as usual, but came back to the White House shortly before twelve to go with my husband to the Capitol to hear him deliver his message to a joint session of Congress. I was living through again, it seemed to me, the day that President Wilson addressed the Congress to announce our entry into World War I. Now the president of the United States was my husband, and for the second time in my life I heard a president tell the Congress that this nation was engaged in a war. I was deeply unhappy. I remembered my anxieties about my husband and brother when World War I began; now I had four sons of military age.

The occasion was such a solemn one that we tried to take everyone we could to the Capitol. Jimmy and his wife, our old friend Mrs. Charles Hamlin, who was spending some time with us, Ambassador William Phillips, Mrs. Woodrow Wilson, Harry Hopkins, Grace Tully, Robert Sherwood, Judge Rosenman, Mrs. Stephen Early, Edith Helm and Tommy, as well as the secretaries and aides, were all in the group that went from the White House to hear the message to Congress. It was a very impressive occasion, one of those occasions when a spirit of unity and strength prevailed. There was no criticism—only an acceptance of the fact that something had happened to us which as a nation we had to face.

We knew that the Pearl Harbor attack had set us back a long way, that before us stretched endless months of building up our forces. We might have to retreat, because we had been a peace-loving people and as a nation had not wanted to prepare for war. We had been denied the wherewithal to fortify our islands in the Pacific by people who backed their representatives in Congress in the feeling that Japan did not want war with us. Many believed that only our insistence on preparation for war would force Japan to make war on us. The mistakes of those who thought that way are obvious today, but before Pearl Harbor they were not so obvious, and many patriotic people honestly believed that Japan was not planning war on us. The war in China was far away, and they thought that was all the Japanese were interested in. They did not realize that we were an obstacle to the fulfillment of the Japanese schemes for complete domination in the Pacific.

In retrospect it is easy to see things that were obscure at the time. My husband had long suspected that these Japanese dreams of grandeur and domination existed. I remember his concern about Guam and the other islands of the Pacific as far back as when he was assistant secretary of the navy. His suspicion of Japan was based on his own ideas of what made the Pacific safe for us, and in all the war games in the Pacific, Japan was always the enemy. But anyone who dared to voice such suspicion would immediately have been called a war-monger. With war all about us, we still lived on an "island" where most people felt war was an impossibility. Wishful thinking is one of our besetting sins. After Franklin's message to Congress, war was a grim reality to the whole country.

From the Capitol I went straight back to the Civilian Defense office and stayed there most of the afternoon. A meeting I had arranged in the White House at which Mrs. Mary McLeod Bethune was to speak, had to be carried on without me. I got home at a quarter before six and Miss Thompson and I were at the Washington airport at ten minutes past seven, ready to start with Mayor LaGuardia to the west coast. As I was leaving, I had a glimpse of Elliott, who arrived with two air force officers, Major G. E. Dany and Lieutenant Keely, to make an overnight stop at the White House. Major Dany was the head of the navigation school at Kelly Field, Texas, and Lieutenant Keely was an instructor. Elliott was taking training in navigation and he was on a final flight before graduation. The course had been speeded up because of the war, and the men were graduated two weeks earlier than had been planned. Immediately after that Elliott went on patrol duty on the west coast.

Dinner was served on the airplane shortly after we left Washington, and the mayor went to bed rather early, because we hit an air pocket while he was eating and a whole glass of milk spilled on his suit. Fortunately Miss Thompson and I had had our dinner before we got on the plane. We were still working in a small forward compartment when they brought me a message that had been received by the pilots: a San Francisco paper had announced that the city of San Francisco was being bombed by the Japanese. I was asked to tell Mr. LaGuardia. Just before our next landing I awakened him, and he put his head out of the curtains, looking for all the world like a Kewpie. When I gave him the message, he asked me to get off when we landed and telephone the Washington airport for verification, saying: "If it is true we will go direct to San Francisco." It was so characteristic of him that I glowed inwardly. One could be exasperated with him at times, but one had to admire his real integrity and courage. I telephoned and found that it was a rumor without verification, so I went back to the plane and the mayor decided we should continue to Los Angeles. Before I telephoned I made life uncertain for the people with me. I told Miss Thompson that I would send her back immediately from the next stop if I found the west coast was being bombed, and I told Joe Lash, who was going out to speak at Occidental College in Los Angeles, that of course he should go back, for no one would want to hear lectures.

As we proceeded, we began to receive instructions. First the pilot had orders to land us at Palm Springs, but finally we were allowed to land at an almost completely deserted airport in Los Angeles. There everything was shrouded in mystery, since most airline travel had been stopped.

Mayor LaGuardia had a field day talking to everybody about fire-fighting equipment and defense preparation. As he could not go down to San Diego, I left him in Los Angeles and went without him; it meant that he was ahead of me the rest of the trip, so I got the full impact of his visits on all the officials. His complete courage and lack of fear had a wonderful effect on everyone; but I did not know and never have known how much all our plans, both his and mine, really helped, since so much equipment was lacking that they could not do many of the things that were considered essential. He did get the organizing of doctors and medical supplies started and he did a great deal to spur the reorganizing of fire departments. I talked about the other activities, going up as far as Seattle on this trip. I worked all day and traveled to my next stop by night train since no planes were flying after dark. It was a queer sensation to be on a train with all its lights concealed—even the headlight on the locomotive was dimmed—and no lights to be seen outside.

Before I left on this trip I had told Mrs. Nesbitt to order black-out curtains for the White House. Almost immediately work had begun on a shelter in the Treasury Department basement; gas masks were given to everyone and air-raid drills were held. I was glad to escape. My husband used to joke about the shelter and say to Mr. Morgenthau: "Henry, I will not go down into the shelter unless you allow me to play poker with all the gold in your vaults."

I was back in Washington by December 15 at about two o'clock in the afternoon. I had been gone seven days and had traveled and worked unceasingly. At five that same afternoon Elinor Morgenthau, and Justice Justine Polier, Betty Lindley and Anna Rosenberg, all of whom were helping Elinor, came to give me the latest news of the OCD from the office front. We discussed plans and policies and then some gossip, but I was getting hardened to gossip. Never did I have a more unfavorable press than at that time, but I did not give it much thought. I knew some day I would be out of it and if it did Franklin no harm, I had no feelings about it for myself. Franklin stayed serene and untroubled through it all.

There was gossip too about Harry's living in the White House. Some people felt that since he had not been elected to any office, he should not live there at government expense. Of course, many people have a proprietory interest in the White House and feel free at all times to speak their minds to the president and his wife; but these particular people never seemed to understand or to believe that all the food eaten in the White House is paid for by the president, as I have explained, and that therefore Harry's living there was no added expense to the tax-payers.

While I would pass such comments on to Franklin, since I felt he had a right to know they were being made, I was sure beforehand that he would pay no attention to them. I have already described how he silenced me when I told him of the criticism sure to follow if he brought James to Washington as one of his secretaries. In this instance he said: "There is a tremendous job to be done. I need what Harry has to give and I need him here in the house." From then on I simply made the necessary arrangements and never said anything more to him on that subject.

The arrangements for Harry were not always simple, since he was ill and often unreasonable and irritable. The White House staff could manage anything, however, and I've always been grateful to all of them, from the ushers and Mrs. Nesbitt down to the men and the maids, for their cooperation. Undoubtedly all of them were often tired and annoyed, but whatever was necessary was always done and on the surface all was serene.

And Harry did indeed do all—and more—that Franklin expected of him. Once the war started and he grasped the seriousness of our situation, he put the running of the war ahead of everything else. As far as he was concerned, war needs were paramount. My husband felt similarly. I, however, could not help feeling that it was the New Deal social objectives that had fostered the spirit that would make it possible for us to fight the war, and I believed it was vastly important to give people the feeling that in fighting the war we were still really fighting for these same objectives. It was obvious that if the world were ruled by Hitler, freedom and democracy would no longer exist. I felt it was essential both to the prosecution of the war and to the period after the war that the fight for the rights of minorities should continue. I wanted to see us go on with our medical problem not only in the field of military medicine but in the whole area which concerned children and young people. I thought the groundwork should be laid for a wide health program after the war. Harry Hopkins could not be bothered. He felt that money could not be diverted to anything which did not have a direct bearing on the fighting of the war. He was probably right, but I never could entirely agree with him.

After the Pearl Harbor attack all activity in the White House centered more than ever on preparations for war. The Supply Priorities and Allocation Board began its meetings, and Franklin had more and more appointments with the military people and with people like Mrs. Anna Rosenberg, who was one of his close links with labor. Next to military operations, labor was the most important consideration in our preparation for war.

The Russian ambassador came on two occasions to see my husband; and Crown Princess Marta of Norway, who must have been deeply troubled through all those days, came to gain reassurance and talk over the situation. Another visitor was Harry Hopkins' son, Robert, who was shortly to go into the service, as well as Harry's youngest son, Stephen, aged 17, who came at about the same time. This youngster was killed in the Pacific very soon after going into the service, and I always felt that his youth made it a particularly sad loss. Stephen and Robert were Harry's sons by his first marriage, which ended in divorce. I could not help feeling great sympathy for their mother, who had brought them up and now saw them swept into publicity as Harry's sons just because he happened to be living in the White House.

Seeing their sons go off to war was hard on both my husband and Harry Hopkins. Both of them would have liked to take their sons' places. They wanted their sons to do what they could for the country, but humanly they wished they could be side by side with them. I think one of the secrets of Harry's eagerness to take any trips Franklin might suggest, and Franklin's insistence on himself taking trips which he felt might be of service lay in the strong subconscious desire to share the dangers their sons were going through.

Meanwhile I continued working at the Office of Civilian Defense, organizing a youth division headed by Jane Seaver (now Mrs. James H. Russell), a very fine young worker. I also tried unsuccessfully to get the cabinet wives to take some responsibility for the hordes of girls pouring into Washington to work in the various departments.

The whole OCD episode was unfortunate. I had been reluctant to take the job and had done so only at the insistence of Harry Hopkins and another of my husband's advisers. Franklin himself was completely neutral, though he told me he thought it would help Mayor LaGuardia. When the mayor found what a controversial person I became he was appalled at having me; and I did not blame him for disclaiming any responsibility for the "dreadful" things that some members of Congress felt I had done. After the mayor resigned from the OCD I was instrumental in obtaining his successor. The mounting wave of attack in Congress finally convinced me that I was not going to be able to do a real job in the OCD, so on February twentieth, I too resigned, leaving Judge Landis a pretty prickly problem which he handled very well.

During this period Theodore Dreier came to tell me about Germany and to show me some films. He had been a reporter there, one of the last to come out. When I wrote about his visit in my column, the typesetter, thinking I had made a mistake, changed his name to Dreiser. Theodore Dreiser was very angry and wired me: "Please make correction in your column. I would not be found dead within a mile of the White House." I wrote explaining that it was not my mistake, and heard nothing more from him until after Germany attacked the USSR, when he wired me asking me to join some committee or other which he was heading. After his death his widow wrote to me that her husband had been misled and that he really did not dislike either my husband or myself!

It is history now that as soon as Prime Minister Winston Churchill heard of the Pearl Harbor attack he made up his mind to come to the United States. His trip was a "top secret" and none of us knew until shortly before he arrived that he was coming.

A few days before his visit, my husband sent for Miss Thompson and asked her whom I had invited to stay in the house over Christmas and asked also to see the list of people invited to dinner. In all the years that we had been in the White House he had never paid much attention to such details, and this was the first time he had made such a request of Miss Thompson. As I said before, he counted on my remembering to ask people. On this occasion he gave no explanation and no hint that anything unusual was going to happen, so Miss Thompson and I could only conclude that he felt a sudden curiosity.

When we learned that Mr. Churchill was coming on December 22, everyone scurried around to get ready. The Monroe Room on the second floor had to be turned into a map room and an office for the British delegation, and we shifted beds around to make room for all our Christmas guests. When I knew definitely how many of the British were going to be staying in the house on Christmas Day, I hurriedly sent someone to buy gifts for them to put around our Christmas tree. Last minute shopping in Washington was not easy—by the 23rd the shops were pretty well sold out, and I felt we did a very inadequate job.

My husband on that memorable day of December 22, saw the Russian ambassador, the Chinese ambassador and the Dutch minister, besides filling innumerable other engagements. He left shortly before six in the evening to meet the British prime minister, and they all arrived at the White House at six-thirty. We had quite a houseful, but it represented only a very small quota of those who came over with Mr. Churchill. We met for the first time the prime minister's aide, Commander P. C. Thompson and his secretary, John Martin, both of whom stayed in the house and were later to become real friends of ours. The commander was called "Tommy" and Miss Thompson had to be careful not to answer when she heard the prime minister calling him. Two Scotland Yard men and a valet also stayed in the house.

I had been asked by Franklin to have tea ready in the West Hall for our British guests, but I found on their arrival that they preferred more stimulating refreshments. We were seventeen at dinner that night, including the British ambassador, Lady Halifax, Lord Beaverbrook, Secretary and Mrs. Hull, Undersecretary of State and Mrs. Welles, and Harry Hopkins. At ten o'clock the gentlemen left us to consult together, while the ladies made conversation until after midnight, when their husbands returned a bit shamefaced to take them home. I had come back to Washington that morning on the night train from New York City and had spent a good part of the day at the Office of Civilian Defense. I had gone to the Salvation Army Christmas party, to a Catholic Charities Christmas party, and the Alley Christmas tree programs, so I had added a good deal to the already heavy official program of the day. I still remember that as time wore on that evening I suddenly caught myself falling asleep as I sat trying to talk to my guests.

The next morning, the 23rd, my husband carried on his usual program while I went to the Office of Civilian Defense, returning at half-past eleven to receive with him the office staff and to wish them a merry Christmas. How hollow the words sounded that year! After lunch at the White House I returned to the OCD, but was back at the White House in time to receive the Russian ambassador and Mrs. Litvinoff at quarter before five, and to greet a number of other people who came to tea afterwards. After a four o'clock press conference, my husband, the prime minister and the more important advisers sat down for concentrated work. At dinner we had only eleven and the evening was devoted by the men to further work.

On this visit of Mr. Churchill's, as on all his subsequent visits, my husband worked long hours every day. The prime minister took a long nap every afternoon, so was refreshed for hard work in the evening and far into the night. While he was sleeping, Franklin had to catch up on all of his regular work. Even after Franklin finally retired, if important dispatches or messages came in, he was awakened no matter what the hour, and nearly every meal he was called on the telephone for some urgent matter. It always took him several days to catch up on sleep after Mr. Churchill left.

This was to be the first Christmas without my mother-in-law and I had dreaded it for my husband's sake; but the sudden influx of guests and the increasing work made it practically impossible for him to think too much about any personal sorrow. Franklin's half sister-in-law, Mrs. J. R. Roosevelt, came down as usual, but it was difficult to believe that it was Christmas, for though Diana Hopkins was there none of the grandchildren were. On Christmas Eve I went to the usual parties for poor children in the morning, then to the OCD for a few hours, and then on to the Volunteers of America. At four o'clock my husband and I received the members of the household and their families in the East Room. The Crown Prince and Princess of Norway and their children, with Mr. and Mrs. Ostgaard and Mr. Weddell of their household, were our guests and after the household party was over we all went to see the lighting of the municipal Christmas tree in the south grounds of the White House. This was the first time that the tree had been decorated in the south grounds; always before the celebration had been held in Lafayette Square. Franklin spoke from the south portico and the usual prayers and carols were broadcast, but there was little joy in our hearts. The cold gripped us all so intensely that we were glad of a cup of tea on our return to the house.

That evening we were joined at dinner by Bernard Baruch, who is one of Mr. Churchill's oldest friends, and again the gentlemen left us to go to work after dinner. I had the Christmas stockings to fill, though there were very few, and Miss Thompson and I went as usual to the midnight service at St. Thomas' Church. I have always liked the midnight service on Christmas Eve; after a busy evening of preparation it gives one a little time to rest and think of the real meaning of Christmas from which all the giving of gifts springs.

On Christmas Day we went to the Foundry Methodist Church for an interfaith service, accompanied by all our house guests. The party included our official guests and Harry Hopkins and Diana, Mrs. J. R. Roosevelt, and Harry Hooker. We were nineteen at lunch. In the afternoon the military staffs met with their chiefs, but we had our Christmas tree at four-thirty and all the Norwegian royal family joined us augmenting the number of children. Christmas dinner that night was the biggest Christmas dinner we ever had—sixty people sat down at the table—and after dinner there was a movie and Christmas carols by visiting carolers, but the men again worked until well after one o'clock in the morning.

My friend, Mayris Chaney, was with us this Christmas for dinner and the night. The day Mr. Churchill arrived, young George Fischer, a son of Louis Fischer, the writer, had come down to spend the night, not expecting anything like the galaxy of important people whom he met in the house. When he was told that he had to wear a dinner coat he had a very difficult time trying to borrow from his friends and his final ensemble was not quite all that it should have been.

Several years earlier I had learned from Louis Fischer something about conditions in the USSR when he told me that his wife and his two sons were not being permitted to leave the country and join him in the United States. He asked me if there was anything I could do about it. I talked it over with Franklin, who suggested that since it might be unwise to do anything officially, I might ask Ambassador Oumansky to tea in my sitting room in the White House, tell him the whole story and get his reaction. I followed that suggestion and Mr. Oumansky said he would find out about the situation. However, I heard nothing from him until one day we happened to meet on the plane from New York to Washington. It was a rough flight and neither of us had any desire to talk, but just before I left the airport the ambassador came up to me and said: "The people you are interested in will soon arrive in this country."

A number of people have accused me at various times of having no sense of propriety, because frequently I had what they called "unimportant" people to meet important ones. The truth is that the "unimportant" people usually had been asked long beforehand, or had stand-

ing invitations, and when the important people came I still wanted
my friends and managed somehow to get them into the White House,
in spite of overcrowding and the evident disapproval of some members
of the White House staff. Then too, throughout the war years the
comings and goings of official people were shrouded in mystery, and
it never was as simple as it now sounds to make arrangements for them.
They arrived and they left suddenly and none of us were warned beforehand. This fact often accounted for my having conflicting engagements and for the presence of people whom I might not have invited
had I known in advance what was going to happen.

I recall that during this first visit of the British prime minister I had
invited Mr. and Mrs. Louis Adamic, Monroe Robinson, my cousin,
and several others to dinner on January thirteenth. Of course, when I
invited Mr. and Mrs. Adamic I had no idea that Mr. Churchill would
be there. At the last minute I included a distant cousin of Franklin's
and a young British girl, both of whom were working at the British
embassy, because I thought they would be interested in meeting the
prime minister. After dinner I took Mr. and Mrs. Adamic, Monroe
Robinson and Miss Thompson to the Philadelphia concert, and the
evening seemed to me of casual interest.

The reason for asking Mr. and Mrs. Adamic was the fact that I
had read a book of his: *Two Way Passage*, which I thought interesting.
Because I was always looking for new points of view to interest my
husband, I had given him the book to read also. Then when I found
that Mr. Churchill was to be our guest, I thought it would add to the
interest of the dinner if I passed my copy along to him.

No one was more surprised than I when Mr. Adamic wrote a whole
book, *Dinner at the White House*, based on this one dinner. He
seemed to think every smallest detail of the evening had some particular significance or meaning behind it. It was the supreme example of
how much can be made of very little. In the book Mr. Adamic repeated
a story which was most derogatory to the British prime minister; in
fact the whole book was anti-British and anti-Churchill. Mr.
Churchill hotly resented it and sued Mr. Adamic in Great Britain
where the libel laws are somewhat different from ours.

Of course, Mr. Adamic to the contrary, the whole evening had been a completely casual affair. That was one of the things which I found it very difficult to learn—in fact I never did learn it in all the time we were in the White House. At the end of twelve years I was still doing what I thought were casual things without ever realizing how momentous apparently they seemed to other people.

On January 1, we took the prime minister and quite a party to Christ Church in Alexandria, Virginia, for the New Year's Day service. This is the church that George Washington attended, and Mr. Churchill was much interested in seeing it. I remember quietly passing some money to my husband for the collection because I knew he rarely carried any. As I did this, I wondered whether the prime minister had the same habit, but felt sure that if he had, his aide would be prepared. When these little things are taken care of by others as a rule, it is easy always to expect them to be arranged. Miss LeHand and I always had money ready, because Franklin would often forget and be surprised when he needed it and had none. When we were not along he would borrow from Gus Gennerich or Mike Reilly of the Secret Service.

Throughout Mr. Churchill's visit, there were many consultations, and representatives of all the different branches of the government were called in—not only the secretary and undersecretary of state, Mr. Hull and Mr. Welles, but the military authorities, Admiral Emory Land, who was responsible for the development of our shipping facilities, and the leaders of Congress who spent much time with the pesident. For Great Britain, there was Lord Beaverbrook, who played an important part in public relations, Sir Arthur Salter and many others.

In these first talks which my husband and the prime minister had, they faced the fact that there was a long-drawn-out war ahead during which there would be many setbacks, and that both of them, as leaders of their nations, would have to be prepared to bolster the morale of their people. To explain to one's country that there must be a long period while the military forces are being trained and armed, during which production will be one of the most important factors, and that meanwhile people must be patient and hope at best "to hold the line," is no easy or popular thing to do.

I always had great admiration for the way in which Mr. Churchill did this. In some ways he was more blunt with the people of Great Britain than my husband ever was with us. The British people were closer to the danger and I suppose for that very reason could better understand the blunt approach.

CHAPTER FIFTEEN

THE PATTERN IS SET : 1942

ONE OF the things that bothered us most after the war began was the fact that the Secret Service insisted that the public should no longer be allowed to visit the first floor of the White House. Franklin and I, anxious to build up the public's interest in the White House, had been happy to see it gradually growing. The number of visitors had increased each year, and even though the household staff found it extremely difficult to cope with them, we liked it. At times in the spring during the last year or two before the war the routing through the house had been a real problem. Once the war began, however the Secret Service would allow no visitors. Everyone who worked in the White House, or who lived there, had to be fingerprinted and have a pass to show at the gate when he or she came in. Every expected visitor had to be listed and a note stating who he was and what he was coming for was given to the ushers, who in turn gave the information to the guard at the gate. The gates were kept locked and one could go in and out only one way. These precautions were irritating to both Franklin and me, but willy-nilly we had to conform. However, there was justification for them because the secret-service men did pick up some mentally unbalanced people who were trying to see the president. One woman who tried to get in bit the guard's thumb when he stopped her, and bit it so badly he had to have medical attention.

The last straw was placing gun crews on the roof of the house and on the wings. It seemed ridiculous. I did see a good deal of sense, however, in the order against flying over the White House. My husband approved of this too, because quite aside from the possibility of enemy aircraft, it meant he was not awakened by planes during the night. I think this would have been a good ruling even before the war, because for many people the temptation to fly a little too low over the White House was very strong. I am sure the restrictions were all necessary in spite of our objections. A man must be protected while he is the President of the United States—before and after his terms of office he can look out for himself!

That year for the first time we entertained the Cabinet members at dinner in the White House. As I explained before, in former administrations each member of the cabinet, in turn, gave a dinner for the president and his wife, but because it was so difficult for Franklin to manage steps, it was decided that in his case the cabinet would give a joint dinner each year, which was usually held at a hotel. This year, however, the secret service felt it was not safe for the president to dine at a hotel. Franklin was very much amused, and during dinner said: "What a wonderful opportunity this would be for Hitler if he could just drop a bomb on the White House and catch so many important people at one gathering. If all of us except Frances (Perkins) were killed we would have a woman president."

In retrospect, the thing that strikes me about these days is my triple-barreled effort to work with the OCD, carry out my official engagements and still keep the home fires burning. I wonder particularly how I ever managed to get in all the trips I took. At the same time my husband was having more and more meetings with the cabinet, military advisers, foreign diplomats and labor people. In one morning he saw Major-General Joseph W. Stilwell, the Greek minister and David Dubinsky.

On February 20, I put in a long day at the Civilian Defense office, ending with a party in the departmental auditorium for the staff. That was the day I resigned from OCD. I do not think I was ever happier than when the weight of that office was removed from my shoulders. Afterwards people sometimes suggested that this or that which was being done must annoy me, or that I must regret certain changes, but the truth is that once I ceased to have responsibility I never wanted to criticize anything that was done! I was glad to have turned it over to somebody else. I had done the best I could while I was there, but as long as I held a government position, even as a volunteer, I offered a way to get at the president and in war time it is not politically wise to attack the president. The episode was short but it was one of the experiences I least regretted leaving behind me. ·

The list of White House guests was interestingly varied during the first half of 1942. It seems to me that everyone we were to know well during the next few years began coming at about that time; and all the royal families whose countries had been overrun sooner or later appeared, looking for assistance. Each was given a formal dinner; whatever else they got, of course, I do not know.

One of the most interesting and peculiar visitors was Alexander Woollcott, who came to the White House in January and spent four days with us. I doubt if it would have been possible to have had Mr. Woollcott as one's guest very long in any ordinary household, because he required a good many things that the ordinary household could not easily provide. For instance, he wanted coffee at all hours, and he invited guests for meals in his bedroom or in a sitting room where he could be alone with them. My work and my engagements kept me away from the house a good part of the time, but one late afternoon I returned just as he was leaving for an engagement. As I came in the door he said: "Welcome, Mrs. Roosevelt, come right in. I am delighted to see you. Make yourself at home."

Among our other guests in 1942 were Prime Minister Mackenzie King, and President and Madame Quezon. In May, Foreign Minister Molotov came, accompanied by his interpreter, Mr. Pavlov. I was not at home when they arrived so he was given a stag dinner, but the following morning Mr. Molotov came into my sitting room with Mr. Pavlov, to have a talk with me. He talked about social reforms in his country and in mine, and he hoped that I would someday soon visit the USSR. I had already been told of an incident that had caused some quiet amusement. One of the White House valets was quite astounded when he unpacked Mr. Molotov's bag to find inside a large chunk of black bread, a roll of sausage and a pistol. The secret service men did not like visitors with pistols but on this occasion nothing was said. Mr. Molotov evidently thought he might have to defend himself, and also that he might be hungry. I liked him very much. I was impressed by Mr. Pavlov's English, which, he told me, he had learned from American students in Russia. He must be gifted with a good ear for he had no foreign accent. I think Mr. Molotov, too, could understand English, for he often began to answer questions, without waiting for the translation.

The King of Greece was with us on June 10, and on the 14th there was an impressive Flag Day ceremony in the state dining room of the White House, at which the secretary of state and the diplomatic representatives of 27 other nations were present.

I spent a good deal of time in New York City that spring, emptying our house and Mrs. James Roosevelt's. We had lived in those houses since 1908 and one can imagine the accumulation of the years. My mother-in-law never threw anything away. It was a tremendous job.

My husband had not been in either house since 1932, yet he could tell me exactly what he wanted and where it would be. That spring he spent about two hours in the houses and noticed everything that had been moved. For instance, he immediately asked me what had happened to a painting in his mother's library, which I had given to Franklin, junior. Miss Thompson and I had everything listed, and the crates and boxes and barrels were marked so the things could be stored at Hyde Park and my husband could unpack gradually. It did not all go as smoothly as we had hoped, and one or two things he later wanted especially could not be located until I had time myself to delve into the crates and boxes stored in the cellar of the house.

Mr. Churchill was with us again from the 21st to the 25th of June. The friendship and affection between my husband and Mr. Churchill grew with every visit, and was something quite apart from the official intercourse. It was evident that Great Britain and the United States would have to cooperate in any case, but the war could be carried on to better advantage with the two nations closely united through the personal friendship of Mr. Churchill and my husband. The two men had many interests in common in addition to the paramount issue of the war. They were men who loved the sea and the navy. They both knew a great deal of history and they had somewhat similar tastes in literature. It always gave my husband great joy when Mr. Churchill quoted aptly from Lear's "Nonsense Rhymes," which were among Franklin's favorites. Both of them had read much biography. My husband did not have the same interest in art, but both of them loved the out-of-doors and could enjoy themselves either in the country or in the city. Their companionship grew, I think, with their respect for each other's ability. They did not agree on all things; I heard my husband make remarks which were sometimes inspired by annoyance and occasionally by a realistic facing of facts.

I remember very well his irritation at Mr. Churchill's determination that we should attack through Greece and the Balkans. Franklin said that would mean the loss of many men, though strategically it might be a help to Great Britain and might get us to Berlin before the Russians. However, he did not think that was important and he was not going to risk so many men.

But I also remember the day Tobruk fell. Mr. Churchill was with us when the news came, and though he was stricken, his immediate reaction was to say: "Now what do we do?" To neither of those men was there such a thing as not being able to meet a new situation. I never heard either of them say that ultimately we would not win the war. This attitude was contagious, and no one around either of them would ever have dared to say, "I'm afraid." I do not mean that there were not many times when they suffered. I remember that on D Day, especially, Franklin was tense waiting for news. Even then, the only thing he said was: "I wonder how Linaka will come out." Mr. Linaka, a retired naval veteran of the First World War, had worked for my husband on his tree plantations and was now back in the navy. He commanded one of the landing craft on D Day.

Franklin knew and understood Mr. Churchill's background. He seemed to agree when I said on one occasion that I thought the time that would be the hardest for Mr. Churchill would be after the war.

The world that had existed before the war had been a pleasant world as far as he was concerned; therefore his tendency would be to want to go back to it, even though in his mind he might realize that there was no way in which one could go back to a prewar world. Mr. Churchill had acknowledged to me in casual conversation that he knew the world could never be the same. He once even said that all he wanted to do was to stay in office until he had seen the men come home from the war and until they had places in which to live.

In answer to my comment, Franklin said: "You are right. It will be hard for Winston, and I am sure that in some ways it will be easier to make Mr. Stalin understand certain things after the war is over."

My husband often said he felt sure Mr. Churchill would retire from office after the war ended, but I gathered that he expected that he and Mr. Churchill and Mr. Stalin would all still be in office for at least a short time afterward and have something to say about the policies laid down. He felt that the world was going to be considerably more socialistic after the war, and that Mr. Churchill might find it very difficult to adjust to new conditions. A remark made to him by Mr. Stalin in one of their talks stayed in his mind and I think gave him hope that there might be, after the war, more flexibility in communism, or at least in that particular communist leader, than we actually have seen so far. Franklin had been wondering aloud what would happen in their respective countries if anything happened to either Churchill, Stalin or himself, and Stalin said: "I have everything arranged in my country. I know exactly what will happen." My husband said: "So much depends in the future on how we learn to get along together. Do you think it will be possible for the United States and the USSR to see things in similar ways?" Mr. Stalin responded: "You have come a long way in the United States from your original concept of government and its responsibilities, and your original way of life. I think it is quite possible that we in the USSR, as our resources develop and people can have an easier life, will find ourselves growing nearer to some of your concepts and you may be finding yourselves accepting some of ours."

This, of course, was casual conversation, and I give it as I remember hearing my husband repeat it. It did indicate a certain amount of flexibility and encouraged my husband to believe that confidence could be built between the leaders and that we might at least find a way to live in the world together, each country developing along the lines that seemed best for it.

He felt that this would happen also in Great Britain but that perhaps Mr. Churchill might find some of these developments difficult to accept. I do not think Franklin ever thought that understanding with the USSR would be easy, but he had a real liking for Marshal Stalin himself, and when he had that feeling he was likely to believe that the impossible might be made to happen.

My husband had great confidence in his own ability to understand others and to make them understand our motives and the needs and realities of a situation. I think one of his reasons for being willing to meet with the heads of other nations outside the country, when they were unwilling to come here, was his feeling that he could convince them better by personal contact than by letter or telephone. I have heard some statesmen say they did not think it advisable for an American president to go abroad to meet with the top statesmen of the world because we nearly always got the short end of the bargain. This is a statement with which I should hate to agree; it seems rooted in a lack of confidence in ourselves. I think Franklin accepted what other men in high office said, and believed that if he kept his word they would keep theirs. But he never was prone to overlook a breach of contract, and could be extremely severe with anyone he felt was not living up to his part of the bargain.

Franklin knew and loved the British, but he understood their faults. I remember one little episode which was very characteristic of him. The secretary of the Treasury, Henry Morgenthau, junior, brought him a letter from the British chancellor of the Exchequer, addressed, with that touch of arrogance the British sometimes have, simply to Mr. Henry Morgenthau, with no official title. Mr. Morgenthau had not noticed it because he was much more concerned with the contents of the dispatches; but my husband noticed it at once and, when Henry Morgenthau brought him his answer, he said, "The substance of it is all right, Henry, but you have made a mistake." Mr. Morgenthau was embarrassed and asked, "What have I done?" Franklin said, "It should be addressed to Mr. —— with no title, just the way your letter was addressed." The next message from the Chancellor of the Exchequer was properly addressed to the Secretary of the Treasury.

I shall never cease to be grateful to Mr. Churchill for his leadership during the war; his speeches were a tonic to us here in the United States as well as to his own people. The real affection which he had for my husband and which was reciprocated, he has apparently never lost. It was a fortunate friendship. The war would have been harder to win without it, and the two men might not have gone through it so well if they had not had that personal pleasure in meeting and confidence in each other's integrity and ability.

The day before Mr. Churchill left in June, 1942, young King Peter of Yugoslavia came to the White House and afterwards Franklin said to me: "That young man should forget that he is a king and go to work. In the long run he would be better off." I think of that now when I see him with his wife and child. Waiting around for a throne is not really a very satisfactory business.

That spring we had Crown Princess Marta and her children and household at Hyde Park. During the war she usually spent a week or more with us each spring and autumn on her way to some place for the summer or back to Washington for the winter. We came, for that reason, to know them all very well and I shall never forget some of the things I learned about the bringing up of royal children. Prince Haarold seemed devoid of fear, and though he was frail when he first came, I can remember his swimming when the water was extremely cold. I thought he ought to come out and get warm, but I was told that the water in Norway was colder and that he must become accustomed to the cold.

So much was happening in this period that events of a personal nature were almost swamped. One of the saddest occurred at the end of June when Mr. Henry Parish, who had been more than kind to me all my life, died very suddenly of a heart attack. The next day I made a hurried trip on the night train to see Mrs. Parish, who is my cousin and godmother, and returned to Washington to keep some engagements there, then took the night train again to attend the funeral in

New York City and to go to Tivoli, New York, for the interment in the old churchyard which was near the church the Hall family all attended.

The names of the people who came to see me that year recall a great many activities. For instance, Charles Taussig, who did so much for my husband in the Caribbean area, came often, as well as John Ihlder, whose lasting monument will be the improvement in the alleys and housing in Washington; Clarence Pickett, of the American Friends Service Committee, who helped me in many ways and introduced me to many enterprises that were of value to the people as a whole; and Congresswoman Mary Norton. I also came to know a number of labor leaders, such as Daniel Tobin, Philip Murray, William Green, Sidney Hillman, and David Dubinsky, as well as some of the younger men, like James Carey and Walter Reuther, who were coming rapidly to the fore in the labor movement. Dr. Will Alexander, in his work for better race relations, was helping and teaching me many things. Bernard Baruch, our old friend, will always have my gratitude for his advice and help in many enterprises in which I was interested. No amount of prodding by other people ever made Mr. Baruch feel hurt or slighted, and he was always ready to perform any service that was asked of him. I think he is one of the wisest and most generous people I have ever known, and he never forgets or neglects a friend.

One of the guests who gave my husband and me the greatest pleasure was John Golden, who always went to any amount of trouble to put on a performance or to find something he thought Franklin would enjoy. Franklin once told him that the first play he had ever seen was "The Black Crook," which he had stolen away to see without the permission of his parents. John Golden found one of the original copies of the play and had it beautifully bound for him, which gave Franklin real pleasure. He also did a tremendous amount of work for the servicemen, getting them free tickets for plays and movies, giving prizes for the best plays written by enlisted men, and putting on a show, the proceeds of which went to the Army and Navy Relief.

In the month of June we began to see a good deal of Louise Macy, and finally Harry Hopkins told me what he had already told Franklin

—that he was going to be married to her. He said that Franklin had asked them both to live at the White House, and asked me how I would feel about it. Of course, I felt I had to talk it over with my husband. I went to Franklin and asked him whether he had thought through what it would mean to have a married couple, plus Diana, staying in the White House, and whether he realized what it would mean to them? It seemed to me very hard on them to be obliged to start their married life in someone else's house, even though that house happened to be the White House. Franklin said finally that the most important thing in the world at that time was the conduct of the war and that it was absolutely necessary that Harry be in the house. That settled that; and I want to say here that Louise managed what must have been a difficult situation extraordinarily well.

They were married in the White House on July 30, at noon. There was a very small party—just a few members of both families. We had a small luncheon and saw them off at half-past two.

Louise had been a nurse's aid in New York City and continued her work in Washington, which meant she was out of the White House very early every morning, and returned late in the afternoon. In spite of this work she managed to establish a close relationship with Diana and to change an almost waiflike child, hungry for affection, into a child who really felt she had a family and the security of love. It was an extraordinary accomplishment. When they moved to a house of their own, it was touching to see how much Diana enjoyed her new sense of security.

Living in the White House, of course, was quite different from living in any other house. There was no friction from too close contact, such as there would have been in any private house. The ushers and the staff took care of the visitors' needs; and while I met Louise occasionally in the hall as we both went our busy ways, and we saw each other at dinner when we wanted to, life was no more complicated than if we had been living in separate houses.

I did not try to develop any great intimacy—in fact, I was much amused to find that someone who came to stay in the house had asked more questions and knew more about Louise than I ever knew in all the time she lived with us. As I said before, by this time I had come to feel that there were sides to Harry Hopkins which were alien to me and that perhaps we could get along better if we did not build up too much intimacy.

I had always been careful whenever any children were left in my care not to build up in them a feeling of dependence on me, because that relationship should exist only between parents and children, so long as the parents are alive. Neither with my cousin, Elizabeth Henderson, who stayed with us during the school year, nor with Diana did I establish a relationship which could take the place for them of being with their own families.

In August we had our first visit from Queen Wilhelmina of the Netherlands, who was accompanied by Baroness van Boetzelaer, Jonkheer George van Tets, and General H. van Oyen. My press conference ladies wanted very much to meet her, and though I had been doubtful whether it could be managed, she did attend my press conference the morning after her arrival. During the course of the conference she said something about the increase in tuberculosis in Holland under the Nazis, which she immediately afterwards regretted, fearing the Nazis would retaliate against her people. So I had to chase after the women and insist that everything the queen had said about tuberculosis in Holland must be off the record. When the conference was over I accompanied her to the Capitol; then we met my husband and went to the ceremony marking the transfer of an American subchaser to the Netherlands fleet. Both the president and the queen spoke over the radio and she went on board to speak to the Dutch crew which was taking over the ship. After that we all boarded the "Potomac" for lunch and went down the river to Mount Vernon.

That night the queen dined at her own embassy and on the morning of the 7th, she went to my husband's press conference, which was, of course, much more important than mine. Franklin and Queen Wilhelmina had arranged beforehand what she was to say and both of them played their parts well. Conferences were held also with the military authorities. Later in the day Franklin accompanied her to the train when she left.

This was Franklin's second meeting with the queen of the Netherlands. The first meeting had been when he called on her while she was staying with Princess Juliana in Massachusetts, not many miles from Hyde Park. Crown Princess Marta, who was staying with us at the time, went with him and she always told with amusement how Franklin announced to the queen that he had been nervous before meeting her because he had always heard she was one of the most awesome of all the crowned heads. His respect for her increased with each meeting and both he and I came to have a warm affection for her.

Toward the end of August, I spent a few days at Hyde Park, as I did off and on during the summer, and my husband went occasionally to Shangri-la and to Hyde Park, but we were never away from Washington for very long.

During the summer there was an International Students Service conference in Washington, which brought to the city a number of young people from other countries who had already seen considerable war service. I saw a great deal of the young British and Russians, and I liked them all. Some of the British I saw again when they were stationed in the United States; others I have seen on visits to England. One of them, Captain Peter Cochrane, married Louise Morley, daughter of Christopher Morley, and they are one of my favorite young couples. I have seen Lieutenant Richard Miles and Commander Scott-Malden, too, but I have had no word from the young people from the USSR—Lieutenant Ludmilla Pavlichenko, Nikolai Grasavchencho and Vladimar Pchelintsev.

The next event of real importance to me was my husband's decision that I should accept Queen Elizabeth's invitation to go to Great Britain to see the work the women were doing in the war and to visit our servicemen who were stationed there. I did not know at first that one of the reasons my husband was eager to have me go over was that those men would shortly be leaving for North Africa for the invasion.

CHAPTER SIXTEEN

VISIT TO ENGLAND

EVERY TIME Mr. Churchill came to the White House, he spoke of the time when my husband would visit Great Britain, but one felt that he had in mind a visit to celebrate a victory either in sight or actually achieved. I do not think it ever occurred to him that there was any good reason why I should go to Great Britain during the war. He assumed, I think, that I would go in my proper capacity as a wife when my husband went.

However, it evidently occurred to Queen Elizabeth, for Franklin received some tentative inquiries about whether I would be interested in going over and seeing the role that the British women were playing in the war. Naturally the British looked upon my visit as providing an opportunity to get that story told in the United States, for the queen, knowing I wrote a column and made speeches fairly frequently, felt, I think, that I had access to the people here.

When my husband asked me how I would feel about going, I assured him that if he thought it might be helpful, I should be delighted to go. Knowing that the North African invasion was coming off soon, he said that in addition to observing the work of the British women, he wanted me to visit our servicemen and take them a message from him. As I have said before, I had always been sorry that, because of having young children, I had not been able to do any active war work overseas during the First World War. My recent experience working

(*Acme*)

MRS. ROOSEVELT ON A BALCONY OF THE WHITE HOUSE, MARCH, 1940, WAVING TO THE CHILDREN GATHERED FOR THE ANNUAL EGG-ROLLING.

On the walk outside the White House, Mrs. Roosevelt watches the members of the American Youth Congress parade in the rain. February, 1940.

Mrs. Roosevelt besieged by reporters upon her arrival at Chicago to address the Democratic National Convention, July, 1940.

MRS. ROOSEVELT AND MALVINA THOMPSON ARRIVING IN ENGLAND,
OCTOBER, 1942.

MRS. ROOSEVELT WITH MRS. CHURCHILL, RETURNING TO LONDON FROM
DOVER, OCTOBER, 1942.

Mrs. Roosevelt with the royal family at Buckingham Palace, during her visit to England in 1942. From left to right: King George, Mrs. Roosevelt, Queen Elizabeth, Princess Margaret, Princess Elizabeth.

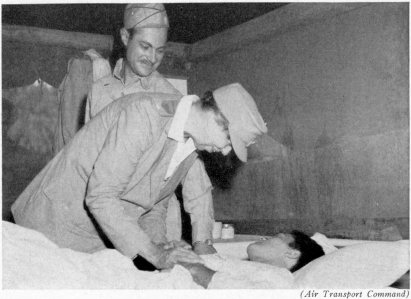

MRS. ROOSEVELT TALKS WITH A WOUNDED SOLDIER DURING HER TOUR OF THE SOUTH PACIFIC IN LATE 1943.

MRS. ROOSEVELT DINES WITH THE ENLISTED MEN AT ONE OF OUR CARIBBEAN BASES, MARCH, 1944.

President and Mrs. Roosevelt with thirteen grandchildren on the occasion of the fourth inauguration, January, 1945. Front row, from left to right: Christopher Roosevelt (Franklin, junior's son); Anne Sturgis Roosevelt (John's daughter); John Roosevelt Boettiger (Anna's son); Elliott Roosevelt, Jr., Kate Roosevelt (James's daughter); Sara Roosevelt (James's daughter). Sitting behind Anne Roosevelt is Haven Clark Roosevelt (John's son). Back row, from left to right: Mrs. Roosevelt, Buzz Boettiger (Anna's son); Sistie Boettiger (Anna's daughter); William Donner Roosevelt (Elliott's son); David Boynton Roosevelt (Elliott's daughter); Chandler Roosevelt (Elliott's daughter); President Roosevelt with Franklin D. Roosevelt, 3rd

FALA, PHOTOGRAPHED AT THE FUNERAL OF PRESIDENT ROOSEVELT.

MRS. ROOSEVELT WITH FALA AND TAMAS IN THE SITTING ROOM OF
HER HYDE PARK COTTAGE, 1948.

in the Office of Civilian Defense had convinced me that being in the White House would prevent me from doing any real job in World War II. I admired and really envied Mrs. Theodore Roosevelt, junior, who during both wars did magnificent work running clubs for servicemen, and when I went to England I visited the club she had established with such incredible energy and persistence. There is so much satisfaction in doing one single concrete job really well. While I was visiting her club, the newspaper people, who followed me throughout the trip, tried to stir up a little excitement by asking if we had talked politics!

The trip to Great Britain seemed to offer me a chance to do something that might be useful. At once I asked Tommy if she would be willing to go with me, since I did not want to obligate her to take a trip that might entail some risk. She was entirely willing and gave as little thought to the possible danger as I did. I suppose the saving fact for all human beings at such times is that they never think anything is going to happen to them until it actually happens. Theoretically and intellectually they recognize the possibility, but in my own case, at least, it was not a sign of courage that I went ahead and did certain things which might have had some slight danger attached to them. It was simply that, like most human beings, I am not given to seeing myself disappear off the face of the earth. If it should happen, having no choice, I would, I hope, accept the inevitable philosophically.

After my husband told Harry Hopkins that I was willing to go (for I think Harry made the suggestion first), I received a formal invitation. I went ahead and made reservations on a commercial plane, I paid for our passage and was given instructions about the amount of baggage allowed, had the necessary shots, and on October 21 appeared at the airport on Long Island at the appointed time, together with Colonel Oveta Hobby, head of the Women's Army Corps, Lieutenant Betty Bandel, her aide, a courier from the State Department, and Mr. Slater, one of the vice-presidents of the American Export Lines. It was a nonstop flight, one of the first to be made. We were luxuriously taken care of and had only one piece of excitement on the way, when we were allowed to look down on a convoy below us—little tiny specks on the ocean. It was hard to believe that those ships were in danger and that some of them might suddenly be torpedoed.

Our first bad weather was in Foynes, Ireland. We had expected to transfer there from our plane to another and continue on to London, but as we landed on the water a small boat came out from shore and we were told that our flight to London had been canceled because of weather. It was pouring rain, and as we transferred from the plane to the open boat to go ashore I realized that my raincoat and umbrella were stowed away in my bags in the wings of the plane. The hat that I had bought new for the trip was ruined and I looked a bit bedraggled when I got on land. Tommy was just as badly off because we had followed instructions to the letter and had only the barest necessities with us in the cabin of the plane.

In the little boat was my uncle, David Gray, then our minister to Ireland, who was much concerned over my having to land in Ireland. We climbed out after making sure that our military ladies were unmilitary in dress; if they had gone ashore in military uniform they would have been interned because that part of Ireland was neutral. It was a bit of a farce because the Irish authorities closed their eyes to much somewhat incriminating evidence.

My aunt, Maude Gray, was waiting to greet us. I was a little annoyed with David, who insisted that no one should know I was there. Crowds of other American plane passengers were also detained by the weather, and as I came up from the float someone said: "Why, there's Mrs. Roosevelt." That made David walk even faster, and after breakfast in the offices of the American Export Company, he hurried me to the home of Lord and Lady Adare where I stayed until the next morning, when the British prime minister sent a plane for us. It landed safely on an inland field; we boarded it and were off again, this time to land in Bristol, where we had our first sight of a bombed city. It came as a shock to me to see the areas of rubble and to look down streets and see no house left standing, but my glimpse was brief. Our ambassador, John G. Winant, met us and we went on board the prime minister's special train for London.

Before I left the United States, Harry Hopkins had told me not to pay too much attention to Mr. Winant, but to be sure to consult Averell Harriman on everything. I had known Mr. Winant for a long time and I had great respect and admiration for him, as did my husband. I made no answer to Harry's suggestion except to say that I had known Averell Harriman since he was a small boy because he had been an intimate friend and schoolmate of my brother's, so I certainly hoped to see him in London. I firmly determined, however, that I would consult John Winant and take his advice. I was sure that Averell Harriman would not have agreed with Harry, because he was in London and knew what a wonderful reputation Mr. Winant enjoyed with the British officials. However, Harry always tended to lean primarily on his own friends and he knew Averell better; I think he never really knew or understood Mr. Winant.

After Mr. Winant met us I was relieved of many anxieties. On the train we went over the proposed itinerary. I thought it was a bit strenuous, but later it was expanded to include much that I had never dreamed of doing at first. Mr. Winant told me that the itinerary had been gone over by the queen and by Stella Lady Reading, who was to take charge of me during a part of the visit. He also said that he would come for me the next morning, and that when we left the Palace his apartment and maid would be at our disposal. I was not conscious of the need for protection, but both the prime minister and the ambassador felt I would be safer and have more privacy in his apartment than in a hotel.

I had been worried by the thought of having to visit at Buckingham Palace, but I finally told myself that one can live through any strange experience for two days. I was determined, even though I had certainly not been asked to come on the trip to enjoy myself, to try to live each moment aware of its special interest. Though certain situations might be unfamiliar and give me a feeling of inadequacy and of not knowing the proper way to behave, still I would do my best and not worry. Nevertheless, as we neared London I grew more and more nervous and wondered why on earth I had ever let myself be inveigled into coming on this trip. I had to be treated as a "Very Important Person" because my husband was President of the United States.

Finally we pulled into the station. The red carpet was unrolled and the station master and the head guard on the train, both of them looking grand enough to be high officials of the government, told me that the moment to get off had arrived. There stood the king and queen and all our high military officials. The only person in the whole group whom I felt I really knew was Stella Reading. I evidently concealed my nervousness, because later Tommy told me that it was only my poise and calm that kept her from having the jitters.

After the formal greetings, the king and queen took me in their car, while Tommy was taken in hand by the lady-in-waiting and two gentlemen from the royal household, and we drove off to Buckingham Palace.

The king and queen treated me with the greatest kindness. The feeling I had had about them during their visit to the United States—that they were simply a young and charming couple, who would have to undergo some very difficult experiences—began to come back to me, intensified by the realization that they now had been through these experiences and were anxious to tell me about them. In all my contacts with them I have gained the greatest respect for both the king and queen. I haven't always agreed with the ideas expressed to me by the king on international subjects, but the fact that both of them are doing an extraordinarily outstanding job for their people in the most trying times stands out when you are with them, and you admire their character and their devotion to duty.

When we arrived at the Palace they took me to my rooms, explaining that I could have only a small fire in my sitting room and one in the outer waiting room, and saying they hoped I would not be too cold. Through the windows they pointed out the shell holes. The window panes in my room had all been broken and replaced with wood and isinglass and one or two small panes of glass. Later the queen showed me where a bomb had dropped right through the king's rooms, destroying both his rooms and hers. They explained the various layers of curtains which had to be kept closed when the lights were on; informed me that there would be a messenger outside my door to take me to the drawing room at the proper hour for dinner, and then left me to my own devices.

Buckingham Palace seemed perfectly enormous to me. The suite I had was so huge that when Elliott saw it he said that after this I would have to take the long corridor at the White House for my bedroom, because the one I had would never again seem adequate. The wardrobes were wonderful—the kind one longs for at home—but the fifty-five-pound limit on baggage made my few clothes look pathetic hanging in those wardrobes. I wondered what the maid thought when she unpacked them. One evening dress, two day dresses, one suit and a few blouses, one pair of day shoes and one pair of evening shoes comprised my wardrobe for a visit to Buckingham Palace! One of the newspaper women, for want of something better to write about, later reported that I had worn the soles of my one pair of shoes through. The head usher at the White House read the story and very thoughtfully sent me another pair.

The first night at dinner the other guests were Prime Minister and Mrs. Churchill, General Smuts and his son, Captain Jacobus Smuts, Sir Piers Leigh, Lord and Lady Mountbatten, Ambassador Winant, Countess Spencer, Elliott and Miss Thompson. After dinner we saw the fine Noel Coward film, "In Which We Serve," based partly on the story of Lord Mountbatten's ship and partly on the story of Dunkirk. It was a novel experience to watch a movie about a man who was himself present, and a very moving experience to see it in the company of people who must have been deeply stirred by it.

Everything in Great Britain was done as one would expect it to be. The restrictions on heat and water and food were observed as carefully in the royal household as in any other home in England. There was a plainly marked black line in my bathtub above which I was not supposed to run the water. We were served on gold and silver plates, but our bread was the same kind of war bread every other family had to eat, and, except for the fact that occasionally game from one of the royal preserves appeared on the table, nothing was served in the way of food that was not served in any of the war canteens.

The next morning Ambassador Winant called for me to take me to a press conference at the American embassy. I faced an overwhelming array of newspaper people in fear and trepidation, but evidently said nothing to cause any anxiety.

My visit to Great Britain was the beginning of a real friendship with Gil Winant. He was a shy person, but he had great intellectual integrity, a vivid imagination which enabled him to understand situations that he had never experienced, and a sensitiveness to other people that enabled him to accomplish things many of his friends thought beyond his powers. He grew to love Great Britain and her people, and I think the statesmen who bore the brunt of the burdens during the war trusted and depended upon him. I know that for a long time he went almost daily at about five o'clock to see Anthony Eden, and though I doubt whether he was exactly the kind of man who would ordinarily have appealed at once to Mr. Churchill, I know Mr. Churchill had a real respect and affection for him.

I myself can never be grateful enough to him for the kindness with which he mapped out my trip and for the things he told me which helped me to carry out my task among the British people better than I might otherwise have done. He was a selfless person who gave little thought to his own comfort, but much thought to helping his friends. He made the time I spent in London both pleasant and comfortable. I shall always miss him, for he came to be one of the people that I looked forward to seeing from time to time. I can not describe what it was he gave his friends. I do not even know that he considered me any more than an acquaintance, but I prized highly what he gave me; and I had a feeling that he shed light in dark places. He worked unceasingly in the hope of a better world for future generations.

With the king and queen I had my first real look at the devastation—blocks upon blocks of rubble. Our first stop was at St. Paul's Cathedral, partly because the king and queen wanted to give the faithful watchers who had saved the cathedral the satisfaction of a visit from them at that time, and partly so that I could stand on the steps and see what modern warfare could do to a great city.

We drove for miles through the poorer sections of the city, from which the people had been evacuated. Some of the streets were literally lined with shell holes, and wherever I looked there was nothing but devastation. When we drove into the City we went through the usual ceremony in which the lord mayor meets the king and allows him to enter—an old custom which still survives in spite of war. I was struck by the amount of destruction in the City, but in spite of the evidences of bombing all around us we had tea with the lord Mayor, in the true British fashion.

During this visit I met most of the royalty in exile. Many of them had visited the United States but some of them I had not known before. I also saw the Russian ambassador, Mr. Maisky—a very cultivated and interesting man who since seems to have disappeared from the diplomatic stage—and his wife.

I spent a weekend at "Chequers," the country estate given by Lord Lee to the British government for the use of British prime ministers. There I watched Prime Minister Churchill playing a game on the floor with his grandson and noticed the extraordinary resemblance between the two. Mr. Churchill once remarked that his grandson didn't look like him, he just looked like all babies. I recollect that at breakfast the following morning, the prime minister was displeased with what was on the table, feeling that it spoke of England's hardships.

Mrs. Churchill is a very attractive, young-looking and charming person. One feels that, being in public life, she has had to assume a role and that the role is now a part of her, but one wonders what she is like underneath. She is very careful not to voice any opinions publicly or to be associated with any political organizations. This I felt was true of the wives of all the public officials whom I met in England. As I have seen more of Mrs. Churchill over the years, my admiration and affection for her have grown. She has had no easy role to play in life, but she has played it with dignity and charm.

For security reasons I had to have a code name, and someone with a sense of humor—I suspected my husband—had decided that "Rover" was appropriate. Tommy was "Assistant Rover." A hypothetical organization called "Rover's Rangers" had been organized by the young men at the United States embassy in London, with my husband as the "Starter."

After lunch one day we were scheduled to visit Elliott's unit at a place called Steeple Morden, but the chauffeur, who, for my protection, was a Scotland Yard man and not a regular chauffeur, lost his way and we could not find the camp. No one who was asked would tell us how to get there—also for security reasons—so finally some one telephoned back to the United States embassy: "Rover has lost her pup" and asked for directions!

With Mrs. Churchill I went to visit a maternity hospital, and also to see how the women in the several branches of the military service were trained. During one of those visits, I remember, the air-raid warning sounded, but the girls went right on with what they were doing and paid no attention. I saw girls learning to service every kind of truck and motor car and to drive every type of vehicle; I even saw girls in gun crews, helping the men to load the guns. I visited factories in which women did every kind of work, and I visited one group of girls whose job it was to fly planes from one part of the country to another. Since it was unwise to keep a concentration of planes anywhere in Great Britain, these girls would take over the plane when a pilot landed and fly it either to a place where it would be well camouflaged or to a repair shop.

One day, with Mrs. Churchill, we started out early in the morning in the prime minister's special train. Our first stop was Canterbury. The dean of the cathedral met us and took us through the cathedral, which had not been hit by bombs though, as everyone knows, the city as a whole was badly damaged. At a woman's institute where we stopped later, the pig club was having an exhibition; one young and active pig had been named "Franklin" and a rabbit "Eleanor." Finally we went on to Dover where we visited the shelters in the Athol caves, built by prisoners of war in the time of Napoleon.

At one time or another during this trip I visited Red Cross clubs of all types—our own American Red Cross, the British Red Cross, and St. John's Guild. At that time, Harvey Gibson, the dynamic head of the Red Cross in Europe, was expanding its facilities in a remarkable manner, and though I occasionally heard that this or that particular club was doing something that my informant considered detrimental to the morale of the men or women, on the whole I thought the Red Cross was doing, in its recreation program at least, an outstanding job. Occasionally at some of the American Red Cross clubs I would come across a boy from Poughkeepsie or some other place in the United States who had seen me at home; and because we were both in a foreign country close to war, we would experience a feeling of intimacy which we would never have known had we met somewhere in the United States.

During this visit to England I started the practice, which I continued on subsequent trips, of collecting from the boys to whom I talked the names and addresses of their families, so that I could write to them on my return to the United States. I had quite a collection before I was through.

I also made a tour of the camps where our servicemen were stationed and ended it by spending one night with Queen Mary at Badminton. This was something that Franklin had particularly wanted me to do because King George V and Queen Mary had been kind to his mother when she visited England. I think he thought of Queen Mary as in some ways rather like his mother, and therefore made a point of my seeing her.

Here again I had the same sense of strain that I had felt before visiting Buckingham Palace. I was told that we must arrive at six o'clock—not five minutes before or five after, but at six sharp. To my surprise, Queen Mary met me at the door and took me to her sitting room, the only small room in that house as far as I could see, and it had a good fire. After a talk, she took me to my room, which though cold and barnlike, was furnished grandly with Chinese Chippendale furniture. She showed me where the bathroom and the w.c. were, and they were cold too.

Tommy's room was as cold as mine. We dressed and went down

to dinner, arriving in good time. At dinner, I sat on the queen's left, the princess royal on her right, the Duke and Duchess of Beaufort, the young relatives who owned Badminton, at either end of the table. General Knox, who seemed to manage the household, Lord Hamilton, gentleman-in-waiting to the queen, and a lady-in-waiting completed the party.

After dinner, which was not a hilarious meal and during which I made valiant efforts at conversation, we went into the drawing room and stood for fifteen minutes. Queen Mary looked very regal and every inch the queen, with many ropes of pearls and many sparkling bracelets and rings. She wore a black velvet evening gown and an ermine jacket. Then she asked me to her sitting room and also asked the princess royal if she wished to accompany us. Tommy was left with the others and soon escaped. I looked in on her when I was politely dismissed to go to bed, and found her already in bed because it was the only way to keep warm. However, I really enjoyed my visit and have a great admiration and real affection for Queen Mary now.

Even on this first visit I recognized her thoughtfulness of others and the Spartan demands she makes on herself. Every little detail of what she considers the proper treatment of guests, she carries through. For instance, on the morning I left she was up before nine o'clock to see me off at the door and to submit to photographs, which I thought showed great self-discipline. In the same way she fulfills every obligation of her position. She has always shown her appreciation of any slight act of friendliness from our family and I am grateful for having known her.

There was one story told about her which I heard on this visit and greatly enjoyed. On one of her drives she picked up an American GI. After a little while she asked him if he knew who had picked him up, and he said: "No, ma'am." She decided not to tell him, knowing it would be easy for him to find out. She asked him questions about his home, his life in the army, and how he liked the British people. As he was getting out she relented and said: "I am Queen Mary," and he responded: "Oh, you are! Well I'm from Missouri and you'll have to show me." Thereupon she gave him some little thing to prove that he had been with her.

She gave me to bring back to Franklin a photograph of herself, fully dressed with hat, veil and gloves, sawing a dead limb off a tree, with one of her dispatch riders, a young Australian, at the other end of the saw. She told me to tell my husband that she cared as much about the conservation of trees as he did and was sending this photograph to prove it. I think nothing I brought him from that trip gave him more pleasure than that photograph and the message, and he always felt that Queen Mary was a grand person.

Under Stella Reading's guidance I visited universities and innumerable factories, stayed on estates where the grounds were now being used for agricultural purposes, and in country houses whose owners, now living in one small part of them, had turned them into nurseries for evacuated or wounded children. I saw the way the Women's Voluntary Services was organized to perform innumerable duties—from moving into a town which had just been bombed and needed everything from food to laundry service, to looking after the billeting of workers who had been moved from one factory to another.

My hostess at one of my stops illustrated the difference in habits and customs between the British and the Americans by telling me of a time when she had invited some American officers from a nearby camp to come in at half-past six for a cocktail. She did not know that they had dinner at six and they did not know that the British did not dine until eight or half-past. Consequently the officers, who were having a pleasant time, stayed until nearly eleven o'clock. Meanwhile the family went hungry and the hard working husbands were none too pleased.

Finally I got one of my real colds, and I remember still the discomfort it caused me. Shortages were already evident everywhere and one could not buy facial tissues. Not until we landed in Northern Ireland and spent the night in Londonderry in the naval captain's house was I able to get some cleansing tissues from our naval hospital there.

Our days usually began at eight o'clock and ended at midnight, but I was so interested that at the time I did not even realize how weary I was gradually becoming. We wrote the column every day at whatever time we could fit it in, and sometimes in rooms so cold that Tommy's fingers would hardly work.

Because in pattern, though not in detail, one day was much like another, perhaps the clearest picture of what our days were like can be gained from an actual diary entry. November 11 will serve as well as any; in variety and interest it was more or less typical.

At eight-thirty we had breakfast with some privates from the women's military organizations [this was in Londonderry], and at nine-thirty we inspected the Naval Base. In one repair shop the men presented me with two ash trays, one marked for the president—"The Boss"—the other inscribed to "Rover."

We stopped at eleven a.m. in the Londonderry Square for the Armistice Day celebration. I placed the wreath given by the American Forces and was followed in the observance by an endless number of other people, including Lady Montgomery, whom I felt it a great honor to meet. She looks like her famous son "Monty," and there is plenty of character in the lines of her face.

The lord mayor asked me to sign his book, and then we were off again to visit the Naval Hospital. At the ceremonies there I was presented with a shillelagh and a cane for the president.

The people of this part of Ireland are much less restrained than the people in England. The crowds got out of hand and the police seemed unable to cope with them as they crowded around us, whereas in England a polite request from the "bobby" is all that is needed.

The Naval Hospital here, which is very well managed, is set up in Nissen huts, with private rooms for officers and for very sick men at either end of each hut. I never realized how compact a kitchen could be created in a Nissen hut; there is not too much space, but just enough. This is true, too, of the operating room.

The doctor, Captain Davis, told me to tell Admiral McIntire that all he asks is to be let alone. He likes his job and is getting on wonderfully. He seems to have very good corpsmen, and to object strongly to Navy nurses. He says women have no place in the services, especially in Londonderry, because he can find no place to house them. One gathers from his conversation that he does not like ladies.

After a luncheon at which I sat next to the Bishop of Derry, we left at once by air for Prestwick, Scotland, landing there at three-forty-five, in time for tea. Then we started for Glasgow, stopping to see some women's institutes on the way. At one place the women presented me with some Scotch shortbread for my husband. (They had saved scarce ingredients to make it, and he was deeply touched when I gave it to him.)

In Glasgow we went first to the American Red Cross, inspected it rather thoroughly, had a little time to rest, wrote the column, had dinner, and then I had coffee with some of the soldiers, which was really fun. Then we went to the opening of the Merchant Marine hostel. I went over that from top to bottom, and then said a few words over the radio. I am deeply grieved that two seamen whom Bob Trout was to interview over the air, were cut off because the other speeches were too long.

By nine-thirty we reached the C. & J. Weir Company factory and spent an hour going over it, then drove through a dense black-out to the Rolls factory. Here the women working on the eleven o'clock shift, some seven hundred and fifty, were gathered together in one room. After we had been through the factory I made a rather brief speech, but the gentleman following me complimented everybody on the platform until I thought we were never going home to bed. We sat through five speeches. Finally we reached Lord Weir's house about twelve, where we met some of the members of his family, were served refreshments, talked a little while and at last went to bed. I wondered if I would ever be able to get up in the morning, for I was weary and my feet didn't seem to belong to me.

In spite of my fears, however, I was up the next morning early to visit a gun crew; then we boarded a boat to go down the Clyde River. This is a man-made river, so narrow that I could watch both sides and see the extraordinary activity going on in the shipyards. The workers knew I was making the trip and were watching for us, so I had to stand on deck in the cold, waving first on one side and then on the other. I never was so cold in my life. We finally landed at Brown's shipyard, where the "Queen Mary" and "Queen Elizabeth" were built, and I went over a large airplane carrier which was under construction. Bombing had gone on up and down the river but work was progressing steadily. To my great joy, Sir Harry Lauder sang for us, and the workers who had crowded around to listen to the speeches joined in with him.

This was a nation at war, going through moments of great uncertainty and stress. But what I have often marveled at has been the people's staunchness and their ability to carry on during the years after the war and to accept the drabness of their life. I should not marvel, however, for in spite of all that had happened to them, I knew then as I talked to them that they would go on living and working for their country. The answers to many questions were in the faces of almost any crowd of Scottish and English people.

One of the workers with whom I talked told me that the hardest thing was to keep on at your job when you knew the bombs were falling in the area of your home and you did not know whether you would find your home and family still there at the end of your day's or night's work. When we lunched with some of the women who were daily feeding the dock-workers, they told me: "We used to look down on the dock-workers as the roughest element in our community. We were a little afraid of them; but now we have come to know them and will never feel that way again."

Women from many different backgrounds, who had never worked together before, were working side by side, just as the men were fighting side by side. These British Isles, which we always regarded as class-conscious, as a place where people were so nearly frozen in their classes that they rarely moved from one to another, became welded together by the war into a closely-knit community in which many of the old distinctions lost their point and from which new values emerged.

There was an old couple who still slept nightly in an underground shelter in London, though they could easily have been evacuated to a country area. They told me they had lived for so long in the shelter that, while they liked to go out in the daytime and sit in their old home —even though there was not enough of it left so that they could sleep there—they preferred to return to the shelter at night rather than to move away.

When I visited a center where bombed-out people were getting clothes and furniture and other supplies, one young woman with a child in her arms and another dragging at her skirt said to me very cheerfully: "Oh, yes, this is the third time we have been bombed out, but the government gives us a bit of help and you people in America send us clothes. We get along and none of us was hurt and that's the main thing."

Back in London I had dinner with Prime Minister and Mrs. Churchill. The dinner was small: the guests were Brendan Bracken, Minister of Information; Lady Denman, head of the women's land army; Lady Limerick, of the British Red Cross; Dame Rachel Crowdy, whom I had met in the United States; General Brooke, Chief of Staff; Henry Morgenthau, junior; and Miss Thompson.

During dinner I had a slight difference of opinion with Prime Minister Churchill on the subject of Loyalist Spain. The prime minister asked Henry Morgenthau whether we, the United States, were sending "enough" to Spain and whether it was reaching there safely. Henry Morgenthau told him that he hoped we were, and I said I thought it was a little too late, that we should have done something to help the Loyalists during their civil war. Mr. Churchill said he had been for the Franco government until Germany and Italy went into Spain to help Franco. I remarked that I could not see why the Loyalist government could not have been helped, and the prime minister replied that he and I would have been the first to lose our heads if the Loyalists had won—the feeling against people like us would have spread. I said that losing my head was unimportant, whereupon he said: "I don't want you to lose your head and neither do I want to lose mine." Then Mrs. Churchill leaned across the table and said: "I think perhaps Mrs. Roosevelt is right." The prime minister was quite annoyed by this time and said: "I have held certain beliefs for sixty years and I'm not going to change now." Mrs. Churchill then got up as a signal that dinner was over.

After dinner Mr. Bracken sat beside me and told me he would take me home. During dinner he had told Tommy that he knew the United States inside out and that he knew the American people. The American people whom he knew were apparently Bernard Baruch, Justice Frankfurter, and the like. After we reached the apartment he came in and talked for quite a while. He was said to be the person closest to Mr. Churchill and was acknowledged by all to be very brilliant. Secretary Morgenthau told me that Mr. Bracken had given him a great deal of information and that he had learned much in an hour's time. I ques-

tioned the latter part of that statement. I felt Mr. Bracken agreed with
me too readily and I feared he was more or less of an opportunist, though
I thought him brilliant and was very glad to have had the chance to
talk with him.

Before I left for home, my aunt, Maude Gray, Tommy and I drove
out one day to Windsor Castle, for I wanted to report to Queen Elizabeth on my trip. While we were talking in her sitting room, the king,
who had spent the day visiting our air force troops, came in with the
children. Both the king and I had rather bad colds, which necessitated a
good deal of attention to our noses. As we drove away from Windsor
Castle my aunt said to me in shocked tones: "Darling, I never was so
humiliated in my life. Your using those nasty little tissues and wadding
them up in your hand while the king used such lovely sheer linen
handkerchiefs! What could they have thought!"

As the time for my return trip approached, my husband and Ambassador Winant and the prime minister discussed how I should travel.
Tommy and I had our return passage on an American Export Lines
plane and saw no reason why we should not go back that way; but at
that time of year, because of the weather, the commercial planes were
going by way of Portugal, Africa and South America, instead of flying
the northern route. Both Ambassador Winant and the prime minister
pointed out that while I might not be concerned personally with the
possibility of the Germans' discovering I was on a plane bound for
Lisbon, and forcing us down, I would be jeopardizing the other passengers. Finally, after many conversations over the trans-Atlantic telephone, my husband, who did not want me to travel on a military plane,
gave in and said: "I don't care how you send her home, just send her."

I had said good-bye to Elliott before he left with his group for
Africa, my heart heavy as I saw him go. We finally left for Prestwick
on November 15 by the night train and the next day we boarded the
plane. I thought the crew looked rather astonished when we walked
out to get on board, but not till we were safely in the air and some
way out to sea did one of them tell us: "We thought we were waiting
for two generals. We could not imagine when two ladies came who
they could be."

The other passengers were a crew of ferry pilots who had delivered a bomber and were on their way back to the United States. The heating system in the plane went wrong and we were extremely cold in spite of all the blankets which were piled on us. We had nothing to eat between lunch time in Prestwick and about two o'clock the next morning when we landed at Gander Lake. Even though there was a lot of snow on the ground it seemed much warmer than in the plane. We were fed and warmed, and finally took off after a delay caused by the icing of the wings. However, we landed safely the next morning in the Washington airport, where my husband met us.

War trip number one was over.

CHAPTER SEVENTEEN

GETTING ON WITH THE WAR : 1943

AFTER WE had been back from London a few days, a Washington columnist wrote for his paper a story asserting that Miss Thompson had asked me for a few days off to go to see her mother, who was ill. I was alleged to have said: "Why Tommy, I didn't know you had a mother, but I am afraid we are much too busy for you to be away now."

It was so ridiculous that neither of us was annoyed. Miss Thompson wrote to the gentleman as follows:

Your column quoting my request for a few days' holiday and Mrs. Roosevelt's alleged reply has just been brought to my attention.

For your information, my mother died in 1928 and in order that there be no confusion about which parent I wanted to visit, my father died in 1932. Nothing could give me more satisfaction than to be able to visit either or both of my parents and get back to my job. If you, in your omnipotence can tell me how to accomplish this, I shall be most grateful.

Needless to say, there was no answer to this letter and no correction in the column.

The day I arrived home we had a large dinner for the president of Ecuador, who was to be an overnight guest. I should have liked at least one evening to catch up on my family, for I had been away several weeks, but that is a pleasure a public person cannot always count on. Naturally Franklin could make no change in an engagement of this kind which had been arranged weeks before.

After that first evening we did have a certain amount of calm and quiet, however, and were home at Hyde Park for Thanksgiving.

Very soon I began to realize that there would shortly be other trips in which I would have no part and about which I had better know very little. The first of these came after the Christmas and New Year holidays were over, when on January 9, 1943, Franklin left for Miami, Florida, taking off on the 12th for Casablanca. It was his first long trip by air across the water and I had hoped he would be won over to flying, but instead he disliked it more than ever. I tried to tell him that the clouds could be as interesting as waves, but he always said: "You can have your clouds. They bore me after a certain length of time."

Admittedly a flight like this in time of war entailed some personal danger, but that was something Franklin never gave a thought to. For a president, there is always that possibility, no matter what he does, and long ago, when Mayor Cermak was killed, Franklin and I had talked it over and decided that that kind of danger was something you could do nothing about. You cannot be protected from a person who does not care whether he is caught or not. But since neither can you live in constant fear and apprehension, the only possible course is to put the thought of danger, of whatever kind, out of your mind and go ahead with your job as you feel you must, regardless of what might be called its occupational risks. In the case of the Casablanca trip, there was also the fact that Franklin was doing an unprecedented thing, and he knew there would be criticism. That again was a consideration he could not let weigh with him. All the arrangements for the trip were made through the secret service; his departure was as secret as possible; the flag which indicates that the president is in residence was never taken down from the White House; and I went on with my daily routine exactly as though he were there.

One morning, just after Franklin left Washington, I went down to the station to meet a train. The train was late so I stopped in the president's room, which was then being used as an information bureau for servicemen. After I had signed innumerable autographs and talked to as many men as possible and had learned that the train would be

very late, I started to walk home in bad weather. A young private, first
class, asked if he could walk along with me. As we went along Pennsylvania Avenue, I asked him when his train left, and finding he had
nothing to do until late afternoon, I invited him to come in and have
lunch. It did not occur to me that there was anything peculiar about
inviting a man in uniform to lunch, but the look on the faces of the
guards and the rest of the staff when I brought him in and announced
that he would stay for lunch was one of extreme disapproval. They
knew I did not know him and they considered it a highly dangerous
performance. I could not see anything dangerous about it. Franklin
was not there, and Louise and Diana Hopkins, Tommy and I were not
going to give him any valuable information; neither were we likely
targets for a subversive act. Nevertheless, there was tension among the
entire White House staff until lunch was over and the young man
was safely on his way back to the station. He apparently was too thrilled
to be able to keep his piece of luck to himself and told the first newspaper reporter he could meet—and then the telephone began to ring.
I had thought that I was only doing a friendly thing, but I realized
it was my own fault when the newspapers got so excited.

While Franklin was away I carried on my usual routine of formal
engagements and, when they permitted, took the opportunity to go
to my cottage in Hyde Park and to my apartment in New York. Louise
and Diana Hopkins were in the house with me in Washington and
Louise, of course, waited for news of Harry as anxiously as I did for
news of my husband and the rest of the party.

When Franklin returned he was full of stories. He loved particularly to tell us how he had made Mr. Churchill unhappy by teasing him
about his "bad boy"—General de Gaulle. Mr. Churchill, of course, was
responsible for General de Gaulle and the general had proved difficult
about going to the meeting. Back of Franklin's teasing, however, there
had been a serious purpose because he had felt that if Mr. Churchill
put the screws on, General de Gaulle would have to come to Casablanca, since Great Britain was providing him with the money necessary to carry on his activities at that time. When the general did go,
it was not altogether a happy meeting, though photographs were taken

of General de Gaulle and General Giraud shaking hands, and conversations were held which all the men felt were useful. When I questioned him about these generals, Franklin said something which interested me very much: "General Giraud is the type of French military man who loves his country and is not in any way a politician, but a good soldier. General de Gaulle is a soldier, patriotic yes, devoted to his country, but on the other hand, he is a politician and a fanatic and there are, I think, in him almost the makings of a dictator." He saw General de Gaulle only once more, when the general came to this country. I never heard Franklin say he had changed his mind about him as a person and I do not think that between them there was any real understanding.

Franklin also loved to tell of riding out in a jeep to see our troops and of the surprise on the faces of the men and his own delight when one man in a back row said in a loud voice: "Gee, the president!" much to the chagrin of the commanding officer, who considered it a breach of discipline.

Another thing Franklin talked much about was the horrible condition of the natives in the places he had stopped. He never minced words in telling Mr. Churchill that he did not think the British had done enough in any one of the colonial areas he had seen on this trip to really improve the lot of the native peoples. He agreed with me that the United States, too, had a serious responsibility in Liberia which we had never lived up to, and I am particularly happy that Edward Stettinius has now gone ahead with the plans for Liberia which he discussed with Franklin at that time. He has formed a company and is starting to develop the natural resources of the country—a project that was only a dream when he talked with my husband after his return from Casablanca.

While at Casablanca, Franklin had had the pleasure of having both Elliott, who was on duty in Africa, and Franklin, junior, who had happened to come in on the destroyer to which he was assigned, spend a little time with him. Franklin, junior, had had no idea his father was there and when he got word to report to the commander-in-chief he had again thought it was Admiral King, as he had at the time of the Atlantic

Charter meeting. He was dumfounded when he arrived to discover his father there.

These meetings meant a great deal to Franklin and also to the boys, and Franklin always came home full of stories of what they had said and done. As the boys look back now, those reunions mean even more to them than they meant at the time, when their minds were busy with the job at hand. Now they like to talk about each detail of the times they spent with their father. For my part, I was always grateful when these meetings were possible, for it meant that I got firsthand news of my sons. Their letters, when they came, were grand, but all the boys were too busy to write a great deal and they never were the best of correspondents.

Franklin missed his birthday this year, since he did not get home from Casablanca until January 31. The next day he reported to the members of the Foreign Affairs Committee, the vice-president and the speaker of the House, and the leaders in the Senate and in the House. Life was very busy for him then, though he did manage to get a week end at Hyde Park now and again.

In early February I made a trip to Portland, Maine, where Cary Bok met me and took me to Camden to visit his shipyard, where he was building wooden vessels. This was something in which Franklin was greatly interested. The ships were being built the same way that our very early ships had been, and many old Maine sailors, who were carpenters and boatbuilders when not at sea, but who had not used their craft for years, found themselves much needed again.

Later in the month I flew to Des Moines, Iowa, with Colonel Oveta Hobby, head of the WAC, to inspect their main training station. While I was there I took a side trip to speak at a college in Columbia, Missouri, and was back in the White House in plenty of time to greet Madame Chiang Kai-shek, who came on February 17 to stay with us. I had previously met Madame Chiang when she first arrived in this country. At that time she was in the Medical Center in New York City for treatment, but had consented to see me. She had seemed to me highly nervous and to be suffering a great deal; she could hardly bear to have anything touch any part of her body. For a long time the doctors were unable to relieve the trouble, which I imagine was the result of long strain and anxiety and the Chinese climate.

Madame Chiang seemed so small and delicate as she lay in her hospital bed that I had a desire to help her and take care of her as I would have if she had been my own daughter. Occasionally I took someone to see her because I felt she would tire of seeing only me, and many people were anxious to meet her.

When it came time for her to leave the hospital we offered her our house in Hyde Park for a few days before she came to Washington. She spent several days there and then, accompanied by two nurses and her nephew and niece, Mr. and Miss Kung, who acted as her secretaries, she came to the White House and stayed until the 28th of the month. She should have been an invalid with no cares; but she felt she had work to do, that she must see important people in our government and in the armed services who could be helpful to China, and that she must fulfill certain official obligations.

I shall never forget the day I went with her when she addressed the House of Representatives, after meeting the senators. A little, slim figure in Chinese dress, she made a dramatic entrance as she walked down the aisle, surrounded by tall men. She knew it, for she had a keen sense of the dramatic. Her speech, beautifully delivered, was a very remarkable expression of her concept of democracy. Theoretically she knew exactly what democracy should be. However, it was not so easy to understand how in practice she thought it should be lived in China, with its particular traditions and habits and customs.

I saw another side of Madame Chiang while she was in the White House, and I was much amused by the reactions of the men with whom she talked. They found her charming, intelligent and fascinating, but they were all a little afraid of her, because she could be a cool-headed statesman when she was fighting for something she deemed necessary to China and to her husband's regime; the little velvet hand and the low, gentle voice disguised a determination that could be as hard as steel.

A certain casualness about cruelty, which was always a surprise to me, emerged sometimes in her conversations with the men, though never with me. I had painted for Franklin such a sweet, gentle and pathetic figure that, as he came to recognize the other side of the lady, it gave him keen pleasure to tease me about my lack of perception. I remember an incident at a dinner party during one of her visits which gave him particular entertainment. John Lewis was acting up at the time, and Franklin turned to Madame Chiang and asked: "What would you do in China with a labor leader like John Lewis?" She never said a word, but the beautiful, small hand came up very quietly and slid across her throat—a most expressive gesture. Franklin looked across at me to make sure I had seen, and went right on talking. He knew that I would understand and make allowances for the differences in background and in customs; nevertheless he enjoyed being able to say to me afterwards: "Well, how about your gentle and sweet character?"

Madame Chiang had been very kind to our son James when, in 1941, Franklin had sent him with another Marine officer to practically every trouble spot in the world to observe how the war was going. His report on his return from China and Africa was the first I had heard from anyone who had actually been strafed by planes. I was then in Civilian Defense and he warned me that people must be trained to withstand noise. It drove people crazy and sometimes got on the nerves of the men so badly that they would stand up and make themselves targets rather than lie on the ground for another minute and listen to the noise all around them.

Jimmy with good reason was very grateful to Madame Chiang. Ever since his operation for ulcers he had been obliged to be rather careful about his diet, but that had been a little difficult on this trip and he had been none too well when he visited the Generalissimo and Madame Chiang. She had immediately understood, and with her own hands had prepared the proper kind of food for him, which straightened him out before he left. You can understand that from that time on Madame Chiang had a special place in my heart.

Her two young secretaries created a slight confusion when they first arrived in the White House because her niece, Miss Kung, insisted on dressing like a man, and the valets, thinking I had made a mistake in assigning the rooms, unpacked Miss Kung under the impression that she was Mr. Kung. Then they went to the ushers' office and reported that I had made a mistake, only to learn much to their confusion that they had unpacked a lady. Franklin was also confused by her type of dress and when she came in to the study where we all met before dinner, he greeted her as "My boy." Harry Hopkins quickly wrote a note saying: "This is Miss Kung." Franklin tried to cover up by saying, blandly: "I always call all young things 'my boy,'" but everyone knew quite well that her clothes had completely fooled him. I do not believe she was offended by his mistake, for that was the impression she was trying to give. She hated being a girl—I suppose in protest against the inferior position sometimes assigned to women in China.

Both Miss Kung and her brother gave us the impression that they felt we, as well as most of the people of our country, thought all Chinese were laundrymen and looked down on them, and they were anxious to dispell that idea. It seemed at times that they had chips on their shoulders, and did not want to be really friendly. At a Sunday night supper when Harry Hooker was visiting the White House, Miss Kung made an attempt to impress him by telling him she was the 76th direct descendant of Confucius. He was rather taken aback and leaned over to me and said: "Eleanor, I did not know that China had a Newport set." It sent me into convulsions of laughter but I am quite sure it meant nothing to Miss Kung. However, towards the end of their visit I felt that we had succeeded in changing Miss Kung's attitude, because she was very cordial to Miss Thompson and invited her to visit China, and she was very sweet to me.

Both Miss Kung and Mr. Kung were considerably irritated by White House rules, such as that the ushers had to be told when some one was coming to see Madame Chiang or anyone else in the house. We had one rather dreadful contretemps when Madame Chiang's doctor from New York City was kept waiting for some time at the gate. The ushers were asked if I had an engagement with anyone of that name, and finally we found that Madame Chiang was expecting him. I was appalled at having wasted so much of the doctor's time and at having treated disrespectfully a man of such high standing in the medical world, but it was not the fault of the White House staff, who were simply obeying the rules.

Two days after Madame Chiang's arrival, the Chi Omega Achievement Award Committee, which had decided to give her their award for the year, made their presentation. This award is given once a year to the woman who has been the most outstanding in her field of work. The idea is to encourage young women as they start their careers. I am a member of the Committee on Awards and I was delighted that Madame Chiang was the recipient.

After Madame Chiang left us she made a long trip by special train throughout the United States, out to the west coast and back. It must have been a strenuous and difficult trip for her, and after her return she questioned Tommy very carefully. Tommy and I had taken practically the same trip, following in her footsteps, a few days behind her, and heard about her everywhere. What mystified Madame Chiang was how it was possible for us to travel alone while she had forty people, yet never enough to do the things that needed to be done. She asked Tommy who packed our bags, and Tommy said she packed hers and I packed mine. She then asked who answered the telephone, and Tommy said that whichever one of us was nearer it answered and that often I impersonated her. She also asked who took care of the mail and telegrams and was told we did it jointly. Her next question was, who looked after our clothes, and Tommy told her that if a dress needed pressing, we asked the hotel valet to do it. Finally she asked about my safety. Tommy explained we did not consider "protection" necessary, since everyone was good to us, but that, of course, in various cities people would sometimes be assigned to meet us at the train and see us off and motor us about if we were going to be in large crowds; that this, however, was entirely dependent upon how the local authorities felt.

I have never asked for or wanted protection and in all the miles I have traveled and the many places I have visited, I never have had an unpleasant incident. People might become a bit too enthusiastic, but it was all kindly meant and I felt it was because they loved my husband. I have had a tail pulled off my fur scarf as a souvenir, but nothing worse than that has ever happened.

Our lack of need of protection was something it was impossible for Madame Chiang to understand, but when one considers the disturbed conditions in China and the extent and long duration of the war there, it is easy to see why she found it hard to comprehend the kind of security we have in this country.

I became very fond of Madame Chiang and I shall always think of her with warm affection, even though I realize that we are worlds apart in our conception of the duties and obligations of the individual in a democracy today, perhaps also in our conception of what the future organization of the world should be when the equality of man is a primary aim. I am glad she is back here, now that China's internal troubles have increased, and I hope she and those she loves find our land a safe refuge.

During the month of April I went on a short trip with Franklin to inspect some war plants in Mexico and to meet the president and spend a few hours in Monterrey. It was a very interesting trip to me, because it was the first time I had been in that country. In Monterrey we saw Mexican soldiers parade, and the school children put on a remarkable exhibition of calisthenics and dancing exercises.

My impression of the city is rather vague, for we drove fast and were watching the crowds rather than the city itself; however, Mexican hospitality, as expressed at the dinner we all attended and in the kindness of everyone with whom we came in contact, made a deep impression on the whole party. We traveled back with a feeling that Mexico was a close neighbor in spirit. My husband, I think, already felt close and friendly to the Mexican people, but to many of us this was a new experience.

That April our daughter, Anna, and her son, Johnny, came for a visit when her husband went into the army. He had served in the First World War and was over-age for the draft, but he had a feeling that because all our sons were in the service he must go in, too, or my husband might feel that he was not doing his share. I was never quite sure that his reasoning was right, though I understood his feeling; nevertheless, it seemed to me that this was a war for which young men were far better suited than older men and that perhaps those who had established themselves in an occupation had a greater obligation to stay and do their job well at home. But I knew only too well how men could feel and I respected John Boettiger's decision.

Like every other family in the country, we watched eagerly for mail from our sons. The ones in the navy came into port occasionally and we had a glimpse of them now and then, but we had less chance to see Elliott. I have a letter from him dated May 23, 1943, which I am putting in here because it is so typical of the letters that many other families must have received. Like so many young men, he felt he knew more about many things than his elders and betters.

DEAREST MUMMY:

I got the socks, they are wonderful and just the right size. Thank Tommy ever so much and give her a kiss for me.

I know you worry about us children in different parts of the world. Don't worry about me. I lead a charmed life. I had a crack-up the other day and escaped with a sore tail although my ship was demolished. The tail fell off another airplane that I flew to England five minutes after we landed. Anyway, if anything should happen remember no one could ask for a better exit line.

We are beating the Germans now, and will finish the job in the next year and a half. Then we can beat the Japs in another year. Our air force is wonderful. The only thing holding it down is the fact that we are not a separate air force. I know father doesn't like the idea, but he's wrong. The R.A.F. and the British Army have a closer cooperation as separate entities than we do as one force. General Spaatz has done a wonderful job, in spite of rather than because of the help of the ground supreme commanders. He is really and truly a great tactical general.

I guess I won't be home for a long time, so keep writing. I love your letters with their news.

> Your loving son,
> ELLIOTT

I am also including a letter from James, which I think is interesting from several points of view. He was with Carlson's Raiders at this time.

San Francisco, California
Wednesday 7/29/42

DEAREST MUMMY:

It was just swell to talk to you on the telephone and you sounded just top of the world and I hope you are. The reason for this visit is because we are about to go on our first job along the lines of our name. We leave about eight days from now and the whole business will take us about three weeks. We go via those things Johnny finds are his new love and the day for the actual work is Brother's birthday, so it will be quite a celebration! So I asked for five days' leave as there were some things that only Rommie and I could settle together. The most important to us is the future after September first. Frankly my insides are little by little getting worse. My weight is shifting a little and an increasing amount of "gas" is for the present just uncomfortable. Originally I volunteered for this work because I felt it was my job to do a front-line job and because I feared that physically the chance would be denied unless I got at it early.

War is not a glorious or exciting thing to me. There is too much to live for at home, away from it. But right or wrong I felt that was my duty. Now comes the chance to stand by the men I've been working with and give them the confidence and leadership which being younger they will need. But Mummy, if we come through this in good shape then my brain tells me that it is foolish to go on to the point of exhaustion. Progressively my judgment and leadership get worse as I feel more lousy, and eventually I am a liability to my own group. Further it only seals also the opportunity of being or trying to be a useful citizen after this is over. Unfortunately I need such things as rest, milk, and food which is not greasy, to stay in shape and one just can't find and shouldn't order things to suit one individual out there or on any 'front.' Someone may suggest that there are good doctors and hospitals out there. But that isn't the point and besides it isn't a question of getting well or being repaired. It's one of keeping well. So I've reached the conclusion that if possible I'd better be just on a training or desk job at home and lead as normal and steady life as it's possible to do these days. Egypt, Midway, Hawaii and now this job should give me some value as a teacher and training officer. General Joe Fegan has told Rommie he would be glad to ask for me in his new job as head of the Marine training center at Santa Marguarita, California. For various reasons I don't want to be in Washington and prefer the west coast and of course, San Francisco, Los Angeles or any other place is well as long as it's a real job to do.

Mummy, I've thought so long on the angle of special interest and favoritism on this. But after all any other officer would never have been given waivers on my defects (eyes 3-20th and stomach) and when this next job is done at least inside I'll feel I have stood the test of making it no matter what the odds.

So whatever can be done or should be done about it I don't want to be retired as physically unfit and truly feel I have much to contribute in a constructive way. Father once told me he would never ask for anything for his sons and he's quite right and shouldn't be put on that kind of a spot.

Much love
JIMMY

John and Franklin, jr., of course wrote of their experiences in the navy, and I thought some of their letters gave a remarkably graphic picture of what life was like for men long at sea. From John came this letter:

U.S.S. "Wasp"   8/12

DEAR MUMMY:

Thanks a lot for your letter. I've been meaning to write but somehow it seems that all I actually get around to is writing Anne. I'm receiving *PM* as regularly as the mails permit and the July 10th edition of the *Times* came through the other day much to the delight of a great many of us. We're enjoying both and they go a long way toward supplementing what we get from *Time* and the daily radio press news. Mummy, I hope you wrote the wife of the gunners' mate who was killed on the June 19th show. He was a very competent boy and was director operator at the time he got it. We were a very lucky ship that day; the Japs seemed to have singled us out and as a result we were high for the fleet in that action.

We've been away from all civilization now for three and a half months. The officers and crew have been ashore once to a lousy sand spit for a beer party—not much in the way of recreation but at least it was a break of sorts. Ever since we got out until this last week we operated almost steadily, just taking time out to load bombs and provisions.

We're all very annoyed with Pa. As long as he was going to Pearl why didn't he send for a good ship! We can provide the fastest surface as well as air transportation. Besides we would have loved to see the States if only for a brief liberty. Anyway we hope we'll get back by next March or April as the ship will need an overhaul by then.

Tell Frank if he brings his ship out this way to let me know. I haven't seen Joe as we haven't been close to where he is stationed. I have run into quite a few people out here but getting around is very difficult—the lagoons are awfully damned big and small boats few and far between.

From what we hear Pa is not going to have much opposition but let me know the real dope. In a way I'm glad I'm away from the hullaballo of the campaign. Aside being away from Anne and the children I don't mind this life too much. It's terribly boring most of the time but it has potentialities of excitement. My gun crew has shaped up into a good group. They were fine under attack and did everything one could possibly have expected. We'll all be damned glad, however, when we get transferred back to the States but for now we'd just as soon get on with the show rather than lie around waiting. None of us can quite figure out why everyone is so damned optimistic at home. It looks good out here and progress is being made but there's a hell of a long tough way to go still.

Mummy, I hope you don't have to do too much this summer and can get some rest at Hyde Park.

Lots of love
JOHN

And from Franklin, Jr.:

U.S.S. "Ulvert M. Moore"   May 27, 1945

MUMMY DEAR:

Today is our 69th straight day at sea on this operation and the strain is beginning to tell on my boys—and I guess too on "the old man." I'd give anything for five hours of uninterrupted sleep. My worries and problems are beginning to multiply as machinery parts and all kinds of little gadgets are beginning to go on the "fritz" for lack of maintenance and overhaul; and the food situation is quite critical (we're completely out of eggs and meat). So you can see the job of keeping a destroyer at sea for this long is rather a difficult one. However, the prospects are now pretty good that in about two or three weeks we will go back to one of our forward bases for a rest and overhaul period. We will be the last ship of our division to go and by that time I'm quite sure the "Moore" will hold the world's record for continuous time at sea for a destroyer-type ship! How like the old sailing ship sagas of "around the Horn in eighty-five days" only they didn't have to worry about these damn "Krazy Kats"—our nickname for the Japs suicide or Kamakaze aircraft. It is very interesting to consider the value to the human race of any nation who holds the value of human life so cheaply.

Much, much love
FRANKLIN, JR.

I imagine every mother felt as I did when I said good-bye to the children during the war. I had a feeling that I might be saying good-bye for the last time. It was a sort of precursor of what it would be like if your children were killed and never to come back. Life had to go on and you had to do what was required of you, but something inside of you quietly died. I began to look with wonder at all the women in the country who must be feeling this same way and I came to admire their courage. Fathers had the same kind of courage, but there was a greater acceptance on their part of the need for war and perhaps a greater pride in the fact that their sons were fulfilling their duty. Men do not instinctively revolt against war as women do.

At the time of the First World War I felt keenly that I wanted to do everything possible to prevent future war, but I never felt it in the same way that I did during World War II. During this second war period I identified myself with all the other women who were going through the same slow death, and I kept praying that I might be able to prevent a repetition of this stupidity called war.

I have tried to keep the promise I made to myself, but the progress that the world is making toward peace seems like the crawling of a little child, very halting and slow. However, that should only make us redouble our efforts, if we can but keep the strength and faith to do so.

May was a busy month in 1943. The president of Bolivia and his foreign minister stayed at the White House on two separate occasions. President Beneš of Czechoslovakia and Prime Minister Mackenzie King each spent a night with us and later the president and the president-elect of Liberia came. Their visit was the direct result of my husband's visit to Liberia on his way back from Casablanca.

We liked both the president and the president-elect. When the latter started to dress for dinner he found that he had only brown shoes. He called his valet, who was at Blair House, and the valet informed him that the only shoes he had with him were those on his feet. I wish I had known at the time, because I could have told him that the same kind of thing had occasionally happened to my husband and my sons and that he should not feel in the least worried. I remember that when Jimmy went with me to President Coolidge's funeral, he had sent a wire asking that his formal morning clothes be sent to him in Northampton, he found when they arrived that while the trousers and the waistcoat were all right, the coat was the coat of his formal evening clothes. He had to keep his overcoat on all during the day!

The real purpose of this visit was to discuss how the United States could help Liberia, and some things which have since been done in the medical field stem directly from those talks.

Early one morning in July I was suddenly called on the telephone and very guardedly told that there had been an engagement in which Franklin, junior's ship had been bombed. They thought it was getting into Palermo safely. That was all. I went to my husband's room and asked him if he knew anything more than I had heard. He said he had just been told the same thing, but he would try during the day to find out about it. It was quite a long time before I heard the details. After the ship had been bombed, it was taken into Palermo, where it continued to be shelled at intervals. It was tied to another ship, and men were injured on both of them. Franklin, junior, had the good luck to be able to save one boy's life by carrying him down to the other ship's doctor. At the time he did not notice that he himself was hit in the shoulder, but to this day little pieces of shrapnel are there to remind him of it.

Weeks later he let me know that the boy whose life he had saved, but who had lost a leg, was at Bethesda Naval Hospital, so we had him to lunch one day. We thought him an extremely nice boy and very courageous.

Eventually Franklin, junior's ship went to Malta for repairs and was still at Malta when he got word that he was to meet his father, who was on his way to Cairo. He was delighted at the chance of seeing him, but when Franklin told him he would like him with him on the trip as his aide, young Franklin's joy changed to determination that nothing of the kind was going to happen. After the repairs on his ship were completed it would have to get home, and he knew it would be an anxious trip because the ship would not really be in top-notch seaworthy condition. He felt he could not let the ship go back without him, after all he and his shipmates had been through together.

Franklin, junior, and his father had quite an argument about where his first duty lay; whether to his ship or to his father's need of his help in traveling. The ship won in the end and his father gave him a letter of orders to return to it. Young Franklin realized that he could never show those orders to anyone, because security demanded that no one know his father was in the area. He had a very amusing and difficult time getting back to Malta with no orders that he could show to get priority for the return trip.

While we were waiting for news of what had happened to his ship I could not help thinking of how difficult it must be for those who could not even try to get anything beyond the original, official notification and simply had to wait until the newspapers or official channels gave further news. I do not know that we got news any more quickly than anybody else, but that experience certainly made me conscious of the need for informing people, whenever possible and as soon as possible, of exactly what was happening.

CHAPTER EIGHTEEN

VISIT TO THE PACIFIC

I DO NOT remember when my husband first suggested that it would be a good idea for me to take a good-will trip to the Pacific, though I do remember the suggestion came because he felt that Australia and New Zealand, being so far away, had been rather neglected in the matter of visitors. Both countries were exposed to attack and the people were under constant strain and anxiety. We had had to send a great number of our servicemen out there—an influx which had added considerably to the strain and which had been, for people whose own men, very often, were fighting in Africa and Italy, a disrupting even though reassuring occurrence. Another reason for the trip was that I had received a number of letters from the women of New Zealand and Australia, suggesting that since I had seen the work the women of Great Britain were doing, I might be interested in coming out to see what they were doing in their far-off countries.

I at once put up a strong plea to be allowed to see our men on Guadalcanal and other islands. I had done considerable visiting in the west coast hospitals to which the early wounded from Guadalcanal and some from the 1st Marine Raider group (with which Jimmy served) were being returned; and I told my husband frankly that it would be very hard for me to go on doing it if, when I was to be in the Pacific area anyway, I were not permitted to visit the places where these men had left their health or received their injuries. He finally broke down and gave me letters to the commanding generals and to Admiral Halsey, saying that he was willing to have me go to Guadalcanal "if it did not interfere with the conduct of the war."

I have since learned from Colonel Hodgson, who later served with me in the United Nations but who at the time was making the arrangements for my visit to Australia, that Franklin told the Australian prime minister and Admiral Halsey that, no matter what he wrote or what he said, I was not to be allowed to go to Guadalcanal because he thought it was too dangerous. However, he did not have the courage to tell me, knowing quite well that I would refuse to make the trip at all under those limiting conditions.

What these gentlemen must have thought about the two conflicting messages they received, I do not know, but I delivered my letters. At that time my sons, except for Jimmy whom I hoped to see in Hawaii, were on the Atlantic side, but I did have some young friends in the Pacific area. Joe Lash was with the weather bureau, and a boy named Cecil Peterson was also on duty out there. Just before leaving I discovered that they were both on Guadalcanal.

Franklin was going to the conference at Quebec on the 17th, the same day I was to leave for San Francisco, but we had a little time together at Hyde Park first. It was decided that my visit should be kept secret, so I went on about my daily business as usual. Prime Minister Churchill, who was staying with us, still speaks occasionally of how surprised he was when I casually mentioned at dinner one night that I was leaving the next day for the Southwest Pacific. He looked aghast and asked: "What have you done about your trip?" I said all the plans had been made and the itinerary worked out. He asked who was going with me; and I said no one, because having been subjected to much criticism on my return from Great Britain, I thought I would avoid some of it on this trip by taking up as little room as possible, since I knew I would have to go in a military plane. I later found to my regret that some columnists were none too kind anyway, and that I might just as well have taken several people—nothing more disagreeable could have been said. Mr. Churchill insisted on cabling to all his people in the Pacific, and they were most kind wherever I met them. I have always been grateful to him for his thoughtfulness.

I had gone to see Norman Davis, chairman of the American Red Cross, as soon as the trip had been decided on, and had asked if it would be of any assistance to him if I went to look over the various Red Cross installations and trouble spots. I hoped in this way to show that I was doing a serious job and not just running around the war area to cause trouble. He promptly said that I could be most useful, because he had been planning to send someone out there to inspect the Red Cross work. He asked me if I would be willing to wear a Red Cross uniform and make a report to him on my return. I talked this suggestion over with my husband, since it seemed to offer a number of advantages. In the first place, uniforms meant less luggage, an advantage when traveling by air; in the second place, in a familiar uniform I would feel easier visiting the hospitals and meeting servicemen. Franklin decided it would be a good idea, so I bought at my own expense the thinnest uniforms I could find, also a heavy one with a warm top coat, because I knew I would encounter extremes of weather. I conscientiously inspected every Red Cross activity in every area I visited and I hope that my reports were some compensation to Mr. Davis for the criticism heaped upon him for permitting me to go in uniform as a Red Cross representative.

Because Franklin felt that, since I was traveling on a military plane, I should not keep any of the money which accrued from my column while I was on this trip, I arranged for half of my earnings to go to the Red Cross and half to the American Friends Service Committee, also dividing between them what I earned for articles written after my return. Later I discovered that certain of the Republican members of Mr. Davis's board were afraid that if it were known I had given this money to the Red Cross, some of the large donors who were strongly opposed to my husband politically would withdraw their contributions. Consequently we never explained how I happened to go in uniform or what the financial arrangements were; however I think it is now quite safe to give the facts.

I flew out to San Francisco on a commercial plane at my own expense, and spent a day there before taking off for Hawaii. George Durno, a former Washington newspaper man whom I knew, then a captain in the Air Transport Command, was assigned to make the trip from San Francisco with me. Much of the time we were on the same plane; the other passengers were officers or messengers traveling their routine way to various destinations. We also carried mail and cargo of various kinds.

My first glimpse of Hawaii was in the early morning hours, and on landing I was hurried into a car and taken straight to Brigadier-General Walter Ryan's house. I still remember the delicious pineapple filled with various kinds of fresh fruit that we had for breakfast in the garden. After Hawaii, we were to visit what my husband called "the islands for guarding the supply route." Here the men had to be constantly on the watch, but they so rarely saw anything that it was very difficult for them to keep up their morale and their interest in the work they were doing. General Harold L. George of the Air Transport Command had discovered a short time before that even mail was not reaching them very regularly, but that was rapidly being corrected.

At best a safe job is not what young soldiers expect or want. One felt the strain on the men. The doctors were trying to do a good job. They gave thorough physical examinations and corrected what defects in teeth or physical condition they could discover, and the Red Cross people were trying to devise methods of recreation; but it was an unnatural life. I was to get my first inkling of how unnatural it was when I landed on Christmas Island, my first stop. The young lieutenant colonel looked at me and said: "You are the first white woman I have seen in ten months."

Over and over again on this trip I wished that I could be changed in some magic way into the mother or the sweetheart or the wife or sister that these men longed to see. It is one thing to tell yourself you are a symbol and that it must give the men a sense of satisfaction to know that their commander in chief is interested enough to send his wife to carry a message to them, but quite another to feel adequate when you know so well what the boys really want and you can do nothing about it.

On Christmas Island I had my first encounter with tropical bugs. I had forgotten to ask the young officer who turned his quarters over to me, after showing me the vagaries of the plumbing, if there were any creatures one should beware of on the island. When I walked into the room after supper and, putting on the light, found my floor completely covered with little red bugs, I nearly disgraced myself by screaming. Remembering in time that I was the only woman on the island, and that a scream would undoubtedly raise an alarm, I stamped my feet instead and all the little bugs scurried down through the cracks in the floor.

I saw everything the men were doing on that island, as I did on all the others I visited. Right from the beginning I followed my sons' advice, which was none too self-flattering, considering that they were officers themselves. They had said: "Mummy, don't take every meal with the brass. See that you have a meal with the non-commissioned officers and get a non-commissioned officer to drive you around, and get one meal with the enlisted men themselves." The only way to accomplish the last was to get up and eat breakfast with the men before six o'clock. Doing this as often as I could, I was always amply rewarded by the conversation which, after the first short period of awkwardness wore away, opened up and gave me an insight into the lives of many United States citizens.

There was a pattern of life, of course, carried out on nearly all the islands. There were movies every night and even when tropical showers came down in torrents, the men turned up their raincoat collars and sat right on through if the movie equipment was covered. Other recreation depended largely upon the ingenuity of the special service people and the Red Cross, and I came home with many requests for equipment. Shipping was always the difficulty in the Pacific; the great cry of the Red Cross or any other agency, when charged with incompetence, was that they could not obtain sufficient shipping space from the military authorities. This, of course, was understandable, since the military authorities were concerned primarily with keeping the men fed and properly outfitted. It was not until we had had men in the Pacific for some time that we realized how quickly supplies deteriorated. In talking to Admiral Ross McIntire, Surgeon-General of the Navy, about the naval hospitals, which everywhere seemed to me very well equipped, I learned that at first they had had no idea how often they would have to replenish their supplies; the realization had come as a considerable shock.

Few people realized how complicated was the organization of the supply points from which shipments were made. I never would have understood it myself if my youngest son had not been assigned for a time as one of the officers under Admiral Mayo at the San Francisco supply depot. When everything from a tank to the smallest nut had to be packed in a ship so that it could be unloaded without disturbing any of the rest of the cargo, the loading could not be done in a haphazard manner but had to be thought out with the greatest of care. The depot itself had to be planned and stocked with such a variety of things that I doubted as I went through it whether any type of business had ever gathered such a conglomeration of articles in any one place.

When I left San Francisco I had known that somewhere along the line I should have to have another shot for tetanus. I had gone through all the other shots with such ease that I walked into the naval hospital on Bora-Bora for this one and never gave it another thought. Then my arm began to swell and for several days I knew how uncomfortable one really could be. However, since there was nothing to be done about it, I tried to forget it as much as possible, because my schedule was all made out and I had to keep moving according to plan. And that plan took me, before I was through, to seventeen islands. In addition, I visited the capital and a number of other places in New Zealand, the large cities on the east coast of Australia and a number of camps and hospitals in the northern part.

I used to wonder how the pilots ever found the little dots of coral islands in that vast expanse of ocean. Having to come down so close to the water to land was a curious sensation at first, but I became entirely accustomed to it.

Having no one with me as a secretary, I had to write my column either at night or during flights in the daytime. I am such a slow typist that this meant an extra two hours' work for me almost every day. However, when I had a long flight I could often write enough for two or three columns, which helped when I had an overcrowded schedule at some stop. Though it is such a short time ago, I doubt very much if I could now stay awake at night to finish my work, get up as early the next morning as I did then, and still keep going through the entire day. As it was, I lost thirty pounds and when I got home I realized I was more tired than I had ever been in all my life. But I was not ill and the work got done—nothing else mattered.

When I reached Noumea and met Admiral Halsey, I presented my letters from my husband. The admiral has told his own story of how much he dreaded my coming. He did not dread it any more than I did, but I determined to do as well as I could, and if it was possible, to get up to Guadalcanal. The admiral refused to give me the slightest inkling of what he had decided about that and told me in no uncertain terms that I would have to go to New Zealand and Australia first and that he would make his decision on my return. I thought I noticed a slight change in his attitude before I left; perhaps some good reports were coming to him from the hospitals and the various places I had already visited. In any case, he sent with me to New Zealand one of his young aides and Coletta Ryan, the head Red Cross worker who was in charge of the clubs in that area.

Wherever I went I met people I had seen before, and I remember my surprise when I found young Robert Atmore of the Choate School running one of the Red Cross clubs in Noumea. That the many trips I had made in the United States during the depression years had an unforeseen by-product was evident as I walked through hospital wards. Occasionally when I spoke to even a very sick boy, he would say he had seen me last when I spoke at his commencement or on some other occasion; then if I recalled something about his home town his whole face would light up, and I would feel that the endless miles I walked every day were quite worth while.

I stayed with the governor general and his wife while I was in the capital of New Zealand, and again with the governor general and his wife on Fiji, invitations I owed to Mr. Churchill's thoughtfulness. Both visits were very pleasant though of course I had to follow my usual routine. In New Zealand especially, I tried to see something of the people of the country and what they were doing, as well as of our own men.

By that time we had only rest camps and hospitals in New Zealand, but I could see the effects of the tremendous influx of our men who had gone from there, first to Guadalcanal and later to other parts of the Pacific. By the time I got there some of the New Zealand men were coming back and I got one amusing letter asking me if I would not see that our men left their girls alone. When I spoke of the letter to some New Zealand people, I was told a story to illustrate the difference between the approach of the average American GI and the New Zealand soldier. A GI was on a bus one day and found himself sitting behind a lovely-looking girl with fair hair. He leaned over and said: "Angel, what heaven did you drop from?" As an opening gambit, that speech probably never would have occurred to a New Zealand man.

In the Red Cross clubs there, one of the girls came up to me and said: "There's a boy here who says he does not want to speak to you or even be in the same room with you, because he understands you advocate that all the marines who came to the Pacific be quarantined for six months after they return, before they are allowed to go home." Here was a story that I had heard before leaving home. My husband had urged me to disregard it when I had said that if it was widespread there was very little use in my making the trip, since I could not accomplish much if the boys believed it. In my talk to the boys that day I mentioned the story, adding that the families of some of the boys who had written back home about it had sent the letters on to me. I told them how surprised I had been, since of course I had never thought of saying anything of the kind. I had a son in the marines, I said, and he certainly would never allow me to have any such ideas. Much later, after I had tested it out and found that as a rule the story was known to the non-commissioned officers and the men, some of the older officers suggested that it might have been a broadcast by Tokyo Rose. Heaven knows how it started, but it plagued me for a long time, and a similar story was told in all parts of the world. The paratroopers in Italy complained that I had said the same thing about them, and I heard it again when I went to the Caribbean. Quite evidently it was propaganda designed to detract from the value of any contacts I might make, whether at home in the hospitals or on various trips.

While I was in New Zealand I visited Rotorua, the home of the Maoris, who had shown our servicemen much hospitality. The Maoris are the original natives on the island, as our American Indians are here. The head guide, Rangi, who showed me about, was a wonderful woman, brilliant and witty and dignified. The area, with its geysers and hot-water pools, is like a miniature Yellowstone Park. In one place the families use the pools for cooking, putting their pots of food over them. I was foolish enough to ask whether this was not unwise and whether their children did not steal from pots belonging to someone else. With dignity Rangi told me their children were taught not to steal. That was a little rebuke which I deserved and I wished fervently I could be certain that the teaching of our children was always so successful, success evidently being a foregone conclusion so far as the Maoris were concerned.

The New Zealanders have imported many things from the United States and they claim that any fish or game brought from our country, once it is acclimated, grows better there than it does here; consequently if you go fishing or hunting, you may get the same kind of fish or game, but it will be much larger than anything you could find in America.

When I reached Australia Colonel Hodgson, Lieutenant-General R. L. Eichelberger and his aide, Brigadier General C. E. Byers, were waiting for me and told me my trip was well planned. I stayed for a while at Canberra with the governor general and his wife, Lord and Lady Gowrie, who were kindness itself; I shall never feel grateful enough to them for all they did to make my visit useful and pleasant. I spoke to vast audiences and visited many hospitals, rest homes for our nurses, and recreation centers for our men. The population of Australia is not very great; but though we were filling up many parts of the country and swamping many of the small towns and villages with GIs, their hospitality was proverbial. Boy after boy told me how kindly he had been treated in Australian homes, and that was equally true in New Zealand; however Australia had a greater number of our men in proportion to her population. Nevertheless, they stood up under the strain in a remarkable manner.

Fortunately I had brought with me the newsreel that had been made on my trip to Great Britain, besides a recent movie which had been made of Fala. Everyone was eager to see all that I had seen and done in Great Britain, and the movies with the king and queen interested them greatly.

When visiting one of the rest homes for nurses, I was told of the difficulties of traveling about Australia. The various states in Australia are even more insistent on their sovereignty than are ours in the United States. However, it did seem to me to be carrying sovereignty too far to have the railroads all of different gauges so that at every state line all the freight and passengers have to be unloaded and transferred to another railroad. Each state has its own governor general and there is, of course, one for the whole of Australia as well. They patterned not only their government but their capital city after ours, and Canberra is a beautiful place which will, I am sure, become more beautiful as the years go by.

In a rest home for nurses I asked one young nurse what she objected to most. I told her I knew she had realized when she came that there would be danger, but that I wondered what had proved to be the most difficult thing to stand up against. She looked at me and without any hesitation said: "The rat that sits in the middle of my floor and will not move no matter how much noise I make." Rats, insects and snakes were things one had to contend with daily in the hospitals on the islands, and one girl told me of waking up to find a snake neatly coiled on the outside of her netting. She could not get up until some one came and did away with it.

Many of these girls were working in hospitals where water was sometimes almost impossible to get; one cupful to a patient a day had to do for drinking and washing. The mud was so deep at times that even with the GI boots, and trousers tucked into the tops, it was difficult to get around. But I never heard any of them really complain.

The daughter of the Reverend Endicott Peabody, the headmaster of Groton School for many years, was out in Australia as a nurse when I was there, but though I tried very hard to see her, we missed each other. I did see a cousin of mine, Dorothy Robinson Kidder, whose husband is in the diplomatic corps and who was stationed in Australia at that time, and I saw many other people I knew, in addition, of course, to innumerable boys in rest camps and training camps, with some of whom I had a chance really to talk.

In northern Australia I watched the training for jungle warfare. I was particularly interested in this because before leaving home, I had had an irate letter from a woman whose son was receiving some kind of training in the swamps of Louisiana which seemed to her cruel, inhuman and unnecessary. I followed the men along jungle paths in Australia, looked on while they were taught how to remain motionless, how to conceal themselves, how to detect the enemy and how to remain unseen. Traps were set, so if a man did not follow instructions implicitly, he was "trapped" and marked "dead." I wished I had seen all this before I answered that mother's letter; I might have been able to explain to her that the training in the swamps of Louisiana was for her son's own safety in the future.

It was also in Australia, in a Red Cross club, that I had an interesting talk with some young men. They were mostly air force boys, some of them from West Virginia, and the discussion turned to John Lewis and the coal strike. I told them of a boy in a hospital who had looked at me, ill as he was, and said: "I come from West Virginia. I'm a miner. It isn't the miners who are wrong; they've got real grievances and they don't understand about us, you know that." Since I understood their feeling that no one at home should be on strike, I was glad I knew mining areas well enough to realize that it was not even entirely John Lewis' fault. It was the fault of all of us, who should have paid attention long ago to the conditions under which the miners worked and not have left it to John Lewis to get for them the only benefits they had received up to that time. But the boys who had been miners themselves, or whose fathers were miners, had a difficult time trying to explain to their companions that there was any justification for a coal strike in war time.

I was always a little sorry when the boys were called together and had to stand in the sun while I made a short speech, because I knew how they hated that. The chance conversations in a Red Cross room, or in a mess hall or in a hospital, I always hoped had some interest for them, and I carried away an endless number of names of mothers, wives, sweethearts and sisters to whom to send messages when I got home.

The story has been told—and it is true—of how after my return I telephoned one girl in Washington and told her who I was and that I had a message from her fiance. She said: "Don't be funny. Who do you think you're fooling?" and refused to believe that the call was genuine until I sent her a little note.

Toward the end of my Australian trip I happened to go on board a destroyer tied up at one of the ports and found that it was the "Helm," which was named for Admiral Helm, Edith Helm's husband. She and I had visited it when it was near Washington, D. C. Many of the crew who had been on board then were now gone, but there were still a few who remembered and we all enjoyed the reunion.

My last night in Australia I dined with Mrs. Douglas MacArthur, but I did not see the general; he was in New Guinea, and felt I should not be allowed to go up there because of the danger. I bade good-bye to General Eichelberger and General Byers with a feeling that I had made real friends, and with a deep sense of appreciation for their thoughtfulness and kindness throughout the trip. They must have been glad to get rid of me, but they never showed it, and I only hope that they felt I did enough good to justify all the time and trouble they took.

Back at Noumea, I still did not know whether I was to be allowed to go to Guadalcanal or was starting homeward. The last evening, after I had spent the day doing all the things that had been arranged for me by Admiral Halsey, he calmly announced that I was to be ready to leave the next morning at eight o'clock for Efate. I was not to mention the name of the island because the Japs had never bombed it and we had some of our biggest hospitals there. He hoped that they did not know we were established there. From Efate I would go to Espiritu Santo and then on to Guadalcanal. You may be sure that I was ready on time the next morning.

Because the next few days were the busiest and in many ways the most interesting of my entire trip, my diary for that period may be worth quoting:

We are not using our usual size plane because it is too big to land on some of the small islands. Miss Coletta Ryan, who is out here to supervise the Red Cross clubs in the Southwest Pacific is making this trip with me, hoping to be allowed to set up clubs in places where they now do not have them. We landed about 11:00 A.M. on Efate and it seemed as though I walked through miles of hospital wards. I am deeply impressed with the work that has been done on that island to prevent malaria and make it a healthful place. In the afternoon, about 4:30, I arrived at Espiritu Santo, which is the headquarters of the navy air force and also a rendezvous for navy ships and for some army personnel. The navy men have built themselves, on a little island across from the main station, a wonderful recreation ground. I saw a great deal in the first hour, and then in the late afternoon the admiral had a reception. We dined with him and went to the movies, where I said a few words to the men and it was almost 11:00 o'clock when we went to bed.

I was called at 1 A.M., since we were to take off at 1:30 A.M. Coletta Ryan and I sat on two little seats opposite each other and over the bomb bay. The young man who gave us blankets when we were cold and offered us cups of coffee, was most solicitous for our comfort. He turned out to be the nineteen-year-old nephew of governor Stainback of Honolulu. It is unbelievable how young some of these boys are, but the responsibility of war matures them quickly. By 6:00 A.M. we were on Guadalcanal, where we had breakfast with the commanding officer on the airfield; he is a great friend of Admiral Halsey's. At one point he was lost and everybody turned out to find him, including the admiral himself.

Then the army officers came to get me, and as we drove off the trucks with the men who were working on the field were just coming in. Coletta Ryan and I leaned out to wave. At first there was complete surprise written on the faces of the men, and then one boy in very stentorian tones said: "Gosh, there's Eleanor." I am never quite sure whether to take this as a compliment or to be a little ashamed of it, but they were so evidently pleased to see women, we had to laugh and go on waving. The commanding officer was plainly horrified to have me treated with such levity, so I tried to make believe I considered it a great compliment.

I visited all the improvements which have been made since this part of the island came into our possession. There are thought to be some Japs still on the other side of the island and there are still air raids.

One of the things which I shall never forget on Guadalcanal is my visit to the cemetery. The little church there was built by the natives and given to the soldiers; they even made an altar and the altar vessels, carving them beautifully and decorating the church with symbols which have special meanings for them—fishes of various kind which mean long life, eternity, etc. It was very moving to walk among the graves and to realize how united these boys had been in spite of differences in religion and background. The boy's mess-kit or sometimes his helmet hung on the cross which some friend would have carved with the appropriate symbol of the Jewish or Catholic or Protestant faith. Words that came from the heart were carved on the base, such as "He was a grand guy"—"Best buddy ever."

The cemetery is carefully tended and flags wave over the graves. The chaplain told me he took photographs and sent them home to sorrowing families in the United States.

Hospitals and cemeteries are closely tied together in my head and heart on this trip and I think of them even when I talk to the boys who are well and strong and in training.

On Guadalcanal, as in many other places, I said a prayer in my heart for the growth of the human spirit, so that we may do away with force in settling disputes in the future.

I asked to have Joe Lash sent for, and also asked for Cecil Peterson. Cecil Peterson and I had a short talk, and I had a brief few minutes with Joe just before lunch but arranged for him to come for me in a jeep after my official visits were over, when I could have an hour with him. I lunched with the officers and continued immediately afterwards on the rounds. We were not able to finish going through the hospital wards because I took an hour off from 4:30 to 5:30 to go to the weather station where Joe was assigned so I could tell Trude about it. At 5:30 I went to the dinner that had been arranged and then back to the hospital to finish the wards. There was an air-raid alert just as we were driving in, which meant that we had to take to the shelter in the hospital grounds, with all the patients who could walk. For a short time there was a rather tense atmosphere, but somebody started to sing and we all joined in. When the all-clear sounded I went through the wards I had not covered before. I was much interested to see what the effects of the alert would be on those who could not leave their beds and go to the shelter. I saw only two men who were badly affected—one a colored boy who lay turning his head from side to side and moaning, seemingly completely unconscious. A sweet little nurse sat beside him trying to quiet him. The other was a white boy who paced the floor in a little room. I tried to talk to him to change the current of his thoughts, but it was impossible and I finally had to give up.

I went back to the little guest cabin, had a bath and sat down on the porch to rest and wait for Joe. Though he arrived late, we did have an opportunity for a fairly long talk, so I shall have much of interest to tell Trude when I get back. Finally he left and I had a few hours' sleep, but we were up again at 4:00 A.M. off the Island by 5:00 A.M. and on our way back to Espiritu Santo.

I left Miss Ryan on Espiritu Santo and heard shortly afterwards that she had been successful in establishing clubs.

The return trip to Hawaii was again made by way of Christmas Island because an attack was being made on the route we originally planned to take and it was thought not safe for me to go that way. My time on Christmas Island was short and I visited only one boy, about whom the doctor was very much worried. At the hospital, I made him promise that he would try to get well if I would try to see his mother on my return. I did see her, and fortunately he recovered and came to see me when he got back to the United States.

This time I stayed some days in Hawaii, where I saw the training given under actual fire—and was greatly impressed by it—visited a great number of hospitals, and a New York State regiment. Judith Anderson met me at luncheon at one of the hospitals. She and Maurice Evans were giving Shakespearean plays on the islands in this group—*Macbeth* at the time— and it was a wild success. She told me with satisfaction that some of the boys would wait outside and ask her "who this guy Shakespeare" was and tell her it was the first time they had seen a real play with living people in it, and ask to be allowed to come again the next night because they did not think they got everything there was in the play. They were audiences such as few actors and actresses ever meet and I think repaid fully everything which Miss Anderson and Mr. Evans put into their trip.

Finally I took off for home. I have a lasting recollection of landing in California and having to sit in the plane while all the outer air was shut off and we were squirted thoroughly with disinfectant.

My stop in San Francisco was very short. I went to a hotel where my granddaughter, Sistie, came to lunch with me; then I took off again and went right through to New York City, where Jimmy and Tommy met me.

I had been to Hawaii, Christmas Island, Penrhyn Island, Bora-Bora, Aitutaki, Tutuila, Samoa, Fiji, New Caledonia; Auckland, Wellington and Rotorua in New Zealand; Sydney, Canberra, Melbourne, Rockhampton, Cairns, Brisbane in Australia; Efate, Espiritu Santo, Guadalcanal, and Wallis.

War trip number two was over.

CHAPTER NINETEEN

FRANKLIN'S SECOND WAR TRIP AND MY THIRD : TEHERAN AND THE CARIBBEAN

HAVING TOLD the story of my two trips to parts of the world where actual war was going on and where, of necessity, one saw the results of the war in the hospitals, I think I should say something of the impressions these trips left with me.

At first I could hardly bear the hospitals. There was, of course, a certain amount of pure physical fatigue from walking miles of hospital wards day after day; but that was nothing in comparison with the horrible consciousness of waste and feeling of resentment that burned within me as I wondered why men could not sit down around a table and settle their differences before an infinite number of the youth of many nations had to suffer.

I think the most horrifying hospitals were those where the men had been mentally affected by the experiences they had been through. I could tell myself, of course, that these men would probably have broken under other circumstances, that there must be something wrong with our civilization when our young people were so vulnerable to mental illness and that we can work to discover the reasons and try to change them; nevertheless my horror at seeing people who had broken mentally and emotionally made me lie awake nights.

I have a great objection to seeing anyone, particularly anyone whom

311

I care about, lose his self-control, whether from drinking or from lack of emotional stability. Drinking to excess is a type of emotional instability only one step short of what happens to people who actually go out of their minds. As I walked through wards in mental hospitals, I kept saying to myself: "Why does this have to happen?"

There were times in the other hospitals when it was hard to accept the gallantry of the men themselves without showing how deeply sorry I was for them. I knew that that was the last thing they wanted and that their brave front of casual cheerfulness was put on to prevent people from showing that they were sorry.

There was one young marine whom I met in a San Francisco hospital who had lost one leg and one arm in the fighting in the Pacific. He had to have many operations. Finally he was fitted with an artificial leg and came walking into the ward to the cheers of all the patients. He went into San Francisco on leave with another handicapped boy who was without arms but could still take him picka-back! Months later, when I again visited the hospital, I was told he was still there and I was asked to talk to him about doing what the doctors told him to do. He promised to be "a good boy." Just before I left the White House for good, I heard that he was married, doing well enough in business to start buying a little house, had a car which his uncle had given him, and was a successful insurance salesman.

Another young man, whom I found at Walter Reed Hospital in Washington, was a shining example of courage, persistence and gallantry. He had been studying to become a concert pianist. During one of the earliest landings in the war his hands had been badly burned and rendered practically useless. To me it seemed a cruel blow. When I talked to him he said he thought with practice he might be able to play the piano again, but he did not like to practice on the piano in the hospital because he was self-conscious in front of the other men. I suggested that he come to the White House where there were three pianos and where he could be entirely alone in one room or another. It took quite a bit of urging to make him agree, but finally he accepted the offer and came regularly. One day he asked to see me and told me with great excitement that he could at last reach an octave. Later he asked me to listen to him play. He played beautifully, and my heart ached for him because his hands would never permit him to play professionally. However he continued his musical studies and is now teaching music.

Many of the other boys I saw in hospitals are now leading happy and useful lives, but they carry with them, day after day, the results of the war. The gallantry of youth, bearing handicaps which will be a cross all their lives, seems to me a theme for some great poet. Though the war had to be fought to preserve our freedom, their full reward for their suffering is not yet in sight. To see that it is paid in full measure is an obligation which all of us who lived through the war owe to the thousands who fought it. If we do not achieve the real ends for which they sacrificed—a peaceful world in which there exists freedom from fear both of aggression and want—we have failed. This is the challenge presented to the citizens of our democracy by the last war and we shall not have paid our debt until these ends are achieved.

These are the thoughts that I brought back from my visit to the South Pacific. My next trip, to the Caribbean area, was interesting but not soul-stirring. The Pacific trip left a mark from which I think I shall never be free. It is because there must be thousands of men and women in this country who were similarly affected by their experiences during the war that I have hope we may eventually build the kind of future that so many men suffered and died for.

One other development gives me great hope for the future. Women have always come to the fore in wartime, but I think in World War II they took responsibility in more fields than ever before—in factories, on the farms, in business and in the military services. They were an indispensable part of the life of the country. This was true in Great Britain, in Australia, in New Zealand, in France, in all occupied countries in Europe, in Russia and in the United States. Women have become conscious also of the need to take part in the political life of their country. In the European countries more women are today playing an active role in public life than would have been possible before the war, and I am sure we are going to see great developments in the Asiatic area too. This, to me, is a very hopeful sign, for women will work for peace as hard as they worked for the war.

That autumn, on November 9, 1943, there was a ceremony in the East Room of the White House in which my husband took great pride. He believed in dramatizing special occasions, and he carefully planned that when the forty-four nations signed the agreement for the United Nations Relief and Rehabilitation administration, it be done with pomp and ceremony. I was particularly glad of the chance to witness the beginning of this giant organization, which was to bring relief to many people before it came to an end. The first administrator was former Governor Herbert H. Lehman of New York, in whose ability Franklin had complete confidence, having worked with him for many years. Mr. Lehman proved by the way he set up his organization and conducted the work that he was a good organizer and had the patience of Job. The difficulties he encountered, both in this country and in many others, made it necessary for him to choose his personnel carefully and demanded at the top level skillful negotiation, in which I think he excels.

On the afternoon of the day this great event took place I had the pleasure of having Ernie Pyle to tea. He wrote a column about that visit and described it better than I can. He mentioned that he was conscious that the elbows of his coat were out. I never noticed that. I did notice, however, his very charming, sensitive face and I wished that we might have had more opportunities to meet. I had read, always with admiration, the columns he had written from the various battle fronts, and I told him I thought he should do for the men in the Pacific what he had done for the men of the African and European areas. I think he made the men in the army more human than any other writer. His death and that of Ray Clapper, one of the finest war correspondents, were a great loss and high-lighted the fact that, to keep us informed at home, men were taking risks and sacrificing their lives even though they were not actually in the fighting forces.

On November 11 Franklin left for his second war trip. He was to meet the Generalissimo and Madame Chiang in Cairo. This would be his first meeting with the Generalissimo, and Madame Chiang was to act as interpreter. Elliott was ordered to join his father for part of the time, and John Boettiger, who was in the army in Italy, was also detailed to be with him. Mr. Churchill met Franklin in Cairo and the talks went well.

Because at that time the USSR was not at war with Japan, Marshal Stalin was reluctant to meet with the head of the Chinese government; consequently when the talks in Cairo were over, Mr. Churchill, Franklin, and Elliott and John Boettiger went on to Teheran to meet Marshal Stalin. This was the first meeting between Marshal Stalin and my husband. Franklin went to it with the determination that, if it was possible, there was going to be good will and understanding between them. When he talked about this trip beforehand he was very much intrigued at the idea of meeting the Marshal. He thought it was a challenge, knowing well how suspicious the government representatives of the USSR were. Realizing that Stalin himself assumed much of the responsibility in the command of the Russian army and the strategy of the fighting, Franklin accepted reluctantly his refusal to go further away from home than Teheran; but though he said very little about it, I knew he was going to exert himself to the utmost to win the confidence of Stalin himself and to establish, if possible, a better relationship between our two governments.

After Franklin had been in Teheran for only a day, Stalin insisted that, because of the rumors of unrest among the native people of Iran, the president must move into the same area of the city that he was in. Mr. Churchill was next door and the Russian soldiers could more easily protect them all.

Afterwards my husband told me that he felt there was a great distrust on the part of Marshal Stalin when they first met, and he had no idea, on leaving, whether he had been able to dissipate any of it or not. He added that he intended to see that we kept our promises to the letter. He hoped that Great Britain would be able to also, and said he would do all he could to help them do it. He felt that by keeping our word we could build the confidence of this leader whose people, though fighting on our side, still did not trust us completely. The USSR needed all the help that we, with our great power of production, could give, while we were more than grateful for the fact that fighting in the USSR kept so many German divisions busy.

My husband enjoyed his first contact with Stalin. It was always a challenge to him to meet new people whom he knew he had to win over to his own point of view, and this encounter was especially important. I know he was impressed by the strength of Marshal Stalin's personality. On his return he was always careful in describing him to mention that he was short and thick-set and powerful and gave the impression of being a bigger man than he actually was. He also said that his control over the people of his country was unquestionably due to their trust in him and their confidence that he had their good at heart. It is hard to describe what gives a man the quality of leadership, but I am sure my husband felt that Marshal Stalin had this quality.

I have often thought that these three men, Stalin, Churchill and Roosevelt, in their very different ways, were extraordinarily good people to have been thrown together to achieve success in this war. All of them, without any question, led their people and gave so unstintingly of their own strength that they inspired confidence and respect.

It was probably difficult for Marshal Stalin to forget some of the things the great leader of the United Kingdom had said in the past, and the fact that we had joined with the British in occupying part of Russia's northern territory at the end of the First World War did not make it any easier to bring about cordial relations. However in 1933 my husband had recognized the USSR, which had been isolated since 1918, and I am sure that at Teheran he made Marshal Stalin feel that his good will was genuine. After this meeting the cooperation among the three men grew steadily closer.

After these meetings Franklin always described the extravagant banquets given by the Russian leaders; the amount of food and especially the amount of liquor impressed him greatly. But the ceremony he liked best to describe was the presentation by Mr. Churchill to Mr. Stalin of a very beautiful sword which he had brought for the Marshal. Franklin said that this evidently pleased Stalin very much and that he showed his pleasure and real appreciation of the gift. It was after this ceremony that the picture of the three men. in which Mr. Stalin looks particularly cheerful, was taken.

Franklin returned to Washington on December 17, exhilarated by the trip, full of new interests and seemingly in better health. Because of his keen interest in everything he saw and everyone he met, each trip seemed to have this effect on him.

During his absence Louise Hopkins and Diana had moved to a house of their own and were really excited about it. Harry went there after this trip. Franklin had known before he left of their decision to move, and had not felt he could oppose it: it was natural that Harry and Louise should want their own home, and the end of the war was now in sight. Harry's health was very poor, and this move, plus his illness, really began to make it difficult for him to work as closely with Franklin as he had done when living in the White House. While he was with us, the two men would often have a meal together, or Harry would drop in to Franklin's room before going to bed, and they would discuss domestic policies, and later the problems of the war. They always talked over trips beforehand, and I am sure Harry was always given certain specific instructions before he left on one.

Anna and her children came early in December and, because it was what the children greatly desired, Franklin agreed that we should all spend Christmas at Hyde Park. All the usual parties for the people in the executive offices and on the household staff were held on the 23rd so that Franklin could leave that night. At Hyde Park we had the usual Christmas tree party for the people who worked on our place and two evening parties in the Franklin D. Roosevelt Library for the soldiers who were attending the Military Police school there. We had quite a family reunion, and everyone on the place was always glad of a chance to see the children and grandchildren. For us it was a joy to have the girls and the grandchildren, but if a son could come for a short leave it was, of course, special cause for rejoicing. Franklin, junior, and his family, and Johnny and his wife and children were with us this year, as well as Anna and her children.

Back in Washington, in January, 1944, we welcomed John's wife, Anne, and Haven and the baby, Nina, for an indefinite visit. Johnny had gone off with his ship on her trial trip and wanted Anne to settle the children in the White House so she would feel free to join him wherever he might put into port, if only for a day.

This visit was the occasion of one of the stories that we always enjoyed in the family. Franklin liked it so much that as usual he continued to embellish it every time he told it—for he loved to tell stories on himself. Johnny called me one evening just before Anne and the children were to come. I was out, so he talked to his father who was already in bed. First he told him when Anne would arrive and then proceeded to tell him about the various things that must be ordered and prepared for their arrival. Finally he said: "Be sure to order the diaper service." Franklin, who had never heard of the diaper service, said, "What did you say?" Johnny replied, "The diaper service," and explained what it was and said the order should be for two hundred. This bewildered his father who asked: "Is there anything wrong with the baby? We always boiled ours." Johnny said: "Oh, father, people don't do things like that any more and there is nothing wrong with my baby. This is just a supply to have on hand." Franklin dutifully made a mental note and was so much intrigued with the whole idea that while he waited to tell me about it, he went over in his mind the conversation he would have the next morning. He thought to himself: "I will call Hacky (Miss Hackmeister, the head telephone operator) and say: 'Hacky get me the diaper service immediately' and Hacky will say 'What did you say, Mr. President' and then I will answer: 'The diaper service, Hacky, I do not know what it is but please get it.' After Hacky completes the call I will say: 'This is the President of the United States and I want to order two hundred diapers sent to me at the White House.'" All of this having been carefully decided in his mind, he put out his light and went to sleep. The next morning was an especially busy one and even I did not get in to see him until fairly late. I had been talking to him for a few minutes when suddenly a look of horror came over his face and he said: "Oh, I entirely forgot about the diaper service." Not knowing that Johnny had called, I was more and more bewildered until finally he told me the whole story and repeated his imaginary conversation. Fortunately it remained in his imagination. He always loved to tell this story and point out that if I had not been gadding, I would have been at home to receive Johnny's call.

Early in January John Boettiger returned from Italy and took his family back to Seattle for a time, but on February 20, Anna arrived for an indefinite stay with little Johnny because her husband expected to be stationed in Washington for a while. The two older children were in boarding school. Anna's presence was the greatest possible help to my husband. Ever since Miss LeHand's illness, though Miss Tully did a remarkable job in taking her place, there had been gaps which could have been filled only by someone living in the house. Now Anna filled them. She saw and talked to people whom Franklin was too busy to see and then gave him a digest of the conversations. She also took over the supervision of his food. The doctor thought he should have a dietitian to plan his menus, and keeping peace between her and the temperamental cook was no easy task. Anna also had her hands full keeping peace between the cook and Mrs. Nesbitt. In fact, she helped Franklin in innumerable ways. Everything she did was done capably, and she brought to all her contacts a gaiety and buoyance that made everybody feel just a little happier because she was around.

The fourth of March the church service which Franklin always insisted on as a reminder of the first inauguration was held in the East Room of the White House. Tommy and I left immediately after for our 13,000-mile plane trip in the Caribbean area. My husband had insisted that I take this trip. He thought that because the war had receded in that area the men stationed there felt they were in a backwater and chafed to be where they could do what they considered a more important job. Nevertheless, we had to have men there to guard and watch for submarines because there was so much traffic to Europe, Asia and Africa. Franklin wanted them to realize that he knew and understood the whole picture and believed they were doing a still vitally necessary job—that they were not forgotten, even though they were not on the front line.

I was getting a little weary of the criticism heaped on me for taking these trips, but because my husband insisted that my visit to the South Pacific had been a success in that it had accomplished what he had hoped for, I decided to make this tour. He mapped it out, and I took Miss Thompson with me. The entire trip from March 4 to March 28, was by air, and in that period we visited Guantanamo, Cuba; Jamaica;

Puerto Rico; Virgin Islands; Antigua; St. Lucia; Trinidad; Paramaribo; Belem, Natal and Recife in Brazil; La Guaira; Caracas; Curaçao; Aruba; Barranquilla; Canal Zone; Salinas; Galapagos Islands; Guatemala; Havana, Cuba. From Havana we flew straight home.

In Guantanamo, Cuba, the navy people, hoping that my husband would come down for a rest and a visit, took me over the quarters they thought he might occupy. I was rather certain that he would not be able to make the trip, but I examined the quarters with interest and found everything very comfortable and convenient. I knew that if Franklin could persuade those who looked after his safety that it was all right for him to go, he would enjoy the contact with the navy, and it would give him satisfaction to see the ships on war duty.

In Jamaica, I spent one night at the colonel's house in the camp, talked to the men after the movie, and did the usual rounds of inspection. The second night I spent with the governor and his wife, Lord and Lady Huggins. Lady Huggins was working on several projects, including a clinic for babies and milk stations, to help the poorer natives. It was a popular belief among the poorer people that the more children one had the surer one was of getting to heaven and close to God. While this might be wonderful for them in the next world, it was not a helpful notion in this one, for the means of sustenance were often lacking and one saw many poorly-nourished children. One woman thirty-six years old had twenty-three children!

Puerto Rico was seething with activity and did not seem to me at all like the rather quiet, restful spot I had visited ten years previously. Rex Tugwell was the governor of the islands at the time of my second visit and he and Mrs. Tugwell made us very comfortable in the historic old house, La Fortelesa. Governor Tugwell was trying out in Puerto Rico some of the ideas he had become interested in during his first survey, and Adrian Dornbush was doing research to develop new uses for Puerto Rican materials—bamboo, sugar cane, palms, and the like.

The young men of Puerto Rico had been drafted into the army, and I still remember the tears of one woman who was running a milk station and her plea to me for her son's safety. I found later he was stationed on a near-by island. Puerto Ricans apparently hate to leave their island and seem to want to return to it even when they have to return to slums which are as bad as any in the world.

All these islands in the Caribbean have charm, and life on them can be delightful, but under war conditions I doubt if any of our men gave much thought to the wonderful combination of moonlight and palms. Busy building roads and camps and cleaning up bad sanitary conditions, they found life on the whole none too interesting.

The flight to northern Brazil and down along the coast gave me a view of a really tropical jungle; I said a little prayer that our plane would land us safely in Belem and would not have to come down in the jungle area over which we were flying.

Belem is an interesting city of old churches and picturesque mosaic-tiled-front houses, but I do not think I would enjoy living there for long, for the climate is hot and damp. The harbor was crowded with fishing boats on which lived swarms of men, women and children. They were not my idea of comfortable and clean habitations.

I was joined in Belem by the wives of some of the Brazilian government officials, who had been sent to meet me, and by our ambassador, Mr. Caffery and his wife. I enjoyed having them all with me on my visit to Natal and Recife, where, as in Belem, I saw all the army and navy activities and inspected the recreation facilities.

I marveled at the hardiness of the Brazilian fishermen, who put out to sea in little boats which looked as though just a few nails held them together. They were really nothing more than rafts with a sail. I was given a model of one to take back to my husband, who was greatly interested in it and in the navigating skill of the fishermen.

The airfield at Recife had a special fascination for me because it was from there the men were checked out to start their long trek across the ocean. I had a chat with a boy who was getting his last orders before leaving for India, where he would be flying the Hump—one of the most dangerous trips of all. He had just been home on leave, and told me that when flying low over some of the midwestern country on his way back to a base near his home, he had looked down and said to himself: "I wish I could say to you people below me 'do you know how lucky you are? What wonderful lives you have? How rich is your security in comparison to the millions of people I have seen in India and China?" He was one of the many boys who in India saw famine at first hand; I doubt if any of them will ever forget it.

The Brazilian people were sorry that I was not going down to their beautiful city of Rio de Janeiro, but Franklin had very carefully stated that I was to confine myself to visiting the places where our men were stationed, and Rio served as a base only during the occasional visits of our warships.

In British Guiana I took off from Georgetown on a short flight with an old-timer, Major Williams, who ran a regular plane service for prospectors and farmers in the jungles and high mountains. He wanted to show me one of the remarkable sights in the interior, Essequibo Falls, said to be the highest in the world, but the fog was so thick I could not see them. However, he was able to fly low enough along the little rivers to show me the small settlements here and there, explaining that when someone was ill or in need of anything, he would land in these little streams and pick up his passenger or deliver what was wanted. Life there seemed a curious pioneer existence to me, but it must have a fascination for quite a number of people, for there was no dearth of men, women and children living in little clearings dotted all over that wild country.

At one of the hospitals I met a boy who had heard the same quarantine story that had been circulated in the Pacific, but he was intelligent enough to doubt it and we had a very nice talk.

Curaçao struck me as being so Dutch that I felt a small piece of Holland had been transplanted to these curious tropical islands. Princess Juliana, as she was then, had been there just a short time before, and the people were still excited and inspired by her visit. The governor of the islands had left his family behind him in Holland when the Germans invaded the country. He told me his wife had said to him: "I will look after the children. If you stay here the Germans will put you in prison, and then you can do nothing for your country during the war." She practically drove him out of Holland. Like so many others, he had great difficulty in getting any news from her during the occupation. What wonderful courage those women had! Think of facing an invading army with five little children to look after and protect!

One place my husband allowed me to go that was not strictly speaking a service base was Venezuela. I was driven from the airport up a very steep road to Caracas. Franklin had said it was one of the most beautiful roads he had ever seen, and I agreed with him after driving over it. We were told the road was built entirely by hand by men and women who had worked on it for seven years; it was a sort of WPA project. My visit was merely one of good will but while I was there I learned something of the awakening interest among women of the country in the better care and feeding of children.

The president of Venezuela and his wife gave a wonderful dinner in my honor. I was told that in the table decorations and in the brilliantly lighted trees there were four thousand orchids. It was on this trip that I first saw orchids in great profusion and I realized that I had never before dreamed how beautiful they could be. It seemed wicked to use them so extravagantly for decoration, but they grew in such abundance and variety that one had to become accustomed to accepting them as a common garden flower and not a great luxury.

After a brief stop in Colombia we flew to the Canal Zone, where I was able to get a good view of the Panama Canal from the air. General Brett and Admiral Train had mapped out quite an active tour there, and I was glad to be able to visit boys in lonely camps, to ride in a PT boat to inspect the base, and in general to see as much of our men as possible.

I had an unexpected pleasure in Panama. The USS "Wasp," the ship on which my son, John, was assistant supply officer, was going through the canal the day I arrived and since he had four hours shore leave, he came to see me. It was the last time I saw him until the end of the war.

On leaving the Canal Zone I paid a brief visit to Ecuador, where a few men were stationed, and then flew to Galapagos Island. Quite a number of people thought this was an unnecessary trip, and various USO entertainers had been persuaded not to go there, much to the disappointment of the men. However, it was one place where my husband insisted I go, because he knew the men there were probably having a duller and more trying time than the men stationed anywhere else in the world. After visiting it, I realized that he was right. The army had men stationed at one end and the navy at the other. Absolutely nothing but a few scrub cacti grew on the wretched island; it never rained, there was no fresh water, and the men had to use distilled water from the sea. As for fauna there were iguanas (which looked like miniature dinosaurs) and two goats, whose horns had been painted red and green by the navy men. What they ate nobody knew. I could see few other living things on the island. The navy non-commissioned officers had built a recreation building for themselves and we were invited to visit it. We were much amused at the sign over the door: "Women Invited"; we were the only two women who had ever been on the island!

I was sorry for the boys who made the daily flights to cover the triangle—Galapagos, Ecuador and Guatemala, and back because, while they had to be endlessly on the watch since they were guarding the mouth of the Panama Canal, they rarely sighted anything, and it is easy to lose your alertness under those conditions. Some of the men at the anti-aircraft gun stations in this area had been here as long as forty-two months, and I told my husband when I got home that I thought that was too long a time for men to be stationed in those lonely places, especially Galapagos.

The climate at the coast station in Guatemala was terrible and the men found the heat and the insects and reptiles hard to bear. Over the door of their recreation room they had a sign: "Home of the Forgotten Men." Guatemala City, however, had a delightful climate and had I been on a pleasure trip, I should have liked to spend more time visiting the old capital and some of the Indian villages.

The president of Guatemala gave a very formal reception for me in his palace; all were seated according to protocol and brought up to be presented to me in groups according to rank or position. The palace is luxurious. Many kinds of mahogany were used in the interior decorations, some of it as light as our pine. As I was entering the building to attend this reception, escorted by our military officers, a flashlight bulb exploded and before I could take a breath Guatemalan soldiers seemed to spring up out of the floor, and our officers seized my arms and rushed me away. It had sounded like a shot and no one was taking any chances.

Another amusing recollection from that trip is of the place where, though the ladies' room was primitive and guarded by a soldier, we found everything a woman could possibly wish for—good soap, towels, hairpins, bobby pins, facial tissues, shoe brush, clothes brush, face powder and puffs. Clearly the most meticulous care had been taken to provide us with everything we might find useful, and I could not help thinking that the officer responsible must have had a thoughtful wife who made her guests very comfortable. By contrast, in some other places the officers treated themselves in Spartan fashion; one man who turned his quarters over to us had only an army cot with a thin mattress as his bed and another cot which he used as a dresser. There was no chest of drawers. There was an electric icebox in which he put things to drink, but I would gladly have exchanged the drinks for a few more amenities in the bedroom.

Since this trip was not within easy reach of the enemy, it was publicized before I left, and countless mothers, wives, sweethearts and sisters wrote to beg me to try to see their menfolk. When I left home, I took with me a file of cards with the names and identification numbers of the men I'd been asked to look up, and as I reached each place, I gave the cards of the men stationed there to one of the officers and asked, if possible, to see them. The young men would be told, without explanation, to be at a certain place—usually an officer's room—at a given time. They would arrive, very nervous and apprehensive, and when I appeared would invariably look surprised and greatly relieved. On my return, I had letters to write to hundreds of people, because during the trip many other boys I met asked me to write to their families back home.

On this trip too I managed to have meals with the enlisted men, the non-commissioned officers and the officers. It meant breakfast at 5:55 a.m. and not 6, dinner at noon, and supper at 5:00 or 5:30 p.m. In one place some Puerto Rican soldiers were very kind and brought

Miss Thompson and me our coffee at breakfast time all prepared the way they like it—mostly sugar and canned milk.

Everywhere I went I was treated with the greatest courtesy and consideration, though some of the top-ranking officers were quite frank in telling me they had not anticipated my visit with pleasure. Nevertheless Ambassador Caffery and some of the generals and admirals were kind enough to write to Washington that my trip had been helpful, and I have always hoped that I was able to give the men some pleasure and encouragement, which had been my husband's thought in suggesting this tour.

We stopped at Havana on the way back, where, as in any foreign country I visited, I met the government officials or their deputies. This always gave me a welcome opportunity to learn something about the country itself and to express the good will of our people toward our neighbors to the south.

On the whole we had remarkably good weather. I always tried to be very meticulous about carrying out any requests of the crew regarding times of arrival and departure, and I cannot remember a single occasion when the weather held us up on this trip. We landed back in Washington after having covered 13,000 miles by air and many, many miles by foot going through hospital wards, camps and so forth.

In two days both Tommy and I felt that the trip already lay far behind; as always the accumulated work demanded such concentration to catch up that we were back in the daily routine almost before we had an opportunity to report on what we had seen and done.

CHAPTER TWENTY

THE LAST TERM : 1944-1945

ALL THROUGH the winter of 1943-1944 my husband had run a low
fever at intervals and we thought he had picked up a bug on the trip or
perhaps had acquired undulant fever from our cows at Hyde Park.
It was a terrible idea, but I suppose one considers every possibility
when nobody seems able to decide exactly why certain symptoms
recur. Franklin did seem to feel quite miserable, which was not altogether astonishing, considering that he had been through so many
years of strain. Finally he made up his mind on April ninth that he
would go down and stay with Bernard Baruch at his plantation, Hobcaw, in Georgetown, South Carolina. Mr. Baruch had offered to take
in his whole entourage.

There were times when being a very independent gentleman, Mr.
Baruch differed from my husband on policies. There were also times,
as often happens to any president, when the people around him became jealous of outside advisers such as Mr. Baruch and made it
difficult for cordial relations to exist. However, my husband was in-
clined to be impervious to stories or rumors about anyone who he felt
could be helpful; and, since Mr. Baruch is one of the people who can
ignore the past, he was always ready to be useful when called upon.
The personal relationship remained unbroken through all the years
Franklin and I knew him.

Hobcaw was just the right place for Franklin, who loved the country and the life there, and he stayed almost a month. One day Anna and I flew down for lunch, along with the prime minister of Australia and his wife, Mr. and Mrs. Curtin, and I came home feeling that it was the very best move Franklin could have made. I have always been grateful to Mr. Baruch for providing him with that holiday.

June 6, 1944, was a red-letter day. We had known for a long time that invasion preparations were being made, but everything was kept very secret. When the time came Franklin went on the air to give his D Day prayer, and for hours our hearts were with the men on the beaches. The news came in little by little. In spite of the sorrow our losses brought to many families, it was a great relief to know that permanent landings had finally been made and that the liberation of Europe had really begun.

Another election lay ahead in the fall of 1944. I knew without asking that as long as the war was on it was a foregone conclusion that Franklin, if he was well enough, would run again. A number of doctors were called in and he was given a thorough physical examination. Since to hand over to anyone else at that particular point would have been extremely difficult, it was finally decided that if he would agree to follow certain rules laid down by the doctors, he could stand going on with his work.

There has recently appeared in a magazine, an article, written by a doctor who does not give his sources of information. This doctor states that my husband had three strokes while he was in the White House; one at least, I believe, prior to this examination. It seems to me that if this statement were true, it would be a reflection on the doctors called in for consultation. I have asked Dr. Ross T. McIntire whether he ever thought my husband had had a stroke and he assures me that he never had one. It would have been impossible for him to have had a stroke without some one of us, who were so constantly with him, noting that something was wrong. I cannot bring myself to believe that the doctors called in for consultation, and Dr. McIntire who was with him all the time, as well as Dr. Bruenn who was with him in Warm Springs, suspected anything of this kind and did not tell me, but did tell the doctor who wrote the article.

The implication in the article is that the family knew of the three strokes and kept them from the public. I wish to state here that no member of the family, including myself, ever suspected anything of this kind or were ever told by any doctor that he suspected anything of the kind. I am sure my husband would have been the last person to permit doctors to slur over anything which might have made him less able mentally to continue his work, and I certainly would have felt that such a thing was unthinkable.

I think all of us knew that Franklin was far from well, but none of us ever said anything about it—I suppose because we felt that if he believed it was his duty to continue in office, there was nothing for us to do but make it as easy as possible for him.

On July 7, while I was in Hyde Park, General de Gaulle lunched with Franklin in the White House. We wondered whether this visit would change his feeling about the general, but their meeting was evidently entirely formal though pleasant, and I saw no difference in Franklin's attitude.

From the 15th of July to the 17th of August, Franklin was away on a trip to the Pacific. He had been in the European area a great deal; now he wanted to establish personal contact with the officers in the Pacific area and go over their plans for the war. Consequently a meeting was arranged in Hawaii. From there he went to Alaska and the Aleutians. It was this trip that gave rise to the extraordinary tale that Fala had been left behind on one of the islands and a destroyer sent back for him. I have no idea where this story started and neither had my husband, though we supposed it was with some bright young man in Republican headquarters. There was no incident during the trip which could have given rise to any such tale.

While Franklin was gone Anna and her husband were in the White House. Her children were with me at Hyde Park, where I spent most of the summer. As usual we had a good many guests. In July I made a trip to Lake Junaluska in North Carolina to speak before a group of Methodist women. I had been very hesitant about going anywhere in the south, because my conviction that the colored people should have full civil rights had, over the years, aroused a good deal of feeling there.

This hostility found an outlet, particularly in election years, in a number of disagreeable letters and editorials and I felt my presence would not be helpful. However, this group was very insistent and I was glad afterwards that I went, for I enjoyed myself and they seemed to think that my coming was worth while. I had great admiration for the courage of Mrs. M. E. Tilly of Atlanta, Georgia, who was the executive secretary of the Methodist women's organization. I was told that whenever a lynching occurred, she went alone or with a friend, as soon as she heard of it, to investigate the circumstances. Only a southern woman could have done this, but even for a southern woman it seemed to me to require great moral as well as physical courage. She is a Christian who believes in all Christ's teachings, including the concept that all men are brothers; and though she is a white southern woman she deeply resents the fact that white southern women are so often used as a pretext for lynching. Later, Mrs. Tilly served with distinction on President Truman's Civil Rights Committee, and has gained for herself the admiration of both northerners and southerners.

We were all saddened by the death of Marguerite LeHand on August second. I was glad that I had been able to see her not very long before when I went to Boston to visit the Chelsea Naval Hospital. She had worked for so many years with my husband and she had been so loyal and devoted, living with us practically as a member of the family, that I knew he would feel sad not to be able to pay a last tribute of respect by attending her funeral. I had to go alone, however, since he could not get back in time.

On September 10 we all left for Quebec for another war conference. Mrs. Churchill was to be there with her husband and Franklin had asked me to go. At first Mr. and Mrs. Hull had planned to go, but Secretary Hull decided that he was not well enough. Later Franklin asked Henry Morgenthau, junior, to come up, to confer on a postwar plan for Germany.

Franklin was very anxious that it should be made impossible for Germany again to start a war. I heard him discuss many plans, even the possibility of dividing Germany into its original principalities. He realized that the industrial power of Germany lay in the Ruhr, and he considered carefully the possibility of international control of that region, but whether he came to any final decision or not, I do not remember ever hearing him say.

He undoubtedly discussed with Henry Morgenthau all of his ideas, including the possibility of reducing Germany to a country more dependent on agriculture than in the past, allowing her only such industry as was essential to a self-supporting state, and making sure that the economy of the rest of Europe would not again be so dependent on Germany for its prosperity.

Here I think it is necessary to review some of the situations described in Henry Morgenthau's articles which appeared in the New York Post in 1947. He tells there of the attitude of different factions in Great Britain while he was abroad in 1944 as well as in our own Army of Occupation, and I think it is important to recall what he says:

"I was astonished to hear that the Big Three had already specifically instructed EAC (European Advisory Commission) to study the problems of partitioning Germany. Stalin, determined that Germany should never again disturb the peace of Europe, strongly favored dismemberment. Roosevelt backed him wholeheartedly and Churchill reluctantly agreed that EAC consider the proposal. Anthony Eden and I were both amazed to learn that EAC was cheerfully drawing its plans not on the basis of German dismemberment, but of German unity. Winant had been at Teheran. But having received no instructions from the State Department to proceed along the Teheran lines, he felt that they might not know of the Big Three decision and that it was not his business to inform his superiors on such a matter.

"This, then, was the situation when I flew back to the United States August 17. The State Department was talking about reconstituting Germany in the family of nations. The British Treasury was interested in Germany as a post-war market. The Army wanted to do a good job. The EAC, blandly ignoring its instructions from Teheran, was planning in terms of a united Germany."

The account given in Henry Morgenthau's article reveals nothing really unusual. Apparently there was a lack of coordination among even the highest levels of government thinking, both in our own country and in Great Britain. The net result of it all seems to have been that the president's intentions were not carried out—intentions which apparently were shared by the Supreme Commander of the European Theater, General Eisenhower.

The Treasury, because of Henry Morgenthau's interest in the prevention of war, decided to study the problem and to give the president the benefit of its studies, even though such a problem was perhaps a little outside its usual province.

The first memo from the Treasury sub-committee which Mr. Morgenthau set up was the basis of what later was known as the Morgenthau Plan: "The provision for the destruction of German armament industry and international control of heavy industry in the Ruhr and Rhineland and the resettlement of Germans on the land."

When Henry Morgenthau showed this plan to my husband, Franklin emphasized three points which he felt were important psychologically in Germany. I think they might well be remembered today.

"The first, that Germany should be allowed no aircraft of any kind, not even a glider.

"The second, that nobody should be allowed to wear a uniform.

"The third, that there should be no marching of any kind."

The prohibition of uniforms and parades, he thought, would do more than anything else to teach the Germans they had been defeated.

I think these articles of Henry Morgenthau's should be re-read in the light of what has been written since then and in the light of what is happening today. They explain clearly the background of the Quebec conference and how Mr. Morgenthau came to be there. At least a month before the Quebec conference, my husband had received memoranda from Secretary Hull, Secretary Stimson and Secretary Morgenthau, members of the Cabinet Committee he had set up to recommend a plan for the post-war treatment of Germany. All were carefully considered, so it is fair to surmise that Henry Morgenthau's plan more closely met the needs of the situation as Franklin saw it. Mr. Morgenthau also tells very clearly about the consideration of the Treasury memo and the Treasury Plan, his own work with Lord Cherwell who might be termed, he says, "Churchill's one-man brain trust," and then about the dictation by Mr. Churchill of his own memo. He gives the memo as dictated by Mr. Churchill and approved by Roosevelt in full, and I quote it here:

"At a conference between the President and the Prime Minister upon the best measures to prevent renewed rearmament by Germany, it was felt that an essential feature was the future disposition of the Ruhr and the Saar.

"The ease with which the metallurgical, chemical and electric industries in Germany can be converted from peace to war has already been impressed upon us by bitter experience. It must also be remembered that the Germans have devastated a large portion of the industries of Russia, and of other neighboring Allies, and it is only in accordance with justice that these injured countries should be entitled to remove the machinery they require in order to repair the losses they have suffered. The industries referred to in the Ruhr and in the Saar would therefore be necessarily put out of action and closed down. It was felt that the two districts should be put under some body under the world organization which would supervise the dismantling of these industries and make sure that they were not started up again by some subterfuge.

"This programme for eliminating the war-making industries in the Ruhr and in the Saar is looking forward to converting Germany into a country primarily agricultural and pastoral in its character.

"The Prime Minister and the President were in agreement upon this programme.

OK

F.D.R.

W.S.C.   September 16, 1944"

After that, there seems to have been the usual trouble among men in high places and the usual difficulty when too many and none-too-accurate news stories leaked out. I do not wonder that Henry Morgenthau was deeply grateful for the letter sent him by Secretary of War Stimson; accusations of the kind that were printed against him must indeed have been hard to bear by a man whose sons were in the fighting forces.

Henry Morgenthau himself tells the story of his last interview with my husband the night before he died. He left him with the firm conviction that Franklin still was determined "not to allow any sentimental consideration to modify the conditions necessary to prevent Germany and the German people from becoming aggressors again." Henry Morgenthau felt that these views were embodied in the Potsdam Agreement. The trouble which has arisen since was not because of that agreement, but because of the lack of further agreement. A careful analysis of much that has happened would probably show that Mr. Churchill always favored a less harsh attitude toward Germany, and as fear of Russia increased, his feeling naturally intensified.

The change in government in Great Britain did not change the policy; it simply transferred the fear of Russia to a different government leader. The foreign policy of Great Britain is always much the same, no matter who is in office. I think it is fairly evident now that the British feel that Germany, as a buffer state and as a market for English goods, is less to be feared than the growing strength of a. communist power. There were people in this country who had much the same idea—and probably some were in the State Department. That may not have been a predominant idea over here, but certainly there were divisions in thinking, as always. We must remember there are people who traditionally want to back the British and people who traditionally do not; and that struggle may also have been going on.

In Robert Sherwood's book, *Roosevelt and Hopkins,* he writes: "I can confirm from my personal knowledge (Secretary) Stimson's statement that Roosevelt subsequently made no secret of his regret that he had ever agreed to initial the proposal. Indeed, on October 20, six weeks after the Quebec conference, Roosevelt gave demonstration of his reaction to the episode by dismissing *all* specific planning for the treatment of Germany; he said in a memo to Hull: 'I dislike making detailed plans for a country which we do not yet occupy,' adding that the details 'were dependent upon what we and our Allies find when we get into Germany—and we are not there yet.' "

I never heard my husband say that he had changed his attitude on this plan. I think the repercussions brought about by the press stories made him feel that it was wise to abandon any final solution at that time

—which was what he was doing in this memo. (Incidentally, I do not agree with Mr. Sherwood that the reason Franklin did not put Harry Hopkins on the temporary joint committee on post-war lend-lease planning was because he was told that Harry was too much under the influence of the British or our other Allies to be a reliable American representative. Franklin would have told Harry what his own stand was on any question that arose and, knowing Harry very well, would have been fairly sure that he could make Harry see things his way. No, it was circumstances that separated them. As I have said, Harry was no longer living in the White House, and in addition he was far from well. He could not carry the active burdens he had once carried. Franklin had so much to do that, no matter how deeply he might have felt, he had no time to keep up any personal relationship that did not also fit in with the demands of his work. This is a hard attitude; nevertheless, it meets the necessities of such a situation.

I have heard Bernard Baruch say many times that "no matter who suffers, the president cannot be wrong." In this case, Mr. Morgenthau suffered, but to me that does not mean at all that fundamentally Franklin's attitude changed. I think this is borne out by the fact that at their last meeting my husband encouraged Henry Morgenthau to write his book on Germany, outlining the ideas he knew Henry held and which to a certain extent Franklin also held, though perhaps they varied in certain details.

While we were at the Quebec conference Mr. Churchill showed us a scale model of a D Day landing harbor in order that my husband might see exactly how it had been used. We were all greatly interested, and Franklin especially so; he insisted that it be taken down to Washington and displayed in the War Department where all the officers could see it.

Staying in the old Citadel in Quebec was a novel experience and I enjoyed walking about the fort, particularly along the ramparts where I could look down on the river. Mr. Mackenzie King was there, and the governor general and Princess Alice, who were kindness itself. One afternoon they took Mrs. Churchill and me for a drive in the country and a picnic tea which I shall always remember with great pleasure.

Both Mrs. Churchill and I were asked to speak in French over the radio, and there were a number of entertainments which we attended. On the 18th, Franklin returned to Hyde Park with Mr. and Mrs. Churchill. Their rest there was necessarily brief because the 1944 campaign was about to begin.

Franklin opened the campaign by speaking at the Teamsters' Union dinner in Washington, Daniel Tobin being an old and warm Democratic adherent. It was at this dinner, I always felt, that Franklin really laid the foundation for Mr. Dewey's defeat by the way in which he told the story of Fala's indignation over the Republican accusation that he had been left behind on an island, and retrieved only at the cost of untold sums of the taxpayers' money. By ridicule, Franklin turned this silly charge to his advantage. Fala with his austere but distinctly Scotch personality gave my husband great joy. In the campaign he would chuckle and say: "I think the people prefer the big man with the little dog to the little man with the big dog."

After that dinner the campaign was on, but I was busy with a number of things which had nothing to do with it. A conference on rural education, organized largely through Miss Charl Ormond Williams' interest, was held in the White House October 4 and 5, and while I know that much of real worth was accomplished, my most vivid recollection is of having one of the delegates ask to see Fala and of my having him brought in, with a piece of cake, so I could make him do his tricks. It gave everybody a little rest from being too serious.

Shortly after my birthday I went at the regular interval to donate blood to the Red Cross. The young lady at the desk was terribly embarrassed because I had passed the sixty mark in years and no one over sixty could be allowed to give blood. I was slightly indignant, because I was unable to see how in a few weeks my blood could have changed; I realized, however that there had to be some definite limit set, and so I felt I really entered old age on October 11, 1944.

At the end of the campaign Franklin and I drove through miles of New York City streets in one of the worst rain storms I ever remember.

We did everything that had been planned, but in between times we stopped in a city garage so Franklin could change into dry clothes. Riding in an open car in that downpour, he was drenched to the skin. We ended up at the apartment, which I had been trying to get Franklin to look at ever since we sold the 65th Street houses. He had told me to get an apartment in New York City in which we could stay occasionally after we left Washington, specifying that it should be a place where he could work in peace and quiet, with no steps anywhere. I had asked him if he cared in what part of town he lived and he had said he had absolutely no preference. He had every intention of spending the rest of his life, after leaving the White House, in Hyde Park and Warm Springs, but realized since he planned to do some magazine work that he must have some place in which to stay in New York City. When I happened to find an apartment on Washington Square, with no steps and with two rooms connected by a bathroom which could be shut off from the rest of the apartment, I decided that it was the ideal spot. But since he had not been in the city I had never had a chance to show it to him, even after I had furnished it and put it all in order. He now said he liked it very much.

I was really worried about him that day, but instead of being completely exhausted he was exhilarated, after he had had a chance to change his clothes and get a little rest. The crowds had been warm and welcoming and the contact with them was good for him. People had seemed not to mind at all standing in the rain so long as they could get a glimpse of him as he waved at them. That must give anyone a very warm feeling. People love you when they believe you have done something really worth while for them, and there was no question but that the people of New York City had been telling him that day how much they cared. Men, women and children had stood for hours, and as far as I could tell it had made no difference that the sun was not shining.

Dr. McIntire had worried about the campaign, but I had told him early in the autumn that I thought Franklin drew strength from contact with people. On the day of our visit to New York City I felt that I had been right and that Franklin was better than he had been at the beginning of the campaign.

That night, October 21, Franklin spoke at the Foreign Policy Association dinner. I heard afterwards that some people thought he looked very ill that night, but I was not surprised because of course he was extremely tired. We went to Hyde Park for the election. When the returns showed that his reelection was assured, he went out on the porch as usual to welcome our neighbors when they came down to greet and congratulate him.

The election over, I went to New York City for a day or two to attend the wedding of Joe and Trude Lash. When I returned to Hyde Park to go back to Washington with Franklin I found that Harry Hooker, our old friend who always was with us on important occasions, had been taken ill. There was no one staying in the Hyde Park house who could look after him, so we bundled him up and took him to Washington. We discovered afterwards that he had had a really serious heart attack and should not have been moved. However, it did not seem to hurt him. We put him to bed in the White House and he stayed for about two months. I could not have managed it at Hyde Park, but in the White House anything was possible. In many ways I think it was better for Harry to be there than in a hospital, and both Franklin and I were happy to be able to keep an eye on him.

Franklin went down to Warm Springs for Thanksgiving and had nearly three weeks there. I was always glad when he was able to go, because he got great satisfaction out of the contact with the patients, especially the youngsters. I think he felt that Warm Springs represented something that he had really been able to do for people who suffered as he had suffered.

Again this year we spent Christmas at Hyde Park. Elliott brought Faye up to meet us and to be welcomed into the family, and spent part of the time driving with his father about the farm and through the Christmas tree plantation. Soon after, Franklin began to plan for his trip to Yalta. I remember that he was so busy it was well into January before he had time to open his Christmas presents. He would not let any of us do it for him, so little by little, as he had a few minutes before dinner, he had the pleasure of opening his gifts, every one of which he enjoyed.

Early in January, realizing full well this would certainly be his last inauguration, perhaps even having a premonition that he would not be with us very long, Franklin insisted that every grandchild come to the White House for a few days over the 20th. I was somewhat reluctant to have thirteen grandchildren ranging in age from three to sixteen together, for fear of an epidemic of measles or chicken pox, but he was so insistent that I agreed.

We bulged at the corners, for it was a tremendous family to house; though it was not so bad as during one of the earlier inaugurations when I had several grandchildren with their mothers and nurses as well as several of my friends staying in the house. That time, when I came to assign beds for two grandchildren and a nurse who were uncertain about coming until the last minute, I found I had to give up my own rooms and sleep in a room on the third floor which my maid used as a sewing and pressing room, and I had to take my mail and work on part of Miss Thompson's desk in her very small office. I was not too comfortable, nor, I fear, too sweet about it.

After the inauguration it was clearer every day that Franklin was far from well. Nevertheless he was determined to go to Yalta, and when he made up his mind that he wanted to do something he rarely gave up the idea. And he did enjoy these trips, particularly when he could go most of the way by battleship. We discussed whether I should go, and he said: "If you go they will all feel they have to make a great fuss, but if Anna goes it will be simpler. Averell Harriman will bring his daughter down from Moscow." Thus it was decided, Anna's husband saying it seemed only fair that she should see one of these conferences—even though he would be left in Washington to look after little Johnny.

Franklin had high hopes that at this conference he could make real progress in strengthening the personal relationship between himself and Marshal Stalin. He talked a good deal about the importance of this in the days of peace to come, since he realized that the problems which would arise then would be more difficult even than those of the war period. He also told me that he intended, if possible, to see some of the Arabs and try to find a peaceful solution to the Palestine situation.

While they were away, Anna kept us posted about her father's health and what was happening on the trip. I thought that in all probability the trip would prove beneficial to Franklin, since he seemed to feel that it was having good results, particularly as concerned his understanding with Marshal Stalin. On the way back, however, General Watson, who had wanted above all else to go on the trip, had a stroke, which I knew must be causing Franklin great anxiety. Before they were out of the Mediterranean he died. Harry Hopkins was also very ill on this trip and got off at Marrakech for a holiday and rest. Altogether dark clouds seemed to be settling over the ship and I was really worried. However, when Franklin landed he seemed better and, in spite of his sorrow, retained some of the pleasant excitement incident to getting home and telling his stories of the trip. This he always enjoyed.

Many things have been said about the "surrender" of the United States' interests in the agreements at Yalta. Edward Stettinius' new book answers these accusations authoritatively, and I hope it will be read by everyone who has for one minute thought that Franklin was not always first concerned with the good of the United States. However, that our welfare was inextricably linked with the welfare of other countries was something he believed deeply—and he also believed we needed the friendship of other countries. He knew that negotiation invariably involved some give and take, but he was a good bargainer and a good poker player, and he loved the game of negotiation. I am sure that even at the Yalta conference, the necessity of matching his wits against other people's stimulated him and kept him alert and interested, no matter how weary he may at times have been.

Yalta was only a step towards the ultimate solution Franklin had in mind. He knew it was not the final step. He knew there had to be more negotiation, other meetings. He hoped for an era of peace and understanding, but he knew well that peace was not won in a day—that days upon days and years upon years lay before us in which we must keep the peace by constant effort.

Though Franklin had felt confident of being able to work with Stalin when he left for Yalta, not long after he got home he began to feel that the Marshal was not keeping his promises. This was something he could not overlook, and I believe he wrote him a number of extremely stern messages. I think he still thought, however, that in the end he could make Stalin live up to his word, and that he, Stalin, and Churchill, having fought the war together, had gained enough understanding and respect for each other to be able to work things out.

In telling of his experiences on this trip, Franklin always said emphatically that one of the most interesting and colorful episodes was his meeting with King Ibn Saud. The king arrived on a destroyer, sitting with all his entourage under a canopy on deck, the sheep which he had brought for food herded at the other end of the ship. Franklin said it was the strangest looking destroyer he had ever seen. Beautiful rugs had been spread and everything done to make the king comfortable in fairly familiar surroundings. Franklin served coffee on their arrival and the king asked permission to have his own coffee-maker prepare the ceremonial coffee, which Franklin drank with him.

The purpose of this visit, of course, was to get some kind of agreement on Palestine; also Franklin wanted to make some suggestions about the development of the Arab countries. He had always felt strongly that they should not turn over all their oil resources to the great nations of the world but should retain enough to use in pumping water to the surface to irrigate the desert for better agricultural development. He was sure that much of the desert land had underground rivers which would make irrigation possible. He also thought that much more could be done in the way of reforestation in these countries. He had mentioned this to the sultan of Morocco when he and Mr. Churchill had dined with him during the Casablanca conference. Franklin said Mr. Churchill did not look too happy over the idea but the sultan seemed enthusiastic.

He tried talking on these subjects to King Ibn Saud only to be met by the statement that the king was a warrior and would continue to be as long as he lived. He said one of his sons—and he had a great many sons—was interested in agriculture and another son was interested in conservation but that he had no interest at all in anything except being a warrior and the king of his nomad people.

Franklin liked Ibn Saud and thought him a fine specimen of the warrior king, but he was discouraged about the chances of doing anything to improve the conditions of Ibn Saud's people. The king did not want his people changed and he felt contact with Europeans would be bad for them. When it came to Palestine, Franklin got nowhere. He always said that his one real failure had been in his talks with this Arabian king.

That they got on well and liked each other was evidenced by the fact that Ibn Saud sent Franklin a beautiful gold sword with many precious jewels in the handle, and that he kept and used the wheel chair which Franklin sent him. He had rheumatism and found it painful to walk. Unfortunately the sword arrived after my husband's death, and it is now in the Library at Hyde Park, the property of our government.

My husband also loved to tell about a formal dinner at Yalta, at which Admiral Leahy felt Anna was drinking too many toasts. Anna enjoyed the admiral's evident concern and did not tell him until afterwards that her glass was being filled with ginger ale instead of vodka.

Franklin went through the difficult task of seeing Mrs. Watson, and attended the funeral of her husband in Arlington Cemetery. I had not only a sense of personal loss in General Watson's death but a great anxiety about the effect it would have on Franklin.

On the first of March he addressed the Congress, and I knew when he consented to do this sitting down that he had accepted a certain degree of invalidism. I found him less and less willing to see people for any length of time, wanting and needing a rest in the middle of the day. He was anxious to get away and I was pleased when he decided to go to Warm Springs where, as I said before, he always gained in health and strength. He invited his cousins, Laura Delano and Margaret Suckley, to go down with him. I knew that they would not bother him as I should have by discussing questions of state; he would be allowed to get a real rest and yet would have companionship—and that was what I felt he most needed.

For the first time I was beginning to realize that he could no longer bear to have a real discussion, such as we had always had. This was impressed on me one night when we were discussing with Harry Hooker the question of compulsory military service for all young men as a peacetime measure. Harry Hooker had long believed in this and had worked for it. I disliked the idea thoroughly and argued against it heatedly, probably because I felt Harry was so much in favor of it that Franklin seemed to be getting only one side of the picture. In the end, I evidently made Franklin feel I was really arguing against him and I suddenly realized he was upset. I stopped at once, but afterwards Harry Hooker took me to task and said that I must not do that to Franklin again. I knew only too well that in discussing the issue I had forgotten that Franklin was no longer the calm and imperturbable person who, in the past, had always goaded me on to vehement arguments when questions of policy came up. It was just another indication of the change which we were all so unwilling to acknowledge.

Anna had returned to find her little boy seriously ill with a gland infection for which he had to have penicillin. For a time we kept him in the White House, but later he was moved to the Naval Hospital and all of us were really anxious about him. Anna had planned to take him to Warm Springs when her father went down but had had to give up that idea; and most of us were still far more worried about little Johnny than we were about Franklin who, we felt, would find in Warm Springs the healing it had always brought him in the past.

On April first, Easter Sunday, Tommy and I went as usual to the Sunrise Service and throughout the following days I carried on my usual round of duties, hearing by telephone daily from Warm Springs. All the news was good until on April 12 in the afternoon Laura Delano called me to say that Franklin had fainted while sitting for his portrait and had been carried to bed. I talked to Dr. McIntire, who was not alarmed, but we planned to go to Warm Springs that evening. He told me, however, that he thought I had better go on with my afternoon engagements, since it would cause great comment if I cancelled them at the last moment to go to Warm Springs.

I was at a benefit for the Thrift Shop at the Sulgrave Club in Washington when I was called to the telephone. Steve Early, very much upset, asked me to come home at once. I did not even ask why. I knew down in my heart that something dreadful had happened. Nevertheless the amenities had to be observed, so I went back to the party and said good-bye, expressing my regrets that I could not stay longer because something had come up at home which called me away. I got into the car and sat with clenched hands all the way to the White House. In my heart I knew what had happened, but one does not actually formulate these terrible thoughts until they are spoken. I went to my sitting room and Steve Early and Dr. McIntire came to tell me the news. Word had come to them through Dr. Bruenn in Warm Springs first of the hemorrhage and later of Franklin's death.

I sent at once for the vice-president, and I made arrangements for Dr. McIntire and Steve to go with me to Warm Springs by plane that evening. Somehow in emergencies one moves automatically. I have always been that way; when anything happens, I freeze. Johnny was still in the hospital and Anna fortunately was in the White House, so she and Tommy and Edith Helm were left to arrange all the details for the funeral service in the White House.

When the vice-president came I could think of nothing to say except how sorry I was for him, how much we would all want to help him in any way we could, and how sorry I was for the people of the country, to have lost their leader and friend before the war was really won.

Then I cabled my sons: "Father slept away. He would expect you to carry on and finish your jobs."

Almost before we knew it we were on the plane and flew all through the night. The next day in Warm Springs was a long and heartbreaking day. Laura Delano and Margaret Suckley, Lizzie McDuffie, our White House maid, Daisy Bonner, the cook Franklin always had in Warm Springs, and Prettyman, the valet, were all stunned and sad but everyone was as self-controlled and calm as possible. Though this was a terrible blow, somehow you had no chance to think of it as a personal sorrow. It was the sorrow of all those to whom this man who now lay dead, and who happened to be my husband, had been a symbol of strength and fortitude.

Finally the slow procession moved to the railroad station and we got on the train and started for Washington. The military guard surrounded the coffin in the back of the car where Franklin had sat so often. I lay in my berth all night with the window shade up, looking out at the countryside he had loved and watching the faces of the people at stations, and even at the crossroads, who came to pay their last tribute all through the night.

All the plans for the funeral were as Franklin would have wanted them. We had talked often, when there had been a funeral at the Capitol in which a man had lain in state and the crowds had gone by the open coffin, of how much we disliked the practice; and we had made up our minds that we would never allow it. I asked that the coffin be opened once after it was placed in the East Room, so that I could go in alone to put a few flowers in it before it was closed finally. He wanted to be remembered as he was when he was alive, and to have his friends at services in the East Room.

It seemed to me that everyone in the world was in the East Room for the funeral services except three of my own sons. Elliott was the only one who, by luck, could get back; he had been asked to fly in the plane which brought Mr. Baruch and several others back from London. Jimmy was able to come east but he did not reach New York City until after the funeral at Hyde Park, so he joined us on the train on our way back to Washington. Langdon Marvin, junior, who was my husband's godchild, came with Jimmy. Franklin, junior, and Johnny were out in the Pacific area.

Franklin wanted to be buried in the rose garden at Hyde Park and left exact directions in writing, but he had neglected to make the arrangements necessary for using private property, so we had to make those at the last minute.

After the funeral in Washington we traveled to Hyde Park. Again no one could sleep, so we watched out of the windows of the train the crowds of people who stood in respect and sorrow all along the way. I was deeply touched by the number of our friends who had left their homes very early to drive to Hyde Park for the funeral, and especially by the kind thoughtfulness of Prime Minister Mackenzie King. My niece (Mrs. Edward P. Elliott) was living in Ottawa at the time and he had invited her to go to Hyde Park on his special train. After the burial I stayed in the house long enough to greet old personal friends and the officials who had come up from Washington, and then my son, Elliott, my four daughters-in-law, Tommy, Harry Hooker and I went back to Washington on the same train as President and Mrs. Truman.

President and Mrs. Truman were more than kind in urging me to take my time about moving out of the White House, but I felt I wanted to leave it just as soon as possible. I had already started to prepare directions so that the accumulation of twelve years could be quickly packed and shipped. As always happens in life, something was coming to an end and something new was beginning. I went over many things in my mind as we traveled the familiar road back to Washington.

I am quite sure that Franklin accepted the thought of death as he accepted life. He had a strong religious feeling and his religion was a very personal one. I think he actually felt he could ask God for guidance and receive it. That was why he loved the 23rd Psalm, the Beatitudes, and the 13th Chapter of First Corinthians. He never talked about his religion or his beliefs and never seemed to have any intellectual difficulties about what he believed. Once, in talking to him about some spiritualist conversations which had been sent in to me (people were always sending me their conversations with the dead), I expressed a somewhat cynical disbelief in them. He said to me very simply: "I think it is unwise to say you do not believe in anything when you can't prove that it is either true or untrue. There is so much in the world which is always new in the way of discoveries that it is wiser to say that there may be spiritual things which we are simply unable now to fathom. Therefore I am interested and have respect for whatever people believe, even if I can not understand their beliefs or share their experiences."

That seemed to me a very natural attitude for him to take. He was always open-minded about anything that came to his attention, ready to look into it and study it, but his own beliefs were the beliefs of a child grown to manhood under certain simple influences. He still held to the fundamental feeling that religion was an anchor and a source of strength and guidance, so I am sure that he died looking into the future as calmly as he had looked at all the events of his life.

At a time of shock and sorrow the lesser emotions fade away. Any man in public life is bound to have had some close relationships that were later broken for one reason or another, and some relationships that were never very close and which simply slipped away; but when Franklin died many men who had felt bitterly towards him and who without question would feel so again, at that moment forgot and merged with the great mass of people in the country who felt that they had lost someone whom they needed. Harry Hopkins looked, the day of the funeral, as though he were just about to die. After his return from Marrakech, he had been practically confined to the house, and since both men were ill, it had been impossible for them to see much of each other. I do not think that they cared less for each other or that there was any break, such as some people believe must have occurred. I think the circumstances and their own health made it difficult for them to meet and consult more often.

Men like Jim Farley grieved that day too. I have not forgotten their grief, and I understand how bitterness can persist and be exploited though deep down there is a real affection.

As I look back now I realize that unwittingly Franklin's parents had prepared him well, through contact with themselves, travel abroad and familiarity with the customs and peoples of many countries, to meet the various situations that he faced during his public life. They certainly never intended him to be in politics, but the training they gave him made him better able to accomplish his tasks.

The so-called New Deal was, of course, nothing more than an effort to preserve our economic system. Viewing the world today, I wonder whether some of the other peoples might not have stood up better in World War II had something like the New Deal taken place in their countries long enough before to have given them a sense of security and confidence in themselves. It was the rebuilding of those two qualities in the people of the United States as a whole that made it possible for us to produce as we did in the early days of the war and to go into the most terrible war in our history and win it. So the two crises that my husband faced were really closely tied together. If he had not successfully handled the one, he could never have handled the other, because no leader can do anything unless the people are willing to follow him.

What brought this more clearly before me were the letters that came in such quantities after Franklin's death, and which are now in the Franklin D. Roosevelt Library. Touchingly, people told their complete stories and cited the plans and policies undertaken by my husband that had brought about improvement in their lives. In many cases he had saved them from complete despair.

These letters continued to come in throughout the summer and President Truman was kind enough to let Mrs. Robert Butturff, who had worked with us for twelve years, come to Hyde Park to help us open them. The last one was opened and read the end of August. I remember distinctly our feeling of relief and accomplishment when the last pile of letters was read. It was quite impossible for me to answer them all personally as I should have liked to do; but I have always felt that in them future historians would find the explanation of why one man was four times elected to the office of President of the United States.

It is hard for me to understand now, but at the time I had an almost impersonal feeling about everything that was happening. The only explanation I have is that during the years of the war I had schooled myself to believe that some or all of my sons might be killed and I had long faced the fact that Franklin might be killed or die at any time. This was not consciously phrased; it simply underlay all my thoughts and merged what might happen to me with what was happening to all the suffering people of the world. That does not entirely account for my feelings, however. Perhaps it was that much further back I had had to face certain difficulties until I decided to accept the fact that a man must be what he is, life must be lived as it is, circumstances force your children away from you, and you can not live at all if you do not learn to adapt yourself to your life as it happens to be.

All human beings have failings, all human beings have needs and temptations and stresses. Men and women who live together through long years get to know one another's failings; but they also come to know what is worthy of respect and admiration in those they live with and in themselves. If at the end one can say; "This man used to the limit the powers that God granted him; he was worthy of love and respect and of the sacrifices of many people, made in order that he might achieve what he deemed to be his task," then that life has been lived well and there are no regrets.

Before we went to Washington in 1933, I had frankly faced my own personal situation. In my early married years the pattern of my life had been largely my mother-in-law's pattern. Later it was the children and Franklin who made the pattern. When the last child went to boarding school I began to want to do things on my own, to use my own mind and abilities for my own aims. When I went to Washington I felt sure that I would be able to use opportunities which came to me to help Franklin gain the objectives he cared about—but the work would be his work and the pattern his pattern. He might have been happier with a wife who was completely uncritical. That I was never able to be, and he had to find it in other people. Nevertheless, I think I sometimes acted as a spur, even though the spurring was not always wanted or welcome. I was one of those who served his purposes.

One cannot live the life Franklin led in Washington and keep up many personal friendships. A man in high public office is neither husband nor father nor friend in the commonly accepted sense of the words; but I have come to believe that Franklin stands in the memory of people as a man who lived with a great sense of history and with a sense of his obligation to fulfill his part as he saw it.

As I mentally call the roll of people who served Franklin, they are many and varied, from those who helped him intellectually and gave him in different ways loyalty and affection in their relationships, to those who served him in little ways, providing food, protecting him, helping him to overcome his physical disabilites. Closest in his daily life were his secretaries, Louis Howe, General Watson, Steve Early, Marvin McIntyre, Bill Hassett, Marguerite LeHand and Grace Tully. Dr. McIntire saw him daily and was a trusted friend. Many people helped at different times with speeches. Sam Rosenman worked with him until he died, not only on speeches but on other special jobs, and his association with Bob Sherwood grew into friendship. His former law partner, Basil O'Connor, was his friend and associate in many things that were close to his heart, though until Mr. O'Connor became head of the Red Cross he never held any position connected with the government. Among the members of his cabinet, some became real friends as well as working associates.

It is curious to realize that out of my years in Washington, though I met many people and learned much about the country and its people, I made very few new friends. My friendship with Miss Thompson deepened and I grew very fond of Edith Helm and of the other people who worked with us in the White House and on the staff generally. Mr. and Mrs. Henry Morgenthau, junior, who had been our friends before we went to Washington, continued to be close friends. Frances Perkins I had known before and liked and I grew to know her better and to count her as a friend. Of many others who were officially associated with me, I have kept pleasant memories but I have deep-rooted ties with none. Among the newspaper women I made a few real friendships. Miss Lorena Hickok became a dear friend; Bess Furman, Ruby Black, Dorothy Ducas, Emma Bugbee, whom I knew in New York before going to Washington, May Craig, Genevieve Herrick, Martha Strayer, Kathleen McLaughlin I came to know well, and I always renew my contacts with them with pleasure.

On the whole, however, I think I lived those years very impersonally. It was almost as though I had erected someone a little outside of myself who was the president's wife. I was lost somewhere deep down inside myself. That is the way I felt and worked until I left the White House.

One can not say good-bye to people with whom one has lived and who have served one well without deep emotion, but at last even that was over. Jimmy and Rommie, Elliott and Faye, Tommy and I were on our way to New York City, and I was now on my own.

APPENDIX I

A PLAN TO PRESERVE WORLD PEACE
Offered for "THE AMERICAN PEACE AWARD"

I

FOREWORD

The United States of America views with anxiety the failure of the world either to restore order in the economic and social processes of civilization or to carry out the demand of the overwhelming majority that wars shall cease. We seek not to become involved as a nation in the purely regional affairs of groups of other nations, nor to give to the representatives of other peoples the right to compel us to enter upon undertakings calling for or leading up to the use of armed force without our full and free consent, given through our constitutional procedure.

Nevertheless, we believe that the participation of the United States with the other nations in a serious and continuing effort to eliminate the causes of war, is not only justified but is called for by the record of our history, by our own best interests, and chiefly by our high purpose to help mankind to better things.

So believing, it is our duty to confer with other peoples, not in gatherings hastily summoned in time of threatened crises, but in a continuing permanent society. In such a way only can we assist in improving the underlying ills which contain the germs of war. In such a way only can we assist when nations, losing reason, take up the sword.

II

PRINCIPLES OF A PLAN FOR A SOCIETY OF NATIONS

1. In the place and stead of the League of Nations there shall be created a new permanent and continuing International Conference to be known as the "Society of Nations."

Argument:

It is believed that public opinion in the United States is, and will be for some time to come, sufficiently hostile to the present formula of the "League of Nations" to preclude any use of the old name for a new conference. The words "Society of Nations" can most readily be directly translated into all languages.

2. The Society of Nations shall consist of those national governments signatory to the agreement creating the Society, and also such other nations as may be elected thereafter by the Assembly of the Society.

Fully self-governing states, dominions or colonies shall be eligible to membership in the Society.

Any member of the Society may, after 3 months' notice, withdraw from the Society provided, however, that the Society may hold it responsible for all obligations incurred up to the time of its withdrawal.

Argument:

The membership of the Society of Nations would follow closely the membership of the present League of Nations, including the right to membership of self-governing colonies.

Notice of intention to withdraw from the Society is placed at 3 months instead of the 2 years required by the present League Covenant. The time is thus reduced because it is believed that a nation insistent upon withdrawing would not hesitate to break the 2-year provision, but would hesitate to violate an obligation to give a comparatively short notice.

3. Action of the Society shall be effected through the instrumentality of an Assembly and of an Executive Committee, with a permanent Secretariat.

The permanent seat of the Secretariat shall be established at Geneva, which, failing other action, shall also be the meeting place of the Assembly and Executive Committee. Meetings of the Assembly and Executive Committee may, however, be held in other places to suit the convenience of the members.

Argument:

The above is similar to Articles II and VII of the League of Nations Covenant, but gives wider latitude to the holding of meetings elsewhere. (The "Executive Committee" will be explained below.)

4. The Assembly shall consist of representatives of the members of the Society. Each member shall have one vote, and may not have more than three representatives.

The Assembly shall meet at least once a year, and when not in session may be called upon to meet in special or extraordinary session by the Executive Committee.

The Assembly may deal at its meetings with any matter affecting the peace of the world or within the sphere of action of the Society.

Argument:

The above is akin to Article III of the League Covenant, but adds the right of the Executive Committee to call extraordinary or special sessions. This is added because it is believed that international crises demanding immediate action by the Assembly may occur between regular sessions.

The sphere of action of the Assembly is necessarily of the widest latitude.

5. The Executive Committee shall consist of 11 members, representing 11 different members of the Society.

For a period 10 years from the date of the first meeting of the Assembly of the Society the United States of America, the British Empire, France, Italy and Japan shall be represented on the Executive Committee, and during this period no representative of a dominion or colony shall sit on the Executive Committee. The other 6 members of the Society to be represented on the Executive Committee shall be selected by the Assembly from time to time in its discretion.

The Executive Committee may deal at its meetings with any matter affecting the peace of the world, or within the sphere of action of the Society.

Any member of the Society not represented on the Executive Committee shall be invited to send a representative to sit as a member at any meeting of the Executive Committee during the consideration of matters especially affecting the interests of that member of the Society.

At meetings of the Executive Committee each member of the Society represented shall have 1 vote and may have not more than 1 representative.

The purpose of the Executive Committee shall be to function when the Assembly is not in session, to determine facts, to make recommendations to the Assembly, to carry out decisions and policies of the Assembly and in general to exercise executive powers in the name of the Society of Nations.

Argument:

The above is a proposal for a distinct change from present League of Nations procedure. It is believed that the existing Council of the League of Nations is too akin to an upper or duplicating Legislative Chamber. The proposal to create an Executive Committee in the place of a Council would give to such Executive Committee the true functions which the name implies.

The number of the members of the Executive Committee follows that of the Council of the League of Nations as amended. The five so-called "Great Powers" are guaranteed representation for 10 years, and during that period colonies, dominions or dependencies of those nations are allowed no seat an the Executive Committee. The 10-year limitation follows the theory of the Washington Conference of 1921, i.e., that after 10 years a further determination of the subject can properly be arrived at.

The object of keeping the Executive Committee in practically continuous session is to obtain immediate action in the event of an unlooked-for crisis, such as the Corfu episode of this year.

6. Decisions at any meeting of the Assembly of the Executive Committee shall require the approval of two-thirds of all members of the Society represented, except that matters of procedure may be decided by a majority vote.

Argument:

The above is a radical departure from Article V of the Covenant of the League of Nations which, in general, requires unanimous agreement of the Assembly or of the Council. It is believed that common sense cannot defend a procedure by which 1 or 2 recalcitrant nations could block the will of the great majority.

7. The present Secretariat of the League of Nations shall form the basis for the establishment of the permanent Secretariat of the Society of Nations.

The first Secretary General shall be named by the Assembly and thereafter shall be appointed by the Executive Committee with the approval of the majority of the Assembly. The staff of the Secretariat shall be appointed by the Secretary General with the approval of the Executive Committee.

The expenses of the Society of Nations shall be borne by the members in the proportion decided by the Assembly.

Argument:

This virtually follows Article VI of the Covenant of the League of Nations, giving to the proposed Executive Committee the powers now held by the Council.

The reference to the expenses of the Society of Nations follows the amendment made by the Assembly of the League of Nations in 1921.

8. The Society recognizing that the maintenance of peace requires further reduction of armaments, the Executive Committee shall study and report to the Assembly plans for such reductions, such plans to be subject to reconsideration and revision at least every 10 years.

In the consideration of such plans, existing regional, continental or local agreements for limitation of armaments may be recognized and similar agreements may be recommended.

Further, the Executive Committee shall make recommendations looking to the eventual termination of the manufacture by private enterprise of munitions and implements of war.

The members of the Society will undertake to interchange full and frank information regarding existing or proposed armaments.

Argument:

The above is based on Article VIII of the Covenant of the League of Nations, but recognizes and approves explicitly such agreements as the Washington Naval and Pacific Treaties of 1921.

The principles set forth regarding manufacture of munitions and exchange of information follow substantially the existing clause in the covenant of the League of Nations.

9. The Assembly shall have the right to establish such permanent or temporary commissions as may be deemed necessary.

Argument:

The League Covenant in Article IX authorized a permanent Commission to advise the Council on the execution of provisions of Articles I and VIII. It is felt that a broad authorization to the Assembly to establish necessary commissions would be more in conformity with all possible needs.

10. The members of the Society of Nations shall undertake to respect the territorial integrity and existing political independence of all members of the Society. In the event of the failure of any member or members of the Society to abide by this undertaking, or in the event of any threat or dan-

ger of aggression, the Assembly, if in session, or if not, the Executive Committee, shall make recommendations to the members of the Society upon the means by which this undertaking shall best be fulfilled.

The Executive Committee shall, as soon as practicable, study and report to the Assembly upon the total elimination of so-called insults to national honor as a cause of war. Injuries or crimes committed against persons or property by citizens of another nation have, in the past, been the proximate cause of war or of warlike acts of aggression. The principle shall be established that, while it is essential that the lives and property of the citizens of one nation shall be safe throughout the world, and while it is needful that national honor be upheld, the Society of Nations shall be substituted for the offended nation as the means or instrument for obtaining adequate redress.

Argument:

The above contains vital departures from the existing Covenant of the League of Nations.

First, it eliminates the much-discussed language of Article X, "Preserve as against external aggression."

11. Any war or threat of war, whether immediately affecting any of the members of the Society or not, shall be a matter of concern to the whole Society, and the Society shall recommend to its members such action as may be deemed wise or effectual to safeguard the peace of nations.

It shall be the friendly right of each member of the Society to bring to the attention of the Assembly or of the Executive Committee any circumstances whatever affecting international relations which threaten to disturb international peace or the good understanding between nations upon which peace depends.

Argument:

The above would seem to meet objections to Article XI of the League Covenant. The latter provides that in the event of war or threat of war, "the League shall take any action that may be deemed wise" etc. It is proposed to change this according to the same principles as the changes to Article X, i.e., making the action of the Society of Nations a recommedation to its members.

In other respects the principles of Article XI are followed.

12. The members of the Society shall agree that if there should arise between them any dispute likely to lead to a rupture they will submit the matter either to arbitration or judicial settlement or to inquiry by the Execu-

tive Committee, and they agree in no case to resort to war until 3 months after the award by the arbitrators or the judicial decision or the report by the Executive Committee. Any award or decision shall be made within a reasonable time, and the report of the Executive Committee shall be made within 6 months after the submission of the dispute.

Argument:

This is substantially the same as Article XII of the Covenant of the League of Nations.

13. The members of the Society shall agree that whenever any dispute shall arise between them which cannot be satisfactorily settled by diplomacy they will submit the whole subject matter to arbitration or judicial settlement.

For the consideration of any such dispute the Court to which the case is referred shall be the Permanent Court of International Justice or any tribunal agreed upon by parties to the dispute or stipulated in any convention existing between them.

Members of the Society shall agree to carry out in full good faith any award or decision rendered, and that they will not resort to war against any member of the Society which complies therewith.

Argument:

The above is substantially similar to the Article XIII of the Covenant as amended. It is, however, even stronger in requiring arbitration of *all* disputes not settled by diplomacy and not merely those "which they recognize to be suitable for submission to arbitration" as provided in the Covenant.

The United States has, with other nations, many Treaties containing drastic arbitration requirements. It is believed that the rule of arbitration or judicial settlement should be made a hard and fast one, covering all disputes not readily settled by diplomatic negotiation.

14. The existing Permanent Court of International Justice shall continue as the Court of the Society of Nations. The members of the Society shall, however, confer through the Assembly of the Society for the purpose of revising the Statute for the creation of the Permanent Court of International Justice.

Argument:

The above speaks for itself. It is felt that inasmuch as the United States did not take part in the adoption of the statute creating the Court, and inasmuch as said statute provides for machinery of a more or less complicated nature, it is felt that the United States should have the opportunity of reopening the questions involved in the creation of the detailed plans for the Court.

NOTE: Article XV of the Covenant of the League of Nations relating to the reference to the Council of the League all disputes between members not submitted to arbitration is left out of the present plan for a Society of Nations as unnecessary. Paragraph 13 above changes the present League procedure by providing for the submission to arbitration of *all* disputes which cannot be satisfactorily settled by diplomacy. This does not prevent the Assembly of the Society of Nations, under the present plan, from taking cognizance of disputes between members or prevent members from asking the Assembly or Executive Committee to investigate and report.

15. Should any member of the Society resort to war in disregard of the Treaty or Agreement creating the Society, it shall, *ipso facto,* be deemed to have committed an unfriendly act against the other members of the Society, which hereby undertake immediately to subject it to the severance of all trade or financial relations, and the prohibition of all intercourse. It is for the Assembly, or if it is not in session, for the Executive Committee, to give an opinion whether or not a breach of faith has taken place. In deliberations on these questions in the Assembly or Executive Committee, the votes of members alleged to have resorted to war and of members against whom such action shall be directed shall not be counted. The Society shall notify all its members the date which it recommends for the application of the economic pressure. Nevertheless, the Society may, in the case of particular members, postpone the coming into force of any of these measures for a specified period, where it is satisfied that such postponement will best facilitate the attainment of the object, or that it is necessary in order to minimize the loss and inconvenience which would be caused to such members.

The Assembly may invite members of the Society to contribute armed forces to be used to protect the covenants of the Society.

Members of the Society shall agree further mutually to support one another in the financial and economic measures to be taken under this clause.

16. In the event of a dispute between a member of the Society and a nation not a member of the Society, or between any nations not members of the Society, the Society of Nations may invite such nonmember nations to accept the good offices of the Society for the purposes of such dispute,

and shall set forth the procedure for the investigation or settlement of the dispute in general accord with the principles of the Society of Nations. If a nonmember nation declines to accept the good offices of the Society of Nations, or fails to conform to its awards or decisions, the Society of Nations may recommend to its members what steps shall be taken against said nonmember nations looking to the preservation of peace.

Argument:

The above closely follows Article XVII of the Covenant of the League of Nations, but is greatly simplified in form, giving more latitude and discretion to the Society of Nations.

17. All treaties entered into between member nations shall be forthwith registered with and published by the Secretariat of the Society.

Argument:

The above is similar to Article XVIII of the Covenant of the League of Nations.

18. Nothing in the creation of the Society of Nations shall be deemed to affect the validity of international engagements, such as treaties of arbitration of regional understandings like the Monroe Doctrine, for securing the maintenance of peace.

Argument:

The above follows word for word Article XXI of the Covenant of the League of Nations. It would seem to give to the United States complete reassurance on the Monroe Doctrine and on regional treaties such as those consummated in Washington in 1921.

19. The principle of mandates as set forth and exercised under the present League of Nations shall be recognized by the Society of Nations, and the Society of Nations shall succeed to the rights and duties of the League of Nations on this subject.

Argument:

This principle carries out Article XXII of the League of Nations Covenant. In the absence of other information it would seem that the existing mandates established under the Treaty of Versailles and the League of Nations are proceeding satisfactorily. No valid reason exists for a discontinuance of these mandates or a prevention of future mandates under proper conditions.

20. The Society of Nations shall take over and assume the duties enumerated under Article XXIII of the Covenant of the League of Nations.

Argument:

This relates to the authority over
- (a) labor conditions
- (b) just treatment of native inhabitants
- (c) traffic in women and children and
  traffic in opium and other drugs
- (d) trade in arms and ammunition
- (e) freedom of communications and of transit and equitable treatment
  for commerce
- (f) prevention and control of disease

Such excellent beginnings have been made by the existing League in these subjects that no change should be made under the proposed Society of Nations.

21. At the request of a majority of the members of the Society acting through their representatives in the Assembly, the Society may undertake special investigations into any economic, financial or commercial situation affecting 2 or more members of the Society. The expenses of such a special investigation shall be borne by the members making the request therefor, and shall be conducted by the Society only for the purpose of reporting upon the facts of the subject investigated.

Argument:

The above provides a new method for using the machinery of the Society of Nations to obtain a special fact-finding report on economic, financial or commercial subjects. It does not in any way affect the right of the Society of Nations to take the initiative in economic situations which threaten peace, but is here introduced for the purpose of doing away with international ills which might later become more serious.

22. Nothing contained in membership in the Society of Nations shall be deemed in anyway to supersede, abrogate or limit the constitutional or other powers of the governmental system of any member nation.

Argument:

This is a statement in positive language of what is undoubtedly the existing situation under the League of Nations, but it is felt that the statement should be thus made in order that no timid misgivings may remain.

NOTE PRELIMINARY TO SUMMARY

The basis of this plan assumes:

First: No plan to preserve world peace can be successful without the participation of the United States.

Second: The United States will not now, or probably for many years to come, join the existing League of Nations.

Third: Any new plan to take the place of the League of Nations must have the support of the United States, and no foreign nation would suggest such a plan without previous knowledge that it was acceptable to the United States.

SUMMARY

Provision is here made for a Senate Resolution adopting general principles of a plan for a Society of Nations, and approving the calling of an International Conference.

The plan itself is, in one sense, based on the general outline of the Covenant of the League of Nations, in recognition of the fact that the present League is an operating body of which 54 nations of the world are members, and which has already accomplished much that is useful. It takes over all that is best in the existing League, including the great humanitarian and economic enterprises of the League—all of this with the belief that the amelioration of international social and economic ills is a necessary part in the prevention of future war.

Many changes, however, are made both in the machinery of the League of Nations, and in the obligations of the individual member nations.

The proposed Society of Nations shall operate primarily through an Assembly, and an Executive Committee thereof, thus eliminating the dual system of the Assembly and the Council of the League of Nations.

The Executive Committee would be a continuously sitting body carrying out the executive work laid down by the Assembly, and acting with the powers of the Assembly when the Assembly was not in session.

This Executive Committee would be composed of 11 members—the five so-called "Great Powers" having one member each for the first ten years, and no dominions or colonies having the right to a member. A two-thirds majority of all members would be able to take action at meetings of the Assembly or of the Executive Committee in place of the unanimous vote rule now in force in the League.

In regard to the powers and duties of the member nations, under the proposed Society of Nations, definite recognition is given to the superiority of the Constitutional law of any nation over any act of the Society.

The much-discussed Article X of the League Covenant becomes under the Society of Nations an undertaking to respect territorial integrity and a declaration of the right of the Assembly to *recommend* to the member nations methods for fulfilling this obligation.

The somewhat complicated machinery of the League relating to disputes is simplified by the provisions that all disputes which cannot satis-factorily be settled by diplomacy shall be submitted to arbitration or judicial settlement. This is in accord with many existing treaties, entered into by the United States.

The Permanent Court of International Justice is recognized and con-tinued, but may be reorganized.

INITIATION OF PLAN

1. The Senate of the United States, as the treaty-ratifying branch of the government, shall pass a Resolution requesting the President to call, in such manner and at such time and place as he may deem best, an Inter-national Conference of representatives of the 54 nations now members of the League of Nations, together with such other powers not now members as the President may determine. The Senate shall, in this Resolution, give expression to its approval *in principle* of the following plan for a *SOCIETY OF NATIONS*, to be organized in the place and stead of the existing League of Nations.

Argument:

It is well recognized that any concrete proposal for participation by the United States in a permanent association of nations or world court, must originate from the United States itself. While the treaty-making power is vested in the President, the events of recent years and the uncertain state of political opinion in the nation at present, requires the approval by the Senate of at least the *principles* of some plan before the details of such plan are discussed with other nations or submitted as a Treaty for ratifica-tion by the Senate: A Senate Resolution such as that proposed above is well within the power of the Senate, and conforms to many precedents. Such a Resolution can either (1) be the original action of the Senate, or (2) follow upon the recommendation of the President of the United States by special message.

2. Upon the passage of the above Resolution by the Senate, approving the following plan *in principle,* the President of the United States through the Secretary of State, shall approach the governments of the nations to be invited, with the object of determining upon the most acceptable meth-ods and place and date for holding the proposed Conference, and shall thereafter formally summon the Conference.

Argument:

It is not believed that the principle nations would decline an invitation from the United States. Their failure hitherto to approach the government of the United States with a view to a modification of the present League, or the formation of a new association, has been due to the obscure political situation in the United States in general, and in the United States Senate in particular.

It is further suggested that the prior acceptance of the *principles* of a new general plan by the United States Senate would give to the other nations of the world a sufficient earnest of our future desire and intention to cooperate.

FINAL NOTE TO PLAN

It is particularly to be understood that the Senate of the United States in giving consideration to a plan such as this for a Society of Nations could confine itself to a declaration of principles. In the consideration of this particular plan the Senate might consider it advisable to omit from any Resolution reference to some details of the machinery of the proposed Society of Nations. To do so would in no way interfere with the plan itself, for in the suggested International Conference modifications of details would, without question, occur.

The principles laid down, however, seem ample to protect the interests of the United States and to provide the means of establishing a permanent gathering of all nations in the interests of peace.

Any member of the Society which has violated any of its obligations as a member of the Society, may be declared to be no longer a member of the Society by a two-thirds vote of all members of the Society represented in the Assembly.

Argument:

The above, based on Article XVI (as amended) of the Covenant of the League of Nations, relates to so-called economic and nonintercourse boycott. This, while an untried experiment in international intercourse, is believed to hold forth great possibilities as a deterrent of war and of aggressive acts.

The paragraph of the League of Nations Covenant relating to recommendations for the use of armed forces against recalcitrant nations is modified to make it acceptable to the United States.

In the event of a failure on the part of a member of the Society to respect the territorial integrity of another member, the Assembly (or the Executive Committee) shall *recommend,* instead of "advise upon the means." Final action must obviously rest upon each nation.

Third, a far-reaching and drastic step is recommended looking to a virtual change in existing international law. A survey of history will prove that most recent wars have been commenced on the pretext at least of some attack on so-called national honor. The "diplomatic indiscretion" prior to the Franco-Prussian war, the sinking of the Maine before the Spanish War, the murder of Sarajevo, the recent Corfu episode, are but examples. It is believed that the Executive Committee can offer a plan to the members of the Society of Nations by which each nation will virtually give up at least for 30, 60 or 90 days its right to commit an act of war, seize territory or property or use its armed forces as a threat. The Society of Nations should first be given what might be called the *Agency* for obtaining adequate redress, apology or compensation for the nation whose honor has been assailed. Should the Society of Nations be unable to obtain adequate redress through its own negotiations, the injured nation would still have its original remedy.

The same remarks may be said to apply to the case of demonstrations made by one nation against the other for the purpose of collecting financial debts. There is no good reason why a clear statement should not be approved by all nations, referring such matters in the first instance to the Society of Nations instead of taking direct action.

The principles of the so-called international economic and nonintercourse boycott are also continued as the principle weapon to be used against recalcitrant members of the Society.

Finally a new step forward is taken with provision for the ultimate elimination of so-called affronts to national honor as a cause for armed demonstration or other acts of aggression. While in no way taking away the safety of a national or his property in a foreign land, it is believed that this provision will eliminate what has been the proximate cause of the majority of recent wars.

APPENDIX II

Franklin D. Roosevelt—Demand Note
dates 2/29/28

	Payment on a/c Principal	Payment on a/c Interest
12/30/29	$ 7,500.00*	$
1/31/30	3,680.20	
1/31/30	10,487.63	
1/31/30		10,083.92
1/31/30		12,100.07
6/9/30	2,000.00	
8/27/30	50,000.00	
8/27/30		1,991.67
8/27/30		53.33
12/1/30	5,000.00*	
2/20/31	1,260.89	
3/1/31	1,106.00	
12/31/31	5,000.00*	
3/25/32	1,000.00*	
12/21/32	1,633.11	
1/13/33		10,000.00
2/14/33	2,000.00	
3/1/33	1,676.56	
4/20/33	3,323.44	
2/5/34		1,207.54
8/25/37	1,985.40	
3/22/39	2,866.69	
12/31/37		14,761.41
7/3/42	5,193.63	

Franklin D. Roosevelt—Demand Note—*Continued*
dates 2/29/28

	Payment on a/c Principal	Payment on a/c Interest
7/3/42	$ 2,612.60	$
7/31/45 (paid to estate)	93,341.68	
7/31/45 (paid to estate)		44,621.73
TOTAL	$201,667.83	$94,819.67

"Under 'Payment on a/c Principal' the four items marked with an asterisk total $18,500 and represent deductions which F.D.R. voluntarily made in the total amount of the note.

In additions to the foregoing, F.D.R. between 1935 and the time of his death gave the Foundation an additional $34,508.91, making total contributions from F.D.R. of $53,008.91.

Of the above $34,508.91 (referred to above), $3,000 represented the value of the gift of the Mrs. James Roosevelt cottage to the Foundation, and $9,508.91 represents the royalties from his book, *The Public Papers and Addresses of Franklin D. Roosevelt,* which Judge Rosenman edited with my husband's help and original comments.

The demand note was prepared and supplied to Mr. Basil O'Connor by the National Foundation for Infantile Paralysis and he sent it to me at my request, I asked them to get permission from Mr. Raskob and Mr. Ford's family to give the amounts of their generous contributions.

Insurance was taken out on my husband's life in favor of Warm Springs, and after his death, out of this insurance, the final payment was made to his estate which cleared up all indebtedness.

APPENDIX III

DEPARTMENT OF STATE

May 25, 1939

STATE VISIT OF THEIR BRITANNIC MAJESTIES
JUNE 1939

MEMBERS OF THE ROYAL FAMILY

**THE KING
**THE QUEEN

*Lady Nunburnholme	} Ladies in Waiting
**Lady Katharine Seymour	
*The Right Honorable William Lyon Mackenzie King Prime Minister of Canada	Minister in Attendance
The Earl of Eldon	Lord in Waiting to the King
The Earl of Airlie	Lord Chamberlain to the Queen
**Mr. Alan Lascelles	Acting Private Secretary to the King
Surgeon Captain Henry White, R.N.	Medical Officer
Mr. George F. Steward	Chief Press Liaison Officer
Captain Michael Adeane	Assistant Private Secretary to the King

* To stay at Hyde Park.
** To stay at the White House and at Hyde Park.

**Lieutenant Colonel
 The Honorable Piers W. Leigh ⎫
Commander E.M.C. Abel-Smith, ⎬ Equerries to the King
 R.N. ⎭
Mr. A.D.P. Heeney   Principal Secretary to the Prime
                                          Minister of Canada

Tuesday, June 6

The Secretary of State and Mrs. Hull, with the British Ambassador and the following committee, will proceed by train to Buffalo, New York:

Mr. George T. Summerlin
The Chief of Protocol

Major General Hugh A. Drum, U.S.A.
Military Aide to the King

Rear Admiral James O. Richardson, U.S.N.
Naval Aide to the King

Captain L.C.A. St. J. Curzon-Howe, M.V.O., R.N.
Naval Attaché, British Embassy

Colonel R.V. Read, D.S.O., M.C.
Military Attaché, British Embassy

Group Captain G.C. Pirie, M.C., D.F.C.
Air Attaché, British Embassy

Mr. Cecil W. Gray
Assistant to the Secretary of State

Mr. Michael J. McDermott
Chief, Division of Current Information
Department of State

Mr. Robert C. Bannerman
Chief Special Agent
Department of State

Mr. George W. Renchard
Department of State

Wednesday, June 7

Eastern Standard
   Time

8:00 P.M.   The reception committee will proceed to the Canadian border at Niagara Falls to welcome Their Majesties the King and Queen on their arrival in the United States.

9:35 P.M.   The royal train will arrive at the Suspension Bridge Station, Niagara Falls, New York. The King and Queen will descend from the train and be welcomed on the station platform by the welcoming committee. The British Ambassador will present the Secretary of State and Mrs. Hull to the King and Queen. The Secretary of State will present the other members of the committee to Their Majesties. Immediately thereafter the Royal Party and the welcoming committee will board the train.

Dress—Informal.

Thursday, June 8

11:00 A.M.   The King and Queen will arrive at Washington. Their Majesties will be escorted through a double line of Marines by the Secretary of State and the British Ambassador to the President's Reception Room at Union Station, where they will be received by the President and Mrs. Roosevelt. Their Majesties' suite will be presented to the President and Mrs. Roosevelt, and the members of the reception committee will then be presented to the King and Queen. The members of the reception committee will be:

   The Vice-President
      and Mrs. Garner
   The Chief Justice
      and Mrs. Hughes
   The Speaker
      and Mrs. Bankhead
   The Secretary of the Treasury
      and Mrs. Morgenthau
   The Secretary of War
      and Mrs. Woodring
   The Attorney General
   The Postmaster General
      and Mrs. Farley

The Secretary of the Navy
and Mrs. Swanson
The Secretary of the Interior
and Mrs. Ickes
The Secretary of Agriculture
and Mrs. Wallace
The Secretary of Commerce
The Secretary of Labor
Senator and Mrs. Pittman
Representative and Mrs. McReynolds
The Chief of Staff
and Mrs. Craig
The Chief of Naval Operations
and Mrs. Leahy
The Commandant of the Marine Corps
and Mrs. Holcomb
The Undersecretary of State
and Mrs. Welles
The Counselor of the
Department of State

The British Ambassador will then present to the King and Queen Lady Lindsay and the members of the Embassy staff. Mr. Mackenzie King will present the Minister of Canada and Lady Marler. Sir Herbert Marler will present his staff. Lord Eldon will present the Minister of the Union of South Africa and Mrs. Close, and the Secretary of the Irish Legation and Mrs. Healy. Mr. Close will present his staff. The President and Mrs. Roosevelt will escort the King and Queen to the guard of honor, drawn up in front of the station. Military honors will be rendered, including the British and American National Anthems and a salute of twenty-one guns. Photographs will be made following the honors. Members of the reception committee and others will enter their automobiles at the side of the reception room, while the President and Mrs. Roosevelt and the King and Queen are receiving the honors and the photographers.

From the station there will be a procession with military escort to the White House, over the following route:

Up Delaware Avenue to the Capitol, passing before and turning around in front of the Capitol, thence down Constitution Avenue to Pennsylvania Avenue. On Pennsylvania Avenue the procession will bear right and proceed on Pennsylvania Avenue to the Treasury; thence south of the Treasury to East Executive Avenue, entering the White House grounds at the southeast gate, and driving to the south entrance of the White House.

Dress—Formal, Day.

12:00 M. The procession will arrive at the White House. Immediately following the arrival at the White House, there will be a Diplomatic Circle in the East Room for the Chiefs of Diplomatic Missions and their wives. The British Ambassador, as Dean of the Diplomatic Corps, will present the Chiefs of Mission and their wives to the King, and Lady Lindsay will present them to the Queen.

Dress—Uniform or Formal Day.

1:00 P.M. Small luncheon at the White House.

Dress—Informal.

2:30 P.M. The King and Queen will drive around Washington for an hour's sightseeing, visiting the Lincoln Memorial, the Cathedral Chuch of St. Peter and St. Paul, Rock Creek Park and other points of interest.

4:00 P.M. Garden party at the British Embassy.

Dress—Formal, Day.

4:45 P.M. Their Majesties will leave the White House passing through a line of Boy Scouts and Girl Scouts drawn up on South Executive Place.

5:00 P.M. The King and Queen will arrive at the British Embassy.

8:00 P.M. State dinner at the White House, followed by a reception and musicale.

Dress—Uniform or Formal Evening.

Their Majesties will remain at the White House for the night.

Friday, June 9

10:00 A.M. The King and Queen will leave the White House for the British Embassy.

10:10 A.M. Their Majesties will receive members of the British colony at the Embassy.

10:45 A.M. The King and Queen will leave the British Embassy for the Capitol.

11:00 A.M.   Their Majesties, accompanied by their suite, will arrive at the Capitol and be received by Vice-President Garner and Speaker Bankhead, who will escort them to the Rotunda where the King and Queen will receive the members of the Senate and the House of Representatives.
Dress—Formal, Day.

11:45 A.M.   The King and Queen, with their suite, will leave the Capitol for the Washington Navy Yard.

12:00 M.   The President and Mrs. Roosevelt will receive Their Majesties, accompanied by their suite, on board the U.S.S. "Potomac." Luncheon will be served on board during the sail to Mount Vernon.

1:30 P.M.   Arrival at Mount Vernon.

1:45 P.M.   The King will lay a wreath at Washington's tomb at Mount Vernon. Return to Washington will be by automobile.

2:30 P.M.   Visit to the Civilian Conservation Corps camp at Fort Hunt, Virginia.

3:00 P.M.   Departure from Fort Hunt.

3:25 P.M.   Arrival at Arlington Cemetery, where the King will lay a wreath on the Tomb of the Unknown Soldier and on the Canadian Cross. Representatives of the United States veterans' organizations will be present at the Tomb of the Unknown Soldier.

3:45 P.M.   Departure from Arlington.

3:55 P.M.   Arrival at the White House.

4:30 P.M.   Informal tea at the White House.
Dress—Informal.

7:55 P.M.   The King and Queen will leave the White House for the British Embassy.

8:05 P.M.   The President and Mrs. Roosevelt will leave the White House for the British Embassy.

8:15 P.M.   Their Majesties will give a dinner at the British Embassy in honor of the President and Mrs. Roosevelt.
Dress—Formal Evening.

10:45 P.M.   The President and Mrs. Roosevelt will leave the British Embassy for the White House.

11:30 P.M.   Their Majesties, accompanied by their suite and American aides, will entrain at Union Station for New York, proceeding directly from the Embassy to the Station.
No ceremony.

Saturday, June 10

Daylight Saving Time

9:00 A.M.   The royal train will arrive at Red Bank, New Jersey.

9:10 A.M.   The King and Queen and other members of the Royal Party will leave Red Bank station by automobile and proceed to Fort Hancock, Sandy Hook.
Dress—Formal, Day.

9:40 A.M.   The Royal Party will embark on board a destroyer from the wharf at Fort Hancock and proceed with naval escort up the bay to Pier No. 1, North River, The Battery, New York City.

11:15 A.M.   The Governor of New York and Mrs. Lehman and the Mayor of the City of New York and Mrs. LaGuardia will welcome the King and Queen at The Battery (Pier No. 1, North River).

11:30 A.M.   The Royal Party will leave The Battery by automobile and proceed from Battery Place to West Street and the West Side Highway to 72nd Street, east on 72nd Street to Central Park, through Park to East Park Drive; north on East Park Drive to 96th Street; east on 96th Street to East River Drive; north on East River Drive to 125th Street; over Triborough Bridge and Grand Central Parkway to World's Fair Boulevard and the entrance to the New York World's Fair.

12.00 M.   Their Majesties will arrive at the New York World's Fair and proceed to Perylon Hall, where they will be met by the President of the New York World's Fair and Mrs. Whalen and will sign in the Fair's Guest Book. The King and Queen, followed by the Royal Party, will proceed to the square in front of the United States Federal Building, where a guard of honor will be drawn up before the building. Their Majesties will receive military honors.

12:40 P.M.   Their Majesties will proceed to the Federal Building where they will be received by the United States Commissioner General and Mrs. Flynn.

12:50 P.M.   The United States New York World's Fair Commission will give a luncheon in honor of the King and Queen in the Federal Building.

1:50 P.M.   The King and Queen will visit the Canadian, Southern Rhodesian, Irish, and British Pavilions, including the Australian, New Zealand and Colonial exhibits.

3:40 P.M.   The Royal Party will leave the Fair for Columbia University, returning over the same route as earlier to 96th Street and Central Park; entering Park at 96th Street; turn north on East Park Drive to 110th Street, leaving Park at the corner of 110th Street and Central Park West; west on 110th Street to Amsterdam Avenue to 116th Street; west on 116th Street to Columbia University.

4:00 P.M.   The King and Queen will be received by the President of Columbia University and make a brief visit to the University.

4:15 P.M.   Their Majesties will leave Columbia University, proceeding west on 116th Street to Riverside Drive; south on Riverside Drive to 96th Street; right-hand turn on 96th Street to Henry Hudson Parkway and north on Henry Hudson Parkway to city limits.

6:15 P.M.   The King and Queen will arrive at Hyde Park.

Sunday, June 11

Their Majesties will spend the day at Hyde Park.

11:00 P.M.   The King and Queen and their suite will leave Hyde Park by train for Canada, crossing the border during the night.

APPENDIX IV

LIST OF PEOPLE ATTENDING LUNCHEON
Thursday, June 8, 1938
at one o'clock

The President and Mrs. Roosevelt
Their Britannic Majesties
H. E. The Rt. Hon. William L. Mackenzie King
The Lady Katharine Seymour
Mr. Alan Lascelles
Lt. Col. Piers W. Leigh
Miss Marguerite LeHand
Hon. and Mrs. James Roosevelt
Mr. and Mrs. Elliott Roosevelt
Mr. and Mrs. Franklin D. Roosevelt, Jr.

INDEX

379